International Relations
on Film

INTERNATIONAL RELATIONS ON FILM

Robert W. Gregg

LYNNE
RIENNER
PUBLISHERS

BOULDER
LONDON

Published in the United States of America in 1998 by
Lynne Rienner Publishers, Inc.
1800 30th Street, Boulder, Colorado 80301

and in the United Kingdom by
Lynne Rienner Publishers, Inc.
3 Henrietta Street, Covent Garden, London WC2E 8LU

Library of Congress Cataloging-in-Publication Data
Gregg, Robert W.
  International relations on film / by Robert W. Gregg.
    p.   cm.
  Includes bibliographical references and index.
  ISBN 1-55587-659-5 (hardcover : alk. paper) ISBN 1-55587-675-7
(pbk : alk. paper)
  1. International relations in motion pictures. I. Title.
PN1995.9.I57G74   1998
791.43'658—dc21   97-40574
                                                          CIP

British Cataloguing in Publication Data
A Cataloguing in Publication record for this book
is available from the British Library.

Printed and bound in the United States of America

5 4 3 2 1

For Patty and Stephen

Contents

Preface

The idea for this book grew gradually over several years as I experimented with the use of feature films in my undergraduate course in world politics. It was my experience that films provided a change of pace in the classroom, illustrated points I wished to make about the conceptual vocabulary of the field, and stimulated debate about a variety of issues. Moreover, the use of films was fun for me and, I believe, for my students, helping to make the subject more interesting and accessible by opening up the possibility that popular culture, which is so much a part of our lives, may have something to tell us about the world we live in. Eventually, an understanding dean granted me permission to create a new course entitled "International Relations in Film and Fiction," in which I was able to indulge my enthusiasm for film as a learning tool.

This book is first and foremost about international relations and the ways in which feature films illustrate aspects of that field or shed light in its dark corners. It is not primarily a book about film, with international relations only the glue to hold it together. No attempt is made in these pages to serve as a reviewer of the films I cite, much less to comment on the techniques employed by those who made them. The films I discuss have found their way into the book only because I believe that viewing them and thinking about them can enhance our understanding of international relations. In providing a conceptual framework for the relevance of the films discussed in the book, I have quite deliberately drawn upon familiar mainstream literature in the international relations field. Several books are mentioned and quoted frequently, and the reason is simply that they are works that I have found particularly useful in my courses over the years. Some sources might be characterized as old friends, such as Stanley Hoffmann's *Duties Beyond Borders* and Richard Ned Lebow's *Between Peace and War*, while others are provocative invitations to debate, such as Francis Fukuyama's thesis on the end of history and Samuel Huntington's on the clash of civilizations.

Many films are discussed at length in the book—well over one hundred in fact—and many others are mentioned briefly. Not surprisingly, I have favorites among these films. While I try to avoid "grading" the films, it will quickly become apparent to the reader that some are also among my old friends. A generation of students will attest to my fondness for *Dr. Strangelove*, and I still find it easy to wax ecstatic about films such as *Lawrence of Arabia, Forbidden Games*, and *Sugar Cane Alley*. I am also partial to the British TV series *Yes, Prime Minister*, several episodes of which arguably do as good a job of explaining foreign policy as many a long chapter in the textbooks. Incidentally, the reader will notice that I typically identify films with their directors. This should not be construed as an uncritical acceptance on my part of the *auteur* theory of filmmaking, which holds that the director is the primary creative force behind a film. Filmmaking is obviously a process to which many people make important contributions, but the use of the director's name—for example, Stone's *Salvador*, Bertolucci's *1900*, or Attenborough's *Gandhi*—follows a common practice and seems an acceptable shorthand.

I confess to being a film buff, but I am loathe to put together a list of my own "top ten" among the films I cite. I hope that the reader will have seen—or will want to see—most of the movies mentioned in the book. And I hope that seeing them and thinking about them will both stimulate interest in international relations and contribute to a better understanding of its many complexities.

Many people had something to do with bringing this book to fruition, but none more than Lilian Duarte. She brought to her work with me a sophisticated grasp of international relations, a wealth of knowledge about films, an abundance of creative ideas, and a sharp eye for problems in the manuscript. I also benefited greatly from the assistance of Peter Kelley and David Kassebaum in tracking down information about obscure films. The students in my "International Relations in Film and Fiction" class made teaching such a subject immensely satisfying; they also made many useful suggestions about films, some of which I have been able to incorporate into this book. A number of faculty colleagues gave me valuable advice at one stage or another of the process, but any errors of fact or dubious judgment calls are entirely my own responsibility. A special word of appreciation is also due to Ed Palaszynski, without whose help at critical moments it is doubtful if this book would ever have seen the light of day. I am also very grateful to Shena Redmond and Jean Hay of Lynne Rienner Publishers for the skill and patience with which they guided me through the publication process. Finally, I want to thank my wife, Barbara, both for her encouragement and for her understanding during the many weeks when my favorite spot in the house was the chair in front of our VCR.

Robert W. Gregg

1

Understanding International Relations: The Role of Film

Feature films—the movies we see in our neighborhood theaters or on the VCRs in our living rooms—can make an important contribution to our understanding of international relations. We are at a juncture in history when the world around us seems to be careening out of control. Familiar landmarks have disappeared and policymakers are struggling to get their bearings. If we cannot know for sure where we are going, it may help to know where we have been and how we got to where we are. Film can never be a primary source in this quest for knowledge about international relations; it can, however, be a valuable adjunct.

International relations is a large and complex subject. Scholars try to analyze it, teachers to explain it, students to understand it. The results are inevitably uneven. Part of the problem is that international relations have been taking place over a very long period of time—much of international relations is now history. But history casts a long shadow, and there is still truth in the old adage that those who do not learn from the past are destined to repeat it. There is good reason to believe that this adage applies particularly to international relations. Some knowledge of history is clearly important to an understanding of international relations; a fuller knowledge is obviously better.

Another explanation for the difficulty in making sense of international relations lies in the fact that the subject belongs to no one discipline. It is, in effect, a multidisciplinary field, dominated perhaps by political science and economics, but also drawing on insights from such disciplines as history, sociology, anthropology, and geography. Philosophy has also contributed much to the evolution of thinking about international relations, as have physics and biology, from which students of the field have borrowed freely if sometimes inappropriately as they seek to make their analyses more scientific. Thus one should ideally have at least a nodding acquaintance of the intellectual tools and concepts of several disciplines in order to understand international relations.

1

To complicate things further, there is the matter of levels of analysis. There is scarcely a textbook in the field that does not emphasize the fact that there are many perspectives from which to view international relations, each of which has its scholarly devotees, but no one of which can tell the whole story. These levels of analysis range from the systemic or macro level, the level of global interactions, down to the level of the individual decisionmaker within the state. Each level of analysis emphasizes particular influences affecting the course of international relations and offers its own distinctive explanations for trends and events. Inasmuch as there is no one correct level or perspective, a full understanding of international relations would seem to depend on an admittedly herculean effort to employ them all.

Given the magnitude and complexity of international relations—the long time line, its multidisciplinary character, the multiple levels of analysis—we can acknowledge the impossibility of mastering the field and turn our back on the world, focusing instead on simpler, more manageable things. Many do precisely that. Or we can pretend to have knowledge we do not possess and speak with misplaced certitude about matters we do not fully understand. There is no shortage of people in this category either, some of them unfortunately in a position to do harm. Or we can make the best judgments we can in the absence of full information and then, recognizing our limitations, strive to learn more about this fascinating and frustrating subject. Quite obviously the latter strategy is preferable. And it is one in which a judicious resort to the contributions of popular culture can be of more than a little help.

We all know, if we think about it, that we are surrounded by evidence of the ubiquity of international relations.[1] It is present in television news broadcasts and on the shelves of our supermarkets. It can be found in the cars on our streets (and often in our own garages), as well as in the faces we see and the accents we hear in our malls (and often in our neighborhoods). We are reminded of it by the labels on the clothes we wear and in the strange customs we encounter when we travel abroad on business or pleasure. We are brought face to face with it when our friends and relatives in uniform are dispatched to some troubled corner of the earth or when the country of our ancestors becomes the scene of a tragedy, natural or manmade. And it is there, over and over again, in the movies we watch in our theaters or from the couch in our living room.

Film as a Window on the World

Films are one of the most common and most powerful instruments for dispensing information about the world we live in and the myriad interactions among its countries and peoples. We do not, of course, typically go to the movies or rent a video cassette with the specific objective of enhancing our knowledge of international relations. It is far more likely that we view a particular film because we like an actor or an actress starring in it, because we have read and enjoyed the book, or because the reviewers give it two thumbs up or otherwise promise a pleasant evening's diversion. But it is always possible that a film will stretch our minds or at least fill in a few of the blanks in our body of knowledge, even as it entertains us. Few of us will know as much history as we should, however, or have the time or the aptitude to familiarize ourselves with the several disciplines that inform the study of international relations, or have the inclination or the opportunity to immerse ourselves in each of the several levels of analysis that together provide a full and balanced picture of any given event or issue. In view of these inherent limitations on our knowledge of international relations, it makes sense that we take advantage of every available means for stretching our minds and learning more about this complex field. Film is one such means.

No thoughtful person would wish to argue that the movies are the best source of information and insights into the complexities of international relations. For a great many reasons, film watching is a poor substitute for reading the works of great thinkers, subscribing to major scholarly journals, or even listening to National Public Radio. We would not wish to become like Chance, the gardener-hero of Hal Ashby's film *Being There*, whose knowledge of the world was shaped entirely by television. Nor should we encourage the elevation to high office of people who confuse what transpires on the silver screen with the far more complex and dangerous reality of contemporary international relations. Ronald Reagan, when asked if he had been nervous debating President Carter during the 1980 election campaign, replied: "Not at all. I've been on the same stage with John Wayne."[2] Such a statement does not, of course, demonstrate that Reagan's performance as president was significantly shaped by his years as an actor in Hollywood, although there is no shortage of critics who believe that it was. But whatever one's opinion of America's fortieth president, we know that the movies can never be a substitute for other means of learning about international relations.

Yet films can enhance our knowledge of international relations. In the first place, they demonstrate over and over again the old axiom that a picture is worth a thousand words. In effect, they dramatize the abstract idea and the mundane event. Even inherently exciting subjects such as war and espionage, which have long been prominent staples of film fare, can be brought more vividly to life on the screen than on the printed page or in the lecture hall. We learned this lesson in both the Vietnam War and the Gulf War. In the case of the former, pictures of the carnage contributed in no small measure to the rising tide of public hostility to the war; in the Gulf War, the daily diet of film depicting the triumph of the technologically sophisticated weapons being used against Iraq certainly helped to sustain public support for government policy.[3] And if film footage, courtesy of CNN and the other networks, made us armchair participants in those conflicts, how much more dramatic can feature film be because of the director's capacity to stage the action and bring us ever so much closer to it. A case in point is the horror of trench warfare in World War I. It has been well described in numerous books,[4] but those descriptions pale beside the French attack on the fortified German position known as the anthill in Stanley Kubrick's film, *Paths of Glory*. And much as headline stories about the killing of Archbishop Romero and the American nuns in the Salvadoran civil war commanded our attention, the impact of Oliver Stone's treatment of those events in *Salvador* is even more compelling.

But it is the capacity of film to dramatize the undramatic that merits special attention. We shall always know more about wars than we do about the more obscure aspects of international relations, simply because war is inherently more dramatic and because the stakes are so unmistakably high. The movies are arguably of even greater service to an understanding of international relations when they confront us with aspects of the subject that might otherwise languish on the periphery of our attention—concepts, issues, events that seem remote and dry and relatively uninteresting until explored by moviemakers. Take the case of imperialism, the subject of numerous studies and tracts by scholars and polemicists—Lenin probably the best known among them. In Gillo Pontecorvo's film *Burn*, it ceases to be simply a generic term for the relationship between European powers and the peoples in the Southern hemisphere and becomes a dramatic and often violent confrontation with economic causes we can comprehend and consequences that are visibly tragic. Similarly, much has been made of the cultural roots of chronic tensions between the United States and Japan, but scholarly efforts to describe those cultural differences are dramatically if controversially upstaged by Philip Kaufman's film treatment of the subject in his adaptation of Michael Crichton's novel, *Rising Sun*. These films grab our attention and in their own modest way can help us unlock at least some of the puzzles that make up international relations.

Movies typically dramatize by personalizing. The great concepts that have dominated the dialogue about international relations—concepts such as sovereignty, nationalism, balance of power, hegemony, and deterrence—are all abstractions and hence tend to be faceless and impersonal. Film, by its very nature—if it is to find an audience and hold its attention—must make such abstractions concrete. Films focus on individuals who become surrogates for groups, for armies, for governments, for nations. Ideas are personified. Conflicts between ideologies and interests take the form of conflicts between individual protagonists. And this transformation wrought on the screen helps to make international relations accessible. Whereas we may be annoyed by the vocabulary of the scholar or diplomat and dismiss it as jargon, we are more likely to pay attention *and* to understand when the big words, the abstractions, are presented in recognizable human form.

And while it is often difficult to relate to large numbers, the problems of a few people, as we get to know them and follow their lives, frequently make a strong claim on our attention and our emotions. Virtually all the films discussed in this book personalize the issues they address. The consequences of nuclear radiation are seen in the deaths in the years following Hiroshima of many characters in Shohei Imamura's film, *Black Rain*. The tragedy of sectarian conflict in Northern Ireland is humanized in the affair between a Catholic boy and the widow of a man gunned down by the IRA in Pat O'Connor's *Cal*. And the horror of the genocidal behavior of the Khmer Rouge in Cambodia is brought dramatically to life through the story of Dith Pran in Roland Joffe's *The Killing Fields*. These are people— and issues and events—we are unlikely to forget.

Films also have the capacity to enhance our knowledge of international relations by building bridges to increasingly remote but still important times and events, allowing the viewer to imagine what it was like to have been there. As any teacher can attest who has stood in front of classes whose students become younger every year, events that once were contemporaneous or at least recent become increasingly ancient (and murky) history for the students, requiring more and more effort to make them seem relevant. None of us, of course, teachers and students alike, has first-hand knowledge of Columbus's voyages of discovery, the Thirty Years War, the Battle of Waterloo, or the late nineteenth-century competition among European states for colonies in Africa. Relatively few are alive who followed the great debate over the League of Nations Covenant and its ultimate rejection by the U.S. Senate. The Japanese attack on Pearl Harbor and the atomic bombing of Hiroshima and Nagasaki occurred before the majority of the world's population now living were born. Even the Cold War, the dominant meta-issue in international relations for most of the last half-century, is rapidly fading into history, the magnitude of its impact on the lives of hundreds of millions of people increasingly hard for a new generation to imagine. The movies can help us to identify with these events and with the historical context in which they took place. They also remind us that many contemporary issues have historical antecedents— that our problems are not new, however much they may have been modified by advances in science and technology and however much the particular parties may have changed.

At their best, films may serve as valuable history lessons. For example, India's struggle for independence and the pivotal role that Mohandas Gandhi played in that process is brought vividly to life in Richard Attenborough's film of the life of the Indian apostle of nonviolence. The story of the Manhattan Project, which ushered in the nuclear age, is made far more accessible (if controversially so) for many of us in Roland Joffe's *Fat Man and Little Boy* than it probably will be via books. And even historical periods and processes less focused on specific figures than Gandhi or specific events than the creation of the atomic bomb can be given a sense of immediacy by filmmakers. A case in point is Jan Troell's *The Emigrants*, which offers us a picture of what it must have been like to pull up roots and join the migration of economically hard-pressed peoples from the old world to the new in the nineteenth century. Thus in a modest way films help us to compensate for the fact that as a people we tend to be ahistorical.

Finally, and perhaps most importantly, feature films can contribute to a better understanding of international relations by serving as catalysts for debate and further inquiry. The causes they espouse (or denigrate), the figures they lionize (or vilify), the issues they dissect (or leave tantalizingly vague)—all are typically the subject of the kind of post-viewing discussion and argument with which we are all familiar and in which we have ourselves engaged. It need be but a small step from such casual postmortems to a more reflective exploration of the ideas raised by films on international relations subjects. With relatively few exceptions, the films discussed in this book raise important questions even as they seek to entertain us—questions about the ethical character of particular policies, about the personal demons that drove particular statesmen, about the decisions taken or not taken that have affected the course of history, about the developments and trends that should give us pause as we contemplate the human condition at the close of the twentieth century.

Historical License in Film

Learning about international relations from film has its hazards, and this is nowhere clearer than in the treatment of historical figures and events. With rare exceptions, feature films do not exceed two and a half hours in length. Thus at a very minimum they must condense history. And of course they typically do much more. As a commentator on Shakespeare's historical plays has written about the bard, "Although there are limits on the liberties he can take—there is no point at all in writing a play about Richard III if you have him *win* at Bosworth—he can, and does, change the personalities of historical figures, invent characters, compress the chronology, alter geography, devise confrontations that never took place, commit anachronisms, and so forth."[5] Much the same could be said of filmmakers. No film purporting to deal with history—as do many of the films concerned with international relations—presents it exactly as it happened. There are almost always different versions of events and different interpretations of character and motive, which is why there can be so many books by historians dealing with the same subject. The great Japanese filmmaker Akira Kurosawa made essentially the same point in his early classic *Rashomon*, which has nothing at all to do with international relations but might be instructive for those trying to make sense of conflicting explanations for the phenomena of world politics.[6]

All films reflect the knowledge, the perspective, and the vision of those involved in their making. Even the most convoluted plots are necessarily simplifications. The camera cannot be everywhere; all of the thoughts of all the principals cannot be captured on the sound track. But far more importantly, filmmakers editorialize. A literal rendering of history is often dull, full of ambiguities that do not satisfy those filmmakers and probably would not satisfy their audiences. The editor of a recent book on Hollywood's interpretation of history, contrasting the craft of historians with that of filmmakers, puts it this way:

> Historians listen for echoes of the past. But the echoes are often faint, and our hearing aids are primitive. By imperfect means we try to translate these muffled sounds so that they speak to the present. What historical filmmakers do is analogous; but they choose simple languages that will be accessible to most viewers. Filmmakers often translate the past into a handful of reiterated "story lines" and themes: X is a hero, and Y a villain. Evil lurks beyond our borders and sometimes even within. Leaders must be strong, the people vigilant. Pride is punished, and humility rewarded. And on and on.[7]

And so as viewers we must be on guard, especially where the skills of director and cameraman and cast are such as to sweep us up in the story and invite us to suspend judgment. Much concern has been expressed, for example, over Oliver Stone's treatment of President Kennedy's assassination in the film *JFK;* critics of Stone's conspiracy thesis worry that millions of people will now accept his version of events (what one critic calls "that black hole of deceit"[8]) because it is so compellingly presented by a master filmmaker with a strong point of view. Films can have that kind of power. Stone may be the most often cited example of a director with an axe to grind and the talent to make it convincing. But he is not alone. We should also keep in mind Stanley Kubrick's intense dislike of the military, Stanley Kramer's sentimental liberalism, Sergei Eisenstein's role as propagandist for the Soviet regime, and Samuel Fuller's right-wing anticommunism, to cite but a few instances of directors whose films have a strong point of view.

Yet we would be the poorer without such filmmakers and the films they have created. They editorialize, often shamelessly as well as sometimes brilliantly. And in doing so they frequently distort the record— omitting here, embellishing there, manipulating our sympathies all the while. But they also focus our attention on important issues, challenge conventional wisdom, and, most importantly, make international relations come alive.

The question of whether the liberties taken with history and historical figures by a filmmaker are so egregious as to undermine the value of the film for our purposes is obviously something that has to be answered on a case-by-case basis. Several examples from the extensive repertoire of films about international relations will make the point that the historical film is frequently inaccurate; whether the inaccuracies are important is something else again.

Take the case of Basil Dearden's *Khartoum*, a film that seeks to recreate that episode in the history of British empire in which General Charles Gordon sought to hold the outpost of Khartoum on the upper Nile against the siege and eventual attack of Sudanese forces under the command of an Islamic zealot called the Mahdi. This crisis, which ranks with the Sepoy Mutiny in India as one of the memorable nineteenth-century disasters for British imperialism, can only be fully understood in the context of the larger story of the Suez Canal, suppression of the slave trade, confiscatory taxation, Sudanese nationalism, and what one historian has termed "the impaired sovereignty of the Egyptian Khedive."[9] Moreover, the crisis occurred at a time when London was hoping to establish a Cape-to-Cairo rail and telegraph link in Africa. The French, nervously contemplating such a development, tried to block it by creating a transcontinental link of their own, this one from west to east. In 1898 the two European rivals came close to war over the issue in the Fashoda crisis, precipitated by a foolhardy French move that had no chance of military success.[10] But in the decade prior to that crisis, the siege of Khartoum and Gordon's violent death only days before a relief column reached the town created a legend that simply had to be made into a movie. *Khartoum* has been criticized for tampering with history, especially in having Gordon and the Mahdi confront each other face to face at a critical juncture during the siege, when in fact there is no evidence that the two men ever met. Is this a fatal falsification of the historical record? Almost certainly not; and it is clearly not as important as the fact that the broader historical context has been almost entirely omitted. Here, as in other cases, what stirred the imagination of the filmmakers was the contest of wills between two stubborn (some would say charismatic) men, not the history lesson.

Gandhi and Columbus are two other historical figures, each incomparably more significant than either Gordon or the Mahdi, who have been the subject of film biographies that have been criticized for their historical inaccuracies. The complaint about *Gandhi* has not been that events are falsified. On the contrary, in episodes such as the Salt March and the British massacre of unarmed civilians at Jallianwalla Bagh, the film is remarkably true to what is known to have happened. The problem is rather that Gandhi is presented as a more saintly figure than in fact he was. The viewer seeking to know the Mahatma will learn little of the private man who could be a tyrant and who had a strange obsession with the workings of his bowels; the film deals with none of this. But in the final analysis, these errors of omission are unimportant for understanding India's struggle to throw off the British yoke.[11]

The Columbus films are a different matter. Writing about the famous Italian navigator, Ella Shohat and Robert Stam argue that "idealized versions of his story have served to initiate generation after generation into the colonial paradigm. . . . Cinematic recreations of the past reshape the imagination of the present, legitimating or interrogating hegemonic memories and assumptions. Mainstream films on Columbus prolong the pedagogy of pro-Columbus textbooks, thus indirectly influencing perceptions of colonial history."[12] And two recent mainstream films on Columbus— *Christopher Columbus: The Discovery* and *1492: Conquest of Paradise* — have in fact been controversial because they present the navigator as an heroic figure and advance agent of modernity in spite of the disease and death he brought to the New World. Although Ridley Scott's *1492* is somewhat more deferential to revisionist thinking than John Glen's alternative version of the Columbus story, both films treat history selectively. As with Gandhi, Columbus the man is misrepresented, his beliefs and personality modified to fit the purposes of the directors and the styles of the actors playing him. But unlike *Gandhi*, *1492* and *Christopher Columbus* also distort history—or omit historically important context and events—in ways that do matter.

Holes in the Whole: What Films Don't Do

Movies also pose problems other than those concerning historical accuracy for those who would use them to learn about international relations. Prominent among these is the fact that while feature films have much to say about some aspects of the field, they are virtually silent about others. The result is a picture of the puzzle of international relations from which important pieces are either missing or seriously underrepresented. The most conspicuous of those missing pieces is international economic relations. There is only very minimal film treatment of international trade or international finance, in spite of their demonstrable importance to the larger subject of international relations.

Occasionally a film takes us inside the corporate boardroom or the industrial assembly line, but rarely is such a film about international relations. Ron Howard's *Gung Ho,* a comedy about a Japanese takeover of an American automobile plant, is an exception, although its value for understanding international relations lies less in its commentary on international economics than in its exposure of cultural misunderstanding. One could, of

course, look to certain films set in times past, such as those cited above, produced on the cinquecentennial of Columbus's "discovery of America." After
all, his voyages had the purpose of discovering a sea route to Asia, thereby
facilitating trade, and they led to the great age of Spanish mercantilism. But
film treatment of the Columbus story actually has very little to say about the
international economic relations of the fifteenth and sixteenth centuries. It is
not uncommon for films to be made in which economic issues are at least indirect causes of what unfolds on the screen; one thinks especially of films
such as *Burn,* in which trade is identified as the rationale for colonialism,
or Philip Noyce's *Clear and Present Danger,* in which drug trafficking, an
economically lucrative international business, provides an excuse for Tom
Clancy's hero, Jack Ryan, to risk his life in a good cause. As a general rule,
however, economic issues get short shrift in feature films. The moviegoer
could be forgiven for missing the economic sub-text.

This is hardly surprising. Filmmakers have simply not found a way to
dramatize these issues in ways that will attract financing and draw an audience. There are exceptions, of course, but they often come to us from
Third World filmmakers and deal with the problems of poverty and development (or failed development) in the global South. Such films typically
have limited circulation in the West. However, it is only recently that international political economy has become a major focus of international
relations textbooks and, with the Cold War over, that international economic issues have begun to supplant security issues as the primary concern
of foreign policymakers. So perhaps the imbalance that characterizes the
international relations film "library" is partly a case of lag time between
what is happening in the real world and the discovery of these "new"
themes and issues by the film industry. In any event, for the time being
film treatment of international relations tends to overlook its critical economic dimension, leaving a large and admittedly important gap in the whole.

There are also other respects in which film treatment of international
relations is uneven. The field has generated a number of important theoretical debates, but not all of the contenders in these debates are well represented on the screen. Three such debates have been the realist-idealist,
the scientific-normative, and the behavioralist-postmodern. But one would
not know about those debates from going to the movies. Films do not, of
course, explicitly espouse any theoretical perspective; filmmaking is
largely atheoretical. But even a relatively cursory analysis will make clear
that some perspectives are much better represented on the screen than others. This is a situation that owes more to the nature of film and the film industry than to any conscious strategy of exclusion.

Of all the contending schools in international relations theory, the realist
school has been dominant in films about international relations. As understood by students of the subject, realism holds that we live in a state-centric
world. In such a world, states have no choice but to pursue their own

interests. Power is all important in such a context, and states will do what they can to maximize their power. As Thucydides observed in one of the classic statements of the realist position, "The strong do what they have the power to do and the weak accept what they have to accept."[13] In such a world, conflict is ever present. And war, the extreme form of conflict, is common. Some realists find the roots of this phenomenon in human nature, while others prefer to explain it as the consequence of international anarchy, which is to say the absence of any authority higher than that of the state. The latter are commonly referred to as neorealists. Whatever the root cause, the world is something of a jungle and international relations is prone to violence.

Not surprisingly, such a perspective commands a great deal of screen time in films about international relations. Conflict is exciting. Conflict sells. Films dealing with international relations are disproportionally concerned with war, espionage, revolutionary nationalism, and other forms of conflictual behavior. The participants may vary from large armies to individuals who serve as surrogates for some larger group or interest. The state-centric core of the realist paradigm is present in the overwhelming majority of the films discussed in this book. Frequently it is transparently obvious; the state and its agents—governments, armies, spies—are conspicuously engaged in doing the state's business, openly or clandestinely, heroically or disreputably, successfully or unsuccessfully. Examples of such films are legion. They include such diverse entries as Stanley Kubrick's *Dr. Strangelove*, in which an American president tries to stop a nuclear attack on Russia launched by a psychotic general; Franklin Schaffner's *Patton*, in which the U.S. Army fights the Germans from North Africa through Sicily to the Battle of the Bulge; Tony Richardson's *The Border*, in which agents from the Immigration and Naturalization Service try to cope with the inexorable tide of illegal immigrants from Mexico into the United States; and Michael Winner's *Scorpio*, in which the Central Intelligence Agency seeks to eliminate an alleged double agent during the dark days of the Cold War.

In other cases, we see the enemies of the state seeking to undermine its authority or even its existence, often with the objective of taking over the government and acquiring state authority in the process. Here, too, there is a rich harvest of films, in many of which the director sides with those who are challenging the state. Among these are Gillo Pontecorvo's *Battle of Algiers*, in which the Algerians rise up against French colonial rule; Euzhan Palcy's *A Dry White Season*, in which a white South African, his consciousness raised, challenges his government's apartheid regime; Oliver Stone's *Born on the Fourth of July*, in which the central character changes from eager supporter to bitter opponent of his government's war in Vietnam; and even Jiri Menzel's *Larks on a String*, in which the director uses the medium to ridicule communist rule in Czechoslovakia.

Idealists have challenged the realist paradigm, arguing that realism is not realistic; idealism holds that "morality, law, and international organization can form the basis for relations among states; that human nature is not evil; that peaceful and cooperative relations among states are possible; and that states can operate as a community rather than merely as autonomous self-interested agents."[14] Moreover, idealism is critical of the realist preoccupation with power and even with its fixation upon the state, preferring instead to treat the world as less a collection of states than a community of people. Films do occasionally stress these idealist themes, and it is not uncommon to find spokespersons for them in films that otherwise take place in a realist context. An antiwar film such as Jean Renoir's *Grand Illusion* is a familiar example; although it is set during the Great War, its theme is the common humanity of soldiers on both sides of that conflict. But in the main, idealism is less filmable than realism, community sells fewer tickets than conflict. It is probably no accident that the United Nations, after more than fifty years, has so rarely been seen on the screen, its most famous moment coming when Cary Grant is mistakenly believed to be the killer of a diplomat in the UN delegates' lounge in Hitchcock's *North by Northwest*.

If realism and the state have dominated films about international relations at the expense of idealism, so too has the normative position prevailed over the scientific one. This may seem paradoxical, inasmuch as normative scholars, such as those who embrace peace studies, also reject realism. But whereas they insist that realism's claim to objectivity is false, they themselves renounce objectivity, arguing that students of international relations should stop trying to explain how the world works and concentrate instead on how it *ought* to work—and then take an active role in making it work that way. The makers of films about international relations do not all subscribe to the agenda of peace studies by any means, but, as we have seen, filmmaking is by its nature a subjective undertaking. There is no obligation on the part of the filmmaker to set aside personal values or abandon a particular story line in the service of objectivity. In this sense, movies typically have a normative, not a scientific, bias.

International relations scholars may insist on scientific rigor, on the careful testing of hypotheses, on the systematic investigation of patterns of behavior with the aid of reliable data, and so on. No one expects filmmakers to proceed in this way. One has to look elsewhere for instruction on the merits of the scientific approach to an understanding of international relations phenomena and for the results and implications of scientific inquiry into specific issues of importance in the field.

The last of the major debates within the fraternity of international relations scholars has been that between behavioralists and postmodernists. The former are concerned with what actors do and with the application of the scientific method to the analysis of their behavior. The latter are concerned with words and texts, and take the position that there is no single, objective reality. In this view, even the state is a fiction

> that we (as scholars and citizens) construct to make sense of the actions of large numbers of individuals. For postmodernists, the stories told about the actions and policies of states are just that—stories. From this perspective, it is an arbitrary distinction that leads bookstores to put spy novels on the fiction shelf whereas biographies and histories go on the nonfiction shelf. All are forms of discourse, none are objective realities, and all are filtered through an interpretive process that distorts the actual experiences of those involved.[15]

Thus postmodernists are always looking for hidden meanings; unlike behavioralists, they do not expect to pin down reality. As the author of one prominent textbook in the field says, postmodernists "want to celebrate the diversity of experiences that make up IR without needing to make sense of them by simplifying and categorizing."[16] It is clear that feature films do not reflect the behavioralist persuasion. Nor are most filmmakers self-consciously postmodernists. But the postmodernist would advise us to deconstruct the films we watch, to look for the unstated assumptions, the hidden agendas of those who made them. Of course some filmmakers make little attempt to hide their agendas. Stone doesn't; neither does Costa-Gavras. Yet even in such cases, there is more than meets the eye, according to the postmodernist critique. Feminist postmodernists, for example, insist on deconstructing the language used in the discourse of international relations; they often find a sub-text full of sexual imagery and the possibility that wars and the weapons with which they are fought provide sexual gratification for male politicians and soldiers.[17] The many films cited in this book that deal with war do not typically make such statements (*Dr. Strangelove* is a conspicuous exception), but postmodernists believe we should not take any films at face value.

The Matter of Eurocentrism

Perhaps most important on any list of hazards to bear in mind when watching films about international relations is the matter of Eurocentrism. This is the argument that films—and indeed popular culture more generally, not to mention the liberal arts curriculum of our colleges and universities—view the world through European (Western) eyes, forcing the reality of "cultural heterogeneity into a single paradigmatic perspective in which Europe is seen as the unique source of meaning, as the world's center of gravity."[18] Inasmuch as the overwhelming majority of films discussed in this book are based on Western sources and screenplays by Western writers, have Western directors, and were produced with Western audiences in mind, it seems appropriate to take seriously the thesis that there may be a cultural bias, presumably unconscious in most cases, in those films.

The charge of Eurocentrism has been most vigorously pressed against films dealing with the so-called Third World, especially those in which Westerners interact with the inhabitants of that world. The perspective in such films, according to this indictment, is disrespectful of other peoples and cultures and portrays Western values and ideas as vastly superior to those of the less civilized "others." Moreover, Eurocentric films, we are told, posit "the availability of Third World space for the play of First World interests and curiosity."[19] This observation was made by two critics of Eurocentrism in popular culture, Ella Shohat and Robert Stam, in a commentary on Steven Spielberg's immensely popular *Raiders of the Lost Ark*, a film they cite over and over again as a way of demonstrating that imperialism has survived the end of colonialism and that the West continues to exploit and misrepresent the Third World in popular culture (and by implication in foreign policy).

Not only has "the Indiana Jones series recycled Rider Haggard and Kipling for the Reagan-Bush era, resurrecting the colonial adventure genre with insidious charm,"[20] it has also helped to perpetuate the myth of Western superiority. Although Egypt is the film's setting for a titanic struggle for possession of the Ark of the Covenant between Harrison Ford's archetypal Western adventurer and assorted evil Nazis, Egyptians are reduced to "ignorant non-entities who happen to be sitting on a land full of historical treasurers, much as the Arabs happen to 'sit' on oil."[21] Thus is Eurocentrism perpetuated and the non-Western world caricatured.

Shohat and Stam also make considerable use of a much earlier film, *Bird of Paradise*, to press their point. This 1932 King Vidor film, embarrassingly naive and politically incorrect by today's standards, is the story of a romance between an American sailor and a South Seas native woman that ends with her sacrificial death in a fiery volcano. Once again, the film industry has metaphorically sent us a message about the West and the rest. In this case, there is a sexual sub-text the authors want us to deconstruct. The Third World is "a 'virgin' land . . . presumably available for defloration and fecundation; ownerless, it becomes the property of its 'discoverers' and cultivators."[22] But it is also a threatening land (witness the volcano) that must be tamed by the Western adventurer. So the South Seas maiden represents both virginity and libidinousness, and the American sailor the Westerner who will penetrate and master this strange new land.

There are many films that could be cited to make the point that "so embedded is Eurocentrism in everyday life, so pervasive, that it often goes unnoticed."[23] Several of these films will be examined in subsequent chapters. Even those who scoff at the deconstruction of *Raiders* and *Bird of Paradise* might have second thoughts as they ponder the case of a historical biography such as David Lean's *Lawrence of Arabia* or an exercise in colonial nostalgia such as Sydney Pollack's *Out of Africa*. But whether the advocates of multiculturalism in the movies have overstated their case or not, it is necessary to be alert to the possibility that filmmakers who are products of a European-based culture may tend to understate and even denigrate the place in international relations of countries and peoples from the non-Western world.

As with the problems of historical license, the absence of films on some important issues, and the asymmetrical attention to the various schools of thought in the field, Eurocentrism is not so serious a flaw as to negate the value of the movies for understanding international relations. Once we are aware of these inherent difficulties, we can not only proceed to watch and study films with the proverbial grain of salt. We can also, as suggested earlier, use films as a stimulus to further inquiry and debate, turning their limitations to advantage.

Sneak Preview

As some of the commentary in this introduction makes clear, and as common sense will confirm, feature films leave something to be desired as a syllabus for the study of international relations. But they can be a useful and occasionally powerful tool for learning. Their most valuable contribution is to generate and sustain interest, surely a necessary if insufficient condition for the acquisition of knowledge about most subjects. If we view *Lawrence of Arabia* only as a gloriously filmed story of an eccentric Englishman who becomes something of a hero in the backwaters of World War I, we shall of course be richly entertained but we shall learn little about international relations. The enigmatic Lawrence, after all, is hardly one of the major figures of the twentieth century, however interesting he may have been. But if we view the film as a window on the decay of the Ottoman Empire, the emergence of some of the issues that would haunt the Arab world down to our own time, and the problems attendant on a dialogue across a cultural gulf, it can add significantly to our knowledge of that region and to an important dimension of twentieth-century international relations.

Similarly, if we go to see a revival of *Dr. Strangelove* only to laugh at the over-the-top performance of George C. Scott as a gung-ho Air Force general and the incredible telephone conversation between Peter Sellers' U.S. president and his counterpart in the Kremlin, we shall enjoy ourselves thoroughly. But if we also go primed to see the film as a lesson in deterrence theory and the very real problem of decisionmaking pathologies among leaders charged with the conduct of foreign policy, we shall come away with a much better grasp of world politics.

Numerous films offer insights into one aspect or another of the field, including some that are not in any obvious sense about international relations at all. In the chapters that follow, more than one hundred films will be cited and related to the various themes covered in the book—films from the silent era and films released in the 1990s, films in black and white and films in color, message films and comedies, Academy Award–winning films and films that were little seen and have largely been forgotten, films made in Hollywood and films from countries as diverse as Japan, China, France, Germany, Russia, South Africa, Argentina, and Martinique.

In only a relatively few cases is the whole film pertinent to international relations. Many of the films discussed are primarily concerned with the love affairs of their principals or with other matters quite unrelated to international relations, however broadly defined. Obviously it is desirable that all of these films be seen in their entirety, both for the enjoyment of the film and in order to place the "relevant" portions within their proper dramatic framework. But whether the relevance to international relations lies in the movie as a whole or in one brief but salient scene, all the films discussed can add to our understanding of international relations and our appreciation of its variety and compexity.

The remainder of the book is divided into ten chapters and an epilogue; each of the chapters is devoted to a theme or issue area that has received a considerable amount of attention over the years in feature films. Each chapter provides a brief overview of its theme, discussing both major concepts employed by scholars as they have analyzed that aspect of international relations and trends that have characterized the evolution of international relations in that issue area. In each case, films are cited and then used to illustrate the way in which popular culture may illuminate those concepts and trends.

As noted in this introduction, some important aspects of international relations have been largely neglected in feature films. This means, for example, that only one chapter is directly concerned with international economic relations, and that chapter is virtually silent on the important issues of international trade and international finance. The themes that define the following chapters are by no means mutually exclusive. Thus war, which has a chapter of its own, also figures prominently in several other chapters, including those on nationalism and intervention, and even in the one on law and morality. Similarly, some of the films crop up in more than one chapter for the simple reason that they have something to say about more than one issue.

The order in which the book's themes are presented is not intended to suggest their relative importance. A case could be made that the last chapter, which deals with the domestic roots of international relations, should come first. But the fact that few of the films discussed in that chapter are overtly about international relations at all has led to the decision to place it last, where it may stand as a reminder that the problems subsumed under the heading of international relations often have their roots deep in the social fabric of the member states of the international system.

And so "The Dilemma of Sovereignty" will be addressed first in Chapter 2. The state, as we have noted, has been the principal actor on the international stage at least since the Peace of Westphalia, and the state has typically been described by political philosophers and students of international relations as sovereign. Inasmuch as sovereignty means supreme authority, and inasmuch as there are many states, we are left with a world in which states are by definition equal with respect to their rights and duties—that is, they are equally sovereign. Although this concept is honored in many ways, perhaps most visibly in the United Nations General Assembly, where each state has one vote, we know that states are in fact anything but equal and that it is becoming increasingly difficult for even the more powerful states to exercise their sovereign prerogatives in the face of forces that do not respect sovereignty. This most basic if controversial characteristic of the state has only infrequently and then indirectly been the focus of films. But it is so central to an understanding of international relations that attention must be paid to the concept of sovereignty and to several diverse and intriguing film treatments of the subject. Among these are the filmed version of Verdi's opera *Don Carlo*, with its dramatic illustration of the pre-Westphalian order when states were not yet sovereign, and two perceptive comedies, Henry Cornelius's *Passport to Pimlico* and a hilarious episode from the British television series *Yes, Prime Minister*, entitled "A Diplomatic Incident." We shall also discuss films that comment on the increasing permeability of the sovereign state, films such as *The Border* (illegal immigration), *Clear and Present Danger* (drug trafficking), and *Black Sunday* (terrorism).

Closely related to the concept of sovereignty is that of nationalism, and Chapter 3 bears the somewhat ambivalent title, "Nationalism and Its Discontents." The disintegration of the Soviet Union and Yugoslavia in the 1990s has reminded us that ethnonationalism is a powerful and enduring phenomenon, not one that was exorcized by the dissolution of colonial empires after World War II. Although the recent proliferation of sovereign states as a result of decolonization and ethnic strife has led us to think of nationalism as a centrifugal force, integral nationalism has also been an important factor in international relations, as German nationalism in the nineteenth century and again in the middle and latter parts of the twentieth century demonstrates. Nationalism is a theme that has been visited frequently by filmmakers, especially in films that depict the struggle to end colonialism. Filmmakers have helped to remind us that one of the distinguishing characteristics of the modern state is that it is a nation-state. This means that the impulse of nationalism has led to a situation in which most nations either have their own state or contribute to international ferment in their quest for statehood. Among the many films that treat this subject are *Gandhi*, *Battle of Algiers*, and Regis Wargnier's *Indochine*. Sergei Eisenstein's *Alexander Nevsky* is both an evocation of thirteenth-century nationalism and a barely disguised appeal to twentieth-century Russian nationalism. Even films primarily about other matters may contain segments that make powerful statements about nationalism; Mira Nair's *Mississippi Masala* comes to mind. And of course *Lawrence of Arabia*, which will be cited in several of these chapters, is also very much about nationalism. In sum, this issue has a long and rich film history.

Two of the central tenets of the Westphalian order, in which sovereign states are the primary players, have been the principles of self-help and nonintervention. The latter has been so fundamental as to justify a separate chapter, "Civil Strife and Intervention," so titled because intervention has been so common, in spite of the presumption against it, and because the occasion for it has so often been conflict within the state. Not only has the long and sordid history of colonialism demonstrated the frequency of intervention; it also appears to be on the rise at the end of the twentieth century and to be enjoying the cautious if carefully qualified support of the international community, as expressed through the resolutions and actions of the United Nations dealing with human rights violations and humanitarian relief and, most dramatically, in NATO's belated peacemaking efforts in Bosnia. Few issues have produced stronger statements on film than that of intervention. Some of the sharpest criticism of intervention, both in public debate and on film, has focused on U.S. involvement in the affairs of its neighbors in Latin America and the Caribbean. Among the works addressing this issue and joining the chorus of disapproval have been Roger Spottiswoode's *Under Fire*, Costa-Gavras's *Missing*, and, angriest of all, *Salvador*. Indictments of intervention have also been common in the many films about the war in Vietnam, and the problem of how to stanch the flow of illegal drugs at the source has likewise produced commentary on intervention in films such as *Clear and Present Danger*. The movies have rarely championed intervention in the affairs of sovereign states. But increasingly vivid and shocking media coverage of atrocities creates a climate in which intervention may come to be seen as morally justifiable and nonintervention morally reprehensible. Films may contribute to this debate, as in the case of *The Killing Fields*, in which the horrors perpetrated by Cambodia's Khmer Rouge seemed to call for an intervention that did not come until long after the fact.

States have long tried to gain knowledge about the capabilities and plans of rivals by clandestine means, the spy being one of the oldest figures in the literature of interstate relations. This particular form of intervention, widely practiced but still controversial, has proved endlessly fascinating to filmmakers, justifying a separate chapter on "Espionage and Subversion." Espionage appears to have reached some sort of zenith of sophistication in the twentieth century, with the conflicts first between Axis and Allied powers and later between the Soviets on the one hand and the Americans and British on the other giving the film industry a genre second in importance, at least quantitatively, only to war itself. In addition to the ubiquitous James Bond, spies and their contributions to relations between states have been featured in films as diverse as Martin Ritt's version of John LeCarré's grim novel, *The Spy Who Came in from the Cold;* George Seaton's gut-wrenching *The Counterfeit Traitor;* Sidney Furie's sober and even cynical answer to 007, *The Ipcress File;* Louis de Rochemont's quasi-documentary film, *The House on 92nd Street;* and Sydney Pollack's excursion into paranoia, *Three Days of the Condor.* While the many films in this genre may be less important to an understanding of international relations than those in most other categories, it is inconceivable that they be left out of a book dealing with popular culture's treatment of the field.

The conduct of foreign policy requires that difficult decisions be made, decisions affecting the security of the state and the stability of the international system itself. The politics and psychology of decisionmaking in times of crisis became a principal staple of international relations literature during the Cold War, when the presence of nuclear weapons in the arsenals of the major powers seemed to reduce the margin of error for those charged with responsibility for their country's well-being. The Cold War did not, of course, create the security dilemma, nor does the end of the Cold War herald its end, even in confrontations between states armed "only" with conventional weapons. Indeed, so important is the subject of decisionmaking under crisis conditions that Chapter 6, entitled "Decisionmaking and Crisis Management," merits inclusion in a book on international relations on film. Fortunately, the subject has been the focus of a number of interesting films. *Dr. Strangelove*, a black comedy if ever there was one, is perhaps the best-known film treatment of decisionmaking during a crisis; it also has much to say about the closely related subject of nuclear deterrence. British television has produced several insightful explorations of foreign policymaking. In addition to the *Masterpiece Theater* production of *The Final Cut*, there are two perceptive analyses of decisionmaking in the comedy series *Yes, Prime Minister*, one ("The Grand Design") a concise clinic on the logic of deterrence, the other ("A Victory for Democracy") a telling parody of the thesis that foreign policy decisions are the product of a rational process. The fact that crises may be disastrously mishandled due to the human penchant for seeing only what we expect (or want) to see has rarely been better demonstrated than in the "Prelude to War" episode of another television series, *Reilly: The Ace of Spies.* Insightful comments on decisionmaking have also been made in films as different in subject matter as Henry King's *Wilson* (the battle over ratification of the League of Nations Covenant) and *The Wannsee Conference* (the planning of the "final solution" by the Nazis).

History suggests that war is the most dramatic and most enduring form that international relations takes. As such, it inevitably has a chapter of its own, "The Tragedy of War." It is both an interstate and an intrastate phenomenon, and civil wars almost invariably have significant international dimensions and consequences, as recent events in several parts of our troubled world attest. This chapter will, however, deal mainly with interstate warfare, leaving civil war as a factor in several of the issues raised in other chapters. It seems axiomatic that every war will eventually find its way onto the screen, where the issues that led to the war and shaped its outcome will once again be fought out by the filmmakers. The best of war films may ask us to reflect on Clausewitz's famous dictum that war is politics by other means. Films can also demonstrate the evolution of military technology and strategy, making the point that while the killing and dying in Kenneth Branagh's *Henry V* and Stone's *Platoon* are horrible in both cases, the techniques of butchery are very different. Some of the most compelling films on the subject have an unmistakable antiwar message, among them *Paths of Glory*, *Grand Illusion*, and René Clement's *Forbidden Games*. Others, if not glorifying war, view it as high drama with larger-than-life figures at its epicenter. *Lawrence of Arabia*, *Patton*, and Sergei Bondarchuk's *Waterloo* come to mind. As long as nations fight, popular culture seems certain to be there to dramatize the act.

As indicated above, major economic issues such as trade and finance have largely been ignored by film producers and directors. But economic interdependence has occasionally been at least a significant secondary issue in several films; moreover, the problems of development, broadly defined, have surfaced in a fair number of films, including important examples by Third World filmmakers. There has thus been sufficient interest within the industry to warrant inclusion of Chapter 8 on "Economic Interdependence and Development." Two films about U.S.-Japanese relations, *Gung Ho* and *Rising Sun*, while more concerned with cross-cultural communication than economics, do have something important to say about economic interdependence. Even more important are those films with a development focus. The great majority of the world's peoples live in countries classified as "developing," although many seem to be sinking deeper into poverty. This is an economic issue with a human face, a state of affairs that has generated large-scale migration, environmental damage, and other problems that cannot easily be ignored by the more fortunate countries in the developed Western world. However, it is less the response of the affluent to the plight of the poor that has captured the attention of filmmakers than it is the causes and consequences of poverty in which much of what until recently has been termed the Third World seems mired. Thus films such as *Burn* and Euzhan Palcy's *Sugar Cane Alley* do address the issue of development and locate the roots of its failure in colonialism. Other films, including *The Border* and Gregory Nava's *El Norte* focus on one of the principal consequences of the failure of development, migration to more affluent countries. These films remind us that societies are always in the process of being reshaped by migrants seeking a better life, a point illustrated in Stephen Frears's *My Beautiful Laundrette*.

The international system may be anarchical, but its participants do customarily observe certain rules of behavior, evidence that the international system is also an international society.[24] In some cases those rules have acquired the status of international law, in spite of the absence of a superior authority and hence an effective capacity for enforcement. The somewhat different if related question of whether there are "duties beyond borders,"[25] of whether ethical or moral international relations are possible, has long engaged philosphers, social scientists, and even statesmen, who otherwise are presumed to owe their highest allegiance to *raison d'état*. Not surprisingly, these issues of law and morality receive attention in film and merit the inclusion of Chapter 9 on "Ethics and International Law." Many films about war and intervention frequently reflect their directors' strong views on exactly such issues, as do Stone's films *Born on the Fourth of July* and *Salvador.* Others, such as Bruce Beresford's *Breaker Morant,* make the point that even mortal combat has rules. *Black Rain* and Alan Parker's *Come See the Paradise* contribute in their low-keyed way to the continuing debates over the morality of American decisions to drop atomic bombs on Hiroshima and Nagasaki and to intern Japanese-American citizens during World War II. In addition, *Battle of Algiers*, with its depiction of indiscriminate terrorism, and Luis Puenzo's *The Official Story*, with its exposure of human rights violations by the Argentine junta, both raise questions of law or morality, as does Stanley Kramer's *Judgment at Nuremberg*, once again timely in view of efforts to try those accused of war crimes in former Yugoslavia.

It has been the practice of most students and scholars in the field of international relations to stress conflicts of interest and ideology, a fact that reflects the predominance of political scientists among those generating the theories and writing the textbooks. But one of the important factors hampering cooperative problem solving and conflict management has often been the barrier of culture. The problem is of sufficient importance to dictate the inclusion of Chapter 10 on "The Clash of Cultures." Parties to disputes frequently do not communicate well because they approach negotiations with vastly different assumptions and styles rooted in their respective cultures. One distinguished student of world politics has recently argued in a highly controversial essay that ideological conflict is about to be superseded by what he terms "the clash of civilizations," which he defines as large culture blocs.[26] This aspect of international relations has been the subject of such recent films as *Rising Sun* and *Gung Ho*, both of which deal with U.S.-Japanese relations, one of the most frequently cited examples of cultural differences compounding conflicts of interest. No film on the subject has made the culture gap seem less bridgeable than

Brian Gilbert's highly controversial *Not Without My Daughter*, a micro-cosmic look at U.S.-Iranian relations. But cultures in conflict is an important theme or sub-theme in a great many of the films discussed here, ranging from Beresford's *Black Robe* to Louis Malle's *Alamo Bay* and Paul Mazursky's *Moscow on the Hudson*. Then, of course, there is that last word on the clash of cultures, Jamie Uys's *The Gods Must Be Crazy*.

Finally, we must consider the "Domestic Roots of International Relations" in Chapter 11. International relations scholars like to talk about the importance of levels of analysis, and one of the most important of these levels is the societal one and the perspective it gives us when trying to explain international events. Culture, our previous subject, is obviously related to the focus of this chapter. But culture is only one of many factors shaping a country's role in world affairs; the purpose of this chapter is to remind us that there are other societal factors that affect the way a state arrives at policies toward neighbors and adversaries as well as the way in which that state is perceived by others. Conditions and events that may seem at first blush purely internal have an impact on the way a state interacts with the world. Thus it is appropriate to include films that focus on internal factors that have a bearing on external relations. The American experience of westward expansion in the nineteenth century, developed in many westerns, makes films such as John Ford's *The Searchers* relevant for students of international relations. Any of several films about South Africa under the apartheid regime, such as *A Dry White Season*, also meet this test, as do films reflecting the impact of the McCarthy phenomenon in the United States in the 1950s and the Watergate crisis in the 1970s. So, too, do films that deal with the German unwillingness to face up to the evils of Nazism, including Istvan Szabo's *Mephisto;* those that chronicle the stifling grip of communism, among them Ivan Passer's *Stalin;* and such powerful indictments of repressive military regimes as *The Official Story*. This is one of the richest veins to mine for insights into the sources of foreign policy and tensions in international relations.

More than one hundred feature films will be cited in the course of this book. Some will be obvious choices for anyone who has both some interest in international relations and a love affair with the movies. Those who meet these admittedly loose criteria will almost certainly nod in recognition of films such as *Lawrence of Arabia, Gandhi, The Killing Fields, Patton*, and perhaps, depending on one's age and the longevity of one's interest in the movies—*Alexander Nevsky* or even that classic from the beginning of the sound era, Lewis Milestone's *All Quiet on the Western Front*. Other films will be unfamiliar or, if remembered, will be regarded as suspect entries in the library for this book. It is easy to imagine raised eyebrows or even hoots of laughter at the inclusion of the Marx Brothers' *Duck Soup* or the French farce, *The Tall Blond Man with One Black Shoe*. Some will surely question the presence of such Hollywood fare as *Johnny*

Guitar and *Pickup on South Street*. And presumably few readers will be familiar with *Wedding in Galilee* and *Where the Green Ants Dream*. However, every film cited in the book has something to say about international relations if viewed with both a healthy skepticism *and* a willingness to believe that popular culture may enhance our understanding of the complexities of the world we live in.

There must be dozens of additional films that could have been used to illustrate aspects of international relations. The roster of films chosen for inclusion inevitably reflects the preferences and the prejudices of the author. Some films have been left off the list simply because an exercise like this has to stop somewhere. Others have been omitted because, whatever their appeal at the box office, for me they simply do not have sufficient redeeming value. This is not to say that every film included is a good one, much less a great one; I readily concede that several of my choices, viewed in their entirety, are second-rate examples of moviemaking. But I believe that even these have something worthwhile to say about our subject. Other films may be missing because they are unfamiliar to the author. This is especially true of films from Third World countries. I have drawn primarily on movies made in the West, and the United States may well be overrepresented. But the book's inventory of feature films is sufficiently long *and* inclusive to provide a potentially valuable window on the real world of international relations.

If the movies can help us comprehend international relations, past and present, and provide us with clues to the future of this complex subject, we should rush to the local rental outlet, peruse the local papers for announcements of film festivals, and otherwise take advantage of every opportunity to study international relations while we enjoy the derring-do of spies, the heroism of soldiers in battle, and the agonizing of statesmen as they grapple with the latest foreign policy crisis.

Notes

1. One book that was written to remind us of this fact is Hamilton, *Main Street America*.

2. Curtis, "The Wimp Factor," p. 44, 46.

3. A recent study by the U.S. General Accounting Office argues that these state-of-the-art weapons were not all that effective. See Weiner, "Smart Weapons Overrated," A1, A14.

4. See Keegan, *The Face of Battle*, Ch. 4.

5. Saccio, *Shakespeare's English Kings*, p. 14.

6. *Rashomon* tells the story of the death of a samurai and the violation of his wife from four different perspectives, and as the stories unfold we learn more about the people telling them than we do about what actually happened.

7. Carnes, "Hollywood History," p. 84.

8. *Ibid.*, p. 78.

9. Lewis, "Khartoum," p. 164.

10. An excellent short analysis of the Fashoda crisis is to be found in Lebow, *Between Peace and War,* pp. 317–33.

11. See Ward, "Gandhi," pp. 254–57.

12. Shohat and Stam, *Unthinking Eurocentrism,* p. 62.

13. Thucydides, *History of the Peleponnesian War*, p. 402.

14. Goldstein, *International Relations*, p. 95.

15. *Ibid.*, p. 122.

16. *Ibid.*, p. 123.

17. See Cohn, "Sex and Death," pp. 687–718.

18. Shohat and Stam, *Unthinking Eurocentrism*, pp. 1–2.

19. *Ibid.*, p. 222.

20. *Ibid.*, p. 124.

21. *Ibid.*, p. 151.

22. *Ibid.*, p. 142.

23. *Ibid.*, p. 1.

24. See Bull, *The Anarchical Society*, for a discussion of the distinction between system and society.

25. See Hoffmann, *Duties Beyond Borders*.

26. Huntington, "The Clash of Civilizations," pp. 22–49. Huntington has developed the thesis of this article into a book, *The Clash of Civilizations*.

2

The Dilemma
of Sovereignty

Of all the core concepts in the vocabulary of international relations, "sovereignty" is arguably the slipperiest. "Hegemony" would, in all probability, have its supporters for that somewhat dubious honor, if only because scholars seem reluctant to bestow the label "hegemon" on more than two states: Great Britain in the nineteenth century and the United States in the years after World War II. "Power," of course, is also a contender, especially in view of the considerable body of evidence that capabilities frequently do not translate into influence—that power is all too often not fungible.

But sovereignty is certainly among the most problematic and increasingly controversial terms one encounters when studying international relations. One distinguished critic has argued that it is a bad word, "not only because it has served terrible mythologies; in international relations and even in international law, it is often a catchword, a substitute for thinking and precision."[1] Others have been even harsher in their criticism of the term. Alan James, a chronicler of these opinions, has quoted one of them to the effect that to use the concept is to "encumber our thinking with gibberish phrases,"[2] and another as urging people to forget "all that blather" about sovereignty.[3] There is no question that it has been used in different ways at different times by different scholars. Even among those who have embraced the concept, there are some who believe that it may have outlived its usefulness, that both its normative stature and its descriptive value may have been so badly eroded by the realities of modern international relations that it no longer has any relevance.[4]

But whether sovereignty is a good word or bad, whether it is obsolete (or at least obsolescent) or not, it has held its place in the international relations lexicon for so long and shaped so much of the discussion of the nature of the state system that it must be addressed in these pages—provided, of course, that films have something to tell us about it. And they do.

The Birth of the Westphalian Order

The term "sovereignty" is derived from the Latin word *supra*, and hence carries the meaning of superiority. As Ruth Lapidoth reminds us, the concept can be traced back at least as far as the late Middle Ages, when it served two purposes. "Externally, the ruler invoked sovereignty to justify his aspirations for freedom from the influence of the emperor and the Pope. Internally, sovereignty was used to strengthen the control of the ruler or the prince over autonomous vassals and to consolidate his exclusive territorial jurisdiction in contrast to overlapping medieval personal jurisdictions."[5] This duality of sovereignty—its external and internal aspects—has persisted down to the present and is one of the major reasons why the concept has generated so much confusion and controversy. Internal sovereignty has been the subject of most of the theorizing, beginning with Jean Bodin's work in the latter half of the sixteenth century. The discourse on internal sovereignty has been about supreme legal authority within the state; the issue historically was whether the sovereign was absolute or was subject to limitations to be found in the laws of God or nature. What motivated Bodin and later Thomas Hobbes to address the subject was their experience of chronic domestic disorder; Hobbes, who had lived through the English Civil War, proposed a "great Leviathan"—a sovereign—that would save men from lives that, in his famous words, were "nasty, brutish and short."[6] In more recent times, with the decline of monarchy and the rise of democracy, the subject of who is sovereign within the state has assumed more importance; the issue has become one of whether sovereignty resides in the ruler or the ruled, and whether and when there is justification for revolution.

If we define sovereignty in this way, it has of course been the subject of a great many films that directly or indirectly portray the struggle for power within a state's territorial jurisdiction. Films depicting popular uprisings against monarchical governments that no longer enjoy legitimacy fall into this category. Although the monarchy has already been displaced in Andrzej Wajda's *Danton* and Sergei Eisenstein's *October*, these films also qualify; both deal with the issue of who within the state shall be sovereign and with the nature of sovereign authority, the first in the context of the French Revolution and the latter in the context of the Russian Revolution.[7] Similarly, films that focus on efforts by disaffected groups to overthrow constitutionally elected governments, whether successful or not, may be said to be about internal sovereignty. John Frankenheimer's *Seven Days in May* is such a movie. In it, a popular U.S. general, played by Burt Lancaster, is bitterly opposed to the plans of the president (Frederic March) for a disarmament treaty with the Soviet Union. He organizes a coup to overthrow the government and for seven tense days the survival of the Republic is at stake.

External sovereignty is most important for understanding international relations, however. Whereas internal sovereignty has to do with supreme authority within the state, external sovereignty refers to the independence and equality of states. In other words, when we refer to the sovereign state we mean that it is not subject to the control of any other state or external authority. It was not always so. Prior to 1648 and the Peace of Westphalia, which brought an end to the Thirty Years War, there had existed a European order that was in theory if not always in fact hierarchical, the state subordinate to the Roman Catholic Church and the Holy Roman Empire. We know that the Middle Ages were times of anarchy and violence. Those living then knew it, too. But as Lynn Miller has argued, "The medieval European conception of the kind of world they lived in was that it was bounded by a unified Christendom, defined by the supreme authority of emperor and pope, the one the final arbiter in matters secular and the other the highest spiritual authority."[8] In other words, the world may have been anarchical in fact, but it was not so in theory. When Westphalia brought an end to the last of the terrible wars of religion in Europe,[9] it also ended the illusion of centralized authority. In effect, "Westphalia made the absence of central rule the basic condition around which the new international system would be organized, whereas the medieval normative system tried to overcome it by idealizing central rule."[10]

The sovereign state as we know it today is thus a legacy of Westphalia. And the sovereign state is present, either front and center or not far off in the background of most films concerning international relations. But the pre-Westphalian order, in which the various precursors, large and small, of the modern state were presumably subordinate to the will of Pope and emperor, is a relatively rare setting for films, and even when it is, the contemporary viewer may be forgiven for missing the fact that the main ordering principle of international relations back then was different.

The finest treatment of the earlier hierarchical order comes not in a feature film, but in one of Giuseppe Verdi's greatest operas, *Don Carlo*. Most of opera's basic repertory is available for home viewing, either in the form of a feature film (e.g., Zefferelli's version of *La Traviata* and Rossi's of *Carmen*) or, more commonly, as taped during a live performance. But most operas have nothing to say about international relations or say it in such a baroque or melodramatic way as to make them irrelevant for our purposes.[11] *Don Carlo* is a powerful exception to this rule and deserves to be seen by anyone interested in international relations. Perhaps the best version, all in all, is that of the Metropolitan Opera Company, with James Levine conducting and a superb cast.

The opera, based on a play by Friedrich Schiller, is set in sixteenth-century Spain. The action takes place, therefore, well before the Thirty Years War and the Peace of Westphalia. *Don Carlo* has several things to say that are pertinent to an understanding of international relations in that pre-Westphalian time. In a decision that sets in motion one of the principal elements of the plot, the young Elizabeth of Valois is betrothed to the aging King Philip of Spain. This was one of those dynastic marriages made not in heaven, but for reasons of diplomacy: to cement ties between Spain and France. Such marriages were of course a common feature of European diplomacy for centuries. The problem, however, is that Don Carlo, Philip's son, is in love with Elizabeth and she with him. She will do her duty as queen, but Carlo has now become the king's adversary. The adversarial relationship is compounded by the fact that Carlo, encouraged by his friend the marquis of Posa, decides to champion the cause of freedom for Flanders, then part of Philip's far-flung European empire. This dimension of the plot introduces, if you will, the issue of colonialism, or at least a sixteenth-century version of it. The pressure for the dissolution of empires will reappear in later centuries and in many other films, but chronologically this is among the first.

Philip, troubled by the fact that his queen does not love him and that his son and his trusted confidant, Posa, are actively supporting the Flemish cause, seeks guidance from the Grand Inquisitor. The confrontation between these two powerful men, one representing the state and the other the church, is the high point of the opera, a musically and dramatically gripping scene that is, in my judgment, the finest depiction on film of the conflicts between the concepts of centralized and decentralized world order. The aged Grand Inquisitor insists that the reluctant king must turn both Carlo and Posa over to the Inquisition. In the end, the Church prevails (at least in the opera, and as it did in principle prior to Westphalia). As the Grand Inquisitor leaves, Philip concludes the scene with a line that perfectly captures the pre-Westphalian ethos: "So the throne must always bow to the altar!"

Schiller's play and hence Verdi's opera illustrate the fact, alluded to in the introduction, that much of popular culture takes liberties with historical fact. *Don Carlo* is historically inaccurate in a number of particulars, but, as Charles Osborne observes, it reflects the author's concern with poetic truth and the fact that in order to achieve it "he was willing to sacrifice mundane fact whenever necessary."[12] In the final analysis, the historical inaccuracies are relatively unimportant. What matters is that the concept of hierarchical order and the challenge to it posed by the state are effectively conveyed. In this instance, the hierarchical order prevails. It was not always so, for the tension between king and state on the one hand and papacy and Holy Roman Empire on the other surfaced long before Westphalia, demonstrating that the sovereign state emerged gradually over a period of centuries. Evidence of this may be seen in the story of Henry VIII of England and the so-called "king's great matter," Henry's wish to annul his marriage to Catherine of Aragon, who had failed to provide him with a son, so that he could marry Anne Boleyn. Unable to obtain papal approval for his plan, Henry in 1533 secured passage of an act of Parliament that abolished the Pope's jurisdiction and made him supreme head of the church in England. One historian has characterized this as "'perhaps the most important statute of the sixteenth century,' because, in its preamble, it enunciated 'as accepted fact, a new doctrine that the king was supreme head of a realm which was a sovereign state free from all foreign authority.'"[13]

This story has been told in film on more than one occasion, perhaps most thoughtfully in Fred Zinneman's *A Man for All Seasons*. In this Academy Award–winning film, the conflict is between Henry and his lord chancellor, Thomas More, who refuses to swear an oath accepting the king as supreme head of the Church of England and as a result is ultimately imprisoned and beheaded for treason. Once again we have a film that takes liberties with historical fact (in this case it presents More as a heroic martyr when in fact he was a much more complex figure). But it does illustrate the conflict between church and state in that age: "More adhered to an old and hard-won principle governing relations between the Church and the monarchs of the Catholic West. Kings were to protect the Church, but secular governments, ordained by God to suppress sin and keep order, had no authority to define theology."[14] Henry VIII prevailed in his quarrel with Rome and with More, but the larger issue would not be resolved until Westphalia.

Once the pretense that supreme authority resided in the papacy and the empire was abandoned, the state became the locus of supreme authority. Henceforth, international relations were "structured around the legal fiction that states have exclusive (sovereign) jurisdiction over their territory and its occupants and resources."[15] Inasmuch as there were a great many states or other more-or-less separate territorial units, sovereignty necessarily came to mean the independence and equality of states. The emergence of sovereign states was aided by developments that made it easier for kings to exercise control over their territories and provide security for their subjects. Among these developments was the use of gunpowder and the introduction of conscript armies. But states also came to see that the new order was preferable to the old; if they accepted its norms, "violence among them could be reduced to tolerable levels. In that equation, Westphalia sought to reconcile new material capabilities with an essential social value."[16] Unfortunately, not all states have been willing to observe the Westphalian norms; on occasion, and most conspicuously in the cases of Napoleonic France and Nazi Germany, ambitious attempts were made to reestablish a hierarchical order. In both instances, as we know, the logic of the Westphalian order prevailed, if only after years of violent struggle.

Sovereign equality has meant several things in practice, among them that all states are equal with respect to their rights and duties in international relations, that the territorial integrity and political independence of all states are inviolable, and that there exists for all states a duty of nonintervention in the affairs of all other states. Of course states are in fact conspicuously unequal with respect to their physical and other attributes, the most important of which is their power—that is, their ability to make other states do what they might not otherwise do. But juridically they are equal, a condition perhaps best reflected in the one state–one vote rule in the United Nations General Assembly and the many other international organizations whose members are sovereign states.[17]

Sovereignty Denied:
The European Double Standard

For much of the modern era the notion of sovereign equality of states applied only to European states, which had created the new order at Westphalia and were not disposed to admit other political entities outside Europe into their system. Great civilizations had existed in China, in India, in the Muslim world, and in Central America and the Andes long before the Peace of Westphalia, indeed well before Columbus set out on his voyages of "discovery." Some of these civilizations were well known to the Europeans. After all, Marco Polo had travelled as far as China in the thirteenth century and Spain had been under the control of the Islamic omayyad dynasty for more than two centuries before that. The crusades during which Christian Europe sought to recapture the Holy Land from the Arabs began in the late eleventh century, and the Castilian conquistadores had encountered the rich and powerful Inca and Aztec empires a century before Europe was convulsed by the Thirty Years War. No matter. The system of sovereign states that emerged in the seventeenth century was a system of, by, and for Europeans. Whereas European states could claim the benefits of nonintervention in each other's affairs, no such assumption governed relations between European states and the rest of the world. As Lynn Miller has argued persuasively, the Westphalian system was in effect a laissez-faire system and such a system works best in a context of abundance; that abundance was effectively provided for a long period of time by the vast expanses of the non-European world.[18] The European imperial powers, whether acting directly or in support of commercial ventures like the British East India Company, extended the reach of their sovereign authority into Asia, Africa, and the Americas without ever seriously entertaining the possibility that Westphalia's norms might also apply to the peoples of those territories. The result, as we know, was the double standard of imperialism and colonialism.

This double standard has been well treated in the movies, some of them embarrassingly racist by today's standards but probably consistent with the political and social reality of their times. These movies are among the most egregious examples of Eurocentrism in popular culture. A classic example of this kind of filmmaking is George Stevens's 1939 adventure epic, *Gunga Din*. This adaptation of a Kipling poem not only accepts the double standard but revels in it. Three sergeants with the British army on India's rugged northwest frontier spend the film brawling, carousing, and, when necessary, fighting like whirling dervishes.[19] Hopelessly outnumbered in the film's climactic battle by a horde of indigenous fanatics called Thuggees, Cary Grant and his fellow sergeants are rescued by a British relief column thanks to the heroic sacrifice of their Indian water boy, Gunga Din. The Thuggees had hoped, of course, to drive the British out of India, but the film takes the side of the dashing agents of imperialism and the servile and amusing native "boy" who helps them preserve the cause of empire. Bertolt Brecht, no friend of imperialism, had this to say upon seeing the film:

> I saw a British occupation force fighting a native population. . . . The Indians were primitive creatures, either comic or wicked: comic when loyal to the British, and wicked when hostile. . . . One of the Indians betrayed his compatriots to the British, sacrificed his life so that his fellow country-men should be defeated, and earned the audience's applause. . . . My heart was touched too . . . despite the fact that I knew all the time that . . . this Gunga Din could also be seen . . . as a traitor to his people.[20]

Brecht's comment is a fascinating commentary on the power of the medium. Stevens's film is an artful demonstration of the durability of the double standard according to which the rules of the game of international relations were for a very long time different for the West than they were for the rest.

All films about colonialism—and there are many—may be said to be about the double standard: sovereignty for the states of Europe (and somewhat later for territories settled by Europeans, such as the United States, and for states that learned to behave like the Europeans, such as Japan) and second-class status as mere objects of competition among European sovereigns for the rest. Some of these films will be discussed in subsequent chapters, especially Chapter 3 on nationalism with its emphasis on the decolonization process. But one other film merits mention in a discussion of the double standard that took shape after Westphalia: Roland Joffe's *The Mission*. This is a case in which the historical context of the film is both important to an appreciation of the plot and reasonably well presented on the screen.

The film's stars, Jeremy Irons and Robert DeNiro, are two very different Jesuit priests serving at a remote mission in South America in the eighteenth century. Irons, chief of the mission, believes that violence is a denial of God's love. DeNiro is new to the order, having previously been a mercenary, a slave trader, and a murderer; violence still comes more easily to him. The crisis of conscience these two men of the cloth face when the mission is threatened is the dramatic heart of the film. But the film's value for international relations lies in the circumstances that give rise to that crisis. Spain and Portugal had agreed to redraw the boundaries between their possessions in South America, and the treaty would shift control of the Jesuit missions to Portugal. The Jesuits, who had established their missions under protection of the king of Spain and gone about the work of converting the Guarani Indians to Christianity, were no longer in favor in Madrid and Lisbon because the missions had made it more difficult to make slaves of the Indians. Although Spain tolerated slavery, the Portugese were even more aggressive slavers and the consequences for the Guarani of implementing the treaty were very clear.

This situation underscores the extent to which the Westphalian order was still a European order, roughly a century after the end of the Thirty Years War. The European states were sovereign, but the norms of Westphalia did not apply to their colonies. There is an additional conflict in the film and in the history from which it is made. The papacy was involved in a struggle with the two Iberian temporal powers, and much depended on whether the pope would approve the treaty and order the Jesuits to leave South America (a negative decision would have resulted in the expulsion of the order from Spain and Portugal). A papal envoy is sent to the area to take stock of the situation on the ground, as it were; although he agonizes over his decision, he ultimately does the prudent political thing and recommends approval of the treaty, setting in motion the bloody climax of the film in which the Guarani, aided by DeNiro, fight the closing of the mission and are slaughtered. There is no question: the throne no longer feels compelled to bow to the altar. The state has become the dominant actor in world politics.

Within a century of the events of *The Mission*, Latin America was no longer under the control of Spain and Portugal. At the end of the twentieth century, with colonialism dead and ethnic nationalism in full cry, the number of sovereign states approaches 200—roughly the number of separate (and in theory sovereign) political entities in Europe at the end of the Thirty Years War. After Westphalia the many European states and principalities were gradually consolidated, shrinking the number of sovereign entities in Europe to approximately one-eighth the previous number.

Only fifty-one states signed the United Nations Charter in 1945, and they constituted the overwhelming majority of sovereign states in being at that time. An explosion of sovereignties began in earnest in the 1950s, escalated dramatically in the 1960s, and has continued unabated into the 1990s. Although some of these new states have been created as the result of the disintegration of older states (the breakup of the Soviet Union alone has accounted for fifteen new sovereign entities), most came into being as European empires receded from Asia, Africa, the Caribbean, and the Pacific.

Sovereignty Rampant, Sovereignty Under Siege

It is still the larger and more powerful states that dominate international relations, but the club—in the form of membership in the United Nations and other international organizations—is open to all, and the perks that go with it—including the opportunity to obtain a hearing for one's grievances and to cast a vote on all manner of global issues—have proven irresistible. Sovereignty is today claimed and exercised by a great many states that are so small and weak that they are sovereign only in the narrowest sense of the word. The subject has been cleverly satirized in a British comedy of the late 1940s, *Passport to Pimlico*.

Pimlico is very much a film of its time, the period immediately after World War II when England, like many other countries, was struggling to recover from the war and return to normal peacetime pursuits. An acute problem confronting the characters in the film is the persistence of shortages of commodities that English men and women crave. What makes this film so interesting for students of international relations, however, is what it has to say about the vicissitudes of sovereignty. A London neighborhood opts to declare its independence from the crown following the discovery in a local bomb crater of an old and forgotten treaty that proves it is really a part of the medieval kingdom of Burgundy. Burgundy, of course, is no more, but that is no bar to Pimlico using the treaty as justification for severing its ties to Britain, especially when the authenticity of the document is confirmed by no less an authority than that formidable actress Dame Margaret Rutherford.

The original rationale for choosing independence is to escape from rationing and other government-imposed restrictions. After all, a sovereign state need answer to no other state. In spite of their differences, the residents of Pimlico are soon caught up in the excitement generated by their new status. But sovereignty soon proves to be more complicated than anticipated, as British customs officials move in to police the borders and crisis follows crisis for the tiny neighborhood-state. The film is a splendid spoof of sovereignty, but its commentary on the economic problems of economically non-viable small states is not all that far off the mark. Pimlico's troubles—and short-lived sovereignty—may not mirror those of real states, but the caricature is recognizable.

There are today many states nearly as minute as fictional Pimlico, and some are even more vulnerable. All are nominally sovereign. And yet, ironically, the end of colonialism and the extension of the concept of sovereignty to entities as small as Grenada, the Seychelles, and Micronesia[21] was no sooner accomplished than the fragility of the sovereign state became increasingly apparent. Nor was it only the ministate—the modern-day Pimlico—that found itself in trouble. Thus we have the great paradox of the late twentieth century: sovereignty rampant, as demonstrated by the 180-plus members of the United Nations, and sovereignty at bay, as demonstrated by the diminished "capacity of states and their leaders to manage affairs within an enclosed space on a map."[22] Sovereignty has always been a concept rooted in a spatial view of international relations. The territorial state has been sovereign, and on a map the boundaries of territorial states appear clear and precise. Adjacent states are frequently given different colors by cartographers to emphasize their separateness. But these boundaries are increasingly illusory. One influential and oft-quoted student of such matters, Kenichi Ohmae, speaks of "a borderless world."[23]

More than any other factor, the globalization of the world economy has undercut the authority of the sovereign state. We live in an age of transnational firms and global capital flows and sophisticated computer networks. As Walter Wriston has written,

> we are witnessing a galloping new system of international finance. . . . Today, information about all countries' diplomatic, fiscal and monetary policies is instantly transmitted to more than two hundred thousand screens in hundreds of trading rooms in dozens of countries. . . . Money and ideas move across borders in a manner and at a speed never seen before. Markets are no longer geographic locations, but data on a screen transmitted from anywhere in the world.[24]

The challenge to the preeminence of the territorial state as a result of this revolution is unmistakably clear, "the velocity of change . . . so great in all aspects of science, technology, economics and politics that the tectonic plates of national sovereignty and power have begun to shift."[25] The trend seems irreversible.

The sovereign state is under siege in other ways as well. Sovereignty had implied that the state was essentially impermeable, that those residing within its territory could enjoy a rough security from outside forces. Historically those other forces were other states, and although no one expected the Westphalian order to put an end to war, it was assumed that all states, large and small, had incentives to live by the rules, respecting each other's sovereignty. But as we approach the twenty-first century, outside forces other than states—or in addition to states—are conspiring to undermine state sovereignty. The state, never perfectly impermeable, is now dramatically less so. It has been penetrated by actors and forces that are no respecters of the territorial state or its government. There are many termites in the woodwork of state sovereignty.

It is obviously more difficult to defend territory against sophisticated modern weapons of enormous range. Blue water, mountain ranges, and geographical distance no longer provide security. But that may be the least of it. Terrorists regularly and quite deliberately ignore state boundaries, as demonstrated most dramatically by the destruction of the Pan Am flight over Scotland in 1988 and the bombing of the World Trade Center in New York in 1993. Traffickers in cocaine and heroin operate successfully across borders, making a mockery of costly state efforts to police borders and interdict drugs. AIDS has become a worldwide epidemic as infected persons travel from place to place; no state is immune. Refugees and illegal migrants seeking to escape from political persecution or economic misery flood into more stable or more affluent countries across porous borders in ever larger numbers. Nor can popular culture be easily quarantined; the revolution in communications technology has put satellites into orbit and facilitated the transmission of ideas and images across borders as if they were nonexistent. Pollutants of all kinds travel by air and water from their source in one country to their destination in another, demonstrating in the process the inability of the state—any state—alone to provide environmental security.

All of these unwanted forms of penetration are part of a condition now commonly referred to as interdependence. Whatever else interdependence may connote—and for many it has a relatively benign connotation, even one full of promise for a future of cooperative global politics—it means that "the state's traditional freedom of action is rapidly being supplanted by one or another form of dependency, variable in form and substance to be sure, but ultimately part of a single encompassing whirlwind of globalization."[26] Sovereignty has lost its absolute character, or, as James Rosenau has observed, "In some deep and significant sense . . . the authority of states has, like money, moved offshore."[27] It is now necessary to speak of relative sovereignty.

This is a story that the movies have not yet really begun to tell, or at least not to tell well. The threat posed by nuclear weapons has, of course, been presented on screen, probably nowhere more effectively than in *Dr. Strangelove*, to which we will turn in some detail in Chapters 6 and 7. Similarly, international terrorism and drug trafficking have received some attention from the film industry. After all, these are subjects in which conflict is conspicuously present, violence is commonplace, and there is a reasonable likelihood that filmmakers will recover their investment. The emphasis in such films is typically on the contest between the good guys and the bad guys and the rising tension as the plot moves to its pulse-pounding climax, rather than on the demonstration of diminished sovereignty. But the message is there if we are prepared to look for it.

Filmmakers have not yet tried to capture the challenge to state autonomy wrought by the new global electronic infrastructure. Transnational corporations, whose policies are driven by the profit motive rather than by loyalty to either home or host state, have not been the focus of many feature films. Nor have environmental issues received the attention they are due; when it comes we can expect it to take the form of apocalyptic horror stories (although James Bridges' *The China Syndrome* in 1979 did do a fairly good job of anticipating the possibility of one such horror story, Chernobyl).[28]

A few films that deal with the increasing penetration of the sovereign state merit mention, although none of them does justice to the fact that the state could be losing the war, if not the particular battle, at the center of the film's plot. While John Frankenheimer's *Black Sunday* is only one of many 1970s disaster films, and hence a fairly representative example of escapist entertainment, it deals with a real problem: international terrorism by persons opposed to the existence of the state of Israel. Terrorism can be defined as premeditated and indiscriminate political violence directed against civilians, and in this instance the target was the crowd at a Super Bowl game. On numerous occasions, real-life terrorists among enemies of Israel have resorted to dramatic acts of violence, both in Israel and elsewhere. While the Super Bowl has never been targeted, the World Trade Tower, a comparably large and symbolically important facility, has been. In the movie, Israeli commandos and the FBI foil the terrorists at the last minute, but the point has been made that the ability of the sovereign state to maintain societal security is in jeopardy.

Drug trafficking, like terrorism, has a certain appeal for moviemakers, and drug traffickers have also demonstrated how difficult it is for the sovereign state to secure its borders. William Friedkin's award-winning film, *The French Connection*, was a relatively early attempt at dramatizing the international traffic in heroin, but is best remembered for Gene Hackman's sadistic American cop, "Popeye" Doyle, and the spectacular car chase in which he careens down New York's mean streets in pursuit of a criminal on an elevated commuter train above him. A very different view of the subject was presented in Alan Parker's *Midnight Express*. The "criminal" in this case is not a suave, big-time French operator but a young American college student who is trying to smuggle hashish out of Turkey. He is caught and subjected to almost unbearably brutal treatment in a wretched Turkish prison. The highly manipulative screenplay (by Oliver Stone) guarantees that the film will be best remembered not for what it has to say about drug trafficking, but for the controversial message that innocent (and heroic) Americans abroad are at risk in less civilized and cruel societies.

Both *The French Connection* and *Midnight Express* were made in the 1970s; by the 1990s the volume and value of drugs moving in international commerce were significantly larger; the drug of choice had become cocaine and the locus of the drug trade had shifted to Latin America and especially to Colombia, with its notorious Medellin and Cali cartels. The drug-trafficking film of the decade was now *Clear and Present Danger*. This adaptation of Tom Clancy's pot-boiler novel makes the point that the war on drugs has reached another level. No longer does the country whose borders have been breached by the illicit trade in narcotics seek only to apprehend the dealers on the streets of its cities and seize shipments of drugs at its airports and harbors. Instead, it carries the war to the source; in this case, a U.S. paramilitary force under orders from the CIA tries to eliminate the Colombian drug lords in their own country. Although the film has another story to tell—Harrison Ford's quest for the truth his own government is withholding from him—it indirectly contributes to the conclusion that the effort to end drug trafficking is unlikely to be successful—in other words, that as long as there is a demand, drugs will continue to flow across borders, no matter how great the effort to contain the flow.

One of the hallmarks of sovereignty has always been the right of a state to set its own immigration policy—to determine who shall be allowed into the country and in what numbers. But many states are inundated by refugees fleeing persecution, war, and even genocide, and by illegal immigrants seeking a better life. Whereas the concept of *non-refoulement* may have created an obligation to accept refugees,[29] no such obligation exists with respect to immigrants. Yet they continue to come, demonstrating daily the porousness of state borders and the limitations of sovereign authority. This is a problem rooted in the distressing economic conditions of many developing countries; several films dealing with that problem will be discussed in Chapter 8. One of those films, Tony Richardson's *The Border*, deserves brief mention here. The border of the title is the Rio Grande River, which separates the United States from Mexico, and across which Mexicans in large numbers have been entering the United States for many years. Jack Nicholson, playing against type, is a border guard who hates his job and feels some empathy for the Mexicans who are trying to make it across the river. His colleague, Harvey Keitel, and other members of the border patrol are corrupt; they make money on the side by closing their eyes as "wetbacks" are loaded into vans and delivered to equally corrupt American businessmen. Enforcing the country's immigration laws would be difficult under any circumstances; when those charged with enforcement "persecute enough Mexicans to keep government bureaus happy while functioning as slave traders,"[30] the task, according to Tony Richardson's thoughtful film, is impossible.

The Challenge of Supranationalism

An altogether different challenge to the authority of the sovereign state is one that some states have consciously embraced. It is the challenge of supranationalism, and its most ambitious manifestation is the European Union (EU). The Union had its origins back in the 1950s when practitioners of neofunctionalism[31] sought to strengthen economic cooperation among Western European states and simultaneously guarantee that Germany would not again become the scourge of Europe; they did so by first creating the European Coal and Steel Community and then, with the Treaty of Rome, the European Economic Community, hoping to knit together the economies of France, the Benelux states, Italy, and Germany so well that the latter would have no incentive to contemplate war against its neighbors for the third time in the twentieth century. Since that time, the European Community has become both wider and deeper. It has expanded from its original six and as of 1997 had fifteen members, with other states either clamoring for membership or contemplating it. Even more importantly for its impact on the sovereignty of its members has been the gradual deepening of the commitment to integration. Already a common market, the Community formally became a Union in 1992 with the signing of the Maastricht Treaty.

The most important of the extensive powers the Maastricht Treaty confers upon the institutions of the European Union had not yet taken effect in late 1997. There is still no monetary union or common currency, and many critics have argued that there should be none;[32] Jean Monnet's dream of a United States of Europe is still far from a reality. The European Union is nonetheless exceptional, "for it is more ambitious, expansive, and embedded than any other contemporary single set of mechanisms for international cooperation. For this reason, the EU deserves special attention in any discussion of the effects of international institutions on national sovereignty."[33] The salient fact is that there are important areas of law and market regulation in which the decisions of Union institutions are binding without the prior consent of member governments. Whether Europe moves ahead to monetary union and through it to political union or not, the members of the European Union have already transferred some of their sovereignty. The debate about next steps promises to be a difficult one, however. State sovereignty and national identity still exercise a powerful appeal.

No feature film directly addresses the issue of European integration, but the tension between the centrifugal forces of state sovereignty and the centripetal forces of intra-European cooperation have been perceptively explored in an episode of the British television series, *Yes, Prime Minister.* Government and politics have rarely if ever been funnier than they are in the thirty-minute episodes of this program, and it is doubtful if democracy's foibles have anywhere been more accurately and cleverly lampooned. In each episode the none-too-bright prime minister of Great Britain (played by Paul Eddington) and his devious and manipulative cabinet secretary (played by Nigel Hawthorne) strive to create policy, contain crises, and enhance their own reputations. It is the cabinet secretary who almost invariably prevails, although the PM is usually convinced that it is he who has the brilliant idea and has made the right move.

The episode entitled "A Diplomatic Incident" finds the British in a dispute with the French over their respective territorial sovereignties in the new English Channel tunnel. France hopes to claim sovereignty as far as the White Cliffs of Dover, and there is some concern that the PM will mishandle the negotiations in such a way that the French will prevail. Although the discussion of this issue includes a deliciously silly argument over which language shall be used on the menus in the trains' dining cars, there is also debate as to which country would have jurisdiction in the event of a crime on board a train in the tunnel, depending on such factors as the nationality of the victim. All of this is amusing, to be sure, but it is a very effective way of reminding us of the kinds of issues that account for the presence of large numbers of lawyers in foreign ministries. The British and the French are still very much concerned about their sovereign prerogatives, even as economic considerations and modern technology further the cause of European integration.

There is a bonus issue in the episode, and it stems from the desire of the French president, on a state visit to England, to bring along a puppy as a gift for the queen. British law insists that the dog be quarantined for six months at Heathrow airport, and the French regard this as an affront. Moreover, the French demand that they, not the British, provide security for their president while he is in London, and the PM is as unbending in his opposition to this request as he is in the matter of the puppy. A further deterioration in chronically tense Anglo-French relations is narrowly averted when the French are caught red-handed in a violation of British sovereignty (smuggling a bomb into their embassy in an effort to discredit British security), necessitating a face-saving retreat on all of their demands, from channel tunnel to puppy.

Each of these issues contributes something to an understanding of the concept of sovereignty and its practical day-to-day meanings. Those responsible for the film may have had their tongues firmly planted in their cheeks, but they have also contrived to turn an abstract concept into a very tangible thing, complete with vivid examples. Moreover, they have reminded us of the differences between Paris and London that have dogged progress toward European unity. One is reminded of De Gaulle's opposition to Britain's entry into the Common Market, and of Britain's insistence on the right to opt out of that key goal of the Maastricht Treaty, monetary union. But most importantly, "A Diplomatic Incident" confirms in fictional terms what post-Maastricht events in Europe make abundantly clear: a United States of Europe is not the inevitable outcome of the long period of gestation that began with integration of coal and steel production in the

1950s.[34] In no other part of the world has Europe's experiment with supranationalism been copied,[35] and even in Europe may have stalled.

It has been argued that "sovereignty is no longer sovereign; the world has outgrown it."[36] Yet even the authors of this thesis acknowledge that "the fiction of absolute sovereignty has remained surprisingly intact."[37] The consensus among those engaged in this increasingly lively debate would seem to be that the sovereign state is still alive, although clearly under siege and demonstrably weakened. The state remains the principal actor in world politics, coping as best it can with challenges to its authority and not meekly accepting evolution into larger confederated units or devolution into nonstate forms of organization.[38] Not surprisingly, the state and the system of sovereign states provide the context for most of the films discussed in this book. One needs to turn to science fiction, such as the several iterations of *Star Trek*, to escape from the world of sovereign states. But even there, the Federation and its enemies from other galaxies are, in effect, functional equivalents of sovereign states. The norms in space are not unlike those of Westphalia, and there seem always to be races (Klingons?) who, like Napoleonic France and Hitlerian Germany, would challenge those egalitarian live-and-let-live norms and attempt to create a hierarchical order they would then dominate. As Richard Falk contends, "the hold of sovereignty on the imagination remains strong enough that it will be invoked with ardor even as it diminishes in substance."[39]

Notes

1. Louis Henkin, quoted in Lapidoth, "Redefining Authority," p. 8.
2. David Thomson, quoted in James, *Sovereign Statehood*, p. 3.
3. A. A. Leff, quoted in James, *Sovereign Statehood*, p. 3.
4. Lapidoth, "Redefining Authority," p. 4.
5. *Ibid.*, p. 8.
6. The state of nature which Hobbes was describing is not "a true picture of any actual historical condition known to members of the species." See Miller, *Global Order*, p. 80.
7. There is an interesting discussion of the vehement debate that the release of *Danton* in 1983 precipitated among French Socialists and Communists in Danton, "Danton," pp. 104–9.
8. Miller, *Global Order*, p. 22.
9. Violent conflict over religion or issues rooted in religious differences quite obviously did not end with the Peace of Westphalia. Witness recent sectarian strife in India, in the Middle East, and in Northern Ireland. But religious wars on the scale of those that devastated Europe in the sixteenth and seventeenth centuries came to an end when the Thirty Years War came to an end.
10. Miller, *Global Order*, p. 22. Chapter 2 of Miller's book provides an excellent short analysis of the logic and the assumptions of the Westphalian order.
11. There have been several modern operas with themes relevant for students of international relations, foremost among them John Adams's *Nixon in China* and

The Death of Klinghoffer. However, these operas have not yet entered the basic repertory, nor is it likely that they will any time soon.

12. Osborne, *The Complete Operas of Verdi*, p. 353.

13. Geoffrey de C. Parmiter, quoted in James, *Sovereign Statehood*, p. 240.

14. Marius, "A Man for All Seasons," p. 72.

15. Donnelly, "State Sovereignty and International Intervention," pp. 116, 118.

16. Miller, *Global Order*, p. 25.

17. Not all international organizations employ the one-state, one-vote rule, of course; the World Bank and the International Monetary Fund, for example, use weighted voting, thereby according far more votes to the economic powers than to the smaller, weaker states.

18. Miller, *Global Order*, pp. 29–35.

19. See commentary on this film in T. Thomas, *The Great Adventure Films*, pp. 86–91.

20. Quoted in Shohat and Stam, *Unthinking Eurocentrism*, p. 351.

21. These three states have populations, respectively, of 85,000, 68,000, and 99,000. Of the UN's 185 members, the 41 with fewer than 1 million people each have a combined population of less than half of that of the city of Tokyo or the state of California. See Rourke, *International Politics,* p. 162.

22. Falk, "Toward Obsolescence, p. 35.

23. Ohmae, "The Rise of the Region State."

24. Wriston, "Technology and Sovereignty," pp. 71–72.

25. *Ibid.*, p. 75.

26. Falk, "Toward Obsolescence," p. 35.

27. Rosenau, "Sovereignty in a Turbulent World," p. 193.

28. Wriston, in "Technology and Sovereignty," discusses the efforts of the Soviet government to cover up the disaster at Chernobyl and the fact that such a coverup was rendered impossible due to observations by a French satellite.

29. *Non-refoulement*, a principle well established in treaty law, means that a refugee may not be returned to his place of departure if he would be endangered or subjected to persecution there.

30. Kael, "The Border," p. 120.

31. Functionalism holds that "technological and economic development lead to more and more supranational structures as states seek practical means to fulfill necessary *functions* such as delivering mail or phone calls from one country to another or coordinating the use of rivers that cross borders"; neofunctionalism is a modification of functionalism which argues "that economic integration (functionalism) generates a *political* dynamic that drives integration further." See Goldstein, *International Relations*, p. 391.

32. See, for example, Feldstein, "Why Maastricht Will Fail," pp. 12–19; Malcolm, "The Case Against 'Europe,'" pp. 52–68; and Dornbusch, "Euro Fantasies," 75:5, pp. 110–24.

33. E. Smith, "A Higher Power," p. 12.

34. Although the major issue confronting the EU is whether and when the members will adopt a common currency (the Euro), they remain sharply divided even on matters where the Eurocrats already possess substantial regulatory authority. A case in point is the amusing but revealing debate over whether a product labeled chocolate must consist entirely of cocoa butter. See Rourke, *International Politics,* p. 245.

35. Free trade areas and common markets have been established by states in various parts of the world (see the North American Free Trade Area, or NAFTA). But these arrangements for economic cooperation aspire only to eliminate barriers

to trade or otherwise facilitate a free flow of factors of production among the members; they are considerably less ambitious than the European Union.

36. Weiss and Chopra, "Sovereignty under Siege," p. 97.
37. *Ibid.*, p. 98.
38. This is a paraphrase of Spruyt, "Decline Reconsidered," p. 39.
39. Falk, "Toward Obsolescence," p. 75.

3

Nationalism and Its Discontents

Few topics in international relations have been the subject of more policy debate or more scholarly discussion in recent years than nationalism. The breakup of the Soviet Union and Yugoslavia was the principal catalyst for this phenomenon, but "the tide of nationalism and ethnic passions is still rising in a wide arc from central Europe to the heart of Asia."[1] Statesmen, academics, and journalists have been drawn to this dramatic evidence of ferment in a world that many had predicted would become less volatile with the end of the Cold War.[2]

From Nation to Nation-State

Nationalism presumes the existence of a nation. One frequently hears states referred to as "nations" or, alternatively, as "nation-states," but these terms are not synonymous and the distinctions are important. A state, properly speaking, has a defined territory, a population living in that territory, and a government that exercises control over that territory. It is the state that enjoys status as a sovereign entity. This much seems to be well established in international law. There is considerably less precision, however, when it comes to defining a nation. E. H. Hobsbawm has argued that "any sufficiently large body of people whose members regard themselves as members of a 'nation,' will be treated as such."[3] While this will not do as a definition, it does focus on what might be called "we-feeling"—the sense of common identity among a group of people. The question then becomes which factors shape that common identity, that sense of community. What are those things a people share that make them a nation?

The standard list of shared attributes typically includes ethnic homogeneity, a common history, a common language, and a common culture. These criteria are not, of course, fixed and firm; Hobsbawm not only refers to them as "fuzzy, shifting and ambiguous" but adds that they are "as useless

43

for purposes of the traveller's orientation as cloud-shapes are compared to landmarks."[4] It is clear that a nation and a state are not the same thing, although they may come together, producing a nation-state. The attributes of a nation are those of a people and are not necessarily linked to a particular territory; nor do they require the existence of a government.

Other kinds of communities share ethnicity, history, language, and culture. Tribes and castes and even extended families may be such communities. One of the most memorable scenes in the film *Lawrence of Arabia* illustrates this point. As Lawrence (Peter O'Toole) makes his way across the desert in search of Feisal, he and his guide stop by a well to drink and rest. Slowly out of the distance a figure appears, at first indistinct because of the shimmering heat waves rising from the desert floor. The rider approaching on a camel is Sherif Ali (Omar Sharif), and as he draws near the well, he shoots and kills Lawrence's guide. The guide's offense was that he drank from the well of another Bedouin tribe, something he knew he should not do. As Sherif Ali tells Lawrence, "He was nothing; the well is everything." In this corner of the world, in this cultural context, in this film, the community with which one identifies is that of the tribe. The Bedouins of one's tribe are "we," those of other tribes "they." By common agreement, nations are larger and more socially complex than tribes and other relatively exclusive social groups. Thus the Japanese are a nation, as are the French and the Russians and the Egyptians. Certain other peoples are united by culture, language, and common historical experiences, such as the Kurds, the Chechens, and the Quebecois, about whom we have heard a great deal in recent years. The difference, of course, is that each of the former group of nations also has a state—Japan, France, Russia, and Egypt—whereas the nations in the latter group have no state to call their own. There is no Kurdistan. Chechnya does not belong to the United Nations. Quebec is still a province of Canada.

In those cases in which the population of a state has the attributes of a nation, the result is a true nation-state. There may be minority communities within such a state, peoples speaking a different language and otherwise having an identity other than that of the great majority of the population. Few states in the world are entirely homogeneous, but many come close enough to warrant the appellation "nation-state," including some that are ethnically and otherwise diverse. Take the case of the United States. Not a nation according to traditional criteria, it is nonetheless widely regarded as one, having found a surrogate for those criteria in a civic religion or constitutional faith. As Benjamin Barber puts it, "the American constitutional faith is faith in a civil society that, precisely because it separates public from private, permits private differences and private freedoms to flourish without jeopardizing the political commons."[5] In effect, there may be many sources of national identity. Ernst Renan has stated it this way: "The essential element of a nation is that all of its individuals must have many things in common, but they must also have forgotten many things."[6]

Switzerland presents a somewhat different kind of a case. Its German-, French-, and Italian-speaking populations make it a multination-state, although one commentator says it "is better described as a confederation of relatively homogeneous territorial nation states (the cantons) than as a truly multiethnic society."[7] Belgium and Canada have also been textbook examples of states composed of at least two substantial nations. The colonial legacy of arbitrarily drawn borders in Africa has meant that many of the states on that continent lack the attributes of a true nation-state. And the roster of multination-states must now, following the breakup of the Soviet Union, include all of the former republics and especially Kazakhstan and Latvia, in each of which the Russian population is a very sizeable percentage of the whole.[8] If more evidence is needed, it can be found in the civil strife in the 1990s in Bosnia, Rwanda, and Burundi, each a recent reminder of the fact that many of the world's sovereign states are not really nation-states, but rather multination-states.

Just as some states contain within them two or more nations, so some nations exist in two or more states. The Kurdish nation, spread across Turkey, Iraq, and Iran (and even into Syria and the former USSR), is a politically salient case in point, and one of the potentially explosive issues in Russia is the fact that Russians in large numbers are now living as "minorities at risk" in what has been termed the "near abroad." These examples could be multiplied many times over. The fact is that nations and states are not everywhere coterminus, and where they are not the international system faces problems of varying degrees of intensity and urgency.

Not all states are nation-states and not all nations have their own state, but modern international history has been characterized by a seemingly inexorable movement toward a worldwide system of nation-states. Lynn Miller claims that "the final characteristic of the Westphalian construct [is] that the units in question be nation-states,"[9] and Michael Lind goes so far as to assert that "The simple idea that every nation should have its own state—accompanied by the corollary that one ethnic or cultural group should not collectively rule over another—has been the most powerful political force of the past two hundred years."[10] Through most of the eighteenth century, it was still the king who typically defined the state, not the people, which is to say the nation. The event above all others that stimulated modern nationalism and ushered in the age of the nation-state was the French Revolution. The system of sovereign states that emerged after Westphalia has been enormously strengthened by the fact that it eventually became in principle, and in many respects in practice, a system of sovereign *nation*-states.

> The equation of the state and the nation not only invested the state with a legitimacy it had not previously possessed; that equation also gave to

the claim of state equality an appeal and force it had never before enjoyed. For the equality of nation-states evoked, if nothing else, a far more
persuasive analogy with the ideal of individual equality than had the
analogy between states and men. The ideal of the nation carried with it a
quality of 'naturalness,' hence a quality of individuality that could be attributed to the state alone only with considerable difficulty.[11]

Nationalism as Patriotic Fervor

If a nation is a matter of shared identity, nationalism refers to a self-
consciousness about that identity. The nation is a fact, to be described.
Nationalism is that fact set in purposive motion. One of the most persuasive definitions of nationalism has been provided by William Pfaff, who
argues that

> nationalism is an expression of the primordial attachments of an individ-
> ual to a group, possessing both positive and destructive powers, and this
> is a phenomenon which existed long before the group to which such pas-
> sionate loyalty was attached became a modern nation-state. . . . The na-
> tionalist has his heart in his work. . . . He acts from the roots of being, of
> human society, from a given earth and clan—primordial attachments.[12]

Nationalism may mean only the celebration and exaltation of the nation,
but more often than not it has also meant advocacy of independence, self-
determination, or autonomy for the nation. It is the film treatment of nationalism, not the nation, that is of greatest interest to those who would
turn to popular culture for a greater understanding of international relations. To be sure, a great many films deal with particular nations. They explore the cultural traits and histories of nations; they dissect national character. The people we see on screen seem to reflect the nation of which they
are a part, assuming the film maker is knowledgeable and sensitive. There
is such a thing as a French film, a Japanese film, a British film, an American film, and so on; when we hear critics make that claim, we assume
they are saying more than simply that the genre in question is a mainstay
of that country's film output.

But nationalism calls attention to itself in ways that the nation does
not. One minor example occurs in one of the most popular movies ever
made, *Casablanca*. The enduring appeal of this improbable story may be
attributed to many factors, including of course Humphrey Bogart's world-
weary antihero and the many memorable lines.[13] The portrayal of (and the
appeal to) nationalism is one of *Casablanca's* more important features.
France has been defeated by Germany, and the puppet Vichy government
installed to govern portions of the country and its overseas possessions. In

one memorable scene, German officers are drinking and lording it over the anxious French refugees gathered at Rick's cafe in this Moroccan backwater of the war. They break into a song, "Watch on the Rhine," which carries the unmistakeable message that the world belongs to the Third Reich. It is then that French nationalism asserts itself. Paul Henreid, with Bogart's nod of consent, has the cafe orchestra strike up "The Marseillaise," and soon the room is transformed. It is an electrifying and emotional moment; as the motley assortment of people in the cafe join in a rousing rendition of the French national anthem, the viewer cannot help but be moved. Nowhere on film is music as a symbol of nationalism more powerfully used. For a few moments, all of us are French men and women.

Nationalism relies on many devices to mobilize and sustain public sentiment. The national anthem and other songs have served this purpose (Ken Burns's documentary, *The Civil War,* makes this point very effectively with its use of the music to which both the Union and the Confederacy went to war). So too, of course, has the flag, as well as other visual symbols of the nation. As noted earlier, the United States qualifies as a nation-state in spite of its great ethnic diversity, and the ubiquitous presence of the Stars and Stripes is a testament to that fact. But perhaps the best-known example of the flag as a means of generating feelings of nationalism was its use by the Nazis. Flags and banners bearing the swastika were flown everywhere and carried in seemingly endless ranks in celebratory parades. The premier example of this phenomenon on film is Leni Riefenstahl's *Triumph of the Will.* This documentary of the Nazi party rally at Nuremberg in 1934 has been universally praised for its craftsmanship, widely acknowledged as one of the most impressive pieces of propaganda on film, and equally widely denigrated in view of the cause it was meant to serve. This book is concerned with feature films, not documentaries, but *Triumph of the Will* is not a conventional documentary. One critic has claimed that Riefenstahl has transformed reality "into the stuff of repellent Wagnerian legend."[14] Another has explained the film's power in this way:

> The key to the atmosphere and impact achieved in the film is the montage. Riefenstahl consistently intercuts the great and the small. Close-ups of the spectators, long shots of the event as a whole, and shots from the point of view of the Party leaders are constantly mixed together by rapid editing. Thus the illusion is created of the all-embracing presence of both the camera and the film audience. Through the film, therefore, the Party Rally can be experienced in a much stronger, more intense, but also more emotionally manipulative, manner than would have been possible at the event itself.[15]

Triumph of the Will is a powerful demonstration not only that flags and parades can stir strong feelings of nationalism, but that cinema itself can do so. This is something that twentieth-century totalitarian regimes were quick to discover. Lenin said that "of all the arts, for us cinema is the most important"[16] because of its value as a weapon of agitation and propaganda. Both the Soviet Union and Nazi Germany recognized the capacity of films to produce citizen identification with the nation. For Hitler, the nation was all-important, "Deutschland Uber Alles" the paramount goal. For Soviet leaders, of course, class was initially more important than state or nation; however, the circumstances in which the USSR found itself after the revolution dictated that it, too, would need to mobilize nationalist sentiments. Both German and Soviet governments kept a tight rein on their respective film industries and used them to serve their agendas.

The most familiar example of a Soviet film made with the explicit purpose of promoting a sense of nationalism is Sergei Eisenstein's *Alexander Nevsky*. It may also be the best example of such a film made at any time in any country. The film was made in 1938, and although the action depicted on the screen takes place in the thirteenth century, the message was intended for contemporary viewers. Eisenstein, whose silent films such as *Battleship Potemkin* had enjoyed world-wide acclaim, had by the late 1930s fallen out of favor with Stalin. Eisenstein chose the story of Russia's defeat of the Teutonic (German) knights seven centuries earlier as a vehicle both for his own rehabilitation and for the strengthening of national resolve in an increasingly uncertain and dangerous time. "The long alienation between the regime and society,"[17] for which Stalin's collectivization and industrial policies and purges were largely responsible, had weakened the country's sense of nationhood, and although the audience for which *Nevsky* was intended included many peoples like the Ukrainians who were not Russian, the celebration of Russian nationalism just might rouse the patriotism of all Soviet peoples.

In the film, the Germans (costumed and directed to look like evil incarnate) are advancing on Novgorod, having captured Pskov and inflicted all manner of terrible atrocities on its citizens. A delegation seeks out Nevsky, hero of an earlier war with Sweden and surrogate for Stalin, urging him to take command and defend Novgorod. In a telling rejoinder, Nevsky vows to fight, not for Novgorod, but for Russia, and to do so by taking the offensive. In this one exchange, Eisenstein sets the tone for the picture as a whole; it is the Russian nation as a whole, roused from its lethargy and parochialism, that will do battle with the enemy—and prevail. And of course it does, the Russians defeating the Teutonic knights in the justly famous Battle on the Ice of Lake Chudskoe; as the Germans sink one by one in the icy waters, the viewer cannot help but think of the fate that has awaited European invaders like Napoleon and Hitler, trapped in the grip of Russian winters.

Alexander Nevsky, with its powerful musical score by Sergei Prokofiev and its brilliantly choreographed battle scenes, remains one of great evocations of nationalism and among the most compelling of all propaganda films. But democracies have also used film to create a sense of national purpose. Examples are legion, especially during the years just prior to and during World War II. Hollywood did go to war, at first tentatively and amid great controversy while the United States was still officially neutral, and then wholeheartedly after Pearl Harbor. In the latter period, Hollywood's mission, with government prodding to make sure that no one missed the point, was to extol the nation's virtues and remind the viewer what the country was fighting for.[18] Britain, of course, also turned out many films designed to bolster a sense of nationalism and sustain morale in that country's darkest hour, among them Noel Coward's *In Which We Serve* and Lawrence Olivier's *Henry V*. Ironically, one of the best examples of this type of movie was made in America about England, Michael Curtiz's 1940 swashbuckler, *The Sea Hawk*. Like *Alexander Nevsky,* this popular Errol Flynn film was set several centuries in the past and dealt with efforts to heighten national consciousness and rouse the country to an awareness of its danger. In this case, the threat came from Spain and the climax was the defeat of the Spanish Armada, but like *Nevsky*, *The Sea Hawk* was really about something much more contemporary—the German Luftwaffe and the Battle of Britain.

Nationalism became a major ideology in the nineteenth century, undermining the legitimacy of dynastic rule. No longer could monarchs say, as Louis XIV had, "L'Etat c'est moi." The primary catalyst for this change was the French Revolution.

> Rising political groups no longer wanted the state of France to be defined by the king but to be defined in terms of the nation, all the people. And externally, as Napoleon's armies marched across Europe, they disrupted society and mobilized nationalist feelings among German-speaking peoples and others. By the middle of the century, there was widening support for the idea that each nation should have a state.[19]

It was thus inevitable that nations that were fragmented or living under the yoke of an alien power would grow restless and seek to form their own nation-state. The result was a period of integral nationalism, highlighted by the unification of Germany and Italy. Much of the early literature on nationalism treated it as a centripetal force, a natural outcome of the desires of peoples sharing language and culture to be united in a single state. Integral nationalism has not received nearly as much attention from filmmakers as has the breakup of empires and states, or centrifugal nationalism. There has, of course, been far more of the latter, beginning with the disintegration of the Austro-Hungarian and Ottoman empires and more recently with the collapse of European colonialism.

Italian unification, or at least the surge of nationalism which led to it, was a focus of Luchino Visconti's lush, operatic film, *Senso*. Set during the Risorgimento when Venice was under Austrian rule, *Senso* is about an ill-fated romance between an Italian countess and an Austrian officer; he proves to be a scoundrel, and in the end she denounces him and he is executed by the Austrians. The action takes place during the campaign for Italian independence and unification, and the theme of nationalism receives dramatic screen treatment at the very beginning of the film. *Senso* opens during a performance of Verdi's *Il Trovatore* at the Venetian opera house. As the tenor concludes one of Verdi's most impassioned arias, the house explodes in a demonstration of Italian patriotism, the audience raining leaflets down on the Austrian officers in attendance and demanding that they leave Venice. It is a brief scene, and although nothing in the remainder of the film matches its power, it makes *Senso* a memorable window on the subject of European nationalism. Inasmuch as it is a Verdi opera that sets the stage for the outpouring of Italian nationalist sentiments in this film, it should perhaps be noted that Verdi himself was an important catalyst for Italian nationalism. The chorus of Hebrew slaves, "Va Pensiero," in his early opera *Nabucco,* quickly became the virtual national anthem of the country, the Italians seeing in the Hebrews' lament over their captivity a parallel to their own subjugation by the Austrians.

Nationalism as Solvent of Colonialism

Nationalism as a challenge to or solvent of colonial empires receives attention in two sets of films. In the first category are those films that side with the colonial powers, or at least with the troops who man the outposts of empire and have the task of defending those outposts against the numerically superior (and, in the more conspicuously Eurocentric films, less civilized) natives. The other and much more important category includes films that focus instead on the struggle for independence.

   In some of the films of imperial adventure (or misadventure), the heroic Europeans prevail, at least for the duration of the film, and in others they fail nobly, although there is often a suggestion that their defeat will be avenged. Cy Endfield's *Zulu* illustrates the former outcome. In this colorful recreation of the 1879 battle of Rorke's Drift in what is now the Republic of South Africa, a company of 139 men of the British 24th Regiment withstands the onslaught of some four thousand Zulu warriors. Although it is a battle of Zulu spears against British firearms, there seems little likelihood that the thin red line of Her Majesty's soldiers, exhausted by repeated and frightening attacks, will survive; but in the end, the Zulu warriors withdraw, acknowledging the bravery of their outnumbered adversary and leaving hundreds of their own dead on the field. More Victoria Crosses were awarded after Rorke's Drift than for any other single day of combat in British history, and the film helps us to understand why. But *Zulu* comes about as close to being an even-handed account of events as any film about the defense of empire. As one reviewer puts it, *Zulu* is *Gunga Din* for real.[20] The British soldiers do not make fun of the Zulu, and the film clearly conveys the admiration for the warrior nation felt by those responsible for this epic. Nonetheless, the viewer is expected to identify with the beleaguered British troops. The odds against them are enormous, encouraging our sympathy for the underdog. We also get to know them as individuals, so that we can feel their fear as they brace for the next attack, knowing that their numbers are dwindling and that they can expect no relief. The Zulu, on the other hand, are both numerous and faceless. They may be fighting for their nation against an alien and unwanted intruder, but this hisoric fact is not likely to be uppermost in the mind of the casual viewer.

In *Zulu,* the triumph of nationalism is deferred. The subsequent history of South Africa reminds us just how complex the cause of nationalism can be; it was not until well over a century later that the descendants of European settlers turned control of the government over to the majority black population, and many of today's Zulu, who regard themselves as a separate nation, remain dissatisfied with their lot in post-apartheid South Africa. The denouement in *Khartoum* is the opposite of that in *Zulu,* which is to say that the outnumbered British garrison in the Sudan is overrun, Khartoum falling to "the Mahdi's spectacular *jihad.*"[21] Thus the cause of Sudanese nationalism would seem to be better served than that of Zulu nationalism. But of course neither film tells the full story. The Mahdi and much of his army were dead within a matter of months of their triumph, the victims of disease, not British guns, and many years would pass before the Sudanese had their state or the British imperium in Africa came to an end.

Nationalism as a restive force under European colonial rule is on display in many movies, although, as in the cases of *Zulu* and *Khartoum,* the producers and directors are usually more interested in the fate of the Europeans than they are in the native populace that has precipitated the conflict we see on screen by daring to challenge the colonial power. Other films, however, explore the conflict between colonialism and nationalism from a perspective that is openly sympathetic to the latter. Such films are much less likely to belong to the genre of adventure films, are much more likely to present three-dimensional portraits of those fighting for their independence, and are far more likely to offer sustenance to those seeking to learn about nationalism in particular and international relations in general from watching movies. Two films in particular come to mind. They are very different from each other in almost every respect but two: both deal with movements that succeed in bringing independence from colonial rule before the end credits roll, and both are made by directors who clearly identify with those movements.

Richard Attenborough's worshipful biographical film *Gandhi* is one of these; Gillo Pontecorvo's gritty and acutely realistic *Battle of Algiers* is the other. *Gandhi* is both the story of the life of one of the twentieth century's most interesting and arguably most important figures and the story of India's struggle for independence from Great Britain. *Battle of Algiers* has no figure equivalent to Gandhi, unless it is the collective Algerian people; it concentrates on Algeria's struggle for independence from France. This difference helps to explain the very different feel of the two movies. Because *Gandhi* is a biographical film, it unfolds over a period of many years, whereas *Battle of Algiers* takes place in a much more constricted time frame. This fact, along with the documentary style Pontecorvo employs, gives *Battle of Algiers* a feeling of immediacy the Attenborough film lacks.

Perhaps the most important difference for students of international relations lies in the strategies employed by the two nationalist movements. In the Algerian case—and *Battle of Algiers* makes the point unflinchingly—blood must be shed for nationalism to prevail against a stubborn, unyielding foe, the French settlers and their metropolitan supporters. This is a violent film, which accurately captures the extreme measures employed by both French and Algerians during the bitter conflict. *Gandhi,* of course, reflects the Mahatma's life-long belief in *satyagraha* or nonviolent resistance, in this case to British colonial rule. Although there is no shortage of violence in *Gandhi,* the film does convey the message that the strategy of nonviolent resistance did wear down British resolve and contributed significantly to independence. Nationalism triumphs in both Algeria and India. But victory does not come easily and the costs are high. That the Algerians and the Indians were prepared to accept those costs is a telling commentary on the power of nationalism. Whatever else may be said about *Gandhi* and *Battle of Algiers,* they succeed in demonstrating the power of that idea.

Of the two films, *Gandhi* is by far the more verbal. Both the Indians and the British talk a lot, among themselves and with each other, and in the process give voice to the arguments for and against independence of colonial peoples. Gandhi himself is, of course, the most articulate and the most persuasive (Ben Kingsley's Academy Award–winning performance has much to do with this). The clinching argument for national self-determination is made by the Mahatma in a meeting between the British governor-general and his staff and the Indian leaders following the massacre at Jallianwalla Bagh in the spring of 1919; it may be said to be the intellectual climax of the film. "You are masters in someone else's home," says Gandhi, brushing aside British efforts to repudiate the massacre. "You must in the nature of things humiliate us to control us. It is time you left. . . . There is no people on earth who wouldn't prefer their own bad government to the good government of an alien power."

These words are spoken in the emotionally charged atmosphere created by the massacre, and a few words about it (and its presentation in the movie) are in order, in view of its dramatic intensity on film and the challenge it posed for Gandhi's policy of nonviolent resistance to British rule. Britain had imposed certain restrictions on the exercise of civil liberties in India, and Gandhi had called upon Indians to refuse to obey those laws. In spite of a prohibition of public meetings, several thousand people had gathered in the walled Bagh, or garden, in the Sikh holy city of Amritsar. In the film, a speaker, in the spirit of Gandhi's principle of *satyagraha*, is urging the people to resist the British by peaceful means when an English general arrives, blocks the only exit, and orders his men to fire on the crowd. The resulting carnage is horrible to see on the screen, just as it must have been in reality in 1919. The general responsible for the massacre subsequently appears before a hearing during which British officials are clearly appalled by his actions and his defense of them. (It may have been episodes like this that persuaded Ella Shohat and Robert Stam, in their treatise on Eurocentrism, to argue that Attenborough subtly prettifies the British role.[22]) There can be no doubt that this massacre and related events made the peaceful pursuit of Indian independence much more problematic.

Gandhi himself is both resolute and optimistic (although we know, as he did not, that independence will not come for nearly thirty more years). At the conclusion of the postmassacre meeting, one of the British officials asks, "You don't think we're just going to walk out of India?" Gandhi's reply is unequivocal: "Yes, in the end you will walk out. Because 100,000 Englishmen simply cannot control 350 million Indians if those Indians refuse to cooperate. And this is what we intend to achieve—peaceful, nonviolent non-cooperation, until you yourself see the wisdom of leaving."

The goal is clear. And so is the strategy of active nonviolent resistance. What remains is for Gandhi to devise tactics that will convince the British to leave. Much of the film is about these tactics, including a nationwide work stoppage (which Gandhi prefers to call a day of prayer and fasting), the burning of clothes made in Manchester and Leeds and the wearing of homespun, and, most notably, the famous salt march in 1930. According to one American authority, the latter event "was to the Indian independence movement what the Boston Tea Party was to ours."[23] British policy forbade the Indians to make their own salt, forcing them to purchase it from government shops where it was heavily taxed. Gandhi chose to defy this law, and set off on a long walk to the sea where he would make salt from sea water. This unlikely symbolic issue caught fire across India, leading to the jailing of Gandhi and thousands of his followers and forcing London finally to take him seriously.

The salt march, like the massacre at Jallianwalla Bagh, is one of the high points of the film and makes an impressive demonstration of the power of nationalism in action. The remainder of the film moves relatively quickly to its historical conclusion; the issue is no longer whether the British will leave, but when—and, of course, whether India shall become a single state or two states, one Hindu and one Muslim. Independence, having been delayed by World War II, finally comes in 1947.

Battle of Algiers, like *Gandhi* one of the great films about nationalism, is an altogether different kind of experience for the viewer. The Indian struggle for independence is episodic and protracted. The Indians provoke the British; the British respond with legislation, jailings, and occasionally brutal measures; the Indians turn to yet another form of provocation; the British, increasingly frustrated and puzzled by Gandhi's tactics, repeat the cycle. On the whole, it is a battle of wills more than a battle of guns. In Algeria, it is all very different. It is, quite plainly, war. By comparison with the British, the French are ruthless. They do not stop with jailing the rebel leaders; they torture them in stomach-turning scenes (some of which were subsequently deleted when the film was shown in the United States), and they plant bombs in Arab residential quarters. Algerians are not disciples of Gandhi. They are presented as terrorists who will resort to any means to demonstrate their determination to be rid of French control. One of the most memorable sequences in the film has three Algerian women, dressed and made up so as to appear European, calmly pass through police checkpoints and plant bombs in places full of French citizens—a cafeteria, a milk bar, and an airline terminal. When these bombs explode, men, women, and children alike are indiscriminately killed. Their deaths affect us, even if we side with the Algerian cause, because we have seen them in close-up, going about their lives quite innocently, only minutes before the explosions. The film's director, Gillo Pontecorvo, supports the cause of Algerian independence, but he doesn't pretend that the Algerians have clean hands; in such a struggle, both sides do what they believe they have to do.

There is a surfeit of violence in movies today, much of it presented for its shock value rather than because it serves any larger purpose. Pontecorvo clearly had something else in mind. He wants to tell the truth about guerrilla warfare, and there may be no film that comes closer to saying to the audience, "This is the way it is." Gandhi is just as single-minded as the Algerian FLN, but Pontecorvo's film is the more representative portrayal of the struggle for independence from colonial rule. In many instances the colonial powers ultimately did walk away without a fight, the cost of empire having become prohibitive, but violent conflict has been a factor in the triumph of nationalism in more than a few places, and *Battle of Algiers* remains "excruciatingly pertinent in view of the increase in similar anguished confrontations today."[24]

A third film worth a brief mention for its depiction of the struggle to end colonialism is *Indochine,* which also deals with the reluctance of France to abandon her colonies in the face of nationalist uprisings. Most U.S. movies that deal with Vietnamese nationalism are more interested in the effect of the Vietnam War on the United States and its troops than they are in the Vietnamese people and their struggle. *Indochine* provides some perspective on Vietnamese nationalism during the French colonial era. It is not in a league with *Gandhi* or *Battle of Algiers* as a study of nationalism and the fight for independence. It is too much of a romantic historical saga (reviewers have likened it to *Gone with the Wind* [25]), and it is too preoccupied with the story of two women: Eliane (Catherine Deneuve), the wealthy owner of a rubber plantation in French Indochina, and Camille, a young Annamese woman whom Deneuve is raising as her own daughter and who becomes radicalized by a series of plot-driven events; at film's end Camille is a member of a communist delegation negotiating the end of French rule in Indochina. However, over the quarter-century encompassed by the film we are witness to the gradual escalation of conflict between the communists and the colonial authorities as well as to the hauteur and the cruelty of the French, which helps to fuel the Vietnamese rebellion. While the anticolonial struggle is overshadowed by the personal drama (and by the breathtaking photography), *Indochine* belongs on any short list of films dealing with nationalism as a solvent of colonial rule. The slave market scene on the dock at remote Dragon Island ranks with the massacre at Jallianwalla Bagh in *Gandhi* as one of filmdom's more memorable illustrations of colonial authority gone horribly wrong. While we may sympathize with the Deneuve character at the film's end, when "her" Vietnam is gone forever, few viewers will harbor regrets at the demise of this "self-indulgent, exotic colonial paradise,"[26] for we have seen its darker underside and know that Vietnam does indeed belong to the Vietnamese.

Nationalism as Exclusivity

Conflicts often develop as to tactics and timing within nationalist organizations. Occasionally, these fissures have become so deep as to fracture nationalist movements, producing two or more nationalisms with conflicting agendas. Gandhi had always insisted that all Indians, whether Hindu or Muslim, shared a common destiny. History and the film suggest that religious differences were sublimated for much of the struggle against British imperialism, but as independence became more and more probable, the Muslim community, led by Gandhi's erstwhile ally, Mohammed Ali Jinnah, demanded its own state. The result, as we know, was the creation of two sovereign states, India and Pakistan. The film does not begin to show us the magnitude of the bloodshed that accompanied independence and the mass movements of people that followed, but it does not shrink from showing us the tragic collapse of nonviolence, and it reminds us that the shared sense of nationalism needed to bring an end to alien rule may not be the same as that required to create a viable postcolonial nation-state. In the end, India was not one nation but two, with religion the distinguishing factor.

The complex nature of nationalism was further demonstrated in 1971 when East Pakistan broke away to become Bangladesh. The common bond of Islam was not strong enough to keep the ethnically different Bengalis within the state that Jinnah had carved out of India in the late 1940s. With many variations, this story has been repeated in other parts of the Third World in the wake of decolonization. The nationalism of rebellion against colonial powers has been replaced in country after country by more narrowly defined nationalisms, and the greatest challenge facing the leaders of many a "new" state has been to forge a broadly based nationalism in situations in which identities and loyalties are more parochial. One of the best illustrations of this challenge is to be found, not in a feature film, but in a powerful novel of postcolonial Africa, V. S. Naipul's *A Bend in the River*. The fictional head of a newly independent state, loosely based on Congo (Zaire), tries to invent symbols and implement policies that will generate a sense of nationhood among the citizenry. In Naipul's pessimistic vision, this proves to be an impossible mission.

The problem also provides the climax of *Lawrence of Arabia*. The Turks have been defeated and Feisal's army has entered Damascus. Lawrence wants a provisional Arab administration to be in control before the European forces arrive, and the film provides us with a fictionalized account of his efforts to effect that control.[27] A large number of Arab leaders gathers in the Damascus town hall and almost immediately they fall to quarreling among themselves. It quickly becomes apparent that Arab unity, always fragile throughout the film, is a chimera, that tribalism takes precedence over Arab nationalism. Of course the Sykes-Picot Treaty, whereby Britain and France would exercise direct administration and maintain well-defined spheres of influence in the region, had already guaranteed that the Arabs would not be the principal beneficiaries of the end of Turkish rule in the Levant. But the failure of Arab nationalism contributed then, as it has in more recent times, to the problems of that troubled region, where conflicts among the states that emerged from the ruins of the Ottoman Empire have made a mockery of pretensions of Arab unity.

In *Gandhi* and *Lawrence of Arabia,* both pictures of epic scope, nationalism as a vehicle for challenging and ending foreign domination is in the end transformed into nationalism as an assertion of exclusivity. This latter aspect of nationalism is also on display in Mira Nair's much more modest film *Mississippi Masala*. This movie is primarily about an interracial romance in the contemporary American south between an African-American man (Denzel Washington) and an Indian woman (Sarita Choudhury); neither his family nor hers approves of the affair, and Nair provides us with a sensitive and wryly amusing study of racial, cultural, and generational conflict. But the film's opening sequence, much of it unfolding while the credits roll, is a powerful commentary on one of the less attractive expressions of nationalism. It takes place in Uganda just after independence as Idi Amin, the Ugandan strongman, forces the Indians out of the country. It does not matter that these people have lived their whole lives in Uganda, or that they have much to contribute to its success as a new sovereign state. In this example of what today we might call ethnic cleansing, it has been decided that there is no room for the Indians; as one character puts it succinctly to Choudhury's father, Africa is now for the Africans. As so often has been the case, those who are expelled must leave the country quickly, can take only a very few personal belongings with them, and are harassed as they go. We see it in *Gandhi,* as Hindus and Muslims trudge in long lines in opposite directions to their new homes. We see it in *Mississippi Masala,* as the Indian family travels by bus to the Entebbe airport for the flight that will take them to America. In a harrowing scene, the mother is forcefully removed from the bus and threatened by an African policeman, although her only offense is that she is an Indian at a time and place when African nationalism has turned ugly. Amin did indeed expel the Indians (and subsequently turned on "Africans" who were not of his tribe in a brutal demonstration of the nationalism of exclusivity). Nair, in a few brief moments, captures this face of nationalism—intolerance of those who are different, whether because of race, religion, ethnicity, or culture. The Indian family survives to make a new life (with new problems) in another place, but in reality many of those who are different are slaughtered, sometimes in near-genocidal proportions. Bosnia and Rwanda are only the latest tragic examples of this dark side of nationalism, and they are unlikely to be the last.

Resurgence of Ethnic and Religious Nationalism

It was widely believed that nationalism was largely a spent force by the end of the decolonization process. Some territorial adjustments might be needed to correct for the artificial legacies of colonialism (although even those concessions to nationalist sentiments were resisted by most governments, especially in Africa), but most observers assumed that the map of the world was no longer in great flux. By the 1990s, however, nationalism, long held in check by the rough discipline of the Cold War between the superpowers, has erupted once more and has indeed become one of the salient features of contemporary international politics. This development has produced a sharp debate between those who find the prospect of an explosion of more nation-states unsettling and those who not only take a more relaxed view of the matter but tend to view it as preferable to the suppression of minorities within multinational states.

   Gidon Gottlieb speaks for the former position, arguing that "self-determination unleashed and unchecked by balancing principles constitutes a menace to the society of states. There is simply no way in which all the hundreds of peoples who aspire to sovereign independence can be granted a state of their own without loosening fearful anarchy and disorder on a planetary scale."[28] Fearful of the consequences of nationalism run amok, Gottlieb has advocated a provocative but highly problematic approach to the problem of restive national minorities. His concept of a "new space for nations" necessarily requires the deconstruction of the notion of sovereignty, creating a parallel world of nations, with sovereignty over people, to go with the world of states, with their sovereignty over territory.[29] The evidence to date is that the world—and many bitter national minorities, from Chechnyans in Russia to Tamils in Sri Lanka—is not ready for Gottlieb's half-loaf. And so we are left with smoldering and occasionally fiercely burning nationalism on virtually every continent.

Not everyone is troubled by this. Michael Lind, writing in defense of liberal nationalism, finds a widespread prejudice against nationalism as if it were "an anachronistic and dangerous relic of a previous age. . . . This prejudice against nationalism—even liberal, democratic, constitutional nationalism—is a mistake. Reflexive support for multinational political entities, especially despotic ones, is as misguided as the automatic rejection of movements that seek the sovereignty of national homelands."[30] Lind dismisses the argument that global disorder will follow in the wake of the further proliferation of nation-states. We cannot, of course, know how many new nation-states will emerge or what the consequences will be. We do know that nationalism remains a powerful force, rooted not only in shared ethnicity and culture but also "flowing from history, from wrongs suffered, from sacrifices made, and from symbolic and mythical elements that move nations in ways that transcend cold considerations of statecraft."[31]

The bitter, multisided conflict in the former Yugoslavia in the 1990s is surely a prime example of this proposition. First in Croatia and then in Bosnia, peoples of different nationalities who had lived side by side and even intermarried in considerable numbers became embroiled in no-holds-barred warfare, committing unspeakable acts against each other, all in the name of narrowly defined nationalism. The worst offenders, it is generally agreed, were the Serbs, of whom a former U.S. ambassador to Yugoslavia says, "Their tragic defect is an obsession with their own history; their hearts are in the past, not in the future."[32] The obsessive and irrational nationalism of such men as Croatian president Tudjman and the Bosnian Serb leader Karadzic is well captured in the ambasssador's story of a conversation with the latter.

> I was startled to hear the extravagance of Karadzic's claims on behalf of the Serbs. He told me that "Serbs have a right to territory not only where they're now living but also where they're buried, since the earth they lie in was taken unjustly from them." When I asked whether he would accept parallel claims on behalf of Croats or Muslims, he answered, "No, because Croats are fascists and Muslims are Islamic fanatics."[33]

The international community's response to this virulent conflict of nationalisms in the Balkans also serves to undermine Gottlieb's argument that the rising tide of nationalism threatens to unleash "fearful anarchy and disorder on a planetary scale." Sarajevo 1994 turned out very differently from Sarajevo 1914. Although the powers eventually took steps to bring the violence in that region to an end, ethnonational conflict raged for several years, especially in Bosnia, without ever threatening a larger war. Whereas in 1914 the assassination of the heir to the Austrian throne—an act rooted in nationalist aspiration—had ignited a chain reaction that quickly engulfed Europe in the great tragedy of World War I, in the 1990s none of the powers felt its interests threatened by events in that troubled region. The problem was not that the powers felt compelled to intervene on the side of one or another of the parties to the latest Balkan war, but rather that they displayed a general unwillingness to intervene effectually to rein in nationalistic excesses and stop the fighting. This aspect of the issue of intervention will be explored in Chapter 4.

The crisis of 1914 has never had a satisfactory treatment on film; there is, of course, the promisingly titled *The Day that Shook the World,* but this international production focuses more on the lives of the young student revolutionaries in the days leading up to their assassination of Archduke Ferdinand than on the nationalist cause that motivated them. The collapse in the 1990s of the Yugoslav state that had been cobbled together after World War I has already been the subject of films such as *Vukovar* and *Before the Rain.* The former is the story of a mixed marriage between a Croatian woman and a Serbian man, set in the Croatian city of Vukovar, itself largely ruined by the bloody war between the competing nationalisms of her people and his. The marriage represents the multinational society that might have been; the reality is far grimmer—death, destruction, and, somehow worst of all, the rapes that reduce nationalism to some kind of horrible pathology. *Before the Rain* takes place largely in Macedonia, formerly a constituent republic of Yugoslavia, but now independent and decidedly insecure in the cauldron of ethnic and geopolitical conflict in the southern Balkans. Like Bosnia, Macedonia has a volatile population mix; Orthodox Slavs constitute the majority, Albanian Muslims the minority. The potentially explosive tensions between them[34] are the subject of Milcho Manchevski's film, in which the hatred of the two ethnic groups for each other precipitates frightening acts of violence that override the efforts of the courageous few who try to bring an end to the madness. The viewer cannot be sanguine that Macedonia will escape the fate of Bosnia.

Before leaving the subject of nationalism and turning to the related issue of intervention, it would be useful to comment on two other familiar instances of modern-day nationalism. In both cases, the disaffected community has demanded autonomy. In both cases, at least until very recently, that demand had been rejected. The result has been a history of violence on both sides, violence that has kept these issues prominently on the agenda of contemporary international relations.

The first of these cases is that of Northern Ireland, where the Catholic minority has been engaged in a long struggle for autonomy. Many Catholics, and certainly Sinn Fein and its militant wing, the Irish Republican Army (IRA), would like union with the Republic of Ireland, denied them in the Government of Ireland Act of 1920, which led to the union of Northern Ireland (Ulster) with Great Britain. The Protestant majority prefers the status quo, and the presence of British troops to counteract IRA terrorism has only intensified the hostility of the Catholic population. The conflct between the two communities has often been bloody, and in spite of negotiations and occasional hints of progress toward settlement, one commentator argues that "the conflict appears less susceptible to resolution than any other ethnoconflict in the western democracies."[35]

This example of religious nationalism has been visited in several films, including *The Crying Game, In the Name of the Father,* and even *Patriot Games.* But no film better captures this conflict than the intimate and intensely human *Cal.* The focus of the film is the relationship between an inarticulate young Catholic man (John Lynch), who is the reluctant driver of a getaway car for the IRA, and the older widow (Helen Mirren) of a policeman gunned down by the IRA. Cal, who wants to get away from all of the violence but cannot, comes to realize that he was the driver the night the policeman was killed; the guilt-ridden young man is tormented by this knowledge but finds himself drawn to the widow, and eventually these two lonely people make love. This disturbing look at the human consequences of nationalist fervor is set against a background of fear and violence. Cal lives with his father in a hostile Protestant neighborhood; their house is virtually under siege, and it is only a matter of time before the threats against them become reality and their house is burned down. A major part of the film's power lies in its bleak and brooding atmosphere, "a war-torn world, where peace and quiet, like the calm in the eye of a hurricane, loom ominously over the damp city streets."[36] There is no happy ending here, nor would such an ending have been appropriate. At the film's climax, Cal is caught by the British and taken away as the widow watches. Thus ends a doomed love affair and, by implication, the likelihood of reconciliation between the factions in this tragic conflict.

The other familiar instance of volatile modern-day nationalism has been that of the Palestinians. The story of the Palestinians' inability to secure a territorial base for their political aspirations is a familiar one, and need not be repeated here. We know that for decades the Palestinians, working through the Palestine Liberation Organization (PLO) and other groups, waged both diplomatic and terrorist warfare against Israel, always with the objective of creating a state of Palestine (and, for many, terminating the existence of the Zionist state). The problem of the Jewish diaspora has been resolved, but the problem of the Palestinian diaspora remains. The efforts of the Palestinians to achieve their goals have been the subject of a number of films, most of which have been of the action genre and routinely caricature the Arabs. In fact, Western popular culture has, on the whole and over many years, done much to demonize Arabs and Islam.[37]

One of the more hopeful efforts to present the Palestinian problem on screen is to be found in Michel Khleifi's *Wedding in Galilee,* a rare film produced in Israel with an Arab point of view. Although its greatest strength may be its insights into the culture and traditions of the Palestinian community, the film has something important to say about the dilemma of nationalism under foreign occupation. An elder in a Palestinian village wants to hold a traditional wedding for his son, one that will entail a celebration lasting long into the night and well past the curfew imposed by the Israeli authorities. The Israelis are initially adamant in their refusal of his plea, but ultimately agree on the condition that the military governor and his staff be allowed to attend as guests of honor. The wedding party does not go smoothly; an Israeli woman guard becomes sick, young Palestinian boys turn a prize horse loose into a field planted with Israeli mines, the groom is unable to consummate the marriage, and several militant Palestinians, dissatisfied with the decision to invite the military governor, plot to kill him. But the tone is generally light, and this microcosm of conflicting nationalisms manages to convey a message quite at odds with that of most films on the subject, which has been that the "primordial attachments" of nationalism make peaceful coexistence extremely difficult if not impossible. The peace process on which Israel and the PLO embarked in the 1990s initially produced considerable progress, with the Palestinians assuming responsibilities for self-governance in Gaza and some of the communities in the West Bank. Unfortunately, the campaign of violence mounted by the intransigent Palestinian organization Hamas in 1996 and the assassination of Israeli prime minister Yitzhak Rabin in 1995, events leading up to the return to power of the hard-line Likud party, have threatened to derail that process, suggesting that *Wedding in Galilee*'s cautious optimism may be premature.

At the close of the twentieth century, nationalism comes in a variety of forms. For some the distinguishing factor is ethnicity, for others it is language and culture, and more often than not it is some combination of these factors. As the cases of Pakistan (*Gandhi*), Macedonia (*Before the Rain*), Northern Ireland (*Cal*), and Palestine (*Wedding in Galilee*) make clear, religious nationalism, which had all but disappeared in the nineteenth century, is once again a powerful force in world affairs. As one writer has noted, "the unsecularization of the world is one of the dominant social facts of life in the late twentieth century."[38] But whether the problem is pathological ethnicity or the fusion of religion and nationalism, recidivist tribalism[39] today poses a profound challenge to the multinational and multicultural state. Minorities in all corners of the globe seem determined to seek autonomy rather than the more modest objective of respect for their rights within the existing polity—that is, to prefer what Albert O. Hirschman has called "exit" (autonomy) to "voice" (protest with the objective of improving their status within the state).[40]

In the best of all possible worlds, peoples of different ethnicities, religions, and cultures would live harmoniously together in democratic states, sharing a "civic ideology in which difference itself is recognized and honored."[41] But we do not live in such a world. As Benjamin Barber has argued, "where the social order has broken down, there is no recourse but to a civil religion of reciprocal rights and mutual respect";[42] but as Barber himself acknowledges and experience has demonstrated, there is little likelihood that the many fractious and fractured states will be able to emulate the American model, with its carefully nurtured constitutional faith and democratic institutions.

> Is there an equivalent of constitutional faith for India or Nigeria or Yugoslavia or Somalia that would pull the tribes off each other and nurture a framework for political unity? In America, constitutional faith has lost its novel artificial look. It has become conventional. Like an old shoe, it fits comfortably and its wearers need not examine too carefully how it was cobbled. But beyond American shores, constitutional faith has to be manufactured afresh each time a fractious nation-state tries to keep itself from flying apart. In the absence of a history of commitment to common civil practices, such an aridly secular faith is unlikely to draw much fealty. For what is its substance to be? Who is the "we" in Europe's or India's or Russia's "we the people?"[43]

Given these circumstances, nationalism promises to continue to be a source of conflict in international relations, conflict which will often turn violent given the passions which nationalism arouses. And inasmuch as films with strong conflict situations appeal to audiences and hence to producers, we may expect to see more movies about nationalism in the years immediately ahead.

Notes

1. Gottlieb, "Nations Without States," p. 102.
2. See, for example, Mearsheimer, "Why We Shall Soon Miss the Cold War," pp. 35–50.
3. Quoted in Gottlieb, *Nation Against State*, p. xi.
4. *Ibid.*
5. Barber, "Global Multiculturalism," p. 49.
6. Quoted in Nye, *Understanding International Conflicts*, p. 148.
7. Lind, "In Defense of Liberal Nationalism," p. 96.

8. Russians make up 37.8 percent of Kazakhstan's population and 34 percent of Latvia's. For these data, see Marshall, "States at Risk," pp. 210–14.

9. Miller, *Global Order,*" p. 25.

10. Lind, "In Defense of Liberal Nationalism," p. 87.

11. Tucker, *The Inequality of Nations*, p. 21.

12. Quoted in O'Brien, "The Wrath of Ages," p. 144.

13. Who is not familiar with such lines as "I stick my neck out for no one"; "Here's looking at you, kid"; "We'll always have Paris"; "The problems of three little people don't amount to a hill of beans"; "Go ahead and shoot, you'll be doing me a favor"; "Louis, I think this is the start of a beautiful friendship"?

14. Hunter, *Movie Classics*, p. 225.

15. Lloyd, *Seventy Years at the Movies*, p. 150.

16. *Ibid.*, p. 63.

17. Conquest, *Stalin: Breaker of Nations*, p. 177.

18. Lloyd, *Seventy Years at the Movies*, pp. 157–63.

19. Nye, *Understanding International Conflicts*, p. 149.

20. T. Thomas, *The Great Adventure Films*, p. 262.

21. Lewis, "Khartoum," p. 164.

22. Shohat and Stam, *Unthinking Eurocentrism*, p. 123.

23. Ward, "Gandhi," p. 254.

24. Vermilye, *500 Best British and Foreign Films*, p. 48.

25. See, for example, the review by Canby, "Deneuve as Symbol," p. C9; and K. Thomas, "Indochine," p. F4.

26. K. Thomas, "Indochine."

27. For a fuller (and more factual account) see J. Wilson, *Lawrence of Arabia*, especially Ch. 26.

28. Gottlieb, *Nation Against State*, p. 26.

29. *Ibid.*

30. Lind, "In Defense of Liberal Nationalism," p. 88.

31. Gottlieb, *Nation Against State*, p. 28.

32. Zimmerman, "The Last Ambassador," p. 3.

33. *Ibid.*, pp. 17–18.

34. For a discussion of this possibility, see Glenny, "Heading Off War."

35. Gurr, *Minorities at Risk,* p. 170.

35. Vermilye, *500 Best British and Foreign Films*, p. 82.

36. Harff, "Minorities, Rebellion, and Repression," p. 221.

37. On this subject, see Said, *Covering Islam.*

38. George Weigel, quoted in Huntington, "The Clash of Civilizations," p. 26.

39. "Recidivist tribalism" is Benjamin Barber's phrase. See his "Global Multiculturalism," p. 52.

40. See Hirschman, *Exit, Voice and Loyalty.*

41. Barber, "Global Multiculturalism," p. 53.

42. *Ibid.*, p. 54.

43. *Ibid.*, p. 49. But note that the 1996 campaign for the Republican presidential nomination in the United States provided considerable evidence that American nativism may be on the rise, potentially creating problems for Barber's thesis.

4

Civil Strife and Intervention

One of the cardinal norms of the Westphalian order of sovereign states has been that of nonintervention. The Thirty Years War had been fought over religious issues, and in the wake of its terrible devastation the crowned heads of Europe decided that henceforth each monarch would determine the religion of his subjects and that no outside power had a right to challenge that decision. Although the catalytic issue in the birth of this new order in the seventeenth century was religion, sovereignty came to imply nonintervention much more generally—that "who governs [a state] and how they govern is not a question that permits outside meddling."[1] Indeed, this norm became one of the essential attributes of an international order to which Hedley Bull has given the paradoxical title "the anarchical society." Whereas the concept of an international system only connotes that there is sufficient interaction between states "to make the behavior of each a necessary element in the calculations of the other,"[2] an international society necessarily entails a "consciousness of certain common interests and common values" so that states "conceive themselves to be bound by a common set of rules in their relations with one another."[3] Bull and other theorists identify many such rules, among them rules of coexistence necessary for the maintenance of international order.

> At the heart of this complex of rules is the principle that each state accepts the duty to respect the sovereignty or supreme jurisdiction of every other state over its own citizens and domain, in return for the right to expect similar respect for its own sovereignty from other states. A corollary or near-corollary of this central rule is the rule that states will not intervene forcibly or dictatorially in one another's internal affairs.[4]

Nonintervention in Theory and Practice

While many might be tempted to argue that the rule of nonintervention is honored as frequently in the breach as in the observance, it remains an important principle in international relations, especially in view of its role in sustaining state sovereignty at a time when the state is under siege and sovereignty is demonstrably not what it used to be. But if nonintervention as a general proposition still commands widespread support, what exactly is it that constitutes intervention? What is it that is prohibited under the rules of the Westphalian order? Bull, in the quotation above, qualifies it with the adverbs "forcibly" and "dictatorially," suggesting that efforts on the part of one state to influence the internal affairs of another state may not be objectionable if military means are not employed and if control is not sought. It is probable that most people associate intervention with the use of military force or at least with the kind of heavy-handed domination once exemplified by the Soviet Union's role in its Eastern European satellites or by the U.S. role in Central America's so-called "banana republics."

Broadly defined, however, intervention can assume less obvious forms, including isolation of the kind the international community imposed on South Africa's apartheid regime and the promise of rewards or the threat of punishment to induce a country to adopt or abandon a particular policy.[5] Indeed, it can be argued that it is impossible for states *not* to intervene in each other's affairs. Carried to the extreme, such an argument would hold that in some circumstances a state can have a significant effect on another state—it can intervene—by doing absolutely nothing. Let us assume, for example, that State A enjoys the feeling of security engendered by a long-standing and close relationship with a relatively powerful neighbor or patron, State B, but that State B declines to become involved when State C attacks State A. State B is officially neutral in the resulting war, but it has effectively intervened on the side of State C by not coming to the assistance of State A. There are many variations of this argument that nonintervention may constitute intervention, but most students of international relations have preferred to set the threshold somewhat higher, insisting that intervention must at least entail "the purposeful and calculated use of political, economic, and military instruments of one country to influence the domestic politics or the foreign policy of another country."[6]

Most would argue that, to qualify as intervention, such "purposeful and calculated" acts must be undertaken without the consent (and contrary to the wishes) of the duly constituted authorities of the other state, which is to say that those acts have as their purpose to bring about changes that are unwanted by the government of that state (including in some cases even the overthrow of that government). Construed in this way, nonintervention is a conservative norm which is biased in favor of the status quo. And, for the most part, its role in international relations *has* been to support the status quo. The nonintervention norm has typically been invoked in defense of the prevailing status quo when governments find that their policies or their very existence are threatened by the interference of other states. However, it is entirely conceivable that intervention may be for the purpose of bolstering an existing government or ensuring that its policies *not* be changed. In such cases, consent is obviously much more likely. Popular culture has given us films of both types—films that depict intervention as hostile to sitting governments and their policies, and films that depict intervention as a way of protecting sitting governments and guaranteeing that their policies continue in effect.

Although military intervention is the most visible form of intervention, it is far from the only technique states use in their efforts to influence the course of events in other states, and it is certainly not the most common. Intervention is frequently clandestine, taking such forms as bribery and the manipulation of elections. Attempts by the government of the United States to influence the outcome of elections in other countries have been well documented, and range from efforts to block communist accession to power in Italy in 1958 to the campaign to prevent Salvador Allende from winning the presidency of Chile in 1970. Clandestine intervention has also been undertaken with the purpose of fomenting coups d'etat or, short of that, of sparking a crisis that will bring down a government or otherwise alter the course of events in the targeted state. Two famous examples are the successful U.S.-aided plots to overthrow the government of Mohammad Mossadeq in Iran in 1953 and that of Allende in Chile in 1973. Paramilitary support for insurgents seeking to topple governments was commonly practiced by both the United States and the Soviet Union during the Cold War, the assumption being that intervention by proxy was less risky than direct, overt use of force to bring about the desired result. State-sponsored terrorism is another form of intervention, one that has become more common in the latter part of the twentieth century, with states like Iran and Libya commonly identified as culprits. States engaging in these types of covert intervention typically deny culpability.

It is not uncommon for states, especially those with the military and economic power to make their influence felt, to intervene in much more conspicuous ways, and to do so openly. Gunboat diplomacy is a classic example of this form of intervention; indeed, the dispatch of ships to troubled waters is virtually a standard operating procedure for countries with substantial navies, and has normally been done to deter another state from taking some action it appears to be considering. In a recent instance, the United States sent two aircraft carrier task forces to the waters off Taiwan in 1996 to counter military exercises by the People's Republic of China aimed at influencing a Taiwanese election (in effect, this crisis contained two simultaneous and dramatic acts of intervention, one by the PRC and one by the United States). The provision of foreign aid, either economic or military, is another well-established form of intervention, as is the withholding of such aid. If channeled to insurgents, such aid qualifies as paramilitary intervention. But it is also used to shore up regimes deemed important for security reasons and to create dependable patron-client relationships. Once again the Cold War provides numerous examples, beginning with U.S. aid to Greece and Turkey in the late 1940s. Termination of aid (or the threat of terminating it) can also be used to influence the policies of the targeted government, as demonstrated repeatedly by U.S. linkage of foreign aid to countries' voting behavior in the United Nations. A variation of this kind of intervention was the Jackson-Vanik amendment to the U.S. foreign trade bill of 1974, whereby Congress tried to force the Soviet Union to liberalize emigration policy for Jews by withholding most-favored-nation treatment. The policy failed to achieve its purpose, as the Soviet government made Jewish emigration more rather than less difficult. In the case of economic sanctions, a state that is particularly desirous of bending another state to its will normally seeks to drum up broad international support for the sanctions. Examples include U.S. efforts to punish the Soviet Union for its role in Afghanistan by means of a grain embargo and a boycott of the Moscow Olympic Games; these sanctions produced decidedly mixed results.

At the lower or least bellicose end of the spectrum of interventions are diplomatic initiatives, such as the withdrawal of an ambassador. But are all of these efforts to influence the behavior of other states cited in the preceding paragraphs really instances of intervention and as such proscribed by the norms of the Westphalian system? Or is it necessary to revert to Bull's qualifying adverbs and say that what states are prohibited from doing is intervening forcibly and dictatorially in the internal affairs of other states? There is, it would seem, no clear line of demarcation between intervention and mere attempts to exercise influence. The United Nations Charter contains what many would view as the consensus position on the subject in Article 2. In Paragraph 4 of that article, the Charter stipulates that "All Members shall refrain in their international relations from the threat or use of force against the territorial integrity or political independence of any state." This provision, arguably the very heart of the Charter, tends to support Bull's thesis that the nonintervention norm pertains to things done forcibly or dictatorially. But another almost equally famous Charter provision, Paragraph 7 of the same article, says that "Nothing contained in the present Charter shall authorize the United Nations to intervene in matters which are essentially within the domestic jurisdiction of any state or shall require the Members to submit such matters to settlement under the present Charter." This paragraph argues for a much broader understanding of the concept of nonintervention. Not surprisingly, sovereign states have historically been quick to invoke Article 2, Paragraph 7, whenever their government or its policies are attacked in a UN forum. Thus even verbal condemnation is viewed by the targeted state as a form of proscribed intervention in that state's internal affairs.[7]

In the Western hemisphere, the Charter of Bogota goes even further than the United Nations Charter in its defense of nonintervention. The Charter, strongly influenced by Latin American experience with European and U.S. intervention, states that "no state or group of states has the right to intervene directly or indirectly, for any reason whatever, in the internal or external affairs of any other state. The foregoing principle prohibits not only armed attack but also any other form of interference or attempted threat against the personality of the state or against the political, economic, and cultural elements."[8] The United Nations Charter and other international treaties complicate the matter by identifying a number of specific member obligations, such as those in the field of human rights, thereby leaving the door open—or at least ajar—for collective intervention by the international community when a member does not honor those obligations. While intervention in such circumstances is still controversial, it enjoys greater legitimacy than intervention by states acting alone or without the authorization of an international organization. However, one of the greatest impediments to an emerging norm of collective intervention on behalf of the international community is the concern, especially among Third World countries, that "what might appear to be the action of an international community is in fact the reflection of the interests of dominant states, and perhaps a vehicle for realization of those interests."[9] After all, history is replete with instances in which intervention has been justified by the invocation of principles that purported to transcend narrowly defined national interest but in fact did no such thing. One thinks of "the white man's burden," the Monroe Doctrine and the Open Door policy, and, of course, the shibboleths of Marxist-Leninist ideology.

The United States in Latin America: Magnet for Filmmakers

It is in the context of this history and this debate that films dealing explicitly or implicitly with intervention need to be viewed. There are a number of such films, most of them set in situations wholly or primarily of civil strife. As the examples cited on the preceding pages suggest, the country most frequently cast in the role of intervenor is the United States. This is not because the United States has necessarily been the most egregious violator of the nonintervention norm. Powerful states—global or regional hegemons—tend to intervene in the affairs of other states because of the scope of their interests and responsibilities (or at least their perception of those responsibilities). And the United States has long been a powerful state, at first within the Western hemisphere and then globally. During the Cold War the United States sought to counter Soviet machinations and the challenge of radical movements deemed inimical to U.S. interests in many Third World countries. The result was a pattern of intervention Tony Smith has called "anti-imperialism imperialism,"[10] and U.S. filmmakers were attracted to it as a subject. Not surprisingly, many of them were critical.

Three of the best known of these films were produced within a few years of each other during the Reagan administration in the 1980s. Each deals with U.S. intervention in the affairs of a Latin American country—Nicaragua, El Salvador, and Chile, respectively. Two deal with efforts by the United States to support right-wing governments, governments threatened by left-wing movements that were anathema to the U.S. government. The third is about U.S. intervention in support of a military coup against a left-wing government. Thus all three interventions, whether conducted on behalf of governments or insurgents, had a Cold War rationale: to ensure that communism, already entrenched in Cuba, made no further inroads in the Western hemisphere.

The films in question are Roger Spottiswoode's *Under Fire,* Oliver Stone's *Salvador,* and Costa-Gavras's *Missing.* They might well be described as a screen triptych on intervention. They also have in common the fact that in each case American journalists play important roles in the film's plot. In fact, journalists appear with such frequency, and with such impact on the story line, in so many films about intervention that the phenomenon needs to be addressed separately. But first there is the issue of government intervention.

Under Fire is set in Nicaragua in 1979 during the Sandinista rebellion against the Somoza regime. Anyone viewing the film today will know, of course, that the Sandinistas won and that the government of the United States spent the better part of the next decade trying to find a way to reverse the outcome of the civil war. The Reagan administration actively supported the Nicaraguan contras, calling them freedom fighters, and fought some of its hardest battles with Congress over both the legality of its Nicaraguan policy and financial support for it.[11] This policy produced, as one of its sorriest legacies, the so-called Iran-Contra affair. It also led to a World Court pronouncement on the subject of intervention when Nicaragua sued the United States over U.S. mining of Nicaraguan waters. Although the U.S. government refused to acknowledge the Court's jurisdiction in the case, the decision is important for what it has to say about the nonintervention norm. It unambiguously rejected the U.S. rationale for its action: "The Court cannot contemplate the creation of a new rule opening up a right of intervention by one State against another on the ground that the latter has opted for some political ideology or political system."[12]

Under Fire deals in fictional terms with events that preceded all of this and helped to set in motion the U.S. fixation on Central America in the 1980s. For much of the film, the outcome of the civil war is in doubt; indeed, Somoza is portrayed as cheerfully confident and the Somocista Guard is still going about its deadly business. We have, in effect, been taken back to the time before the Sandinistas were in power, a time when the United States was still underwriting Somoza. It had been U.S. policy to support Somoza (and other dictators like him),[13] in spite of the transparently odious nature of his regime, simply because he was anticommunist. According to the logic of the Cold War, he may have been a bastard, but he was our bastard.

Of the three films about U.S. intervention in Latin America, *Under Fire* pays most attention to the relationships among the journalists. This has the effect of pushing the issue of U.S. intervention to the background, but it is present as leitmotif throughout the film. Moreover, four of the film's characters, each in his different way, represent the United States and the idea of intervention. One of these is a photojournalist, played by Nick Nolte, who becomes sensitized to the atrocities of the Somoza regime, abandons his journalistic objectivity, and affects the course of the civil war through the film he shoots. Another of the characters who symbolize aspects of U.S. intervention is a totally amoral soldier of fortune who has joined up with Somoza's forces. A third is a Frenchman who is on the CIA's payroll and who clearly embodies what the makers of the film regard as the most deceitful and ugly side of the U.S. role in that struggle. Finally, there is a U.S. aide to Somoza himself, a true believer in the "dictatorships and double standards" doctrine of Jeanne Kirkpatrick, according to which the United States should take the side of the Nicaraguan dictator because the alternative is, in the aide's remark to Nolte, that the "commies take over the world." "Good intervention" (if bad journalism) wins out in *Under Fire,* but the filmmakers make it clear that it is a close call. Had not Nolte provided a faked photograph showing that a charismatic Sandinista leader was still alive when he was in fact dead, the Carter administration would probably have sent additional aid to Somoza, which is just what the CIA agent, the aide, and presumably the mercenary wanted.

This film glorifies the Sandinista rebels, vilifies U.S. support for the Somoza regime, and exaggerates the role of war correspondents. But if it is a film with a left-of-center viewpoint, it is also a film in which some of the best lines are given to the bad guys. The aide observes that "all this stuff about a revolution of poets is crap" and that it is "very easy to fall in love with the underdog," which is exactly what our journalists cum heroes have done; the CIA agent, just before he is killed by the Sandinistas, admits that "Somoza is a tyrant, of course—a vulture," but "if we wish to survive, we have a choice of tyrants." *Under Fire* is a film that invites debate about several things; intervention is certainly one of them.

The second film about U.S. intervention in Latin America is *Salvador;* while it is superficially similar to *Under Fire* in its theme, it provides the viewer with a very different experience. While *Under Fire* is alive with tension and action, *Salvador* erupts like a volcano, or, as the *Los Angeles Times* reviewer said, "it broils, snaps and explodes with energy."[14] Even more significantly, it makes the Spottiswoode film about consciousness-raising among American journalists in Nicaragua look and sound like a balanced debate on the pros and cons of U.S. policy in Central America.

Salvador pulls no punches, but then this is an Oliver Stone film, and Stone is not known for subtlety. The U.S. government is indicted throughout this film for aiding and abetting a conservative government, which is either unable to control the right-wing death squads that are terrorizing El Salvador or is itself, through its security forces, complicit in their activities. The anticommunist rationale for U.S. policy is spelled out again and again by different Americans throughout the film, beginning with Ronald Reagan himself, who appears on television at a party where Salvadorans and Americans have gathered to watch returns from the Carter-Reagan election of 1980. It is most succinctly and simplistically stated by a State Department representative who argues that "Nicaragua was just the beginning. Guatemala and Honduras are targeted next. In five years you're going to be seeing Cuban tank divisions on the Rio Grande."

Salvador, like *Under Fire,* is also a film about a photojournalist covering a civil war. In this case, the reporter, played by James Woods, is an irresponsible liar and con man who drinks too much, takes drugs, cadges money, and otherwise makes a most unlikely hero. But he is the hero in Stone's film, for it is he with whom and through whom we see the horrors perpetrated by the death squads and it is he who repeatedly challenges the leaders of the El Salvadoran right wing and their American patrons and apologists. This is Woods's film, and as Pauline Kael observes in her *New Yorker* review, it is his scurviness and corruption—his craziness—that enables him to function in El Salvador's chaos.[15]

The movie goes by at such breakneck speed that it can be difficult to focus on those scenes that call for debate about intervention. Those that will probably stand out in the viewer's mind are of El Playon, the site where the death squads dump their victims; Archbishop Romero's assassination by a henchman of the head of the death squads (a part based on Roberto D'Aubuisson, the right-wing politician and presidential candidate whom the U.S. ambassador called a psychopathic killer); and the rape and murder of American nuns, once again by members of the death squads. Although Stone takes liberties with history in the way he depicts these events, they did actually take place, and their presentation has led some critics to view this as one of Stone's most historically accurate films. The increasingly irrefutable evidence of these horrors led to efforts in Washington to condition U.S. aid to El Salvador on improvement in the human rights performance of the government, and especially on a demonstrated ability to rein in the security forces. That process begins on the screen while President Carter's ambassador is still on duty. He visits the site where the bodies of the nuns have just been discovered, and, outraged by what he sees, angrily tells the colonel representing the government that he is recommending an immediate cutoff of all American aid. That decision is subsequently reversed, however, when the hardliners in the U.S. mission convince the ambassador that a victory by the rebel FMLN is imminent;

now well provided with ammunition and fuel for their tanks, the government forces rout the guerrillas in a viscerally gripping battle.

Salvador is a genuinely disturbing movie, and not everyone will appreciate Stone's portrait of American interventionists or, for that matter, his depiction of the Salvadoran left as uniformly idealistic and the Salvadoran right as uniformly sadistic. The director clearly has no respect for the former; as one critic has observed, this is a film that "is explicit in blaming American paranoia about communism for the wreckage of this tiny country."[16] With all due allowance for Stone's biases, *Salvador* is a riveting film that holds our attention and forces us to think about the issue of intervention.

The last panel in this triptych of films about U.S. intervention in Latin America is Costa-Gavras's *Missing*. Although it also takes place during a period of civil strife (the overthrow of the Allende regime by the military in Chile in 1973), it does not look or feel like a war movie in the way that *Under Fire* and *Salvador* do. There are plenty of soldiers driving through Santiago's streets, shooting curfew violators, rounding up suspected leftists and herding them into a stadium (where many are summarily executed), and generally behaving like the Somocista Guard and D'Aubisson's death squads. But there is no organized enemy fighting back; the coup is over and the military is engaged in what might be called post-coup ideological cleansing. *Missing* is about American participation in the overthrow of the Allende government and its subsequent coverup of that role—in other words, this is another film about U.S. intervention in a Latin American country, with the difference that this time Uncle Sam is helping to topple a leftist regime rather than keeping one from gaining power.

All three of the films we have been discussing are based on real events and many of their characters are based on real people (some, like Somoza, even keep their real names). But *Missing* is more than simply a fictionalized presentation of some troubled pages in the history of U.S. relations with its neighbors to the south. It is based on a book in which an American businessman charged that his son, an aspiring young journalist living in Chile, was secretly executed by the military during the coup and that U.S. officials in Santiago knew of his fate, may have been a party to it, and conspired to keep the father and the young man's wife from learning the truth. Needless to say, the charge that the United States could approve the killing of one of its own citizens because he was believed to have knowledge of clandestine U.S. participation in the coup is an extremely serious one. Costa-Gavras does not say that he accepts U.S. complicity in this man's death (although he lets the viewer believe that it is quite possible), but he surely accepts the argument that the United States aided the overthrow of Allende and that its representatives in Chile lied repeatedly to the father and wife. We now know that the United States did indeed help create the conditions that led to the military coup;[17] in the film, a not-very-subtle

American naval officer is the director's vehicle for telling us that. And Costa-Gavras is even less subtle in his depiction of U.S. embassy and consular officials as slippery, dishonest men more concerned with preserving opportunities in Chile for U.S. businessmen than they are in protecting individual American citizens.

There is, of course, more going on in *Missing* than the director's biting critique of U.S. foreign policy. The father, played by Jack Lemmon, is a conservative businessman who does not understand his liberal son or why he should have gone to Chile and embraced vaguely leftist causes. Initially he is ready to blame the young man for whatever has happened, and he takes at face value the claims made by U.S. officials that they are doing everything they can to help. But the father is transformed by his experience, much as Nick Nolte's photojournalist is in *Under Fire;* he comes to respect his son's values now that it is too late, and he vows to sue the government for its shabby role in the case (the real life father did sue, but, as Costa-Gavras tells us at film's end, the suit was eventually dismissed). While the personal drama is moving and memorable, the value of the film for an understanding of international relations lies in what it has to say about foreign intervention in conditions of civil strife.

It can be argued, with some justification, that these three films are polemics, best suited for showing at an anti-American film festival. But they also serve to remind us that civil wars, especially those with ideological overtones, are a powerful magnet, drawing in outside powers. During the Cold War era, this was the case the world over, with turmoil in Third World countries the occasion for interventions by both of the superpowers. Moreover, in the presentation of their messages these three films also provide us with a picture of some of the techniques of intervention and of the relationships that develop between local governments and insurgents on the one hand and external powers on the other. It should also be mentioned that, while Spottiswoode, Stone, and Costa-Gavras are sharply critical of U.S. government policy, their "heroes" in each case are American citizens.

Before turning to a consideration of other films, it should be noted that in all three countries—Nicaragua, El Salvador, and Chile—something resembling normalcy was eventually restored and that it happened without benefit of U.S. intervention. Nicaragua is today governed neither by Somoza nor by the Sandinistas; El Salvador is not under the control of either the right-wing death squads or the FMLN; and Chile has replaced the Pinochet regime that came to power in the coup with a democratically elected centrist government. Outside intervention was a factor in reconciliation in Nicaragua and El Salvador, but it was the United Nations that played that role and it assumed a very different and much more benign form than the one on display in these movies.

Two other highly political films also concern the role of the United States in Latin America and have plots that deal with aspects of intervention.

They are *State of Siege,* which was also directed by Costa-Gavras, and *Clear and Present Danger,* already mentioned in the chapter on sovereignty. The former is based on actual events. In 1970 a repressive government in Uruguay was combatting a leftist underground organization known as the Tupamaros; during the course of this struggle, the rebels captured and killed an American adviser to the government. Costra-Gavras turned this event into *State of Siege,* and he makes it clear that his sympathies lie with the rebels. Although initially the viewer identifies with the American adviser (after all, he has been kidnapped and held in a small prison cell by left-wing zealots), it soon becomes apparent that his mission was to help the police and the military torture their adversaries. Thus once again we have the United States in an unsavory role, supporting by clandestine means a fascistic government. The shock we feel at the execution of the adviser is more than balanced by the revulsion we are expected to feel over American duplicity and the police-state tactics of the government the United States is assisting.

U.S. intervention in a Latin American country in *Clear and Present Danger* is for the purpose of destoying a drug cartel. In this case, all of the events portrayed are fiction, but the issue of drug trafficking from and through Latin American countries into the United States is real enough. In fact, with the Cold War over, drug lords began to replace communists as the enemy of choice in films of this kind. Early in the film, the fictional American president sets the plot in motion by asserting that "these drug cartels represent a clear and present danger to the national security of the United States." The foreign aid the U.S. government has been sending to the Colombian government has not been sufficient to put the cartels out of business, so the president decides to escalate the war on drugs by authorizing the CIA to send a paramilitary unit into Colombia to eradicate the cartels. The United States has, of course, long tried to win the war on drugs by treating it as a supply problem, which has meant substantial U.S. involvement in the drug control efforts of several Latin American countries. However, *Clear and Present Danger* goes one step further, presenting a U.S. intervention by covert military means about which the Colombian government is not informed. The policy of intervention pursued by the president's men in this film is not only no respecter of the sovereignty of Colombia; it also is presented as a violation of constitutionally mandated procedures in the United States, reminding the viewer of the Watergate and Iran-Contra scandals (in both of which top government officials tried to deny knowledge of and responsibility for what happened, just as they do in *Clear and Present Danger*). In the film adaptation of Tom Clancy's political thriller, Harrison Ford, as intrepid and scrupulously honest CIA official Jack Ryan, eventually turns the tables on both the Cali cartel and his devious superiors in Washington. But it is the clandestine intervention in Colombia and the consequences of that ill-conceived move that matter here.

Overt military intervention by the United States, or for that matter by other countries, in the affairs of Third World states has not been the common film theme that more clandestine intervention has. The Clint Eastwood movie *Heartbreak Ridge,* which is mainly concerned with a rough and tough Marine Corps sergeant's last tour of duty, does take us ashore with U.S. troops in Grenada when the United States intervened there to rescue U.S. students, defeating a small band of Cuban workers and overturning the island's left-wing government in the process. But viewers of this film will learn nothing about the nature of Grenadan politics, the rationale for the U.S. action, or the consequences of the invasion. We only know that the Eastwood character can end his checkered military career on an upbeat note, walking off into retirement to the stirring beat of a patriotic Sousa march. For screen presentations of full-scale intervention by military forces one must turn to films about colonialism, some of which are cited in Chapter 3, and to films about war, especially the many focusing on the Vietnam War, the subject of Chapter 7.

The films about U.S. intervention in Central and South America may have been intended to affirm the principle of nonintervention by criticizing U.S. policies, but they can also be used to demonstrate just how difficult it is to apply that principle. It would appear to be possible for intervention to be both legal and moral, to be legal but not moral, and to be neither legal nor moral. Most critics would claim that the intervention in *Missing* is both legally and morally wrong because a democratically elected government is the target of that intervention. But what of the intervention in *Under Fire,* the intervention to help the Somoza government cope with Sandinista insurgents as opposed to the subsequent intervention to aid the contras in their efforts to topple the Sandinista government? While Somoza was not democratically elected, he was the head of a recognized government and had the right to ask for Washington's support; Washington had a legal right to extend that support. Was U.S. intervention morally justified? For how long was it legally justified? Until insurgency turned into a full-scale civil war? Until the collapse of the Somoza government? And what if Washington had chosen to withdraw its support from Somoza and aid the insurgency? Stanley Hoffmann, in his thought-provoking book *Duties Beyond Borders,* wrestles with the problem posed by cases such as that of Nicaragua, asking "whether the absence of legitimate domestic foundations eliminates its rights as a member of international society."[18] Hoffmann argues that

> "the tyranny of established government gives rise to a right of revolution," not to a right of foreign intervention. There is, therefore, a "dual reference" for the doctrine of legitimacy. Internal legitimacy is "monistic" or singular—it depends on the presence of democratic institutions. International legitimacy is pluralistic—in the sense that a state can be a legitimate actor and subject of rights even if its government is illegitimate

at home: "people have a right to a state within which their rights are violated."[19]

The issue is considerably more complicated than is suggested by the quotation, as Hoffmann himself attests. There is a presumption that intervention at the request of a friendly government facing an insurgency is acceptable under international law, or at least if the government is somewhat more representative of the people than the insurgents, the intervention would be morally valid. But that caveat illustrates the difficulty with generalizations. It is frequently not clear which is the lesser of two evils, or, conversely, the more legitimate of two claimants—the government or those trying to overthrow it. Hoffmann has no difficulty, however, branding as morally wrong an intervention by force against "a legitimate revolutionary movement," whether in power or not. Needless to say, this doesn't settle the question of just what it is that constitutes a legitimate revolutionary movement, although Hoffmann cites several examples of intervention by the United States he regards as morally wrong because they were directed against revolutionary movements that meet his test of legitimacy, including, among others, Chile in the 1970s and Nicaragua in the 1980s.[20]

In any event, policymakers and the public will almost certainly disagree about the legal and moral rights and wrongs of specific interventions. And they will bring those disagreements to their reactions to films depicting such interventions. It comes as no surprise that a recent *National Review* essay entitled "Your 100 Best Conservative Movies" does not include any of the films about U.S. intervention in Latin America, all of which were critical of American support of right-wing governments and sympathetic to one degree or another with the cause of left-wing insurgents.[21]

The UN, Peacekeeping, and Humanitarian Intervention

The interventions discussed on the preceding pages are all of a unilateral nature. Multilateral intervention, or intervention by or in the name of the international community, has also been carefully circumscribed, but it has not carried the same opprobrium as unilateral intervention by one state in the affairs of another. For example, although developing countries will usually accept aid from any source disposed to provide it, it has long been conventional wisdom that they prefer multilateral assistance to bilateral assistance due to the fact that the latter typically comes with strings attached and expectations regarding behavior that can be construed as an impingement on sovereignty.

Although recent events in Somalia, Bosnia, and Haiti have stimulated debate about collective intervention, it is not a new issue. Whereas the nonintervention norm was presumably still in place (or, perhaps more accurately, restored to its place) as one of the basic rules of coexistence after the end of the Napoleonic Wars, the major European powers asserted their right to intervene to protect any European monarch threatened by revolution (thereby helping to make the point that the nonintervention norm was indeed a conservative one). The Concert of Europe was not a formal international organization in the sense that the United Nations is today, but the powers (England, France, Austria, Prussia, and Russia) were in some respects a prototype of the modern-day Security Council, and they did intervene collectively to restore absolute monarchies in Naples and Spain as a result of decisions reached at the Congresses of Troppau and Verona.[22] Collective intervention in the nineteenth century was short-lived, however, and the principle was not resurrected until the twentieth century with what have been termed the first and second tries at world order, the League of Nations and the United Nations.

Although the experience of these organizations (and regional ones such as the Organization of American States) with collective intervention has on the whole been disappointing, the debate now taking place among scholars and statesmen suggests that the issue enjoys a new salience and that the nonintervention norm (and hence the very concept of sovereignty) is weakening. As one recent essay on the subject of intervention announces in its title, "sovereignty is no longer sacrosanct."[23] One international lawyer goes so far as to argue that "instead of the view that intervention in internal conflicts must be presumptively illegitimate, the prevailing trend today is to take seriously the claim that the international community ought to intercede to prevent bloodshed by whatever means are available."[24] As noted earlier in this chapter, the United Nations Charter contains language that not only upholds the norm of nonintervention but also applies that norm to actions of the UN itself. This would seem to make multilateral intervention on behalf of the international community as problematic as unilateral intervention. But the relevant provision of the Charter, Article 2, Paragraph 7, contains a critically important qualification. While it says that the UN shall not intervene in matters essentially within the domestic jurisdiction of a state, it goes on to stipulate that "this principle shall not prejudice the application of enforcement measures under Chapter VII." Chapter VII of the Charter authorizes the Security Council to determine the existence of threats to the peace, breaches of the peace, and acts of aggression, and to take such actions as are necessary to deal with them. These are the so-called collective security provisions of the Charter, and they open the door to multilateral interventions ranging from calls for compliance with Council resolutions to military operations designed to force such compliance.

The United Nations is now more than half a century old, and in that time the Security Council has authorized military action against a sovereign state only twice, against North Korea in 1950 and against Iraq forty years later. In both instances the Council found that aggression had occurred and, although it did not have the military means to take action itself, as envisioned in Chapter VII, it deputized coalitions led by the United States to repel the aggressors.[25] More relevant to the evolution of doctrine regarding nonintervention, however, has been the response of the United Nations to situations in which the Council was unwilling to invoke the Charter against a malefactor or in which the situation seemed not to fit Charter criteria for intervention. The name commonly given to these UN missions that fall short of enforcement is "peacekeeping." This form of intervention, which is nowhere mentioned in the Charter, had its beginnings in 1956 during the Suez crisis when Israel, Britain, and France invaded Egypt with the objective of reversing Egyptian president Nasser's nationalization of the Suez Canal. A collective security response was unthinkable, so the secretary general, Dag Hammarskjold, with Security Council authorization and the help of imaginative statesmen, created and dispatched a force to that troubled region with the mission of separating the combatants and thereby facilitating a reduction in tension. The ground rules for subsequent peacekeeping missions were road-tested here; the principal ones were UN neutrality as between parties to the dispute, non-use of force except in self defense, and, most importantly, consent of the host state to the stationing of peacekeeping forces on its territory. And so it was that the UN intervened, but on the condition that its presence was acceptable to the parties; the principle of nonintervention had undergone an important adaptation, but the rationale for that principle, state sovereignty, had been sustained.

Peacekeeping has metamorphosed over time as new crises have presented new problems and as the UN has learned from experience. In what might be called the first phase of peacekeeping, a phase that lasted for roughly two decades and reflected the constraints imposed by the Cold War, the principal purpose of UN missions was interposition between parties to international conflicts. The ground rules pioneered during the Suez crisis were gradually routinized, especially after the debacle in the Congo in the early 1960s. The latter crisis, which nearly destroyed the UN, foreshadowed the recent (and, in the eyes of most observers, failed) missions in Somalia and Bosnia, largely because the UN was unable strictly to observe the rules of neutrality, consent, and non-use of force.[26] Although the United Nations righted itself after the debacle in the Congo, its role in peacekeeping was substantially circumscribed until the thaw in the Cold War in the late 1980s, at which time it launched a series of missions in countries that had been the scenes of conflicts previously insulated from UN intervention by Cold War politics. In this phase of peacekeeping, the UN began to assist the process of nationbuilding in the wake of civil wars, even to the extent of supervising elections (see especially the UN missions in Namibia, Angola, Nicaragua, and El Salvador).[27] The relative success of these missions, together with the UN's creditable performance in the Gulf crisis following Iraq's invasion of Kuwait, created a perception that the United Nations might at long last be ready to assume the role of principal agent of international peace and security which the organization's founders had hoped it would play.

Unfortunately, things did not work out that way. The UN's performance in the third phase of its history as a peacekeeper has only served to tarnish its reputation. It has intervened in strength in several crises, but in almost every case has found itself trapped in a situation where it could not consistently remain neutral, where it was not clear whether its presence enjoyed consent, and where the nonuse of force rule was recurrently violated. Not surprisingly, the result has been a veritable cottage industry of revisionist analysis that challenges the time-honored ground rules for UN peacekeeping. Perhaps the most cogent statement of the revisionist position is that of Richard Betts, who argues that the UN has prolonged suffering where its intervention was meant to relieve it.

> How does this happen? By following a principle that sounds like common sense: that intervention should be both limited and impartial, because weighing in on one side of a local struggle undermines the legitimacy of outside involvement. This Olympian presumption resonates with respect for law and international cooperation. It has the ring of prudence, fairness, and restraint. It makes sense in old-fashioned U.N. peacekeeping operations, where the outsiders' role is not to make peace, but to bless and monitor a cease-fire that all parties have decided to accept. But it becomes a destructive misconception when carried over to the messier realm of "peace enforcement," where the belligerents have yet to decide that they have nothing more to gain by fighting.[28]

In effect, the United Nations is now operating in a gray area for which clearly defined guidelines have not yet emerged, much less been codified by practice. Intervention in such circumstances is clearly a parlous undertaking.

Bosnia provides the latest, but surely not the last, evidence of the proposition that peacemakers are more often than not reviled as they seek to mediate disputes or prevent or terminate violent conflict. Third parties may wish to be neutral as to the claims of the parties in conflict, seeking only a fair and just settlement or at least an end to bloodshed. Unfortunately, even well-intentioned neutral intervention may in practice favor one party over the other or be perceived to do so. The result, all too frequently, is a transfer of animosity to the peacemakers, who become convenient scapegoats. This problem receives attention in the Klingon trilogy of *Star Trek: The Next Generation.*

Captain Picard (Patrick Stewart) assumes the unenviable role of arbiter of succession for the Klingon Empire. His task, in effect, is to mediate a dispute between two Klingon factions, each of which has a claim to the throne. Picard refuses to support the emperor, Gowron, against the rebel faction, knowing that becoming involved will only drag the Federation into a Klingon civil war. But in his capacity as arbiter he rejects the claim to the throne of the emperor's enemies, the powerful Duras family. In the short span of one episode, "Redemption," Picard has alienated first one and then the other party to this dispute, even as he tries to do the just and fair thing. Not surprisingly, civil war does break out, and Picard eventually (in "Redemption II") abandons his policy of nonintervention and takes steps which force the Duras faction's Romulan allies to withdraw from the fray, thereby guaranteeing Gowron his throne. While there is of course no exact earthly counterpart to this intergalactic story, those who have followed the UN's troubled missions from the Congo to Somalia and Bosnia, in each of which neutrality proved impossible, will surely understand Picard's dilemma.

The film industry has not yet visited the subject of UN intervention via peacekeeping. There is just a hint of the UN's presence in Macedonia in *Before the Rain*. Although we are provided with brief glimpses of UN peacekeepers driving about in their armored vehicles, they are nowhere in sight when intercommunal violence breaks out; indeed, one suspects that the director may have included those few seconds of film footage of UN peacekeepers only to suggest that the international community will be ineffectual in dealing with Macedonia's tragedy.[29] In any event, intervention by the international community still awaits its first treatment in a feature film. However, there is no shortage of crises that have been the subject of films *and* that have also been the locus of major UN peacekeeping efforts. For example, the United Nations was instrumental in producing the settlement of the prolonged civil war in El Salvador, but its involvement came much later than the events depicted in Oliver Stone's *Salvador*.

One of the most difficult UN missions—a mission that straddled the relatively successful phase of UN peacekeeping and the much more recent and troubled third phase—took place in Cambodia. The events that created the conditions that ultimately brought the United Nations to Cambodia are presented in unforgettable fashion in Roland Joffe's *The Killing Fields*. One of the reasons why anyone interested in international relations should watch *The Killing Fields* is that it confronts the viewer with a painful question: why didn't the international community intervene sooner to stop—or at least to ameliorate—the genocidal policies of the Khmer Rouge government in Cambodia? It thus forces us to think about one of the urgent issues on the international agenda at the end of the twentieth century, that of whether an obligation exists, not to refrain from intervention out of respect for state sovereignty, but to intervene for humanitarian reasons. Are there, in other words, offenses committed by governments against their own people that are so heinous as to justify—even to mandate—intervention that overrides the old Westphalian norm against it?

This is not, of course, a new question. The Holocaust raised the same question more than half a century ago, although the atrocities committed by the Nazis were at the time less widely comprehended and more difficult to combat because of the military might of the German state. The same may be said of the situation in the Soviet Union under Stalin. In both of those cases, the objective of bringing a halt to genocide would have been morally justifiable. But would forceful intervention to achieve that objective also have been morally justifiable? It is at this point that we come up against Stanley Hoffmann's ethics of consequences.

> Any moral statecraft has to be an ethic of consequences, in the sense of being concerned for the foreseeable effects. . . . The criteria of moral politics are double: sound principles, and effectiveness. A morally bad design—say, naked aggression—does not become good because it succeeds. But a morally fine one—say, a rescue operation for the freeing of hostages—does not meet the conditions of the moral politician if the details are such that success is most unlikely, or that the costs of success would be prohibitive.[30]

Reasonable people can debate, years after the fact, what should have been done (and when) about the genocide committed by the century's two greatest tyrants, but everyone knows that forceful and timely intervention would have entailed enormous risks and unknowable consequences. The Cambodian challenge, difficult as it was, was of an altogether different magnitude. After all, Vietnam invaded Cambodia in 1979 and overturned the Khmer Rouge government, putting an end to its particular brand of genocide.[31] The international community did not act until many years later, and in the meanwhile kept the Vietnamese-installed government from occupying the Cambodian seat at the United Nations on grounds related to traditional conceptions of state sovereignty.

During the years of Khmer Rouge rule, an estimated 40 percent of the Cambodian population was either killed by the regime or died of starvation and disease. *The Killing Fields* shows us what the revolutionary regime did to produce that terrible statistic. The film is primarily about the relationship between an American war correspondent, Sydney Schanberg (Sam Waterston), and his Cambodian interpreter and assistant, Dith Pran (Haing Ngor). When the Americans in Phnom Penh are evacuated following the takeover by the Khmer Rouge, Dith Pran is left behind and soon finds himself struggling to survive in a brutal slave labor camp where the government forcefully reeducates its citizens and where Cambodians like Pran must appear illiterate to avoid summary execution. Eventually Pran escapes and in the course of his journey finds himself literally in the killing fields, acres of swamp land filled with the bones and rotting corpses of his countrymen, killed by the hundreds of thousands by the ruthless architects of a new society. The horrors of the slave labor camp, which Haing Ngor himself experienced, are so shockingly presented on screen that the viewer cannot help but ask how such evil was possible—and how the civilized world could have tolerated it. Similar questions have been raised by media coverage of the horrors of mass slaughter in Rwanda and by the savagery of ethnic cleansing in Bosnia. The response of the international community in these cases and in others suggests, as noted earlier, that the nonintervention norm is weakening.

If the day comes when human rights regularly take precedence over sovereign rights, historians will likely focus on the adoption of Security Council Resolution 688 as a pivotal event in the evolution of the new norm. This resolution authorized military intervention in northern Iraq to protect that country's Kurdish minority from Saddam Hussein's army. It was adopted after the end of the Gulf War, and had nothing to do with reversing Iraq's aggression against and occupation of Kuwait. Instead, it represented an unprecedented intervention in the domestic affairs of a sovereign state without the consent of that state's government. While it is true that the Council invoked the magic words in Chapter VII—"threat to international peace and security"—to justify its action, and carefully avoided assertion of a right of humanitarian intervention, the resolution remains "a dramatic harbinger reflecting the quickening pace of humanitarian developments and the extent to which sovereignty is under seige."[32]

However, from a realist perspective Resolution 688 may not be particularly noteworthy. After all, "the victors in war often make demands that compromise the sovereignty of the vanquished, and in this context the resolution offers no new precedent or justification for international intervention."[33] It has to be remembered that the international community had done nothing when Saddam Hussein employed chemical warfare against his Kurdish minority in 1988, and even Resolution 688 produced three negative votes and two abstentions, reflecting the suspicions of many countries that humanitarian intervention may simply be imperialism in disguise. In spite of the fact that Saddam is still constrained by UN resolutions, enthusiasm for enforcement of those resolutions is lukewarm and increasingly hard to sustain. Moreover, the states that might be expected to lead a UN-sanctioned intervention in other places have been conspicuously reluctant to place their soldiers at risk in situations where there is no compelling national interest to do so.[34] It is obviously much too soon to write the obituary for the nonintervention norm.

In most of the recent instances of intervention by the international community, the crises that led to intervention were in part a product of earlier outside intervention. *The Killing Fields* shows us the Nixon administration's bombing of Cambodia (and U.S. efforts to cover it up)—part of the strategy for winning the war in neighboring Vietnam—and strongly suggests a link between the bombing and the postwar tragedy. Similarly, the breakdown in civil order in Somalia that led to U.S. and UN intervention there, has been attributed in part to the earlier Cold War competition between the United States and the Soviet Union, which put too many weapons into the hands of too many people in the Horn of Africa. Even in the case of the former Yugoslavia, critics have laid some of the blame for the three-sided civil war on the successful German-led campaign for premature recognition of the sovereignty of the breakaway republics.

The concern of the international community for human rights and its willingness through international organizations to castigate governments for abuses of those rights have grown appreciably in the last decades of the twentieth century. This, too, represents a challenge to the nonintervention norm. The evolution of the international regime for human rights, still modest in its reach and clearly more of a declaratory regime than one with enforcement capabilities, will be considered in Chapter 9. At that point we shall consider films like *The Official Story* and *Beyond Rangoon,* which raise questions about the place of human rights considerations in foreign policy.

Mercenaries and Journalists

One sub-theme of the subject of intervention that has interested filmmakers is intervention by mercenaries—that is, by soldiers of fortune who are not agents of a sovereign state, although they may indirectly be serving the interests of one. One such mercenary plays an important role in the evolution of the plot of *Under Fire.* In films such as *The Wild Geese* and *The Dogs of War,* the intervention of mercenary armies in African countries *is* the plot. In both of these films, the mercenaries are handpicked for their dangerous assignments by veterans of this kind of warfare, Richard Burton in the one case and Christopher Walken in the other. In both cases they are in the employ of Western businessmen (who turn out to be duplicitous) and their targets are brutal and corrupt African regimes. Thus these films make the mercenaries out to be heroes; the jacket of the videocassette for *The Dogs of War* speaks of the "thankless, perilous lives of mercenaries and the dirty battles they fight because no one else will." This romanticization of the soldier of fortune does not square well with the historical record, and such films are really little more than adventure yarns with a lot of violence. They are also a variation on such old-fashioned films as *Gunga Din,* with brave white standard-bearers of Western civilization (and commercial interests) fighting evil non-whites in exotic locations. *Gunga Din,* for all its dated racism and nostalgia for heroic nineteenth-century colonialism, is far the better movie, if only because it does not take itself so seriously. Perhaps the most prominent real world parallel of the events in *The Wild Geese* and *The Dogs of War* occurred during the Congo crisis in the early 1960s, when mercenaries were involved in the failed secession of that country's Katanga province. Those soldiers of fortune, like the ones depicted in the films, were serving Western business interests, in that case mining companies with a stake in Katanga's mineral wealth. They were not heroic and their mission hardly served the interests of regional or global stability. The Congo (later Zaire, and now the Democratic Republic of Congo) subsequently stagnated under one of the most wretched regimes on the African continent, only to resurface recently as a focus of international attention when long-time strong man Mobutu was driven from power. The insurrection that brought Mobutu down had its roots in the chaotic politics of the years immediately following independence, and it gained new life, ironically, when the international community failed to address in a timely or effective way the recent ethnic troubles in neighboring Rwanda.

Finally, one interesting aspect of several of the films dealing with intervention needs to be mentioned. As noted earlier in this chapter, journalists are featured prominently in the films about U.S. intervention in Latin America. For that matter, journalists play significant roles in a substantial number of films discussed in this book, suggesting that Hollywood and other centers of filmmaking find the journalist useful as a vehicle for commenting on issues (much like a Greek chorus) or as a spokesperson for the director and his views. In *Lawrence of Arabia,* Arthur Kennedy plays a newspaper man who is instrumental in acquainting the world with Lawrence's exploits and who ultimately is disillusioned by the enigmatic hero's descent into savagery in an attack on a defenseless Turkish column. Martin Sheen plays a somewhat similar role in *Gandhi,* helping to dramatize the Mahatma and his tactics of nonviolence, as well as serving as witness to British repression of Gandhi's followers. The principal protagonist in Peter Weir's *The Year of Living Dangerously* is an Australian reporter on assignment in Indonesia on the eve of the overthrow of the Sukarno regime; he misuses information to which he has become privvy, and the results are devastating. This is one of several films in which the journalist influences the course of events, rather than simply serving as the public's eyes and ears.

The journalist as agent of change can be seen most conspicuously in *Under Fire.* In that film, as noted earlier, a photojournalist, played by Nick Nolte, abandons his journalistic objectivity and decides to help the Sandinista cause. He shoots a picture of the dead rebel leader that makes it appear he is alive; this act, intended to revitalize the morale of the rebels, backfires, leading to the murder by the Somocistas of many of those whom Nolte had befriended. Unlike Nolte, James Woods, the journalist in *Salvador,* does not need to learn who the "good guys" are; he is a committed left-wing journalist from the beginning. But he, too, participates in the struggle, supplying photos of victims of the death squads that help families learn of the fate of their loved ones and verbally harassing the right-wing officials at press conferences. And in *Missing,* the plot turns on the fate of a young journalist whom the military junta believes knows too much about the circumstances of the coup that brought it to power.

While journalists play what appear to be unrealistically large roles in most of these films, it is a fact that journalists—both print and electronic—do occupy increasingly important positions in contemporary world politics. Aided by modern, even revolutionary, means of communication, they guarantee that the public will know quickly, graphically, and often in great detail about events occurring almost everywhere on the globe. Their ability to be on the spot and to create the impression of authoritative coverage of those events makes it difficult for governments to conceal what is happening or to put the desired spin on their policies. Mass publics may not, as many studies demonstrate, be very knowledgable about the world we live in. They may not be able to locate Somalia or Bosnia or Iraq on a map, much less know anything about local problems, but they are much more likely to be aware that there is a crisis "out there" and that involvement in it has generated a debate about the national interest. And elite publics, those who have most to say about the direction of their countries' foreign policies, do have a better grasp of these foreign policy conundrums, thanks to the ubiquitous journalists. In this sense, our films do not exaggerate the latter's role in international relations.

Notes

1. Holsti, *International Politics,* p. 196.
2. Bull, *The Anarchical Society*, p. 10.
3. *Ibid.*, p. 13.
4. *Ibid.*, p. 70.
5. Lyons and Mastanduno, *Beyond Westphalia?* p. 10.
6. Schraeder, *Intervention in the 1980s,* p. 2.
7. See UNGA Res. 2131 (XX), December 21, 1965, the "Declaration on the Inadmissibility of Intervention in the Domestic Affairs of States and the Protection of Their Independence and Sovereignty."
8. Charter of Bogota (1948), Article 15.
9. Lyons and Mastanduno, *Beyond Westphalia?* p. 13.
10. See T. Smith, *The Pattern of Imperialism.* Intervention is not, of course, a synonym for imperialism, although imperialism is certainly a particularly ambitious form of intervention. But Smith's definition of imperialism (p. 6) may help to put the problem in perspective: "Imperialism may be defined as the effective domination by a relatively strong state over a weaker people whom it does not control as it does its home population, or as in the effort to secure such domination."
11. See Arnson, *Cross-Roads.*
12. 1986 I.C.J. 133. Quoted in Mullerson, "Self Defense in the Contemporary World," p. 16.
13. For a distinction between traditional and modern dictators, see Rubin, *Modern Dictators.*
14. See review by Wilmington, "Salvador Has Action as Loud as Its Words," 6/6.

15. See review by Kael, "Pig Heaven," p. 77.

16. Silberman, "Stone, Oliver," p. 420.

17. See, for example, Farnsworth, "Chile," and Sigmund, "Chile," pp. 127–56. The sources assessing the U.S. role in the coup that provides the context for *Missing* are also discussed in Toplin, *History by Hollywood*, pp. 104–24.

18. Hoffmann, *Duties Beyond Borders*, p. 58.

19. *Ibid.*, pp. 67–68.

20. *Ibid.*, p. 72.

21. Warren, "Your 100 Best Conservative Movies," pp. 55–61. The essay lists many anticommunist films, tributes to soldiers of fortune, and even one on the inhumanity of mass revolution, *The Scarlet Pimpernel*.

22. The Concert proved to be very short lived, and was effectively at an end by the early 1820s, with England the principal defector. Harold Nicolson, writing about the Conference of Laibach in 1822, puts it this way: "The Great Coalition was thus finally dissolved; the Concert of Europe had disintegrated; the Holy Alliance had succeeded in destroying the Quadruple Alliance; the Conference System had failed." See his *Congress of Vienna*, p. 268.

23. Chopra and Weiss, "Sovereignty Is No Longer Sacrosanct."

24. Damrosch, *Enforcing Restraint*, p. 364.

25. In the Korean case, UN authorization of a military response to North Korean aggression was possible only because the Soviet Union had absented itself from the Security Council and was thus unable to cast a veto. In effect, the UN legitimized U.S. decisions that would have been taken with or without UN authorization. By the time of the Gulf crisis in 1990, the Cold War had ended and the Council was able to authorize member states to use "all necessary means" to expel Iraq from Kuwait, although the critical resolution (SC 678) made no reference to the U.S. role or to the coalition assembled under U.S. leadership.

26. The United Nations did ultimately bring the Congo crisis to an end by forcefully putting down the secession of the mineral-rich Katanga province, thereby making it possible to claim that, in spite of the near-disaster, the mission had finally succeeded.

27. For a useful summary of these (and other) UN peacekeeping missions, see Durch, *The Evolution of U.N. Peacekeeping*, and Durch, *U.N. Peacekeeping*.

28. Betts, "The Delusion of Impartial Intervention," p. 20.

29. The United Nations mission in Macedonia is a case of preventive deployment, designed to prevent (or at least detect) spread of the conflict in the former Yugoslavia into that country. Its mission has not been to prevent interethnic violence in Macedonia.

30. Hoffmann, *Duties Beyond Borders*, pp. 28–29.

31. One instructive instance in which a state intervened in a neighboring state to put an end to the latter's genocidal practices occurred when Tanzania invaded Uganda and overthrew the regime of Idi Amin.

32. Weiss and Chopra, "Sovereignty under Seige," p. 102.

33. Lyons and Mastanduno, *Beyond Sovereignty?* p. 15.

34. This reluctance to intervene on the part of the major powers, so conspicuously in contrast to their behavior during the colonial era and the Cold War, is discussed in, among other places, Mandelbaum, "The Reluctance to Intervene."

5

Espionage and Subversion

In what is probably the classic denunciation of spying as an instrument of statecraft, a U.S. secretary of state once insisted that "gentlemen do not read each other's mail." Henry L. Stimson made this remark in 1929 when he closed down his department's cryptographic section. Given the ubiquitousness of spies, not only in fiction and film but in the employ of governments worldwide, one can only conclude either that very few of them are gentlemen or that gentlemen do in fact read each other's mail—not to mention committing acts of sabotage, generating massive disinformation campaigns, and even occasionally assassinating enemies. Stimson later changed his mind; when, during World War II, he found himself once more in a cabinet post, this time as secretary of war, he appears to have had no compunction about spying on the Germans and the Japanese. And although it may be argued that that was wartime, when anything goes, the fact of the matter is that espionage is the most common form of intervention by one state in the affairs of another, especially where the states in question are large enough and involved enough in world politics to have both an interest in and the capability of spying on each other.

Of all the themes addressed in this book, espionage is probably the least important to a rounded picture of international relations. This is not to say that it is unimportant, because it can be the means whereby the course of war is changed, security of states is enhanced or compromised, negotiating advantage is won or lost, and amicable relations between states are strained or soured. But spying lacks the conceptual weight of most of the themes we are exploring; its absence from these pages would leave the smallest hole in the whole of our understanding of what international relations is all about. However, the spy figures so prominently in the films that introduce us to the complexities of international relations that it is inconceivable that we should reduce the subject to a footnote (or even subsume it under the rubric of "intervention"). Espionage is worth its own chapter, not only because it has been a staple of interstate politics for so long, but because it has been used so often by filmmakers to comment on the major confrontations and crises that have plagued the international system, especially in the twentieth century.

Espionage as Diplomacy by Other Means

Espionage is, in effect, diplomacy by other means. Diplomacy encompasses three tasks. One is negotiation. The picture of the diplomat that most people probably carry in their heads is that of a negotiator, someone sent abroad by his or her government to persuade another government to enter into an agreement on terms favorable to the diplomat's country. A second task of diplomacy is that of representation, or communicating to other governments a country's policy objectives and official position on issues; this is what ambassadors and their staffs routinely do. The third task of diplomacy most frequently involves espionage, and that is the task of gathering information and reporting it back to the diplomat's home government. The problem that necessitates—or at least invites—espionage is that sovereign states typically do not wish other states to know everything there is to know about their capabilities and their intentions. Although much of intelligence gathering is routine and even mundane, and, in the case of all but outright enemies, accomplished openly with the cooperation of the host country, states do have secrets. The more adversarial the relationship among states, the greater the desire for secrecy. Precisely because the relationship is adversarial and hence fraught with some degree of danger (real or perceived), the parties will seek to penetrate that veil of secrecy in order to find out just what the other country is capable of doing, what it is planning to do, and details of how and when. Espionage, or spying, then becomes an integral part of interstate relations.

The fact that espionage is employed to gain information the host state does not wish to divulge does not mean that the other tasks of diplomacy—negotiation and representation—are always characterized by openness and candor. On the contrary, diplomats frequently conceal their country's "bottom-line" position in negotiations in the hope of obtaining a better deal, and they often quite deliberately provide the host government with misinformation or disinformation in their country's pursuit of advantage in the "game" of international relations. This is why it was possible for Sir Henry Wotton, an English official in the early seventeenth century, to define an ambassador as "an honest man sent to lie abroad for the good of his country."[1] But it is in the quest for more information about the other country, the adversary, than it is willing to divulge that states employ clandestine means of intelligence gathering. The most important of these means historically has been the human agent, the spy, and most films dealing with the subject feature spies—men and women engaged in cloak and dagger adventures in a shadowy world where a careless mistake can mean discovery (or worse). In more recent times, while the human agent survives, high-tech intelligence gathering has assumed much greater importance, and it, too, has become a staple feature in films about espionage.

Films about spies and spying have been set almost entirely in the twentieth century, first in the context of the confrontation between the Axis and the Allied powers in the period just prior to and then during World War II, and later in the context of the Cold War between the Soviet bloc and the West. Some of these films attempted to recreate actual events, while others were clearly fictional; but even in the latter case, moviemakers used the ideological struggles of the day, as well as the techniques of real-life spies, to create the appearance of verisimilitude. While the espionage we see on screen takes place mainly in the period between World War I and the end of the twentieth century, it should be noted that the spying has been a part of statecraft for centuries.

Ronald Seth, in his book *The Anatomy of Spying,* introduces the subject with three brief case studies of spies who made a difference—"as a result of the activities of the spies themselves, the subsequent course of history was different from what it might have been if they had not operated."[2] Two of the three episodes took place long before the modern era. One occurred in the mid-sixteenth century and involved a network of spies, assembled by an agent of the English crown, that provided the commanders of the English fleet with precise information about the Spanish Armada, including the time of its arrival off the Channel coast, thereby enabling Drake and Frobisher and the rest to defeat the enemy and prevent Philip's conquest of England. As students of European history will know, the destruction of the Armada is usually attributed to a violent storm; however, the intelligence gathered by the spies was a significant factor in the outcome, and serves as a reminder that espionage antedates the twentieth century by a great many years.

Seth's other example comes from an even earlier era, the time of the war between Rome and Carthage (203 B.C.). Resorting to subterfuge (soldiers, disguised as slaves, provoked a stampede of horses, thereby gaining access to the enemy's fortifications). a Roman general acquired information that led directly to the defeat in battle of a valuable Carthaginian ally. Deprived of the support of its ally, Carthage was no match for Rome in the battle of Zama, and the rest, as they say, is history.[3]

It is principally the spies working for the Germans, the Japanese, the Russians, the British, the French, and, of course, the Americans in the twentieth century who have engaged the interest of the film industry. Moreover, the names that most people associate with this controversial profession are, not surprisingly, those of twentieth-century spies, especially those who betrayed their country's secrets to the enemy during the Cold War—the Rosenbergs, Klaus Fuchs, Burgess and MacLean, and

Aldrich Ames, to name but a few. One early twentieth-century spy who not only has appeared on film but has had an entire television series devoted to his exploits is Sydney Reilly. Reilly, reputed to be the model for Ian Fleming's famous fictional spy, James Bond, is presented in this series as a tough-minded risk taker who works for the British but is not above pursuing his own private interests in the tumultuous first two decades of the century. No hero or superpatriot, Reilly inhabits a dangerous gray area in the relations among states in which his cold, calculating manner and cynicism serve him well as he outwits assorted arms merchants, Russians, Germans, and even some of the people back in London for whom he works. Two of the strongest episodes in the series have Reilly, ostensibly a British shipping agent in Manchuria, feeding the Japanese navy with information that enables it to destroy the Russian fleet and win the Russo-Japanese War, and later infiltrating a German shipyard and stealing plans for an important naval gun with implied consequences for the course of World War I. *Reilly: The Ace of Spies* provides a contemporary audience with one of the better windows on the world of espionage, disabusing the viewer of any notion that the work of the spy is either glamorous or in some strange sense moral.

Films about espionage fall into a number of sub-genres. Leonard Rubenstein, in *The Great Spy Films,* classifies them under such intriguing titles as "The Feel of Politics," "The Problem of Loyalty," "The Touch of Romance," and "The Edge of Paranoia."[4] One thing most of these films have in common is that they are adventure films, in which the viewer is caught up in the suspense of what will happen to the protagonists as they fight their shadowy war for possession of each other's secrets. What makes them relevant for an understanding of international relations, however, is not the fate of particular characters, or even the impact of changing technology on the conduct of foreign policy, but on what they have to say about the nature of world politics. As Rubenstein observes,

> the spy's adventures occurred within the larger social or political issues
> that had immense importance for, and often played an active role, in the
> film's plot. . . . The spy was never a purely lone hero; behind the agent's
> antics lay a bureaucratic structure of clerks, typists and radio operators
> whose orders were issued by the same politicians and generals who pre-
> pared the armies for the future war the spy was already fighting.[5]

In effect, films about espionage provide a window onto the state of world politics and the principal antagonisms among the major world powers at particular times in history. Thus the growing menace of Nazi Germany can be seen in some of the espionage films made in the late 1930s and early 1940s, and the evolution of the Cold War can be followed in the screen treatment of Soviet, American, and British spies, defectors, and double agents. With relatively few exceptions, films about espionage are anchored, firmly or loosely, in real life events.

This was not always so. The first major film about spies, made in 1928 at the end of the silent era, was Fritz Lang's *Spione*, or *Spies*. While influenced by the fascination with spies generated by revelations about espionage in the Great War and by the Russian revolution and its impact on Europe, *Spies* is not about any particular country's espionage activities. It does not presume to tell us about specific events in Europe in the 1920s or earlier, but only about spies and how they operate. The spies presented on the screen in the Lang film—especially the principal spy, Haghi, played by Rudolf Klein-Rogge—are most villainous villains. In fact, Klein-Rogge is made up (quite deliberately, according to Lang) to look suspiciously like Lenin, so perhaps the director did, after all, intend the film to be an oblique commentary on the threat posed by the Soviet Union as well as the larger tensions in Europe at the time. The spy as villain has been a common theme in films, reflecting not only a Stimson-like disdain for what spies do but a belief that their actions are both criminal and evil. Such a view has inevitably undergone substantial change during times of war, both hot and cold, when a distinction is usually made between "their" spies and "our" spies. The former remain villains, of course, because the cause for which they work is evil, while the latter are heroes, doing what they must to thwart the enemy, even if that means resorting to the same tactics as those used by enemy spies.

Nonetheless, spies and the organizations for which they work have rarely been shown in a positive light on the screen. Individuals caught up in the dirty work of espionage may in some cases be given heroic treatment, but the viewer is usually left with the impression not only that Russia's KGB and Germany's Abwehr are loathesome organizations, but that America's CIA and Britain's MI-5 are almost equally cynical and unscrupulous. This is a position that especially reflects American ambivalence about spying. As one commentator has observed, even during the Cold War—not to mention those times when the nation's security was less obviously threatened,

> the intelligence services had their critics—not merely professional critics who felt that they were doing a poor job, but principled critics who took issue with the job itself. Such critics could also be found in other Western democracies, but with a difference. There, these critics, overwhelmingly of the Left, saw their intelligence services as servants of an ideology they mistrusted or abhorred. American critics mistrusted the CIA not because it was a faithful servant, but because it threatened to slip the leash of the master; not because it advanced American values, but because it stood in contradiction to them.[6]

This distrust of spies and the organizations for which they work recurs over and over again in the films we shall be mentioning in the following pages, including such prominent examples of the genre as *The Spy Who Came in from the Cold, Scorpio, Three Days of the Condor,* and even a wartime film such as *The Counterfeit Traitor.*

In films about espionage, spies and other persons associated with clandestine intelligence gathering typically fall into one of two categories. First, there are citizens of Country A who are trying to ferret out information for their government about (and usually in) Country B. Secondly, there are citizens of Country A who are working for Country B, passing secrets about their own government's policies to its enemy. The people who are engaged in these activities are a diverse lot. Some, of course, are professionals; spying or providing support for spies is what they do for a living. Others have been recruited for special assignments; when not spying they may be businessmen, journalists, academics, or simply tourists. Other persons find themselves engaged in espionage because they have access to valuable information *and* are vulnerable to blackmail, need money, harbor a deep-seated grievance, or are so committed to a cause that they feel a moral compulsion to become involved.

The spy on a dangerous mission inside an unfriendly country, the traitor secretly feeding information to his country's foes, the counterintelligence specialist who doggedly pursues an enemy agent—these are but the tip of the espionage iceberg. They are of most interest to moviemakers because their activities are exciting, or can be made so by a well-crafted story line. But behind them are dozens, even hundreds, of generally faceless persons who make up the intelligence communities of the states of the world. Some of these people play secondary roles of some importance in films; this is especially so of those members of the community known as controls, the men and women who, in espionage jargon, "run" spies. However, the great majority of them, like the supply train behind the army in war films, are seen only rarely, and then usually in sterile offices and laboratories, coaxing information out of computers, deciphering cryptic messages, studying grainy photographs and maps, or even doing such mundane things as reading foreign newspapers and journals.

There have been films in which this decidedly unglamorous, backstage aspect of espionage assumes an importance usually denied it. Perhaps the best example of a film of this kind is *The House on 92nd Street*. While most of the movies discussed in this book are identified with their director, this 1945 landmark film owes more to its producer, Louis de Rochemont. An experienced maker of newsreel documentaries, de Rochemont and his director, Henry Hathaway, created a film that looks and sounds very much like a documentary; it uses footage provided by the FBI (even J. Edgar Hoover himself is seen briefly at one point), as well as an off-screen narrator who never lets us forget that we are watching an actual case of attempted German espionage. But the strength of the film lies in its emphasis on the techniques of espionage and counterespionage. The principal characters are not especially interesting, and if there is a hero it is the FBI itself and the many unheralded, anonymous agents who are seen working methodically and successfully to break the enemy's spy ring.

What one remembers most are the details about one-way mirrors, radio relay stations, photographic surveillance, and other tricks of the trade.

The Spy Film Genre and the Nazis

The House on 92nd Street is one of a number of films that focus on the threat posed by Nazi Germany, the international drama that made the spy film a major staple of moviegoing fare. One of the first films to depict German espionage efforts, albeit in fictional terms, was Michael Powell's 1939 thriller, *The Spy in Black*, in which the spy in question was not one of Hitler's men but a World War I U-boat commander ordered to Scotland to spy on the British Royal Navy at a time when German fortunes were running low. Once the war started, spy films tended to become propaganda exercises, but *The Spy in Black* is a much more thoughtful example of the genre. The U-boat commander, played by Conrad Veidt, is not the stereo-typically arrogant German but a cool professional with limited confidence in the government that has sent him on this mission. His contact in Scot-land is a schoolmistress, played by Valerie Hobson, who turns out to be working for the British, not the Germans, and the strength of the film lies in the complex and respectful relationship between these two adversaries.

With storm clouds rapidly gathering over Europe, the film industry turned its attention to even more sinister—and more contemporary—spies than the one played by Veidt. Although Hollywood found it necessary to ex-ercise caution in denouncing Germany at a time when the United States was officially neutral, the Nazis gradually became the villains *du jour,* and Nazi spies made increasingly frequent appearances on the screen. Anatole Lit-vak's *Confessions of a Nazi Spy,* released in 1939, focused on the activities of the German-American Bund in the years prior to the war and reflected the willingness of Warner Brothers, the most socially conscious studio, to attack the Nazis (Germany was much displeased, and launched a diplomatic coun-teroffensive that resulted in the banning of the film in eighteen countries).[7] A very different kind of a film in which the Germans are once again the vil-lains is *Foreign Correspondent,* Alfred Hitchcock's second picture after coming to Hollywood. By this time (1940), the Wehrmacht had conquered France and stood poised on the Channel for an assault on England. But the United States was still neutral, and Hitchcock's film was a plea for Ameri-can involvement in the war. At the end of the film, the hero, an American journalist played by Joel McCrea, is broadcasting from London during a German air raid. His report is propaganda, of course, but it also marks the end of any pretense that neutrality is an honorable or safe course in this war.

Hello, America. I've been watching a part of the world being blown to pieces. A part of the world as nice as Vermont, Ohio, Virginia, California and Illinois lies ripped up bleeding like a steer in a slaughterhouse. . . . I can't read the rest of this speech I have because the lights have gone out. So I'll just have to talk off the cuff. All that noise you hear isn't static, it's death coming to London. . . . It's too late now to do anything except stand in the dark and let them come as if the lights are all out everywhere except in America. Keep those lights burning, cover them with steel, build them in with guns, build a canopy of battleships and bombing planes around them, and, hello America, hang onto your lights. They're the only lights in the world.

Once the war began, few "good" Germans appeared in films. Perhaps the most prominent exception was the movie version of Lillian Hellman's play, *Watch on the Rhine*. When the play opened on Broadway, war was raging in Europe but Pearl Harbor had not yet brought the United States into the fray. By 1943, when the film was released, the United States was deeply involved in the war and had begun to reverse the tide of battle against the Axis powers. The Hal Wallis film, directed by Herman Shumlin, looked back to the prewar era and presented as its hero a German citizen (Paul Lukas) married to an American woman from a prominent and affluent family (Bette Davis). This German is not a Nazi agent, but rather a part of the anti-Hitler underground who has come to the United States to raise money for that cause. The principal adversary in this film is not a German but a Romanian whose support for the Nazis is more mercenary than ideological. *Watch on the Rhine* is unrepresentative of wartime spy films, most of which were merely propaganda exercises with stereotypical characters. It did, however, contribute to the public understanding of espionage as a far more complex phenomenon than the one portrayed in most films of that era.

One of the more interesting films about espionage during World War II is George Seaton's *The Counterfeit Traitor*. Made in 1961, well after the demise of the Third Reich, *The Counterfeit Traitor* is based on a true story of a Swedish businessman who was coerced by British intelligence into espionage work in Germany on behalf of the Allies. This is a grim film which makes it unmistakably clear that spying in time of war is not only a highly dangerous undertaking but one in which even the most basic norms of interpersonal morality may be suspended. The Swedish businessman, Erickson (William Holden), is blackmailed by the British, who circulate false information to the effect that he is a Nazi sympathizer; not only must Erickson use his business trips to Germany to gather information about the German oil industry, he must sustain the lie about his sympathies by speaking contemptuously about the Allies and about Jews. His assignment has effectively ruined his reputation in Sweden, and although he ultimately succeeds in providing the British with the information they need, he has also had to witness Nazi atrocities at first hand, including the execution of an idealistic agent (Lilli Palmer) with whom he had developed a close relationship. Erickson survives by his wits and nerve, but the emotional cost to him is immeasurable. This is a nerve-wracking film to watch, but it presents a dimension of the war that rarely made the headlines but that rings true to a degree that most spy films do not.

While films about espionage involving the Allies and Nazi Germany are relatively common, far fewer focus on the role of spies in the conflict in Asia and the Pacific. One exception is John Huston's 1942 film, *Across the Pacific*. Unlike such films as *The Counterfeit Traitor* and *The House on 92nd Street*, which were based on actual cases, *Across the Pacific* is entirely fictional. Its plot is based on the premise that Japan planned an attack on the Panama Canal concurrently with the one on Pearl Harbor, and it is up to the film's hero, Humphrey Bogart, to prevent such a disaster. The Bogart character is in effect a double agent whose quarry, played by Sydney Greenstreet, is a covert spy for Japan. This is very much a wartime film serving a wartime purpose, in which Bogart, making full use of the famous Bogart persona, effectively discharges his mission and ultimately machine-guns to death the spies and soldiers who were to have sabotaged the canal. *Across the Pacific* manages to be quite realistic in the way it treats the difficult task of dissimulation, which is so essential to the success of the double agent. While it hardly stands out as one of the most important treatments of the subject, it remains an intriguing entry in the catalog of films about espionage from the World War II period.

Spying, as Secretary Stimson's remark makes clear, had not been an important part of the U.S. foreign policy repertoire prior to the war. The exigencies of the titanic struggle with the Axis powers changed that forever. The Office of Strategic Services (OSS) came into being because it had become imperative that the United States use every means available to learn of the enemy's plans and counter them in a timely way; its role was critical in breaking German and Japanese codes, demonstrating once and for all that reading another country's "mail" may make the difference between victory and defeat or at least in the duration of war and the cost of victory. When the prickly wartime alliance of convenience between the Soviet Union and the Western allies turned into a full-fledged cold war, any idea that the United States might get out of the business of espionage quickly became moot. In 1947, as tensions were being ratcheted up in Eastern Europe, the Central Intelligence Agency (CIA) was created as part of a major reorganization of the American defense and security establishment;[8] espionage would receive the sustained and systematic attention of the U.S. government, now apparently locked into a protracted struggle with an adversary that was obsessively secretive and itself deeply involved in spying and other subversive activities.

The Cold War: Spying at Its Apogee

The Cold War soon became *the* dominant meta-issue in international relations, and U.S. citizens became acutely aware of it, not only through news about crises in Greece and Czechoslovakia and Berlin and then war in Korea, but in stories about communist spies at work in Washington. It was not long before the United States found itself caught up in a spy scare, with allegations that Soviet agents were stealing American secrets and that some Americans were conspiring to help them. There was, of course, truth in these charges. Soviet spies were active, and there were inevitably some people in the United States who, for reasons both idealistic and base, were willing to pass secrets to Moscow. The tempest over this issue soon turned ugly, as the United States became infected with the disease called McCarthyism.

The senator from Wisconsin was not the only person to claim that Americans were working for the enemy and to make ferreting them out a national preoccupation; the House Un-American Activities Committee (HUAC) had launched an investigation into communist subversion in Hollywood as early as 1947. But it was McCarthy whose demagoguery did more than anything else to give the issue its prominence. His speech in Wheeling, West Virginia, on February 9, 1950—a speech in which he claimed to have in his hand a list of 205 known communists in the U.S. State Department—moved the Red menace to the top of the national agenda. McCarthy was lying, of course, something he did both easily and recklessly (the paper in his hand contained no list, and he never identified a single communist at State, much less 205 or 81 or 57—he subsequently changed the number at will). But he had tapped into an American anxiety, something he both fed and exploited, and for several years "no man was closer than he to the center of American consciousness or more central to the world's consciousness of America."[9] The dark suspicions he and the like-minded members of HUAC stoked had a chilling effect on popular culture. HUAC zeroed in on wartime films that had praised America's Russian ally, branding them pro-Soviet propaganda;[10] its investigation of alleged subversives in the film industry resulted in jail sentences for the so-called Hollywood Ten, who refused to answer the question, "Are you now or have you ever been a member of the Communist Party?"[11]

The witch hunt also led to a defensive reaction in the nation's movie capital, which began churning out virulently anticommunist films, either as a form of expiation or due to the convictions of right-wing producers and directors. Such films "openly condemned Communists, associating them with espionage and with plots involving the violent overthrow of the American government."[12] Most of these films are quite forgettable; one of the better examples is probably Sam Fuller's *Pickup on South Street.*

> Military valor, the pervasive threat of communism and of crime syndicates, the necessity for vigilante justice, rabid pro-Americanism—these are recurrent Fuller tropes injected into his dime-novel scenarios . . . Fuller's most active period coincided with the height of Cold War anxieties. Weaving variations on the communist threat, the Fuller canon is rife

with motifs of infiltration and deception, yet Fuller typically presents spies, double agents, and stool pigeons in a gutsy resistance against reds.[13]

Pickup on South Street shows us nothing new regarding the techniques employed by spies, but it effectively captures something of the mood of the times. All of the principal characters are lowlifes—a pickpocket, an underworld informer, a tough moll from the wrong side of the tracks; but when the pickpocket (Richard Widmark) accidentally steals film of missile plans for American communists to pass to the Soviet Union, a plot is set in motion that leads ultimately to Fuller's conclusion: even unsavory common criminals will eventually do the right thing and cooperate with the authorities to defeat the "commies." As with so many of the spy films of that era, *Pickup* stressed two themes: that the United States was threatened by a relentless enemy who was aided by the traitors in our midst, and that it was time for all true Americans to be vigilant patriots.

The Cold War lasted for more than forty years and inevitably produced a great variety of spy films. Most of these films are more concerned with the drama of espionage, the adventures of spies and counterspies, of agents and double agents, than they are with shedding light on the complex and tense relationships between East and West during those years. The films based on Ian Fleming's James Bond novels were the most popular, and many of them were quite good examples of their kind. But not even the one most specifically linked to the East-West conflict, *From Russia with Love,* can be considered a serious contribution to an understanding of international relations. Given the series' increasing preoccupation with sexuality and state-of-the-art hardware that frequently strained credulity, the Bond films must be relegated to a footnote in any discussion of international relations in popular culture. Bond's more believable colleague in the spy business was Len Deighton's Harry Palmer, played in the movies by Michael Caine. In the first of that series, *The Ipcress File,* Palmer, a spy with a shady background and ill-concealed contempt for his more sophisticated superiors, tries to discover why some of Britain's top government scientists are disappearing. In view of the importance during the Cold War years of atomic secrets and the frequency with which physicists and other scientists were involved in spy cases, there was potential for an interesting fictional look at what *The Ipcress File* calls the "brain drain" issue. But the film is more interested in exploring increasingly deadly conflicts among supposedly allied espionage organizations, with the result that it is best relegated to that popular sub-genre of spy films, the one populated by double agents.

One of the more interesting films in the latter category is Michael Winner's *Scorpio.* It is not clear until nearly the end of the picture that the spy in question, Cross (Burt Lancaster), is in fact a double agent, but the plot is driven by the assumption by his superiors in the CIA that he is; the uncertainty about this most pivotal issue in the film—both on the part of the audience and the man the CIA has hired to kill Cross—is part of its appeal. Both Cross and his KGB counterpart, Zharkov (Paul Scofield), are sympathetically portrayed; the two veteran spies have far more respect for each other than they do for their bosses, and the film's best scene may be the one in which they discuss the nature of their jobs over a few too many drinks. In fact, as one critic argues, it is *"Scorpio's* conversations [that] give the film its uniquely complex political coloration"[14] and make it one of the strongest indictments of the Cold War on film. One of the film's most memorable lines is given to Zharkov, who tells a Soviet official that he resembles another man "who didn't leave his name, but was trying to build socialism in one country out of the bones from a charnel house." There may be no better epithet for Stalin in all of popular culture.

Arguably the most depressing film about Cold War espionage was the screen adaptation of John Le Carré's novel, *The Spy Who Came in from the Cold.* Director Martin Ritt, who was among those blacklisted in Hollywood during the anticommunist crusade of the 1950s, turned this somber, even grim, modern-day spy film into an indictment of "the cold-blooded expediency [that] was the sole criterion used by espionage chiefs on both sides of the Berlin Wall."[15] Alec Leamas (Richard Burton), an experienced spy with no illusions, is sent to East Germany where he is to pose as a defector. His mission is to get rid of Mundt, the head of that country's counterintelligence service, by convincing the East Germans that the man is a double agent working for the British. But Leamas discovers near the film's end that he has been deceived by his own superiors, that Mundt really is a double agent and that the real target of the mission all along was an East German agent who had begun to suspect Mundt's true role. To achieve this result, the British callously betray both Leamas and his entirely innocent woman friend, who are gunned down in the film's climactic scene as they try to scale the Wall to safety in West Berlin. *The Spy Who Came in from the Cold* is unlike virtually all other spy films in that it is almost entirely devoid of the usual action sequences; the only gun fired in the entire film is the machine gun that kills Leamas and his lover at the very end. Le Carre and Ritt are telling us that espionage is a morally ambiguous and dirty business. Rarely has the Cold War looked so sordid, the causes for which it was ostensibly fought so unworthy.

The spies who populate Cold War films are a varied lot, and include several like Erickson in *The Counterfeit Traitor* who are forced to live the life of the spy. One such reluctant spy is Barley Blair, played by Sean Connery in another film based on a John Le Carré novel, *The Russia House.* Unlike *The Spy Who Came in from the Cold,* which appeared at the height of the Cold War, Fred Schepisi's *The Russia House* arrived on screens just as the Soviet Union was about to collapse. Although the latter film lets us know that private citizens in both Russia and the West can and do meet informally and enjoy each other's company, it provides no hint of a thaw in the Cold War at the governmental level, especially in the agencies dedicated to espionage. The plot is set in motion when a Russian defense scientist, Yakov (Klaus Maria Brandauer), tries to put a manuscript in the hands of Blair, an English publisher whom he has met at a dinner party and come to regard as something of a kindred spirit. The manuscript is not really all that important, but rather "a passionate muddle of technical data and visionary philosophy . . . a message to the world."[16] Unfortunately, the manuscript is intercepted by MI-6 in London, and the intelligence professionals immediately assume that they are in possession of an extremely important if cryptic document that might conceivably alter the balance of power in the world. In no time the CIA is also involved, and Blair is pressed into service to make contact with Yakov. The three principals in this movie are all amateurs—Blair, Yakov, and the Russian book publisher who initially acted as a go-between (Michelle Pfeiffer); they are refreshingly decent and very human, unlike the professionals, who operate on automatic pilot as mutually suspicious, devious cold warriors. Indeed, the Connery and Pfeiffer characters fall in love, which inevitably complicates things for the intelligence agencies. Although the film demonstrates the fact that by the later stages of the Cold War spying had become more technologically sophisticated (we see the spy agencies monitoring Blair's work in Russia from listening posts in London and Washington), it is clear that at least in filmdom there is still no substitute for human intelligence gathering.

The films mentioned in the previous paragraphs may have emerged from the imaginations of novelists and the writers of screenplays, but the events they depicted had rough parallels in the real world (and a few were based on actual cases). Occasionally the industry produced a "what if" film, one that clearly had no real-life counterpart, such as John Mackenzie's *The Fourth Protocol,* based on a novel by Frederick Forsyth. By the time this film hit the market, there was considerably less mystery about the construction of atomic bombs than in the early years of the nuclear age. In addition to the familiar members of the nuclear club (the United States, the Soviet Union, Great Britain, France, and China), other countries were widely believed to possess nuclear weapons, and yet others were known to be trying to develop them. The fact that a relatively small and portable nuclear weapon could be made, and the possibility that a rogue regime—or even a nonstate actor—might consider the use of such a weapon preemptively or even in an act of terrorism, sustained anxiety in many quarters. *The Fourth Protocol* taps into that anxiety, and goes so far as to suggest that the plan to detonate an atomic bomb is not hatched by an irresponsible madman in some Third World country, but by the men in the Kremlin. The bomb is to be smuggled into Britain in several pieces, assembled by a KGB agent (played by Pierce Brosnan), and used to wipe out a U.S. Air Force base, not to mention the English residential area surrounding that base. The plan, if successful, promises to destroy NATO's credibility, and Brosnan appears to be just the kind of meticulous, cold-blooded agent who can make the plan work. Ultimately, however, he encounters a tenacious adversary in the person of British intelligence officer Michael Caine, who has to combat not only the Russian agent but his own superiors as well.

This is one of the films which *The National Review* recently listed among "Your 100 Favorite Conservative Movies," its place on the list earned by its depiction of "the evil of our enemies."[17] The author of the article qualifies his praise for the film, however, noting that it is weakened by a liberal ending. While the average movie-goer is more likely to find it improbable than liberal, the film's denouement does provide an unusual twist: the plot has been jointly hatched by high-ranking officials in the KGB and MI-6, with the implication that they share an interest that overrides a concern for their country's security—that of advancing their own careers. After the tension generated by the film's main plot device, the conclusion leaves a decidedly sour taste.

The Intelligence Community Under Fire

With the exception of those made in support of the war effort in the 1940s and in response to the communist scare of the 1950s, it is apparent that most spy films are in fact highly critical, if not of individual spies, at least of the institutions they serve. In one movie after another, the spymasters are amoral if not immoral, totally cynical, manipulative of their own agents, and often no better than their enemy counterparts. Although Cross (Burt Lancaster) turns out to have been a double agent in *Scorpio*, justifying the CIA's suspicions, the agency's behavior on the screen is far more offensive than Cross's. The viewer is made to identify with Cross, though not his duplicity, and to feel revulsion toward the agency.

This film was made in 1973, of course, a time when the executive branch of the U.S. government was generally on the defensive. President Nixon was fighting for his political life over Watergate; the Congress, reflecting institutional frustration over what it regarded as irresponsible use of presidential authority during the Vietnam War era, passed the War Powers Resolution, which set a time limit of sixty days for deployment of troops in combat without congressional authorization; and evidence was mounting that the CIA had been engaged in covert operations incompatible with American values (the Church Committee, chaired by Senator Frank Church, D-Idaho, would issue its detailed indictment of the agency in 1975). As the Watergate saga unfolded, it became clear that Nixon had also abused the role of his intelligence-gathering services in that sordid affair; within a year not only had the president resigned, but the Congress had acted to rein in an "out-of-control" Central Intelligence Agency by establishing special committees to monitor its activities and requiring executive consultation regarding its covert operations. It is hardly surprising, given a public mood demanding that the government be more accountable, that the CIA, Washington's least-accountable institution, should become the target of sharp criticism in popular culture. Perhaps the most negative treatment of the CIA to come out of Hollywood during this period was Sydney Pollack's *Three Days of the Condor,* released in 1974.

Not at all a conventional spy film, *Condor* focused not on CIA agents penetrating enemy security or enemy agents working clandestinely in the United States, but on a rogue faction within the CIA that was operating ruthlessly outside agency channels. "Condor" is the code name for a member of the agency, played by Robert Redford, whose job is quite simply to read spy novels in a quest for information about espionage that may have escaped the attention of his superiors. Inadvertently he stumbles on an agency network operating in the Middle East, and the result is the murder of all of his colleagues (he escapes elimination only because he is late returning from lunch). One assumes that the top brass in the CIA will quickly size up the situation, act against the renegade faction, and save Condor. The film reflects the mood of the time, however, so Condor's superiors worry more about protecting the agency's good name than they do about Condor or the plot he has uncovered. At film's end, when Condor has just shared his story with the *New York Times,* his superior at the CIA walks away, leaving the audience with the impression that Condor's story "might not be printed, would change nothing if it were," and might lead to Condor's murder if it were published.[18] This indictment of the CIA mirrors the hostility to the cloak-and-dagger profession then common in the United States, especially on college and university campuses, where agency recruiters were picketed and faculty decided that they should no longer accept agency research funds.

If there has been no shortage of films depicting the misdeeds of espionage agencies, neither has there been a paucity of films ridiculing the ineptitude of spies and the governments for which they work. In the real world, the CIA has been much criticized for not predicting the collapse of the Soviet Union. One of the agency's foremost critics, Senator Daniel Patrick Moynihan (D-New York), declared that "The CIA failed in its single, overriding defining mission, which was to chart the course of Soviet affairs."[19] This view has been challenged by defenders of the agency,[20] but it is nonetheless widely shared, as is the conviction that the CIA also failed to detect the extent of Iraq's nonconventional weapons capabilities as revealed in the aftermath of Operation Desert Storm. The case of Aldrich Ames, who had been betraying U.S. agents in the Soviet Union for years, has also been a major embarrassment for the CIA. After Ames's arrest, agency sources were quick to dismiss him as "a drunk and a mediocre case officer . . . inept, dull, unsophisticated and lackadaisical."[21] This is hardly surprising, given the human desire of his colleagues to distance themselves from a traitor. But this marginal officer had, after all, been entrusted with a highly sensitive post, and his lavish spending on a modest salary had failed to set off alarm bells within the organization. The Ames case is a serious one, of course; his activities are alleged to have resulted in the death of at least twelve U.S. agents, not to mention the loss of innumerable secret documents. But it also invites parody. After all, here are the experts in keeping and discovering secrets outwitted for years by someone who was widely regarded as not particularly sharp and who, as if to prove it, left a rather considerable trail. There has been no spy film on the Ames case as yet, but the French did produce a delicious comedy on the ineptitude of their own intelligence agency at very much the same time Hollywood was giving us *Scorpio* and *Three Days of the Condor*.

This French film, whose popularity inevitably produced an American sequel some years later, is *The Tall Blond Man with One Black Shoe*. The plot is set in motion when the head of French counterintelligence becomes suspicious that a subordinate is conspiring against him. He determines to trap the subordinate by setting him off in pursuit of a nonexistent secret agent. The man selected without his knowledge to be the bait in this game is a concert violinist, picked for the role only because he is wearing unmatched shoes. The violinist, played by Pierre Richard, is not only unaware that dozens of French agents believe he is a spy in possession of some important secret; he is also blissfully unaware that they are following him and scrutinizing his life history for some clue to the nonexistent secret. Richard is a complete innocent, of course, a bumbler who even manages to turn an attempted seduction by a female agent into total chaos while the spies watch on closed circuit television. Although the film is one long and clever joke, it also manages to show us, albeit tongue in cheek, much of the now-familiar repertoire of tricks we have come to associate with spies from years of watching them on the screen. Just as Ames, "the third-worst officer among two hundred at his rank,"[22] fooled the CIA for years, so does *The Tall Blond Man with One Black Shoe* fool the French intelligence professionals—without even trying.

One reason Aldrich Ames and others like him can become double agents without being detected is that colleagues cannot imagine that one of their number could be a traitor. An official report criticizing the CIA's handling of counterintelligence cases in the 1980s ascribed the problem in part to a "fundamental inability of anyone in the SE [Soviet-East European] division to think the unthinkable—that a DO [Directorate of Operations] employee could engage in espionage."[23] Such thinking provides the plot line in another comedy about spies, an episode of the British television series *Yes, Prime Minister*. The title of the episode, "One of Us," more or less tells the story. It appears that a former head of MI-5 has died and left papers in which he confesses to having passed secrets to Moscow for the better part of two decades, a revelation that promises to make serious trouble for the government, especially in view of the fact that an earlier inquiry had exonerated him. The explanation offered by several of the principals for the embarrassingly superficial investigation is that the man was "one of us"—part of a close-knit network of officials with similar backgrounds and values and hence someone above suspicion, around whom it is necessary to close ranks. In the end, the cabinet secretary who had headed the investigation is cleared of the charge of incompetence in the case by a prime minister grateful for his help in improving the PM's sagging approval ratings. This episode is replete with quips that satirize both the security community and government in general: "Government security inquiries are only used for killing press stories," "Giving information to Moscow is serious . . . but a scandal like this could gravely weaken the authority of the service," and "If once they accepted the principle that senior civil servants could be removed for incompetence, that would be the thin edge of the wedge." Like all of the episodes in this series, "One of Us" is played for laughs, but underneath the clever dialogue is a perceptive caricature of an important issue.

The major focus of all the spy films discussed in this chapter is on human intelligence gathering, known in intelligence jargon as HUMINT. Failures of human intelligence, together with dramatic progress in high-tech means of information collection, have produced talk of phasing down the role of the human spy and relying increasingly on satellites and other technological wonders that seem able to outperform human agents. Moreover, as a British expert on the subject writes, "What adds to their appeal is that satellites, unlike human beings, do not betray. The Ames affair is an ugly reminder of the fact that people have minds of their own, prone to baseness at worst and to bias at best. In contrast, the camera, the microphone, and their state-of-the-art descendants lack the mind, will, or reason to do anything other than record what is there."[24] As the author goes on to argue, however, high technology is both "partially sighted and hearing impaired";[25] it may be valuable in cases where the target country itself has relatively sophisticated capabilities, but aerial reconnaissance and international inspections are considerably less fruitful in gauging the intentions of an erratic leader of a rogue state. It is almost certainly too soon to write the obituary for the spy, good news for this particular film genre. We shall see more and more of high-tech equipment in spy films, but the appeal of such films will doubtless continue to be rooted in the tension generated by the conflict of wills and skills of the men and women who fight the clandestine espionage wars.

For those who fear that the spy film will be a casualty of the end of the Cold War, it should be noted that the major intelligence agencies (and even those of some smaller states) have discovered a new *raison d'être*— economic espionage. The CIA and other intelligence services have long placed spies under what is known as "nonofficial cover" (NOC), and there is evidence that the NOC of choice these days is that of the businessman whose task it is to penetrate the companies and commercial ministries of economic competitors.[26] *Clear and Present Danger,* discussed in Chapters 2 and 4, reminds us that the CIA has yet another post–Cold War mission as long as the drug trade flourishes. The moral of the story seems to be that the spy is here to stay; if that it true, the spy film is likely to survive as well.

Notes

1. See Craig and George, *Force and Statecraft,* p. 11.
2. Seth, *The Anatomy of Spying,* p. 20.
3. *Ibid.,* especially pp. 21–26.
4. Rubenstein, *The Great Spy Films.*
5. *Ibid.,* p. 12.
6. Sherr, "Cultures of Spying," pp. 56–57.
7. Rubenstein, *The Great Spy Films,* p. 114.
8. The Central Intelligence Agency is only part of the intelligence community in the United States, and not the largest part at that. That honor belongs to the National Security Agency, whose mission is encoding U.S. communications and breaking the codes of other countries. Other parts of the intelligence community include the Defense Intelligence Agency and the National Reconnaissance Office, which, like NSA, are in the Department of Defense. The Department of State has its own much smaller intelligence arm.
9. Rovere, *Senator Joe McCarthy,* p. 4. The McCarthy story has been told in a number of books, but this early account of the senator's rise and fall remains the most readable.
10. Among the egregious examples of films in this category are *Mission to Moscow* (with its whitewash of Stalin's purge trials of the 1930s), *The North Star,* and *Song of Russia.*
11. See Belton, *American Cinema/American Culture,* Ch. 11, for a discussion of this phenomenon.
12. *Ibid.,* p. 245. Examples include *My Son John, Big Jim McLain, I Was a Communist for the FBI,* and *Walk East on Beacon.*
13. Hirsch, "Fuller, Sam," p. 164.
14. Rubenstein, *The Great Spy Films,* p. 99.
15. *Ibid.,* p. 56.
16. See review by Rafferty, "The Spy Game," p. 84.
17. See Warren, "Your 100 Best Conservative Movies," p. 56.
18. Rubenstein, *The Great Spy Films,* p. 103.
19. Quoted in Berkowitz and Richelson, "The CIA Vindicated," p. 36. A distinguished former OSS officer and assistant secretary of state for intelligence and research has argued that the contribution of espionage "to wise decisions in foreign policy and defense is minimal. But the cost in lives, treasure, and intangibles is high. . . . The United States should get out of the business of both espionage and covert political action." See Hilsman, "Does the CIA Still Have a Role?" pp. 110, 116.
20. Berkowitz and Richelson, "The CIA Vindicated," pp. 36–47.
21. Shulsky and Schmitt, "The Future of Intelligence," p. 63.

22. *Ibid.*

23. *Ibid.*, p. 64, note 3.

24. Sherr, "Cultures of Spying," pp. 57–58.

25. *Ibid.*, p. 58.

26. See Dreyfuss, "The CIA Crosses Over," and Shulsky and Schmitt, "The Future of Intelligence."

6

Decisionmaking and Crisis Management

As the very name implies, international relations is necessarily an interactive phenomenon, requiring for its existence two or more actors. While it is possible for states (or other players on the world's stage) to experience unplanned, chance encounters, most of what we call international relations takes place as a result of conscious policy choices. State A is pursuing a particular foreign policy, and in the process of doing so finds it necessary to deal with State B, whose interests (and hence policy preferences) are not the same. The policies in question may concern a matter of great consequence; conversely, what is at issue may be of only minor importance. The policies may be diametrically opposed, or the differences may only be those of nuance. Whatever the case, the intersection of the two foreign policies produces international relations between States A and B. It is possible to analyze this relationship by focusing only on the interaction between the two states, and if we do so we shall probably be interested in their relative power, their bargaining strategies, and, more generally, systemic factors affecting the relationship.

It is also useful to look at the decisionmaking processes within the two states that shaped their respective foreign policies in the first place and that determine how they will respond now that they are engaged with each other in the international arena. When we turn our attention to these matters, we have shifted to different levels of analysis. We are looking at domestic political systems, at the ways in which governments are organized, at the relationship between the public sector and civil society, and even at the roles and belief systems and psychological makeup of influential individuals.

Rationality Versus Reality in Decisionmaking

As suggested in Chapter 1, the realist school tends to regard the state as a unitary rational actor. The casual observer of world affairs probably does so, too. We hear about Chinese policy regarding intellectual property, the British position on a common currency within the European Union, and India's response to Pakistan's nuclear ambitions, and so on, and we overlook the complexities and the conflicts that characterize the process of arriving at those policies. Although we know logically that such policies are not always arrived at easily, there is nonetheless an inclination to think of states—especially states with closed political systems and those with which we are less familiar—as "black boxes" within which, hidden to us, rational decisions are being made. According to this model, states identify their objectives, lay out alternative policies for realizing those objectives, weigh the costs and benefits of the various alternatives, and select the policy that will maximize benefits and minimize costs—that is, the optimal policy.

There are, of course, many problems with this model as a description of how decisions are actually arrived at within states. First, the goals a state wishes to achieve may conflict with each other; adopting a policy most likely to realize one goal may reduce the prospects of realizing another. This can be seen in recent efforts by the United States to increase trade with China while at the same time trying to reduce that country's export of materials used in nuclear weapons production, end its piracy of U.S. software and compact discs, moderate its policies on human rights, and exercise restraint vis-à-vis Taiwan. Second, the rational actor model assumes that the decisionmakers possess sufficient information to make rational choices. But information is almost always incomplete and imperfect, with the result that decisions have to be made under conditions of uncertainty. It is rarely clear just what the consequences of various alternative policies will in fact be. Another important problem with the notion that states behave rationally in selecting foreign policies is that states are not unitary actors. Although few states divide governmental power and responsibility to the degree that the United States does, decisions in most states typically have to be hammered out in bargaining between branches of government and government agencies that have parochial interests that diverge and conflict. The familiar adage, "Where you stand depends on where you sit," may have been coined in an American context, but it applies universally.

Yet another problem with the notion that states are rational actors lies in the fact that decisionmakers often rely on standard operating procedures (SOPs) rather than going through the time-consuming process of constructing policy alternatives and then subjecting them to cost-benefit analysis. Most ministries or agencies involved in decisionmaking have developed over time a repertoire of responses to problems that are compatible with their interests and capabilities, which have been tested, and which seem relatively safe, especially in circumstances where information is limited and time is short. In effect, decisionmakers tend to be habit-driven actors, disposed to go with what they know, making only incremental changes. And these several caveats regarding the rationality of foreign policy decisions must be supplemented by two others: that societal factors constrain decisionmakers, especially in pluralistic societies, and that decision-makers are, in the final analysis, human beings who are not immune to the problems of cognitive limitations, emotional stress, and physical disorders.

There are many models of decisionmaking, no one of which fully explains the process. Perhaps the best known of the works on foreign policy decisionmaking is Graham Allison's *The Essence of Decision: Explaining the Cuban Missile Crisis.*[1] Allison identifies three models, one of which is the aforementioned rational actor model. The other two are an organizational process model, which stresses the tendency of organizations to rely on SOPs and incrementalism, and a bureaucratic politics model, which emphasizes the conflict among self-interested groups within government and thus sees policies as the product of compromise. These models have different explantory power in different contexts. The bureaucratic politics model, for example, is obviously more likely to be helpful in understanding decisionmaking in democracies than in dictatorships. Decisionmaking in democracies is most useful for us here, inasmuch as the most interesting films on the subject depict that process in countries such as the United States and the United Kingdom. Yet all of these analytical models may provide insights into decisionmaking behavior, as the author of one prominent textbook on world politics tells us.

> In general, routine situations that have limited economic or security implications such as the arrest of a citizen abroad or still another UN vote on sanctions against Iraq are more likely to elicit the organizational process decisionmaking model. The rational actor model better suits full-scale crises, such as reaction to the invasion of South Korea by the North or the invasion by Iraq of Kuwait. The bureaucratic politics model becomes most appropriate when decision time is long and economic interests are great. Examples include the U.S. withdrawal from Vietnam, the size of the U.S. defense budget, or U.S. restrictions on Japanese auto imports.[2]

These generalizations must not blind us to the fact that almost all decisions about foreign policy reveal some of the characteristics of each of Allison's three models. Thus organizational parochialism and interagency conflict are not suspended during crises, in spite of the contention that states function more nearly as rational actors under crisis conditions. It must be remembered that states and their governments do not pick and choose from among these decisionmaking models; the models are only analytical constructs.

Students of decisionmaking have identified several patterns of behavior among those involved in the policy process that illustrate the difficulty of arriving at the optimal policy choice. One of these is that subordinates frequently keep information from the person ultimately responsible for a policy decision—the president, the prime minister, even the foreign minister—or that they tell him (it is rarely her) whatever they believe will persuade him to do what the subordinates want to do. Related to this practice is what could be called the "Option B" ploy: the president or prime minister is presented with several alternatives, but all but one are politically or otherwise infeasible, leading to the policy choice desired all along by the advisers. Then there is the well-known strategy wherein advisers cast their recommendations in terms of a worst-case scenario, putting the decisionmaker in the position of risking terrible consequences for the country (and for his own career) if he ignores that advice.

Another tactic with the potential to defeat rational choice is the press leak. There is often no better way to scuttle a policy unwelcome to some agency or even to an individual official than to leak details to the media, thereby guaranteeing a debate on terms and at a time not of the policymaker's choosing. Even if a policy has been decided upon and orders to carry it out issued, bureaucracies opposed to the policy have a way of dragging their feet and even ignoring instructions when it comes to implementation. A variation on this practice occurred in 1948 when President Truman supported the partition of Palestine, only to have the U.S. ambassador to the United Nations announce another policy favored by the State Department's Arabists. These are only a few of the many tricks of the trade that demonstrate not only that the state is not a unitary rational actor but that, at least in Washington (and almost certainly in a great many other places), no one is truly in charge, despite appearances to the contrary.[3]

Many of these facets of foreign policy decisionmaking have been effectively captured on film. Perhaps it is not surprising that some of the best treatments of both organizational process and bureaucratic politics models are to be found in comedies. Indeed, the British television series, *Yes, Prime Minister,* includes two episodes that offer a veritable clinic on the subject. One of these episodes is entitled "A Victory for Democracy," and it provides the viewer with one of the few instances in which the well-meaning but somewhat dim-witted prime minister, James Hacker, is able to get the best of his devious cabinet secretary, Sir Humphrey Appleby. Its value for understanding the decisionmaking process lies mainly in what it has to say about the efforts of the careerists in the Foreign Office to pursue policies of their own choosing regardless of the prime minister's preferences.

There are two strands to the plot. One involves a rumored coup by Marxist guerrillas on St. Georges, a fictional island country in the British Commonwealth, and the likelihood that communist East Yemen will invade in support of the guerrillas. The other concerns a British vote against Israel in the United Nations. The Foreign Office prefers a hands-off policy toward events on St. Georges, largely because it does not want to lose a British contract to build an airport there, and supports the anti-Israel vote because it wishes to court the Arabs and not put the supply of oil from the region at risk. The Foreign Office and the cabinet secretary try to keep the prime minister in the dark about the trouble brewing on St. Georges, knowing that he will want to intervene in defense of democracy. Both believe that it is dangerous to let politicians become involved in diplomacy; Sir Humphrey observes that "diplomacy is about surviving until the next century [while] politics is about surviving until Friday afternoon."

The dialogue is full of witticisms that caricature the decisionmaking process and provide colorful illustrations of some of the bureaucratic stratagems mentioned above. For example, when asked what the Foreign Office will do if the prime minister insists upon options, the reply is a variation on the Option B tactic: he will be given three options, one of which will be totally unacceptable while the other two, upon close inspection, will be exactly the same. The notion that organizations respond to crises by resorting to SOPs is illustrated, tongue in cheek, by a senior Foreign Office careerist and Sir Humphrey, who together explain the four-stage strategy that is the standard response in time of crisis: "In stage one we say nothing is going to happen. In stage two we say something may be going to happen, but we should do nothing about it. In stage three we say maybe we should do something about it, but there is nothing we can do. In stage four we say maybe there's something we could have done, but it's too late now."

That subordinates do not always implement policy decisions with which they disagree is illustrated in the case of the vote at the UN. The prime minister had indicated that he wanted his ambassador to abstain, only to discover that Britain had supported the resolution condemning Israel. The Israeli ambassador, an old friend of the PM, waves off his apology and proceeds to educate the prime minister on the way these things happen: an instruction from the PM becomes a request from the foreign secretary, then a recommendation from the minister of state, then finally just a suggestion to the ambassador. "A Victory for Democracy" also manages to have something to say about personal bias. An adviser to the prime minister who has been seconded from the Foreign Office not only shares the view that there are things the PM should not be told; his sympathies obviously lie with the Arabs. When told by the prime minister, now wise to what has been going on, that he is to be rewarded with the ambassadorship in Tel Aviv, the horrified adviser blurts out that the Israelis won't want him because they know he is on the Arab side. The prime minister's reply to this display of candor is, as might be expected, "I thought you were on our side."

One of the worst-kept secrets about the foreign policy establishment of most countries is that the several branches of the military are rivals, jealously striving to protect their roles and shares of the defense budget. There may be a theoretically optimal way of protecting the nation's security, but the services will predictably define the national interest in terms of their own needs, and will, in moments of crisis, invoke SOPs that make use of their capabilities. The *Yes, Prime Minister* series captures this phenomenon in another of its episodes, "The Grand Design." The PM has decided to shift the British deterrent from nuclear weapons to conventional forces, which means that he can cancel an order to purchase Trident missiles from the United States. When he announces his plan to the head of the British army, he expects a negative reaction. But instead the general applauds the decision, as students of military politics might have predicted. The general says that the navy will, of course, want to keep Trident because it is launched from its submarines; and he dismisses the Royal Air Force, saying that all it is interested in is flying around dropping things on people. As for the general's own branch of service, a shift to conventional forces will have the effect of making it the preeminent leg in Britain's defense triad. The dialogue in this brief scene captures better than many a textbook the reality of bureaucratic politics in the making of foreign policy.

Cognitive Limitations and Bias

If decisionmaking in foreign policy is complicated by organizational parochialism and bureaucratic infighting, it is also handicapped by the inescapable fact that policy makers may experience altogether human problems in arriving at rational decisions. A psychological analysis of decisionmaking calls our attention to two approaches to the process. One is the cognitive approach, associated with scholars like Robert Jervis, which "emphasizes the ways in which human cognitive limitations distort decisionmaking by gross simplifications in problem representation and information processing."[4] The other is the motivational approach, often identified with the work of Irving Janis and Leon Mann, which focuses on the fact that decisionmakers are emotional beings who experience conflict and psychological stress when faced with the need to make difficult decisions in a context of doubt and uncertainty.[5] As Richard Ned Lebow says in his summary treatment of these perspectives on decisionmaking, "For Jervis, we see what we *expect* to see, for Janis and Mann, what we *want* to see."[6]

The cognitive approach to an understanding of misperception among decisionmakers tells us that human beings—not excluding presidents, prime ministers, diplomats, and others involved in steering foreign policy—resist cognitive dissonance. In effect, we strive for cognitive consistency, a tendency that "has some adverse implications for decisionmaking because it suggests the existence of systematic bias in favor of information consistent with information that we have already assimilated."[7] According to this view, people making policy do not come to the task with open minds, receptive to new information that conflicts with preconceived beliefs about the world and their country's allies and adversaries. Instead, they may be disposed to discount or screen out that which contradicts those beliefs. This phenomenon has made it difficult for Americans and Russians, Indians and Pakistanis, Arabs and Israelis, and many other long-time adversaries to seize opportunities to reduce tensions; policymakers on each side have tended to hold images of their adversary that make acceptance even of possibly benign overtures very difficult. This is not to say that those images are wrong or that skepticism is unwarranted, only that they *may* lead to errors in the conduct of foreign policy. The reverse may also be true, of course—that is, policymakers may ignore danger signals because they are inconsistent with their mental image of another country.

This problem has been captured in another film made for television, one of the early episodes in *Reilly: The Ace of Spies*. In the early years of the twentieth century, Sydney Reilly (Sam Neill) has been stationed in Manchuria, at the time a part of the Russian empire in Asia. Although he is officially a shipping agent, he is in reality a spy for the British, who have entered into an alliance with the Japanese. He acquires knowledge of Japanese plans for invading Manchuria and tries to convince his superiors in London that a Japanese victory, which he considers probable, will alter the balance of power in the Pacific. Not only do the British dismiss his cables; the Russians are equally unwilling to give credence to reports that they face a Japanese invasion. Reilly is only too willing to take advantage of the situation to make a financial killing, but the relevant portion of the episode concerns the refusal of the Russians to consider the possibility of a Japanese attack until it is too late. The film contains the preeminent example of Jervis's dictum that decisionmakers see what they expect to see. The Russian commander in Port Arthur is supremely confident that the Japanese will not attack; on the eve of the attack he insists will not come, the commander is busy planning the admiral's ball and dismisses the ominous news that the Japanese delegation has broken off talks with Russia and has left St. Petersburg. "In the history of our civilization," he lectures an aide, "a yellow race has yet to make an attack on a white one. I do not think the Japanese are likely to set a precedent." Sure of his knowledge of the adversary and convinced of the superiority of the Europeans over an "inferior" race, the Russian commander filters out all information that does not conform with his preexisting beliefs until it is too late to deal with the devastating reality of a Japanese attack. The need to maintain cognitive consistency has led to fatal misperception.

Although this episode in *Reilly* is the most compelling example of the problem, it also surfaces in other films in which officials are struggling to find an appropriate policy in difficult circumstances. *Gandhi* contains several scenes in which British officials (played by such distinguished British actors as John Mills and John Gielgud) try to formulate policies with which to neutralize Gandhi and his followers. In all of these scenes the British are shown to be laboring under the handicap of beliefs and images about India and Indians (and about British rule in India) that make it difficult to see the changing situation clearly.

It is conceivable that persons in positions of authority may possess belief systems so strong and so resistant to new information that they are driven to pursue irrational and even dangerous policies. There have been real life cases of the kind, including, for example, General Douglas MacArthur's miscalculation of China's intentions during the Korean War. MacArthur, brimming with confidence and convinced that the Chinese would not enter the war, followed his dramatic victory at Inchon in the fall of 1950 by crossing the 38th parallel and driving north toward the Yalu River, planning to unify Korea by force. As history tells us, it did not work out that way. Chinese divisions mounted a devastating counterattack that drove the American armies back with large casualties, extending the war by two and a half years in the process. As one student of that war has observed, "It was not the absence of intelligence which led us into trouble, but our unwillingness to draw unpleasant conclusions from it."[8] In other words, MacArthur's intolerance of cognitive dissonance was a major factor in the disaster.

Two Cold War films make something of the same point. Both involve a crisis generated by American military leaders whose image of the enemy is so fixed (and paranoid) as to make rational argument impossible. One, John Frankenheimer's *Seven Days in May,* concerns a plan by the chairman of the Joint Chiefs of Staff (JCS) to stage a coup and replace the president, whose support for a disarmament treaty with the Soviet Union he considers treasonous. The other is Stanley Kubrick's *Dr. Strangelove,* a black comedy whose plot is set in motion by an Air Force general who orders his bomber wing to attack Russia. Quite obviously the officers responsible for these crises are extreme instances of cognitive deficiencies; the general in *Seven Days in May* is more than a right-wing anticommunist, he is a megalomaniac (but so, some say, was MacArthur), and the general in *Dr. Strangelove* is almost certainly a psychotic. In both instances critical decisions are made by men whose belief systems are so rigid as to leave no room for alternative perspectives; their minds are closed, and the consequences are extremely serious—even fatal in the case of the Kubrick film.

The planned coup in *Seven Days in May* may be dismissed as something that could not happen in the United States, with its tradition of civilian supremacy over the military. But the policy conflict over the best way to preserve the nation's security in the face of an implacable enemy and in the context of the nuclear age is real enough. The debate over the size of defense budgets, the acquisition of particular weapons systems, and the wisdom of arms control treaties has been loud and long in the United States and in other countries as well. While the Pentagon brass, unlike the character played by Burt Lancaster in the Frankenheimer film, have always in the end lived with presidential and congressional decisions about these matters, they have played a vigorous role in the process of shaping those decisions. Like Lancaster, real life military leaders do tend to paint worst-case scenarios; they simply do not go to such extreme lengths to make their point.

The plot line in *Dr. Strangelove* is almost as improbable as that in *Seven Days in May,* although it may be somewhat easier to imagine the unauthorized detonation of a nuclear weapon than a coup against the U.S. government. Like the other film, *Dr. Strangelove* is very much a product of the Cold War and the fears of nuclear Armageddon. The Cuban missile crisis had brought the world to the brink of war between the superpowers only a year before the release of *Seven Days in May* and only two before *Dr. Strangelove* arrived on screen. There were many who were demanding that the government "ban the bomb," while others believed that war was inevitable and that what was called for was a preemptive first strike to wipe out the dreaded enemy. The latter position is that of General Jack Ripper, commander of Burpleson Air Force Base, in the Kubrick film. Ripper, played by Sterling Hayden, is the personification of anticommunist paranoia. He believes in a monstrous communist conspiracy, which, among other things, is contaminating our precious bodily fluids through fluoridation of water supplies, thereby making him impotent (many people less psychotic than Ripper did in fact believe that fluoridation was a communist plot). Once Ripper's bombers are winging their way toward their targets inside Russia, the film is about the frantic efforts of marginally more sane politicians in both Washington and Moscow to figure out how to recall the planes and save the world. The decisionmaking process we see unfold on the screen is a broad-brush parody of what takes place when governments are faced with difficult decisions in moments of crisis. The American president is totally ineffectual, the Soviet premier is drunk, and the chairman of the Joint Chiefs of Staff is nearly as irresponsible as Ripper, arguing that the United States should take advantage of the crisis to launch an all-out attack on the Russians—"catch 'em with their pants down" is the way he phrases it.

No other film makes foreign policy decisionmaking look quite so much like amateur night.[9] The president, whose very name, Merkin Muffley, connotes weakness, is played by Peter Sellers in what is perhaps his greatest role (or roles, for he plays three of them). When the chairman of the Joint Chiefs of Staff wrestles the Russian ambassador to the floor during a meeting that is supposed to find a way of preventing World War III, Sellers is shocked: "You can't fight here—this is the War Room!" Sellers's telephone conversation with Soviet Premier Kissoff is a classic. One critic describes it as "a Bob Newhart–like routine in which he talks in a wheedling tone, as if he were trying to convince a 5-year-old child to accept an emergency collect call."[10] And George C. Scott is at the top of his form in his role as General Buck Turgidson, the chairman of the JCS, who vigorously defends obviously flawed military policies and procedures (admitting only that "the human element seems to have failed us here"), sees a "commie" trick in each new development in the crisis and has sex on his mind throughout the movie. Indeed, one could make the point that virtually all of the major characters are trying to outdo each other in a demonstration of decisionmaking ineptitude.

Crises and the Deterrence Dilemma

The threat of nuclear disaster in *Dr. Strangelove* clearly qualifies as a crisis and serves as a reminder that not all decisions are equal. Although routine decisions may turn out to have bad consequences for the state, the process of arriving at those decisions does not as a rule appear to be fraught with danger. Filmmakers dealing with international relations subjects frequently gravitate to crises for their material, since the efforts of decisionmakers to avoid impending catastrophe guarantee excitement in ways that more leisurely decisionmaking does not.

What constitutes a crisis may be a matter of perception. The term is now used so casually that almost any problem may be labeled a crisis. However, political scientists have sought to reach broad agreement on the essential characteristics of a crisis, in order to distinguish the decisionmakers' task from that facing them in noncrisis situations. One of these is the element of surprise; this is not to say that the event precipitating the crisis necessarily comes without prior signals, only that there is a sudden escalation of tension. Another element is the perception that a state's vital interests are threatened. A third is the fact that those confronted with the need to make a decision face very real time constraints.[11] These characteristics of crisis inevitably mean that decisionmakers will be operating in a stressful environment in which they will experience heightened anxiety.

The most acute crises are those in which the ability of the decisionmakers to "manage" the crisis determines whether the outcome is war or peace. And the most acute of these acute crises in the modern age is the one in which the war, if it comes, is likely to be nuclear. It is no accident that the Cuban missile crisis has been so intensely studied, for it is generally regarded as the crisis in which the world came closest to nuclear war.[12] Moreover, no crisis, with the possible exception of those facing the European powers in 1914 and 1938, has produced more "lessons" for statesmen and scholars alike. It was the experience with this crisis in 1962

> which helped to instill the belief within the policy-making community that crisis is the primary means by which nuclear superpowers test one another's mettle and that the peace of the world depends upon the

successful mastery of such clashes. After Cuba, Robert McNamara went so far as to claim that "There is no longer any such thing as strategy, only crisis management."[13]

The most perceptive analyses of crisis decisionmaking are those of scholars such as Richard Ned Lebow and Janice Gross Stein, and the brinkmanship crisis has been the focus of most of their work.[14] Such a crisis occurs when "a state knowingly challenges an important commitment of another state in the hope of compelling its adversary to back away from his commitment."[15] Although the challenging state expects its adversary to back down, it is running the risk that it will not and that the outcome may be war—or, almost equally unsatisfactory, that the state initiating the crisis may itself have to back down to avoid war. In effect, such a crisis resembles a game of chicken. The Cuban missile crisis is perhaps the quintessential example of a brinkmanship crisis in which the initiator, the Soviet Union, having miscalculated the resolve of its adversary, had to back down. Events on the eve of World Wars I and II produced very different results, however; the July 1914 crisis eventuated in war and the Munich crisis of 1938 vindicated Germany's strategy when France and Britain chose to appease Hitler over Czechoslovakia.

The literature suggests that perhaps the most decisive factor shaping these crises is the commitment of the challenged state. Was Russia's commitment to Serbia's independence in 1914 both clear and credible? What of the French commitment to preserve Czechoslovakia's territorial integrity? Or the U.S. commitment to keep nuclear missiles out of Cuba? Frequently, commitments are not well defined or communicated in unmistakable terms; they may lack credibility due to a deficiency of capability or will. This matter of credibility became a major problem during the Cold War, when both of the superpowers sought to deter the adversary by threatening to use nuclear weapons.

The problem was—and still is—that it is difficult to make the threat to use nuclear weapons credible. Both the Americans and the Russians possessed—and still possess—enormous inventories of nuclear weapons with which to annihilate each other. And both were—and still are—vulnerable, lacking the capacity to prevent that annihilation, partly as a result of conscious choice, the theory being that if the outcome of a nuclear exchange were "mutually assured destruction," neither side would be tempted to start a war.[16] However great the capacity to wreak devastation on such an unprecedented scale, there remains the question of will. Would any state actually use nuclear weapons to defend its commitments, knowing that to do so could be tantamount to committing suicide? In other words, if nuclear weapons failed in their primary mission, which is to deter, would they then be used to defend? Or, given the seeming irrationality of nuclear war, would the threat to use nuclear weapons be revealed as a gigantic bluff? Uncertainty about the answers to these questions was among the principal factors preserving peace between the superpowers during the years of the Cold War. But the logic (or illogic) of nuclear deterrence received considerable attention, both in print and in film, for many years, and it is doubtful if we have heard or seen the last of it.

The threat of nuclear retaliation to defend national interests ultimately depends on reputation. Or, as one student of the subject puts it, "Deterrence as a psychological relationship cannot, then, be adequately comprehended without treating the behavior of the deterrer as an extension of its nature and character."[17] If this is true, then states must always be on the lookout for ways to enhance a reputation for being willing to honor commitments, especially when there are bound to be doubts about a willingness to use nuclear weapons. It has been suggested that the United States, anxious to establish and sustain such a reputation, felt an obligation throughout the Cold War to resist, by military means if necessary, any communist probe that threatened the balance of power. Former secretary of state Dean Acheson, referring to the Korea crisis, addressed this policy imperative in his memoirs: "To back away from this challenge, in view of our capacity for meeting it, would be highly destructive of the power and prestige of the United States. By prestige I mean the shadow cast by power, which is of great deterrent importance."[18] Thus U.S. policy in Korea, in Vietnam, even in places like Grenada, could be viewed in part as a demonstration of resolve designed to make the nuclear deterrent more credible than it might otherwise be. Soviet behavior could be explained in much the same way (especially after the "loss of face" over Cuba).

One film from the 1970s, Robert Aldrich's *Twilight's Last Gleaming,* bases its rather improbable plot on just such an explanation of U.S. Cold War behavior. Another renegade air force general, this one played by Burt Lancaster, has learned that during the early years of the Vietnam War the U.S. government adopted a strategy of becoming involved in limited wars throughout the world in order to put the Russians on notice that it would not tolerate any extension of the latter's sphere of influence. In other words, the United States would bolster its credibility by the demonstration effect of military action. And the U.S. secretary of state argues that such a policy "is necessary in a nuclear-armed world in order to avoid any possibility of a face-to-face confrontation that could result in a nuclear holocaust."[19] The premise is plausible; the plot, however, has General Dell (Lancaster) seizing an ICBM missile silo in Montana and threatening to trigger a nuclear war with the Soviet Union if the American president does not publicize the minutes of the secret meeting at which the U.S. strategy was adopted. Thus General Dell joins General Ripper in moviedom's pantheon of irrational military leaders. And the U.S. president, rather than sharing the dirty secret with the public, chooses to do away with the general by nuking him; quite appropriately, the plan misfires, and both the general and the president perish.

Twilight's Last Gleaming has interesting things to say about the dilemma of how to make nuclear deterrence credible. The most important film treatment of the deterrence conundrum is, once again, *Dr. Strangelove,* which we have already identified as an insightful look at crisis decisionmaking. Hypothetically, the surest way of making the threat to use nuclear weapons credible would be to make their use automatic in the event of an attack.[20] This is exactly what has happened in *Dr. Strangelove.* The Soviet Union has developed a doomsday machine that will automatically set off nuclear weapons in the event of a nuclear attack, producing, in the words of the Soviet ambassador, "a doomsday shroud—a lethal cloud of radioactivity which will encircle the earth for ninety-three years." The concept is explained to a shocked and incredulous president and his advisors by Dr. Strangelove (Peter Sellers in another of his roles): "Deterrence is the art of producing in the mind of the enemy the fear to attack. And so because of the automated and irrevocable decisionmaking process which rules out human meddling, the doomsday machine is terrifying and simple to understand, and completely credible and convincing."

Knowing the existence of such a device, no sane person would ever launch a nuclear missile. But no one in the United States—not General Ripper, not General Turgidson, not President Muffley—knew of the existence of the doomsday machine. It appears that the Russians were going to announce it at the next Communist Party Congress, too late in this apocalyptic film to prevent the end of the world. The moral of the story, therefore, is that for a deterrent to deter, its existence must be communicated to adversaries. Strangelove says it succinctly: "The whole point of the doomsday machine is lost if you keep it a secret."

Nor is it only with respect to the doomsday machine that there is a failure of communication in the film. President Muffley and Premier Kissoff waste valuable time in their telephone conversation; Kissoff doesn't have the phone number of the Soviet defense headquarters, so he tells Muffley to call Omsk information; the president doesn't have the recall code, so he can't order the bombers to abort their mission; when he obtains the code, he can't get through to one of the bombers because its communications system has been destroyed by Russian defenses; Ripper's executive officer (Sellers in his third role), having figured out the recall code, has trouble getting through to the war room because he has to use a pay phone and doesn't have the right change. Kubrick is telling us that we had better not depend on our ability to communicate with each other to resolve crises.

The credibility of nuclear deterrence is also examined in a humorous but informative scene in an aforementioned episode of *Yes, Prime Minister,* "The Grand Design." The new PM, James Hacker, is briefed on Britain's strategy for defense of the realm and learns that he has it within his power, by pressing "the button," to launch nuclear missiles against the Soviet Union. He finds this responsibility daunting, and seeks the counsel of his chief scientific adviser. The PM insists that he would press the button only as a last resort, but the adviser walks him through a series of scenarios in which the Russians never present an unambiguous threat of attack but rely instead on "salami tactics," until their tanks and troops are poised on the English Channel. To each successive scenario, the flustered prime minister says "no," he would not press the button. The adviser, relentless in his probing of the PM, asks "What is the last resort? Piccadilly?" Hacker poses the question any statesman relying on nuclear weapons for deterrence must at some time ask: "How could we defend ourselves by committing suicide?"

In "The Grand Design," the prime minister thinks he may resolve this dilemma by shifting to conventional forces, a policy position toward which his scientific adviser has been skillfully leading him. But as the episode (and the PM's cabinet secretary) make very clear, Hacker is simply trading one problem for another. After all, conventional forces are much more expensive (as indeed they are in real life); as Sir Humphrey Appleby, the cabinet secretary, observes, it is much cheaper just to press the button.

Even in crises in which nuclear weapons are not a factor, deterrence can be problematic, as the Falklands crisis of 1982 and the Gulf crisis of 1990 attest. Argentina was not deterred from invading the Falkland Islands, probably because the British had been sending ambiguous signals—that is, not making their commitment to defend the islands clear and convincing—and because the Argentine junta was under increasing domestic pressure to invade or be swept out of power.[21] Iraq's invasion of Kuwait in 1990 also sheds light on the requirements of effective deterrence. Following Operation Desert Storm, many concluded that Saddam Hussein must have taken leave of his senses when he decided to attack and absorb Kuwait. Yet Saddam could be forgiven for not anticipating the severity of the response to his action. Collective security under the United Nations Charter was virtually a dead letter. Neither neighboring Arab states nor Israel were in any position to aid Kuwait; the United States had neither the contingency plans nor the personnel and equipment in the region to challenge an army the size of Iraq's; and the U.S. government had been reassuring Saddam almost up to the moment of his attack of its desire for normal relations. Quite simply, "there was no precedent at all for an international coalition as broad and effective as the one Iraq came to face."[22] If there is a lesson here, it is the one cited earlier: that a state bent on changing the status quo and willing to risk war to do so will be deterred, if at all, only by the knowledge, clearly communicated, that its adversary possesses the capability and the will to resist the challenge.

Decisionmaking: Variations on a Theme

Not all films concerned with decisionmaking deal with events that qualify as crises, even if those that do not are often given crisis overtones to make them more dramatic. One such film is *Fat Man and Little Boy,* Roland Joffe's account of the Manhattan Project, which produced the first atomic bombs. The element of crisis that informs the film is the race with Nazi Germany to be first to create the bomb; the consequences of losing that race are too obvious to require much comment. After VE-Day, the race is obviously over and is replaced by the debate among the atomic scientists over whether to detonate the bomb they have worked so long and hard to produce. That issue, which we shall revisit in the chapter on law and morality, is not fully developed in Joffe's film, although the director seems to want the audience to share his antinuclear sentiments. Nor does the film ever take us away from Los Alamos and into the White House for the debate within the highest levels of the Truman administration about using the bomb against Japan. What it does do is explore the relationship between General Leslie Groves (Paul Newman), who heads the bomb project, and J. Robert Oppenheimer (Dwight Schultz), chief of the project's scientific team, men of very different temperaments. We are witness to a series of contentious debates and decisions, all taking place within the framework of the larger framing decision (made before the film begins) to launch the Manhattan Project. As one reviewer wrote, "The push and pull of Groves and Oppenheimer remains the fascination of the story," with Groves becoming "the unlikely Devil to Oppenheimer's Faust."[23]

Another film in which decisions are made within what appear to be crisis-like conditions is *Clear and Present Danger.* This film, already mentioned in earlier chapters, merits a brief comment here for its depiction of a common and little-noted feature of decisionmaking—the phenomenon of deniability. When the U.S. president learns that a businessman friend with ties to a Colombian drug cartel has been murdered, he wants to do something about it but is well aware that his options are constrained by both law and politics. When asked by his chief of staff what course of action he would suggest, the president replies that "the course of action I'd suggest is a course of action I cannot suggest." The implication is clear, and the film's plot is built around that course of action, a paramilitary attack by CIA operatives on the drug lords. The president, of course, can and does deny knowledge of any such plan. This fictional instance of deniability has real-life counterparts, perhaps the most famous being the so-called Iran-Contra scandal during the Reagan adminstration.

Most films which address the subject of decisionmaking in international relations focus on that process within a single state and government. *Tora! Tora! Tora!* is an exception. This film, the product of an unusual collaboration between moviemakers in Japan and America, depicts the attack on Pearl Harbor and the events leading up to it from both points of view. While the film is hardly an insightful treatment of decisionmaking in Washington and Tokyo, much less a classic, it does demonstrate that the crisis in the Pacific was perceived very differently in the two capitals, and it tries to capture something of the processes whereby the two enemies arrived at the decisions that would plunge them into a bitter and prolonged war.

The crisis that preceded the Japanese attack on Pearl Harbor was one of mounting tensions in which Japanese policies and U.S. responses to them put the two countries on a collision course. Japan's desire for a greater East Asian co-prosperity sphere was pursued by military means, initially in China and eventually in Southeast Asia. The United States sought to restrain Japan by means of increasingly severe economic embargoes. The denouement is summarized in Gordon Craig and Alexander George's brief case study of this exercise in attempted coercive diplomacy.

> Negotiations proved fruitless, each power resolutely demanding total concession. A critical turning point that severly escalated the diplomatic confrontation occurred on July 25, 1941, when the United States imposed a total embargo on oil and froze Japanese assets in American banks. U.S. strength and resolve were on the increase, and the threat of escalation was now clear. In November, Japan was presented with demands that included withdrawal from all occupied territories, repudiation of the Tripartite Pact (the alliance with Germany and Italy), and an end to expansion. Faced with visions of economic strangulation, Japan chose the alternative, war with the United States. Pearl Harbor was, in this sense, a rational response to the choice posed by the American ultimatum, for the alternative—acceptance of U.S. demands—was even more unpalatable than war with a stronger opponent, the outcome of which was uncertain.[24]

Tora! Tora! Tora! captures little of the internal debate over these policies in either country, but it does manage to make clear that that debate goes on concurrently in at least two states, and that decisions by one produce feedback that affects decisions by the other. The most interesting portion of the film (other than the recreation of the attack itself) is the first part, in which the Japanese argue over the wisdom of making war on the United States and American officials, using their cryptographic breakthrough (the Magic intercepts), try to figure out what Tokyo is going to do and when.

All things considered, the film is historically accurate, presenting the story in an evenhanded way.[25] If anything, the Japanese are portrayed as the better planners and executors of policy, the Americans as bureaucratic, complacent, and ineffectual. That there was disagreement within the Japanese government as to how to handle the threat posed by U.S. opposition to Japan's war in China and American economic sanctions is made clear, as is the debate in Washington about interpreting and communicating intelligence about Japan's plans. What is missing from the film is a sense of context. The viewer must look elsewhere for information about such critical background factors as Japan's brutal aggression in China and the ultimately uncompromising American response to it. One thing we do know is that the decision to attack the United States was probably the only thing that could have overcome U.S. isolationism and brought it into the war, guaranteeing the total defeat of Japan. Admiral Yamamoto, commander of the Japanese fleet, says as much, both early in the film, when he argues against the war, and at its end, when his colleagues are prematurely celebrating the victory his planning made possible: "To awaken a sleeping giant and fill him with a terrible resolve is sowing the seeds for certain disaster."[26]

Versailles, the Holocaust, and Other Disasters

In *Tora! Tora! Tora!* and most films cited in this chapter, decisionmaking takes place in a bilateral context. But most states are today also members of a great many international organizations and participate in other multilateral fora, and are therefore necessarily involved in negotiating with many other states to produce treaties, resolutions, and other forms of international agreement. Decisionmaking may entail what Robert Putnam has called two-level games.[27] The product of negotiations in a multilateral setting must also be acceptable at the state level, where it must run the gauntlet of the many interested and frequently conflicting participants in the state's decisionmaking process. And those many participants, in turn, will have shaped their country's input into the negotiating process at the multilateral level. Putnam describes it this way:

> Each national political leader appears at both game boards. Across the international table sit his foreign counterparts. . . . Around the domestic table behind him sit party and parliamentary figures. . . . The unusual complexity of this two-level game is that moves that are rational for a player at one board . . . may be impolitic for that same player at the other board. . . . Any key player at the international table who is dissatisfied with the outcome may upset the game board, and, conversely, any leader who fails to satisfy his fellow players at the domestic table risks being evicted from his seat.[28]

No film captures this phenomenon better than *Wilson*, Henry King's 1944 biographical treatment of the career of the twenty-eighth president of the United States.

Wilson is an old-fashioned film. One has only to look at a much more recent film about an American president, Oliver Stone's *Nixon*, to appreciate the difference in cinematic styles of the 1940s and the 1990s as well as the different agendas of the two directors.[29] Nonetheless, *Wilson* is the rare film that demonstrates that decisionmaking in international relations is often indeed a two-level game. The part of this biopic that is relevant, of course, deals with the negotiation and ratification of the peace treaty at the end of the Great War. For some students of the office, "the American Presidency, and with it our whole system of government, reached its highest peak of democracy, efficiency, and morality in the first four years of

Woodrow Wilson."[30] The second term was an altogether different matter, highlighted by the Senate's rejection of the president's beloved League of Nations.

Responsibility for the U.S. failure to embrace the League has been debated extensively, and the consensus seems to be that there is enough blame to go around, what with the Lodge-led insistence that the United States must remain isolated from European politics and Wilson's obstinate defense of the organization, which was to be the vehicle for realizing his vision of a new, liberal world order. But the essential point presented in the film is that the agreements hammered out in Paris by the leaders of the Allied powers—Wilson, Britain's Lloyd George, France's Clemenceau, and Italy's Orlando—then had to run the gauntlet of American government and politics. Wilson is shown arguing with Clemenceau and assuring him that the Senate will ratify the League Covenant and that the United States will act in accordance with the Covenant and come to the aid of France if it is ever again attacked by Germany. He is then shown trying unsuccessfully to persuade Lodge and his Senate colleagues to support the League. The agreement reached in Paris has foundered on the shoals of America's constitutional system, and the president's heroic cross-country campaign to mobilize public opinion on behalf of the League fails dismally and leaves Wilson a sick and defeated man.

Three other films deserve mention in this brief survey of the way foreign policy decisionmaking is portrayed in popular culture. One is the third and final installment of *Masterpiece Theater's* inquiry into the life and times of another fictional British prime minister, the totally unscrupulous Francis Urquhart, *The Final Cut*. Urquhart (Ian Richardson) not only seeks to eclipse Margaret Thatcher's record as the longest-serving PM in British history; he also hopes to use negotiations over Cyprus to enhance his reputation and gain for himself a wealthy retirement. Although a work of fiction, *The Final Cut* provides the audience with realistic insights into the workings of the British parliamentary system and uses a real international problem, the long-simmering crisis over Cyprus, as the fulcrum for its plot. Cyprus, a former British colony, has, of course, been the scene of tensions between its Greek and Turkish communities ever since independence in 1961. This conflict has produced the interposition of a United Nations peacekeeping force, an invasion by Turkey, and the long-standing division of the island into two parts. In the film, Urquhart is on the brink of producing the negotiated settlement of the Cyprus issue that has eluded real-life peacemakers. The only remaining issue concerns water boundaries, and they are to be determined by a panel of jurists, two selected by each of the two communities and the fifth by the British. Arrangements such as this are entirely consistent with accepted techniques for international problemsolving; in this case, however, Urquhart subverts the supposed impartiality of the panel, manipulating the unsuspecting British jurist into a vote awarding the Turkish Cypriots waters that Urquhart and the Turks, but not the Greeks, know to contain oil deposits. The revenues from these deposits will guarantee the PM his comfortable retirement.

When the truth comes out, the Greek Cypriots are outraged, hostages are seized, the peace treaty is in jeopardy, and Urquhart's own secretary of state for foreign affairs quits the government and challenges the PM for his job. It appears that Urquhart is destined to lose *both* the prime ministership and the trust fund for his retirement, but the wily PM, remembering how the successful 1982 British invasion of the Falklands saved the prime ministership of Mrs. Thatcher, decides on a bold intervention in Cyprus by British commandos to reverse the decline in his fortunes. Unfortunately for him, things do not work out as well as they did for Mrs. Thatcher; ignoring his advisers, he insists on a strategy that produces a tragic outcome to the crisis in Cyprus. The film's elaborate story line contains several other interesting observations on decisionmaking. We are witness to no-holds-barred maneuvering between Urquhart and his rival for the prime ministership; the PM gives egregious and calculated offense to Britain's allies in the European Union; and it becomes apparent that Urquhart has been covering up terrible misdeeds that, if known, would end his political career. *The Final Cut* reminds us that even democracies can produce dishonest governments, and in doing so it makes a useful contribution to an understanding of the decisionmaking process, especially when decisionmakers have personal agendas and believe themselves to be infallible.

A second film is the short, static, but mesmerizing (and utterly appalling) Holocaust film, *The Wannsee Conference*. Filmed in Germany by Germans, it is a reconstruction of the 1942 conference at a lakeside villa near Berlin where Reinhard Heydrich, the chief of the Nazi Security Police, and assorted other personnel from the SS, the German bureaucracy, and the Nazi party planned the extermination of Europe's Jews. The dialogue is based on notes from the actual conference, as well as letters written by Hermann Goering and Adolf Eichmann, and the horror of the film—and it does produce that reaction in the viewer—lies in the fact that the discussion of this unspeakable crime is so matter-of-fact. In fact, some of the participants make jokes, one drinks too much and falls asleep, and several are obviously bored. The only problem is how to determine who is a Jew; that issue is disposed of by a decision to treat anyone with any Jewish blood as a Jew. *Schindler's List* and other films do, of course, present much more graphic scenes of the Holocaust, but nowhere on film is Hannah Arendt's comment about "the banality of evil" more chillingly illustrated than in *The Wannsee Conference*. Nowhere on film is decisionmaking about something so momentous (and so monstrous) made to look so routine.

Finally, there is Peter Brook's film adaptation of William Golding's *Lord of the Flies*. Golding's book is not literally about international relations, of course, nor is the movie. But the story of a group of young British schoolboys stranded on an ocean island following an air crash and their efforts to create a society without benefit of adult guidance is in many ways a parable of international relations in an anarchic world. Some realists have likened the condition of the world, with its absence of any higher authority, to that of a state of nature, and it is no exaggeration to say that *Lord of the Flies* unfolds in a metaphorical state of nature. In the film, which uses Golding's dialogue, most of the boys gradually abandon their chosen level-headed leader, Ralph, and, siding with the belligerent Jack, revert to savagery. As leadership in the decision process passes from Ralph to Jack, a form of what Irving Janis has called "groupthink" takes over.[31] The boys take refuge in group unity and are collectively emboldened to do things, such as commit murder, that they would almost certainly not do in other circumstances (early in the film, one of them observes that "We're not savages; after all, we're English").

This, too, is a horror film, albeit of a very different kind, in which rationality is overtaken by superstition and decency by evil. Although most of the films cited in this chapter are not the case studies in evil that *The Final Cut, The Wannsee Conference,* and *Lord of the Flies* are, decision-making pathologies do seem to be on display in most of them. While this proclivity of the industry to emphasize "things gone wrong" is understandable, it helps to remind us that the rational actor model of decision-making is rarely on display in the real world.

Notes

1. Allison, *Essence of Decision.*
2. Hughes, *Continuity and Change in World Politics*, pp. 218–19.
3. For a discussion of these "tricks of the trade," see Gelb and Halperin, "The Ten Commandments."
4. Lebow, *Between Peace and War*, p. 102. See also Jervis, *Perception and Misperception.*
5. See Janis and Mann, *Decision-Making.*
6. Lebow, *Between Peace and War*, p. 111.
7. *Ibid.*, pp. 103–4.
8. De Weerd, "Strategic Surprise and the Korean War," quoted in Lebow, *Between Peace and War*, p. 148.
9. For an excellent analysis of this film, see Peary, *Cult Movies 3*, pp. 71–76.
10. *Ibid.*, p. 75.
11. These elements of a crisis are presented schematically as a "crisis cube" in Russett and Starr, *World Politics*, p. 234; see also Hermann, *International Crises*, and Brecher and Wilkenfeld, "Crisis in World Politics," pp. 380–417.
12. Among the many recent analyses of the Cuban Missile Crisis are Blight, Welch, and Allyn, *Castro, the Missile Crisis and the Soviet Collapse;* Nathan, *The Cuban Missile Crisis Reconsidered;* and Raymond L. Garthoff, *Reflections on the Cuban Missile Crisis.*
13. Lebow, *Between Peace and War*, p. 291.

14. For discussion of brinkmanship crises, see for example, Lebow, *Between Peace and War,* and Jervis, Lebow, and Stein, *Psychology and Deterrence.*

15. Lebow, *Between Peace and War,* p. 57.

16. This was the rationale of the Anti-Ballistic Missile Treaty of 1972, a companion of the first Strategic Arms Limitation Treaty (SALT I). Its purpose was to prevent either side from using a ballistic missile defense as a shield that would enable it to launch a nuclear first strike without fear of effective retaliation.

17. Morgan, "Saving Face," p. 136.

18. Quoted in *ibid.,* p. 138.

19. McCarty, *Thrillers,* p. 220.

20. A nonnuclear analogy frequently cited occurs in a game of chicken if one of the drivers on a collision course throws his steering wheel out the window, thereby guaranteeing that he will not be able to swerve out of the way.

21. See Lebow, "Miscalculation in the South Atlantic.*"*

22. Kincade, "On the Brink," p. 191.

23. See review by Benson, "Making of the Atomic Age," F1.

24. Craig and George, *Force and Statecraft*, p. 201. The authors also argue that the U.S. had been sending conflicting signals; they do not, however, attempt to absolve Japan of responsibility for the attack on Pearl Harbor.

25. Commentary on the historical accuracy of the film is to be found in Iriye, "Tora! Tora! Tora!"

26. Yamamoto is quoted in *ibid.,* p. 228.

27. Putnam, "Diplomacy and Domestic Politics."

28. *Ibid.,* p. 434.

29. The review of *Wilson* in the *New York Times,* quoted on the jacket of the videocassette, speaks of the film's "uncommon dignity" and "good taste," words that would not be found in the reviews of *Nixon,* no matter how laudatory.

30. Rossiter, *The American Presidency,* p. 78.

31. See Janis, *Victims of Groupthink.*

7

The Tragedy of War

History tells us that war has been a common means of conducting international relations, and that in some periods of time it has actually defined an era. Thus we read about the Hundred Years War between England and France in the fourteenth and fifteenth centuries; the Thirty Years War, which wracked and devastated Europe in the first half of the seventeenth century; and the Napoleonic Wars, which again consumed Europe at the beginning of the nineteenth. A major study employing modern techniques of measurement and analysis, the Correlates of War project, has determined that in only twenty of the years between the Congress of Vienna in 1815 and 1980 was there no international war in progress.[1] Moreover, there has not been a day without war since 1945, which underscores the fact that World War II was no more the war to end all wars than was World War I, in spite of the appalling carnage in each case.

World War II and subsequent wars in Korea, Vietnam, and elsewhere have demonstrated that major international wars are not something peculiar to Europeans. Even within the relatively narrow time frame of the Correlates of War project, the fifth most deadly war (following only World Wars I and II and the Korean, Vietnam, and Sino-Japanese wars) was the Lopez War, about which most of the rest of the world is wholly ignorant. In this struggle between Paraguay and the united armies of Brazil, Argentina, and Uruguay between 1865 and 1870, Paraguay was virtually destroyed and some 90 percent of its male population killed. If civil wars are factored into statistics on warfare, the picture is even gloomier, both historically and in our own time. The twentieth century has been the bloodiest century in history by a large margin, with estimates of war-related deaths in World War II alone, both military and civilian, ranging from 50 million to more than 80 million.[2]

This century of total war has also been the century in which the film industry was created and the movies became a dominant form of popular culture. Inasmuch as popular culture tends to be time-bound, reflecting the interests and tastes of its audience, it is no surprise that films made in a time of almost continuous war and the threat of even more war should include many films about war and that those films should reflect the fact that war both repels and fascinates. That war still has the capacity to fascinate us, in spite of the twentieth century's horrors, was much in evidence during the Gulf War in 1991. Millions of people watched that war on their television sets, entranced; the overwhelming majority approved. In 1996 the Academy Award for best picture went to *Braveheart,* an unusually violent depiction of warfare, albeit in an earlier time with weapons more primitive than those now at our disposal.

At the end of the twentieth century, in spite of strong evidence to the contrary in places like Bosnia and Liberia, some political scientists contend that war is finally becoming obsolete. John Mueller argues that "over the last century . . . the ancient institution of war, without losing its inherent fascination, has become substantially discredited, at least within the developed world, as a mechanism for carrying out international affairs and for resolving conflicts among nations."[3] Mueller compares war with duelling, which has become obsolete in spite of the fact that it still has a romantic connotation, and with slavery, an institution that was at one time as historically important as war but has now been all but eradicated. Not everyone will be persuaded by this argument. However, it is widely believed today that war among the powers of Western Europe is very much a thing of the past. And there are many other interstate relationships, all still characterized by conflicts of interest, in which resort to war as a means of resolving those conflicts appears to be out of the question. In other words, war is not an inevitable feature of international relations for all states, and after the end of the Cold War, which Mueller calls the "quiet cataclysm" and the functional equivalent of World War III, a major or global war is not only not inevitable (as many had predicted not so long ago) but almost inconceivable.

But just as the Cassandras, the criers of doom, have ever been with us, so have those declaring the obsolescence of war. Writing nearly a century and a half ago, Ralph Waldo Emerson prophesied that "War is on its last legs; and a universal peace is as sure as is the prevalence of civilization over barbarism, of liberal government over feudal forms. The question for us is only *How soon?*"[4] Emerson was wrong, of course, as was H. G. Wells, who in 1914 remarked that "this, the greatest of all wars, is not just another war—it is the last war!"[5] The truth is that we cannot know whether war is now obsolescent, as Mueller believes, or still an inevitable feature of world politics. What we do know is that the institution of war has been so much a part of international relations for so long that it simply cannot be ignored in a book about the ways in which popular culture may provide insights into the complexities of world affairs.

The Causes of War

Most films have little to say about the causes of the war or the events leading up to the scenes of combat that unfold on the screen. Rather, they immerse us in the tactics of the armies and the lives and fears of those who
are fighting. There are many sub-genres of the war film: the film depicting
male bonding under fire; the coming-of-age film, in which soldiers grow
up fast (and often die before experiencing life); the film pitting the decent,
caring soldier against the one who becomes savage and cruel in the crucible of combat; the film of heroic endeavor, in which men display unac-
customed bravery, often in face of great odds. Although many of these
films are highly formulaic, some are well made and have interesting things
to say about human nature—and even about the nature of an international
system in which resort to war is an accepted way of resolving conflict.
With only a few exceptions, it is not these "men at war" films to which
one would turn for a greater understanding of international relations.

Nor for that matter are the causes of war well treated on film. There is,
of course, much disagreement as to why states resort to war. Some have argued that human aggression is innate, that it is biologically determined. Inasmuch as states are really collectivities of human beings, such a view would
suggest that wars occur because human beings, like many lower order animals, are instinctively violence-prone. Leo Tolstoy once lamented the inevitable necessity of war because of "an elemental zoological law which bees
fulfill when they kill each other in autumn, and which causes male animals to
destroy one another."[6] Scientists such as Konrad Lorenz and Edward O. Wilson offer some support for the controversial thesis that aggressive behavior—
and hence war—is instinctive among humans.[7] In any event, although war
films are likely to depict aggressive behavior in combat, they have little to
say about innate aggressiveness as a cause of war (although the *Star Trek*
episodes and movies do frequently endow some nonhuman races with that
quality, suggesting that the moviegoing public accepts the possibility of war
as biologically determined, at least in the case of "other" bad peoples).

Other attempts to identify the causes of war look to structural factors.
Economists, for example, would argue that states go to war because they
believe that in some cases that is the only way in which they can acquire
needed resources or markets. Among the reasons that Japan made war first
on China and then on the United States in the 1930s and 1940s was the
quest for economic security (and control of the territory the Japanese government believed necessary for that purpose). The film *Tora! Tora! Tora!*,
discussed in the preceding chapter, makes reference to this cause of war,
although it does not develop the point. Marxists have also insisted on the
economic causes of war. Lenin in particular held the view that the imperi-
alist powers, in their competitive quest for raw materials and markets,

were drawn into a struggle that led inevitably to war. Soviet ideologists elaborated on this argument, contending that capitalist countries in decline would make war in an increasingly desperate attempt to maintain their system. While Marxism has of course influenced a number of filmmakers, the Marxist perspective on the causes of war is not really developed in feature films, even in those designed to extol the virtues of communist society and the evils of capitalism.

It has also been argued that wars are caused by the configuration of power among states, and especially by shifts in relative power. This approach is identified with the realist and neorealist schools. According to this perspective, wars are more likely to occur when equilibrium is disturbed by the rising power of State A and the declining power of State B. This change in the relative power of the two states is conducive to war either because State B feels compelled to make war before its position is too badly eroded or because State A is emboldened to resort to war because it sees a window of opportunity. The likelihood of war is presumably even greater when the change in the balance of power occurs in the context of an arms race. The resulting situation is one that has often been characterized as a security dilemma. State A's efforts to make itself stronger and hence more secure only serve to make State B feel more insecure, which prompts State B to take counter measures to strengthen itself, and so on in an escalating spiral of insecurity. The security dilemma is pregnant with the possibility of war for a variety of reasons: one or both of the parties may overrate the hostility of the other; one or both of the parties may come to believe that war is inevitable; and the militaries that would have to fight such a war if it were to come tend to be biased in favor of preventive or preemptive war (as Bernard Brodie argues, "military doctrine is universally imbued with the 'spirit' of the offensive").[8]

As with economic causation, films typically do not explore the role of power balances and security dilemmas as causes of war, although the wars they present on the screen may well have had their origins in such structural and perceptual factors. It would be instructive to analyze the origins of the major wars of the twentieth century—wars depicted in films from *All Quiet on the Western Front* to *Platoon*—for evidence of just such factors. One early episode of the original *Star Trek* series, made well before the show acquired a cult following, does explore the idea that war can be caused by beliefs in an adversary's implacable hostility, war's inevitability, and the value of the offensive. That episode is "Balance of Terror," in which the Federation and the Romulan empire (or rather the *Enterprise* and a Romulan vessel) wage war. Captain Kirk's decision to attack does not come easily. McCoy argues against it, claiming that millions and millions of lives hang on that decision and asking whether Kirk and Spock want a galactic war on their consciences. But one of the crew insists that by running away you only guarantee war, and Spock clinches the decision for war by noting that weakness is something the Federation dare not show the Romulans. And so the *Enterprise,* acting on the assumption of the enemy's hostility and the inevitability of war, goes on the offensive. The Romulans make war because it is in their nature, the Federation because of a security dilemma in which "attacking now is better than defending later."[9]

Students of war have long debated the relative importance of the underlying and the immediate causes of war, with most historians emphasizing the former. An emphasis on underlying or long-term causes can lead to a conclusion that wars are unavoidable, that sooner or later deep-seated causes of hostility, whether rooted in interest or ideology, will lead to war. It is easy to imagine, for example, that the relations among the European powers had deteriorated so badly by the second decade of the twentieth century that World War I would have happened even if Archduke Ferdinand had not been assassinated. By this same logic, if the Cuban missile crisis had led to a shooting war,

> the next generation of historians, if there was one, would have portrayed the crisis and the war that followed as the natural and even inevitable result of almost twenty years of Cold War between the United States and the Soviet Union. Ideology, the nuclear arms race, competition for spheres of influence, and domestic payoffs of aggressive foreign policies would all have been described as important underlying causes of the war. In retrospect, World War III would appear as unavoidable as World War I.[10]

But the Cuban missile crisis was defused short of war and World War III never took place. This seems to suggest that another cause of war is the ineffectual management of crises, a subject explored in the previous chapter.

One of the most frequently cited works on the causes of war is Geoffrey Blainey's *The Causes of War*. Although criticized by political scientists for its "intuitive, nonreplicable, and ultimately unscientific method,"[11] this is a useful *vade mecum* for those looking for a wide-ranging and provocative commentary on the subject. Among Blainey's commonsensical conclusions are the notions that "there can be no war unless at least two nations prefer war to peace" and that "wars usually begin when two nations disagree on their relative strength, and wars usually cease when the fighting nations agree on their relative strength."[12]

Blainey's proposition that there can be no war unless at least two nations prefer war to peace is demonstrated in the last of the *Star Trek* films featuring the original cast, *The Undiscovered Country*. This film, perhaps more than any other in the series, provides the viewer with hard-to-miss analogies to interstate relations here on planet earth. The Federation and the Klingon Empire, long-time bitter enemies, are to attend a peace conference, at which negotiations promise to be exceedingly difficult in view of their deep and abiding mutual hostility. Captain Kirk (William Shatner) succinctly captures the cognitive dissonance he feels when designated to head the Federation negotiating team: "I've never trusted Klingons, and I never will." As the plot unfolds, it becomes clear that while there are some on both sides who desire to risk for peace (Kirk ultimately among them), there are others who insist on perpetuating the conflict, sabotaging the peace conference, and going to war. The latter have the upper hand until the very last minute, with Chang (Christopher Plummer), the intransigent Klingon chief of staff, parodying Neville Chamberlain's famous post-Munich remark and asserting that there will be "no peace in our time." Quoting Shakespeare, as he does throughout the film, Chang speaks for all those who prefer war to peace: "Cry havoc and let slip the dogs of war."

The various characters in *Star Trek: The Undiscovered Country* quite deliberately suggest parallels between the intergalactic future and events and issues in our own time. When the Klingon chancellor says that his people need breathing space (their planet is allegedly dying), Kirk's rejoinder is "Hitler, 1938," a pointed reminder that one of the twentieth-century's greatest tyrants also sought *lebensraum*. When a member of the Enterprise crew speaks of human rights, the chancellor's daughter observes sarcastically that the very name is racist, that "the Federation is no more than a homo sapiens–only club"; thus do the screen writers ask us to think about one of the great social and political issues of our own era. When Kirk protests his assignment, Spock quotes an old Vulcan proverb: "Only Nixon could go to China." Spock, of course, is tapping into conventional wisdom in American politics with the observation that only a president with impeccable anticommunist credentials could have opened the door to normal relations with the Peoples Republic of China; it would have been political suicide for a liberal Democrat to have done so. The prison to which Kirk and McCoy are sent following their conviction by a Klingon court is a remote, bitterly cold, brutally run place, and is referred to as a gulag, the term used to describe the harsh Siberian camps to which Soviet political prisoners were sent. The film is a treasure trove of such references. In spite of its futuristic technology and story line, *Star Trek: The Undiscovered Country* is very much a film about contemporary international relations.

Blainey's second point suggests that war is perhaps the most effective audit of power, especially if "power" is taken to mean not only capabilities but also will. This proposition provides moviegoers with a useful perspective, inviting them to consider why the states engaged in combat might have believed they could prevail and what the outcome of the war says about the relative power of the antagonists. One film that makes a fairly good case study of "war as an audit of power" is *Waterloo,* Sergei Bondarchuk's recreation of Napoleon's return from exile on Elba and the epic battle that brought the so-called "Hundred Days" to an end, leading to the emperor's second and final exile on St. Helena. The film tells us that

Waterloo was no quixotic adventure by an inferior French army; Napoleon came close to defeating Wellington's army that day; but for the arrival of the Prussians late in the afternoon, he might well have done so. We cannot know what would have happened had Napoleon prevailed, but we do know that Waterloo served to clarify the issue of which side was the more powerful, something that had not been clear on the eve of battle.

Perhaps the most-often-quoted definition of war is that of the Prussian general and military theorist, Karl von Clausewitz: "War is the continuation of politics by other means." This is, of course, a realist position, an assertion that war is an occasionally necessary means of achieving the goals and preserving the values of the state, especially the most basic goal—that of national security. Statesmen must determine what the vital interests of the state are and the appropriate means for defending those interests; war is one such means. Clausewitz's dictum clearly implies "that political considerations necessarily take precedence over military logic."[13]

This thesis and the problems it engenders are central in the debate that emerged in the United States after the frustrating experience of the Korean and Vietnam wars. Craig and George have labeled the two sides in this debate the "Never-Again School" and the "Limited War School."[14] The former supports a strategic doctrine that specifies, in effect, that when the United States intervenes militarily, it "should be prepared to do everything necessary to win or it should not intervene at all"; the latter argues that there may be situations in which important national interests justify military intervention but in which the risk of military escalation is such that the United States would need "to limit its objectives and the military means it employed."[15] Former U.S. secretary of war Caspar Weinberger, a staunch supporter of the Never-Again philosophy, argued his case in a much-cited article in *Foreign Affairs* in which he identified preconditions for the employment of U.S. forces in Third World conflicts. Those preconditions added up to a "comprehensive national strategy which held that henceforth any contemplated use of force on behalf of foreign policy should be rejected unless it adhered to sound military doctrine for warfighting and military victory."[16] Such a strategy stands Clausewitz on his head; instead of military force supporting foreign policy, foreign policy is shaped by military doctrine. We observed this reversal of Clausewitz relatively recently in the cases of Somalia and Bosnia.

Clausewitz's dictum is present as context in a number of war films, although the viewer will usually have to do some work to bring it into focus. In *Tora! Tora! Tora!* Japan makes war on the United States with the purpose of achieving political goals that were not being achieved through diplomacy; war is literally the continuation of politics by other means. On the other hand, General Ripper in *Dr. Strangelove* does not believe that military force should have a political rationale. Explaining his decision to order his bomber wing to attack Russia, Ripper invokes Clemenceau, noting that the Frenchman once said that war is too important to be left to the generals. "When he said that," Ripper continues, "he may have been right. But today, war is too important to be left to politicians." This is about as clear a rejection of Clausewitz's dictum as we are likely to hear.

Generals and Foot Soldiers

The reference to the fictional General Ripper reminds us of the pivotal role that military leaders can play in international relations, both in the decision to wage war and in the conduct of war. Although films on war have been more likely to concentrate on the foot soldiers than on the generals, some of the most interesting and important films of the genre have been about those in command, from *Henry V* to *Patton* and including Napoleon and Wellington (*Waterloo*), Rommel (*The Desert Fox*), and assorted fictional generals, such as the one depicted by George Macready in *Paths of Glory*. This is a rich and varied gallery, full of brilliant tacticians, inspiring leaders, burned-out cases, and self-serving egotists; some of these men in uniform have left an indelible mark on the course of history.

Film treatment of men in command also reminds us that whereas generals once led their troops into battle in person, they have for a long time been relatively distant observers of the battles they have planned. Two of Shakespeare's historical plays concern English kings who fought with their men in battles that were pivotal events in that country's history. Both plays have been made into movies. In Lawrence Olivier's film version of *Richard III,* as in the play, that ruthless usurper of the crown is cut down in the battle of Bosworth Field, his death opening the way for the Tudor dynasty that G. M. Trevelyan has called the greatest of all of England's royal lines. This epochal event occurred in 1485. Seventy years earlier, another English king met with dramatically greater success in the French countryside near the village of Agincourt. There, Henry V personally led his weary men against a far larger and better rested French force and won one of history's most incredible victories. This battle has been chronicled twice on film, *Henry V* having been brought to the screen first by Olivier and more recently by Kenneth Branagh. These films dramatize the fact that once upon a time kings were soldier/generals who were typically in the thick of battle, risking not only their crown but their life in tight, man-to-man combat. Film treatment of warfare in more recent times either ignores the generals or, if it puts them into the picture, shows them planning strategy or observing the struggle from a nearby hill or other vantage point. Perhaps the best illustration of this change is *Waterloo*. Although we see a lot of both Napoleon and Wellington in this film, they do not lead cavalry charges, fire rifles, or swing swords, but rather plot the movements and countermovements of thousands of faceless troops in the vast field of combat stretching out between their command posts. In warfare at the end of the twentieth century, the generals are often even further removed from the action, connected to it from afar by modern means of communication.

Some of the most insightful commentary on military leadership in time of war can be found in Freeman Dyson's commendable book, *Weapons and Hope,* in which he contrasts two styles of military professionalism. His examples are two exceptionally talented German generals from the World War II era, Alfred Jodl and Hermann Balck. "For Jodl, Hitler was Germany's fate, a superhuman force transcending right and wrong. Balck saw Hitler as he was, a powerful but not very competent politician. . . . Jodl went on fighting until the bitter end because he had made Hitler's will his highest law. Balck went on fighting because it never occurred to him to do anything else."[17] At the Nuremberg trials, Jodl was convicted and hanged, while Balck was set free. The judgment reflected a belief that waging aggressive war at the strategic level, as Jodl did, is a crime, whereas waging war aggressively at a tactical level, as Balck did, is not. But Dyson empasizes another distinction, that "between soldiering as a trade and soldiering as a cult."[18] He concludes that Germany was only an extreme case of military professionalism run wild, that it is a form of madness which can infect other countries, leaving a terrible trail of death and destruction and influencing the course of history.

While neither Jodl nor Balck has been made the subject of a feature film, another German general has. Field Marshall Erwin Rommel, whose Afrika Korps dominated the war in the desert of North Africa in the early years of World War II, is the hero of Henry Hathaway's *The Desert Fox.* The sympathetic treatment of this "enemy" general (played by James Mason) has much to do with his role in the failed conspiracy to kill Hitler and sue for peace, which is more the focus of the film than the war itself. But it also reflects the fact that those who fought against Rommel respected both his skills as a military tactician and his qualities as a dignified leader of men. In other words, he was cast in the mold of Hermann Balck, not that of Alfred Jodl. At the end of *The Desert Fox,* the audience is expected to feel great compassion for this man as he resolves to commit suicide, as ordered by Hitler, to save his family from the Fuehrer's revenge.

A general and a king who himself commands his men in combat have been given two of the most dramatic statements about war to be found on film. In each case these leaders are addressing their troops as they prepare for battle, and the two speeches provide a striking contrast in styles of leadership and attitudes toward war. One of the leaders, King Henry V, has the advantage of speaking Shakespeare's words, the stirring Crispin's Day speech. It matters not whether it is Lawrence Olivier or Kenneth Branagh who inspires his men before Agincourt. The words are all, as these final lines of the speech demonstrate:

This story shall the good man teach his son,
And Crispin Crispian shall ne'er go by,
From this day to the ending of the world,
But we in it shall be remembered—
We few, we happy few, we band of brothers.
For he today that sheds his blood with me
Shall be my brother. Be he ne'er so vile,
This day shall gentle his condition.
And gentlemen in England now abed
Shall think themselves accursed they were not here,
And hold their manhoods cheap whiles any speaks
That fought with us upon St. Crispin's Day.[19]

It is doubtful if war has ever been made to sound so glorious, participation in it so much the supreme experience of a lifetime. It must be remembered that the odds against the English were awesome, the prospects of victory bleak.

The speech delivered by General George Patton to his troops at the beginning of the film bearing his name is an entirely different matter. Unlike Henry, who, unshaven and rumpled, climbs atop a crude wagon on a dreary morning to address his men, Patton (George C. Scott), in a crisp, bemedalled uniform, strides back and forth in front of a huge American flag while he addresses the troops. The words he chooses are products of a different style of leadership and, needless to say, of a different age. "No bastard ever won a war by dying for his country," he says; "he won it by making the other dumb bastard die for his country." And even more graphically: "We're not just going to shoot the bastards; we're going to cut out their living guts and use them to grease the treads of our tanks." Perhaps most telling of all: "Americans traditionally love to fight. All real Americans love the sting of battle." Rough stuff indeed, and, we are told by biographers, vintage Patton. We know that Patton was a complex figure, a brilliant general and a thoroughly disagreeable personality (his career was almost terminated when he slapped two hospitalized soldiers he thought were malingering, an event included in the film). According to Paul Fussell, the implicit theme of *Patton* is that of "disgrace followed by redemption."[20]

If *Patton* gives us war with a focus on a controversial general, Stanley Kubrick's *Paths of Glory* finds nothing good to say about its generals and, by extension, the military mind more generally. Set in World War I during a period of protracted trench warfare, *Paths of Glory* concerns a suicidal attack by French troops upon an impregnable German position known as "the anthill." The attack is ordered by a pompous, self-serving general who believes that he will receive a prestigious new command if he takes "the anthill," even though he knows that doing so will cost the lives of half of his men. When many of the troops are slaughtered and the survivors fall back under devastating fire, the general (George Macready) brands them cowards and orders a court-martial of a randomly selected soldier from each of three platoons. The defense is not allowed to make its case, and the three men are convicted and executed. Kubrick is merciless in his condemnation of these "narrow-minded career officers . . . who are obsessed with flag, country, and image and have no regard for the obedient soldiers in the trenches."[21] There is arguably no stronger indictment of the military system and the men to whom the conduct of warfare is entrusted.

Far more films depict the stress and strain of war on the foot soldiers than focus on their commanders. This is particularly true of the antiwar films made in the aftermath of the Vietnam war. The phenomenon of shell shock among frontline troops in earlier wars is also well treated on film, perhaps nowhere better than in *Paths of Glory*. Before the assault on the anthill, the general walks through the trenches, asking various soldiers whether they are ready to kill more Germans. One of those soldiers stares vacantly ahead, barely hearing the question and mumbling incoherently in response. Somebody volunteers the information that the man is shell-shocked; the general angrily insists that there is no such thing as shell shock, brands the man a coward, and orders him removed from the platoon so as not to infect the other men with his cowardice. This is among the scenes that lead Lawrence Quirk, author of the anthology *The Great War Films,* to claim that in this early Kubrick film "the futility and downright insanity of war is set forth especially vividly, and the corruptions of high command politics (in *any* country, not just France—and in all eras and all wars) are gotten across forcefully and compellingly."[22]

Revolutions in Warfare: From Agincourt to the Somme

The history of international relations is clearly much more than the history of warfare, but wars provide us with a picture of changing configurations of power, changing patterns of enmity and alliance, and the ongoing revolution in science and technology. Wars serve to remind us that power can be ephemeral and that the bitter foes of one era may become the staunch allies of another. Thus Sweden, a major participant in the Thirty Years War of the seventeenth century, has been a neutral in all of the wars of the twentieth century. France and Britain, who made war on each other for centuries and nearly went to war as recently as the 1890s, have found themselves on the same side in both World War I and World War II. Wars also offer some of the most effective demonstrations of human inventiveness. While we may regret that so much ingenuity and effort have been invested in perfecting the means of killing, wars do tell us much about revolutions in industry, transportation, and communication, revolutions with impacts far beyond the battlefield.

Films about war capture many of these changes. Indeed, perhaps the most important contribution war films make to an understanding of international relations lies in what they have to say about the changing context in which those relations take place. The world in which Oliver Stone's, Stanley Kubrick's, and Francis Ford Coppola's soldiers fought and died in Vietnam is demonstrably different from the one in which the English defeated the French at Agincourt in Olivier's and Branagh's *Henry V*. We know this, of course, without going to the movies. But the films make the difference much more vivid. What we see on screen as we watch war films set in different eras is a military revolution, or rather a series of military revolutions, which not only change "the face of battle"[23] but give us perspective on the changing nature of the international system itself.

One scholar defines a military revolution in the following way:

> It is what occurs when the application of new technologies into a significant number of military systems combines with innovative operational concepts and organizational adaptation in a way that fundamentally alters the character and conduct of conflict. . . . what is revolutionary is not the speed with which the entire shift from one military regime to another occurs, but rather *the recognition, over some relatively brief period, that the character of conflict has changed dramatically, requiring equally dramatic—if not radical—changes in military doctrine and organization.*[24]

This concept of military revolutions has received much attention recently, due in considerable part to the quick and overwhelming success of Operation Desert Storm. As one commentator has observed, "The lopsided struggle with Iraq has already affected the way Americans understand modern war, inducing the ornithological miracle of doves becoming hawks."[25] Whether changes in military doctrine and organization match those in technology remains a subject of dispute, so the jury is still out on whether a revolution in warfare has really occurred. But we can definitely see the unfolding of earlier revolutions and their consequences in films about war.

One of the first of these revolutions occurred during the Hundred Years War, when the English learned to make good tactical use of archers and dismounted men-at-arms to neutralize the advantage of cavalry and rout the previously dominant French armies. The consequences of this revolution can be seen in two battles in which the English inflicted greatly disproportionate casualties on the French and won famous victories: Crecy in 1346 and Agincourt in 1415. The latter battle is the highlight of the films made about Shakespeare's *Henry V*. John Keegan has given us a brilliant summary of Agincourt in his book, *The Face of Battle*,[26] and Kenneth Branagh's film version recreates with remarkable felicity the principal features of that battle as reconstructed by Keegan. We see the long lines of mounted French noblemen, confident of victory, on the crest of a hill; we see the tired, hungry English archers, several hundred yards away, driving pointed stakes into the ground and readying themselves for the inevitable cavalry charge. The battle begins with the release of volleys of arrows by the archers, and the plain on which the two armies meet is soon turned into a terrible killing field as the French horses and men, most wearing sixty to seventy pounds of armor, crash to the muddy ground, victims of the press of their own numbers, the attacks of the English infantry, and the confusion of close-in combat. It is one of the most harrowing battle scenes on film, a reminder that war has always been hell, especially when the killing occurs at arm's length. At the end of the battle, an exhausted Henry confronts the French herald and says, "I tell thee truly, herald, I know not if the day is ours or no." The reply, after a poignant pause: "The day is yours."

Other military revolutions include those in which "gunpowder artillery displaced the centuries-old dominance of the defense in siege warfare" and the warship was "transformed from a floating garrison into an artillery platform."[27] By the time Napoleon became emperor, the industrial revolution had produced significant changes in weaponry. He integrated that technology with new military doctrine and organizational innovations that made his armies the scourge of Europe. One of the key developments in this revolution was the *levée en masse,* which led to a great increase in the size of armies.

> Men proved much more willing to defend and fight for the nation than the crown. Consequently, France's revolutionary armies could endure privations, and attack almost regardless of the cost in men (since they could call upon the total resources of the nation). In battle . . . skirmishers and individually aimed fire could be integrated to great effect into the rolling volleys of artillery and musketry.[28]

This new form of warfare can perhaps be best seen, ironically, in the film that chronicles Napoleon's final defeat, *Waterloo.* Louis XVIII had by then abolished conscription, so Napoleon had had to reconstruct the demobilized Grande Armée; although considerably smaller than the armies of the Allies, it still numbered around 200,000. So when Napoleon's and Wellington's men arrayed themselves for battle on that June day in 1815, it was an impressive scene, with brightly uniformed cavalry regiments and infantry battalions spread over several square miles of the Belgian countryside. As Keegan points out, Napoleon also had 250 cannon at Waterloo (Wellington was well supplied with cannon, as well), "and it was the presence of these weapons which explains—in crude terms—the altogether greater lethality of nineteenth- over fifteenth-century armies."[29] The canvas on which Bondarchuk's film *Waterloo* unfolds is vast and the director captures the many facets of battle during that era—the heavy artillery fire that leaves a pall of smoke over the battlefield; the dramatic cavalry charges that are exciting to watch if of limited importance to the outcome of the struggle; the largely futile efforts to break the squares in which the infantry position themselves; and, finally, the remarkable collapse of Napoleon's army at the end of that long and bloody day. The "reduction of the Guard to a fugitive crowd"[30] guaranteed Wellington his victory, sent Napoleon to his final exile, and ushered in a century devoid of any major international war. The most important innovations in military technology and strategy in the nineteenth century would take place during the American Civil War.

Henry V and *Waterloo* are based not only on real battles but on real people. Henry is in the midst of the carnage at Agincourt, and Napoleon and Wellington bark orders from their vantage points above the field at Waterloo (Rod Steiger, with his well-known method approach to acting, is especially memorable in his recreation of the Corsican, alternately brooding and volcanic, his stomach rebelling against him under the stress of battle.) The best film treatments of World War I, on the other hand, are based on fictional characters. But they are just as effective in conveying a picture of the state of military technology and doctrine at that point in history as any dramatization of real battles and real generals, and they are much more effective as antiwar statements. World War I brought us the submarine and commerce raiding, the use of radio for communication, mechanization in the form of the tank, and (in an admittedly primitive form) war in the air. However, the picture that comes most readily to mind when thinking about the First World War is not any of these technological breakthroughs but the slaughter and stalemate of trench warfare.

Certainly some of the most memorable movies of that war are those in which armies are seen living in the squalor of the trenches (which one writer has called "the concentration camps of the First World War"[31]), emerging only for suicidal assaults across no-man's-land on similar enemy trenches. For Keegan, writing about the battle of the Somme "there *is* something Treblinka-like about almost all accounts of 1 July, about those long docile lines of young men, shoddily uniformed, heavily burdened, numbered about their necks, plodding forward across a featureless landscape to their own extermination inside the barbed wire."[32] And battles much like the Somme are the focus of footage devoted to fighting in such films as *All Quiet on the Western Front,* Lewis Milestone's 1930 classic, and *Paths of Glory,* in which Stanley Kubrick took his audience back to the western front in World War I some twenty-seven years later. It matters not that in Milestone's film (and Erich Maria Remarque's novel), the men and boys in the trenches are German while in Kubrick's they are French. This is war, circa 1916, and it is a meatgrinder that makes Agincourt and Waterloo, for all of their carnage, look almost chivalrous by comparison.

Germany's armies had stormed west in August 1914, following the plan devised by General Alfred von Schlieffen. Convinced that Germany would have to deal with both Russia and France, and unwilling to wage war on two fronts simultaneously, the Schlieffen plan called for striking first in the west and then, after a quick victory over France, redeploying

German forces against Russia. But the attack on France came through neutral Belgium, which drew Britain into the war, and the German attack was stalled almost within sight of Paris. Instead of a quick victory, the front was stabilized; as we are told in a voice-over at the beginning of *Paths of Glory*, "By 1916, after two grisly years of trench warfare, the battle lines had changed very little. Successful attacks were measured in hundreds of yards, and paid for in lives by hundreds of thousands."

Although the heart of the drama in *Paths of Glory* lies in the trial and execution of three hapless French soldiers, court-martialed to satisfy an evil general, Kubrick's film captures the misery of the trenches and the terrible costs of largely futile attacks on enemy positions across the barren, lunar-like landscape of the war's Western Front. The attempt to capture "the anthill" cannot compare, of course, to such horrors of the war as the battles of the Somme and Ypres (the futility of which is suggested by the fact that these were the scenes of several major battles, the Somme in 1916 and again in 1918, Ypres in 1914, 1915, and 1917). The first battle of the Somme alone claimed over 600,000 casualties on each side, including 60,000 British officers and men on the first day alone. Yet the fictional assault on "the anthill" in *Paths of Glory,* relatively modest in scale and mercifully brief when compared to the real thing, has the ring of truth. And a terrible truth it is.

Not all films about the so-called Great War are set in the trenches or in Europe. Two films that suggest the wider geographical character of the war, as well as its technologically transitional nature, are Peter Weir's *Gallipoli* and David Lean's *Lawrence of Arabia*. The former, focusing on the ill-fated Allied effort to gain control of the Dardanelles, not only reminds us that there were other fronts than the one in France, but also that troops from as far away as Australia and New Zealand were involved in the fighting. The film, which made a star of Mel Gibson, is not only a tribute to the valor of the men from Down Under,[33] but also an indictment of the high-level military bungling that led to the disaster at Gallipoli, with its tragic and unnecessary loss of life. Turkey is also the enemy in *Lawrence of Arabia;* the action takes place during the Arab revolt against the Ottoman Empire and features, of course, the exploits of Lawrence as he welds the various Arab tribes into a fighting force that harasses the Turkish forces along the Hejaz railway and eventually occupies Damascus. Modern technology is only beginning to make its presence felt in this theater of the war, and the Arab capture of Aqaba (spectacular in the film, rather less so in reality, although accomplished in both cases without the knowledge or help of the British) is achieved by irregular troops, coming out of the desert, like the cavalry from another era, on horse and camel. In spite of the film's evocation of Lawrence's charisma and the fascination that comes of watching the Arabs outfight a more modern army, *Lawrence of Arabia* is also, ultimately, an antiwar film.

Revolutions in Warfare: The Age of Total War

By the time Hitler unleashed his armies against Poland in 1939 and the Japanese launched their surprise attack on Pearl Harbor in 1941,

> improvements in internal combustion engines, aircraft design, and the exploitation of radio and radar [had] made possible the *blitzkrieg,* carrier aviation, modern amphibious warfare, and strategic aerial bombardment. Entirely new forms of military formations appeared, such as the panzer division, the carrier battlegroup, and the long-range bomber force. After a scant twenty years, the nature of conflict had changed dramatically, and those—like the British and the French—who failed to adapt suffered grievously.[34]

Most of these elements of the continuing military revolution can be seen on film, which is not surprising inasmuch as World War II has been the focus of more war movies than any other war in history. While most of these films are unexceptional, a few provide insights into the ongoing revolution in weaponry and strategy and reinforce the view that this has indeed been the century of total war.

Among the films that contribute to an understanding of these changes are *Das Boot, Patton, Twelve O'Clock High, The Battle of Britain,* and *Tora! Tora! Tora!* Although submarines, tanks, and airplanes had all made their appearance in World War I, they achieved a far greater importance a generation later as part of the war machines that ravaged Europe, Africa, Asia, and the Pacific. Of these instruments of war, it was the submarine, the German U-boat, that had figured most prominently in the outcome of the Great War. Germany, fearing that it was losing the war of attrition, turned to a strategy of unrestricted submarine warfare in an effort to starve Britain into submission; the result, of course, was to bring the United States into the war. Lebow cites this as a prime example of a spin-off crisis, in which "the initiator feels compelled, usually by perceived dictates of national security, to carry out policies it realizes will put it on a collision course with a third party."[35] When Germany sought once more to blockade Britain in the 1940s, the submarine had become an even more formidable weapon, one responsible for sinking more than 2,800 ships weighing between 14 and 15 million tons.[36] But this deadly war in the Atlantic also produced countermeasures, including convoy escort and radar, which eventually turned the tide against the U-boats, themselves now vulnerable. This war is effectively captured in a German film, Wolfgang Petersen's *Das Boot,* which takes the audience into the cramped, claustrophobic quarters of a vessel only 150 feet long and ten feet wide, there to experience "the hellish, apocalyptic, almost unimaginable chaos of a submarine under intense attack."[37] Not only is this a powerful evocation of the kind of war World War II was; it reminds us that some of the most compelling antiwar films were produced years later in Germany and Japan, the countries that started the war and were physically destroyed by it.

The tank, like the submarine, had been introduced in World War I, but it was World War II in which it played a major role in revolutionizing warfare on land. As many as a quarter-million tanks were built during the war, and tank battles took place on a vast scale. In July 1943, in the greatest of these battles, whole armadas of German and Russian tanks fought each other for control of the city of Kursk; in this last German offensive on the Eastern Front, the Wehrmacht lost nearly 3,000 tanks as well as any possibility of reversing the Red Army's inexorable counteroffensive. And this was only one of many battles dominated by the tank, including those fought in North Africa. One of the latter battles is the high point of an early portion of *Patton*. Although the film is more of a character study of the controversial general than a war movie, and although the scenes of battle sometimes look more like Hollywood-style warfare than the real thing, *Patton* gives the viewer a sense of what tank warfare was like (and reminds us that, even in combat between armored divisions, it has been the accompanying infantry who bear the brunt of battle and must ultimately seize and hold ground).

But it was the war in the air that probably constituted the most significant change in the nature of warfare during World War II. This aspect of it, more than any other, was responsible for the terrible spread of war to civilian populations. Noncombatants had suffered in previous wars, of course; the Thirty Years War, for example, "exacted a terrible toll in human life, particularly throughout Germany and Bohemia, where for three decades rival armies roamed the land, plundering, killing, and devastating those societies on a scale that has perhaps never been equaled since. . . . At least one-third and perhaps as much as half of the population of those regions perished."[38] Yet the ability of vast fleets of bombers to drop untold tons of explosives on urban centers, whether to destroy industry and infrastructure or to terrorize the enemy's citizenry, meant that any pretense that war and killing were confined to opposing armies could no longer be sustained. In the Battle of Britain, the German Luftwaffe launched massive and nearly continuous terror raids on London and other British cities in September and October 1940. The British and Americans subsequently rained even greater tonnage of destruction on German cities; although the raids were intended to destroy German industries (they were later determined not to have been very successful), large numbers of civilians were inevitably killed in the process. By the latter months of the war in the Pacific, the U.S. Air Force was bombing Tokyo and other Japanese cities unopposed. Firestorms caused by raids on Dresden and Tokyo are believed to have killed more than 100,000 people in each case.

This aspect of the revolution in warfare has also been featured on film. *Twelve O'Clock High*, although primarily about the strain of command, gives us a good picture of these bomber raids and of aerial combat when the Germans send fighter planes aloft to shoot down Gregory Peck's crews. The film tells the story entirely from the American point of view; neither we nor the bomber crews ever see the victims of their bomb runs, although we are made painfully aware that many of the planes and their crews do not make it back to their base in England. Among the best films showing the air war and the destruction it wreaked among the civilian population is the ambitious and celebrity-filled British recreation, *The Battle of Britain*. The film contains some of the cinema's best scenes of aerial dogfights, but equally impressive are graphic scenes of the destruction visited upon English cities, a reminder that by 1940 we had entered the age of total war.

One final film from the World War II era requires mention because of what it has to say about yet another facet of the military revolution. *Tora! Tora! Tora!*, discussed in Chapter 6 for what it has to tell us about crisis decisionmaking, is ultimately about the attack on Pearl Harbor. That attack would not have been possible had not the mobile, seaborne airfield—the aircraft carrier—been developed. Indeed, the war in the Pacific would have assumed an entirely different character if there had been no carrier battle groups, and it surely would have gone much less well for the United States if the Japanese had been successful in their attack on Midway in June 1942. Instead, the Americans sank four Japanese carriers with their full complement of aircraft in an engagement that deserves to be called the turning point in the Pacific war. It should be noted that while the Japanese assault on Pearl Harbor is generally regarded in the United States as a disaster, it was, in John Mueller's words, only a military inconvenience[39] and may more appropriately be regarded as a blessing in disguise. Not only did the attack not find any U.S. carriers at Pearl, it destroyed or put out of commission a large number of old and obsolete battleships, forcing the United States to build new and superior replacements and, more important, to focus on the carrier battle group in developing military doctrine appropriate for the war that lay ahead. *Tora! Tora! Tora!* invites us to think about these things, even if it seems merely to be offering a screen replay of the "day that will live in infamy."

The Vietnam War has generated a lot of attention among filmmakers, most of which falls into the antiwar (or at least anti–Vietnam War) category. But many of these films about America's first lost war (few of them can be described as films about the victory of Vietnamese nationalism) also have something to say about yet a different kind of war and another military revolution. Unlike most of the films discussed to this point, films about the war in Vietnam reveal a conflict in which there is no front line and the enemy is frequently unseen, not only because he is out of sight over the horizon but because he is (or may be) everywhere. In most previous wars given much film treatment, men in battle were acutely aware of the direction from which death was likely to come. Not so in Vietnam; death was all around, creating what Quirk calls "the myriad horrors of the unexpected."[40] Frances Fitzgerald, writing about Francis Ford Coppola's *Apocalypse Now,* captures yet another aspect of this "modern" war, claiming that the film's brilliance

> has to do with helicopters and napalm. The film opens with a shot of a wall of palm trees rising out of the ocean and the sound of a chopper's rotor blades. Struts move across the top of the frame and a helicopter passes through. With the *snick-snick-snick* of the rotors growing louder, the chopper looks like a huge malevolent insect. To the sound of The Doors singing, "This is the end," the jungle suddenly erupts in flame.[41]

This is indeed a different kind of war, rendered with varying degrees of verisimilitude in such films as *Platoon, Full Metal Jacket, Casualties of War,* and *Apocalypse Now.*

War Termination and the Antiwar Film

Wars typically end when one side establishes its superiority and the other side acknowledges it; as noted earlier, war often provides an effective audit of power. But this is not always the case; some wars drag on while statesmen try to negotiate an armistice, neither side ready to concede that it prefers a distasteful peace to more bloodshed. Although filmmakers tend to be less interested in war termination than in fighting because the former is inherently less exciting, there have been a few films that have something to say about bringing wars to an end. One such film is Lewis Milestone's *Pork Chop Hill,* set during the Korean War. While the film is basically about a U.S. offensive to capture and hold the hill of the title, an extremely difficult operation in which casualties run high, the action takes place while peace negotiations are going on at Panmunjom no more than seventy miles away. In fact, the order to take the hill has nothing to do with its strategic value, but rather with the politics of peacemaking. The U.S. general staff negotiating with the enemy believe that their hand will be strengthened if the troops can demonstrate American toughness—in other words, they want to negotiate from strength. In fact, the Korean peace negotiations did drag out over a period of years; the episode depicted in the film, based on a book by a general who was there, reflects the director's contempt for war "in all its phony grandiosities and futilities."[42]

Bringing the war in Vietnam to an end also proved difficult. American involvement had initially seemed a logical response to the threat that communism would spread throughout southeast Asia. The victory so confidently predicted in the beginning proved elusive, however, and the Tet offensive of February 1968 both shocked the U.S. government into a realization that a military solution was impossible and dramatically increased public oppo-sition to the war. For the next five years first the Johnson and then the Nixon administration sought and finally obtained a negotiated settlement; but the U.S. strategy for getting the North Vietnamese to accept their terms included intensified bombing and the extension of the war into neighbor-ing Cambodia, which only further reinforced the anger of the antiwar movement. In the end, Hanoi's willingness to endure casualties and depri-vation in the interest of achieving its political goal of national unification led a war-weary United States to settle for an agreement that paved the way, within two years, for the triumph of the communist regime. While most of the films about the war in Vietnam focus on the war itself, two films deal in different ways with the issue of war termination.

One of these is Oliver Stone's *Born on the Fourth of July,* the story of Ron Kovic (Tom Cruise), a patriotic American from a conservative family who joins the Marines and goes off to Vietnam in the belief that war is glamorous and that this war against the atheistic communists must be fought and won. Kovic finds that the war is not at all glamorous; in the fog of battle (which Stone presents both figuratively and literally), he is seri-ously wounded and returns home a paraplegic. The film lets us accompany Kovic on his journey from rehabilitation in a miserable veteran's hospital to boozing, self-pity, and angry confrontations with his family, and even-tually to a political awakening that has him leading a group of Vietnam Veterans Against the War at the 1972 Republican Party Convention. (Critic Pauline Kael compares the film's several episodes to the Stations of the Cross.)[43] Although the heart of the film lies in Kovic's growing conviction that his country lied to him, *Born on the Fourth of July* also provides ex-tensive coverage of the antiwar protests that shook the government and contributed significantly to the end of U.S. involvement. We see volatile demonstrations by university students who did not go to Vietnam, and later by veterans who did; even making allowance for dramatic license, the film illustrates the point that it was increasingly difficult to sustain U.S. in-volvement in the face of so much public opposition. This lesson of the Vietnam era is still with us.

The actual end of U.S. involvement in the war in Vietnam came with the fall of Saigon to the North Vietnamese. The weeks, days, and even hours leading up to this event are the focus of the film adaptation of David Hare's play, *Saigon: Year of the Cat.* The film makes the point, as does the play, that key U.S. officials deluded themselves into thinking they could control the outcome and that they waited too long, evacuating the embassy staff hastily by helicopter at the last possible moment and leaving behind thousands of Vietnamese whom they had promised to protect as well as documents identifying some of them as agents who had worked for the United States. This is, of course, a fictionalized account of those frantic last days before the fall of Saigon, featuring a love affair between a British bank employee (Judi Dench) and a CIA official (Frederic Forrest) who tries unsuccessfully to persuade the ambassador of the impending cata- strophe. But it does capture the crisis atmosphere surrounding the end of that war, and it does make clear that the way in which it ended will have terrible consequences for many in Vietnam.

Saigon: Year of the Cat contains no scenes of combat; *Born on the Fourth of July,* a very long film, devotes only a relatively few minutes to the fighting. Several other war films, all arguably superior to the Vietnam films, similarly devote little or none of their screen time to men in combat but must be mentioned in any commentary on the relevance of films for understanding international relations. One is the Jean Renoir classic, *Grand Illusion,* which appears on many lists of the greatest films of all time and is often called the best of all antiwar films. Most of *Grand Illu- sion* takes place within German prisoner of war camps during World War I, and much of the remainder of the film follows an arduous trek to free- dom of two of the prisoners who have escaped. But this is not a conven- tional prisoner-of-war film, nor is it primarily the story of a heroic escape. As Renoir himself said, it is "a statement of man's brotherhood beyond po- litical borders."[44] The director is concerned with a common humanity, and the result is a sympathetic portrayal of all of the characters, French and German. In fact, the German prison commandant, Rauffenstein (Erich von Stroheim), and a French aviator, Boldieu (Pierre Fresnay), whom he has shot down, both aristocrats and career officers, have more in common than the Frenchman has with his fellow prisoners, Marechal (Jean Gabin) and Rosenthal (Marcel Dalio), the one a mechanic and the other a Jew. Boldieu creates a diversion that allows Marechal and Rosenthal to escape; Rauf- fenstein, after pleading unsuccessfully with Boldieu to surrender, shoots him and then consoles him on his deathbed. To stress further the theme of our common humanity, Marechal falls in love with a German widow who cares for him during the escape and promises to marry her after the war.

Renoir's great antiwar film was made in 1937, when storm clouds were gathering across Europe. The Nazis, who even then were preparing their assault on Germany's neighbors, were unmoved by *Grand Illusion.* It was banned by Goebbels, and after the occupation of Paris all available prints of it were confiscated.[45]

A very different kind of antiwar film was made in France seven years after the end of World War II, René Clement's *Jeux Interdit* (or *Forbidden Games*), which, like *Grand Illusion,* contains only a very minimum of what we think of as war footage yet manages to convey the director's mes- sage that "for me, foremost of the forbidden games is war."[46] The princi- pal victim of war in this film is the innocence of childhood. A five-year- old girl, Paulette (Brigitte Fossey), is orphaned when her parents (and her dog) are killed by a German plane strafing French civilians as they flee the German invasion in 1940. Taken in by a farm family, she and their eleven-year-old son, Michel (George Poujouly), bury the dog and then, to keep it from being lonely, join in a game in which they create a private cemetery, replete with crosses, in which they bury mice and moles and even insects. But the crosses are acquired by stealing them from a church cemetery, and the discovery of their theft leads through the insensitivity and deception of unsympathetic adults to the film's sad conclusion. The girl is turned over to the authorities for placement in an orphanage, and in the film's final scene in a crowded railroad station, a terrified Paulette hears a voice call out "Michel." She runs frantically through the station, looking for her friend, but it turns out to be somone else. As the film ends, Paulette calls out for her Michel and her mother as the camera moves up and away to reveal the child, ever smaller, lost in the crowd. There are few more haunting scenes in film history, and it alone more than justifies the inclusion of *Forbidden Games* on any short list of the great war films.

Another memorable film is *Night of the Shooting Stars,* set in Italy in the closing months of World War II. One of things that has been especially troubling about the war in the former Yugoslavia, especially in Bosnia, is that the Serb, Croats, and Muslims who treated each other so savagely had lived peacefully as next-door neighbors. The Taviani brothers, in their film, confront us with a similar tragedy. We are witness to a bloody battle in an otherwise beautiful Van Gogh–like wheatfield between black-shirted fascists on the one hand and antifascist partisans on the other; these people know each other well, and although what makes them enemies is political ideology rather than ethnicity, the thought that former friends and neighbors could be engaged in such a deadly struggle is deeply unsettling.

Night of the Shooting Stars is the story of a group of Italian peasants who steal away from their Nazi-occupied village in the night, hoping to make contact with American forces that are rumored to be approaching. The villagers are caught up in the battle in the wheatfield, but their decision to flee their homes proves to be a wise one, for the Germans dynamite the church where those who stayed behind are gathered on the fateful day. In spite of these scenes of combat and cruelty on the fringe of the larger war, *Night of the Shooting Stars* is not a gloomy picture, but rather "a joyous salute to the heroism of the Italian people and a testament to the human spirit."[47] It is one of those films that remind us that, even in time of war, life goes on, children grow up, and affairs of the heart take place.[48]

The Japanese people, following the destruction of their country in World War II, have strongly embraced pacifism, even to the point of resisting the use of Japanese Self Defense Forces for UN peacekeeping duty. This powerful antiwar sentiment can be seen in two unusual war films by Japanese director Kon Ichikawa. No short list of war films would be complete without these troubling but strangely beautiful works, *The Burmese Harp* and *Fires on the Plain;* both have been described as poetic. The action in both takes place during the final days of the war, when the Japanese army, defeated and starving, is struggling to survive. In *The Burmese Harp*, a private undergoes a spiritual conversion and, donning the robes of a Buddhist monk, sets out to bury his many dead countrymen in Burma. In *Fires on the Plain*, Japanese soldiers in hiding in the Philippines resort to murder and even cannibalism in a vain effort to survive, while the film's "hero," who is dying of tuberculosis, wanders deliriously through this hellish landscape. One critic has observed that "death in the film simply means an end to suffering and nothingness."[49] No one seeing Ichikawa's version of hell will ever view war in quite the same way again.

Finally, in a much lighter vein, no commentary on war on film would be complete without reference to that zaniest of all "war" films, the Marx brothers' *Duck Soup*. War, after all, is the ultimate demonstration of the realist thesis that the international system is anarchic, and the Marx brothers are the ultimate screen anarchists. The plot, of course, is not to be taken seriously, although Groucho's accession to the presidency of mythical Fredonia contains a cautionary lesson for those who would put their country's fate in the hands of unscrupulous and irresponsible leaders. The war, which takes up barely more than ten minutes of this brief film, is unmitigated mayhem and madness, served up in inimitable Marx brothers fashion. It is also a satirically devastating statement on war's absurdity, and for that reason alone merits a place in these pages.

Notes

1. See Small and Singer, *Resort to Arms.*
2. Sources vary as to the number of war-related deaths. These figures, based on studies by several political scientists, are cited in Hughes, *Continuity and Change in World Politics*, p. 113.
3. Mueller, *Quiet Cataclysm*, pp. 122, 112.
4. Quoted in *ibid.*, p. 187.
5. Quoted in *ibid.*, p. 190.
6. Quoted in *ibid.*, p. 112.
7. See Lorenz, *On Aggression*, and E. Wilson, *Sociobiology.*
8. Quoted in Snyder, "Perceptions of the Security Dilemma in 1914," p. 162.
9. *Ibid.*, p. 155.
10. Lebow, *Between Peace and War*, p. 3.
11. See Blainey, *The Causes of War;* the critique is found in Small and Singer, *International War,* p. 220.
12. *Ibid.*, pp. 220–21.
13. Craig and George, *Force and Statecraft*, p. 268.
14. *Ibid.*, p. 261 ff.
15. *Ibid.*, pp. 261, 262.
16. *Ibid.*, p. 268.
17. Dyson, *Weapons and Hope*, p. 154.
18. *Ibid.*, p. 155. Dyson further develops this distinction, using the antebellum American South and Robert E. Lee for purposes of illustration. "Long before the war began, the Southern states had established a cultural tradition which encouraged

their best minds to become professional soldiers. The tradition of exaggerated respect for military prowess was doubly disastrous for the South. It led to the overconfident enthusiasm and the illusions of military superiority with which the South went to war at the beginning. And it produced the spirit of sacrificial dedication in which the Southerners fought on to the bitter end, when the prolongation of the war was bringing to their country nothing but ruin and destruction. Robert E. Lee was a great general and a great gentleman, but all his tactical skill and strength of character only made the suffering of his people heavier" (p. 156).

19. The speech may be found in, among other places, the Arden Shakespeare series, Craik, *King Henry V,* pp. 287–91 (the lines quoted are on p. 291).

20. Fussell, "Patton," p. 244.

21. Peary, *Alternate Oscars,* p. 138.

22. Quirk, *The Great War Films,* p. 155.

23. This is the perceptive title of John Keegan's highly regarded study of warfare, *The Face of Battle.*

24. Krepinevich, "Cavalry to Computer," pp. 30–31 (emphasis in original).

25. E. Cohen, "The Mystique of U.S. Air Power," p. 110.

26. Keegan, *The Face of Battle,* pp. 78–116.

27. Krepinevich, "Cavalry to Computer," pp. 32–33.

28. *Ibid.,* p. 34.

29. Keegan, *The Face of Battle,* p. 144.

30. *Ibid.,* p. 178.

31. Quoted in *ibid.,* p. 260.

32. *Ibid.*

33. "Gallipoli is as much an essential part of the Australian ethos as, say, the Alamo is to Texas: a military defeat that became rationalized over the years into a moral victory." Quoted in Quirk, *The Great War Films,* p. 232.

34. Krepinevich, "Cavalry to Computer," p. 36.

35. Lebow, *Between Peace and War,* p. 41.

36. Harbottle, *Dictionary of Battles,* pp. 34–35.

37. Turan, "Das Boot," p. 470.

38. Miller, *Global Order,* pp. 20–21.

39. See Mueller, *Quiet Cataclysm,* Ch. 7, pp. 85–110.

40. Quirk, *The Great War Films,* p. 242.

41. Fitzgerald, "Apocalypse Now," p. 284.

42. Quirk, *The Great War Films,* p. 169.

43. Kael, "Potency," p. 122.

44. Paris, *The Great French Films,* p. 76.

45. Although the negative was destroyed during World War II, another negative of the film was found after the war in Munich, thereby guaranteeing that Renoir's classic would again be available for viewing. This story is told in Paris, *The Great French Films,* p. 78.

46. *Ibid.,* p. 146.

47. Vermilye, *The Great Italian Films,* p. 238.

48. Other films have also explored this theme; among the best are Jiri Menzel's *Closely Watched Trains* and John Boorman's *Hope and Glory.*

49. Peary, *Guide for the Film Fanatic,* p. 150.

8

Economic Interdependence
and Development

Now that the Cold War is over, and with it the chronic anxiety over a military confrontation between East and West, many scholars and statesmen are prepared to argue that economic warfare will replace the ideological and geopolitical warfare that for so long dominated international relations. In the United States, for example, there has been no shortage of pundits ready to proclaim that, with the Soviet Union dead and Russia grievously wounded, Japan is now the principal enemy, with Germany not far behind. Commenting on this phenomenon, Paul Kennedy observes that "the language used to describe international trade and investment today has become increasingly military in nature; industries are described as coming 'under siege,' markets are 'captured' or 'surrendered,' and comparative rates of R&D expenditures or of shares of high-technology goods are scrutinized as anxiously as the relative sizes of battlefleets before 1914."[1]

The view that the twenty-first century will be marked by economic warfare has been shaped in part by the fact that Japan and Germany have become economic superpowers and that China is poised to become one, and by the perception that their economic policies are designed to achieve a noneconomic goal, that of national power. In other words, these states are seen as pursuing objectives that smack of mercantilism and pose a threat to the open world economy.[2] This view reflects the realist vision of international relations, one fixated on the importance of relative power and the inevitability of conflict among states, one that worries about the collapse of the more familiar "containment order, which was based on the balance of power, nuclear deterrence, and political and ideological competition."[3] These observers look back almost nostalgically at the Cold War and see increasingly vigorous economic competition not only as a successor to the political/military competition that characterized the Cold War but also as symptomatic of the breakdown of alliance discipline in the wake of the collapse of the Soviet Union and the discrediting of communism.[4]

Not everyone is so pessimistic, or, if you will, such an unreconstructed realist. Alternatively, it has been argued that the post–Cold War era, in spite of the resurgence of nationalism in many places, is not essentially one of chaos, with economic warfare ascendant, but one in which the liberal economic order established after the end of World War II is alive and well. Thus, while the Cassandras bemoan the end of the containment or bipolar order, others emphasize the survival of the basic principles of what they regard as an even more important order.

> These less celebrated, less heroic, but more fundamental principles and policies—the real international order—include the commitment to an open world economy and its multilateral management, and the stabilization of socioeconomic welfare. . . . The major industrial democracies took it upon themselves to "domesticate" their dealings through a dense web of multilateral institutions, intergovernmental relations, and joint management of the Western and world political economies. . . . Embracing common liberal democratic norms and operating within interlocking multilateral institutions, the United States, Western Europe, and, later, Japan built an enduring postwar order.[5]

The author of these words, John Ikenberry, is optimistic about the survival of that postwar order, which he finds even more robust than during the Cold War. Others go even further. Francis Fukuyama, in one of the most widely discussed theses advanced in recent years, goes so far as to say that the end of the Cold War heralds "the end of history"—that is, "the endpoint of mankind's ideological evolution and the universalization of Western liberal democracy as the final form of human government."[6] If one accepts this view, the triumph of Western liberalism over absolutism, fascism, and finally communism is no longer in doubt, even if some countries are still mired in history and destined to experience violent conflict as they struggle to enter the posthistorical world. But "international life for the part of the world that has reached the end of history is far more preoccupied with economics than with politics or strategy."[7]

These declarations of the triumph of the West and the liberal international order do not mean the end of vigorous economic competitiveness. But they do suggest that the death of Marxism-Leninism "means the growing 'Common Marketization' of international relations,"[8] and they refute the notion that Japan and Germany will opt to trash the economic system from which they have benefited so handsomely. Fear of Japanese and German economic domination, especially in the United States, has abated somewhat in recent years. While both countries remain economic superpowers, Germany has been struggling with high unemployment and Japan, its economy in the doldrums, is clearly no longer "the vibrant dynamo of legend, which once flooded the world with its exports, but an aging doyen of economies that is choking on regulation."[9] Whether we have reached the end of history or not, Fukuyama is right when he asserts that economics has become the new high politics; while economics does serve political purposes in most countries some of the time (the mercantilist position), the "triumph" of the market means that increasingly politics serves economic purposes in virtually all countries (the liberal position).

For several decades after World War II it was customary to speak of a First World (the industrialized West), a Second World (the communist bloc), and a Third World (the developing countries). But the Second World is but a memory, and the Third World is struggling to come to terms with an international system that is not dominated by the East-West conflict. The ideology associated with the First World—call it economic *and* political liberalism (or capitalism and democracy)—has not travelled easily to the states of the old Second and Third worlds. But these states, like those of the industrialized West, have been caught up in an increasingly interdependent world characterized by an ever-tighter integration of economic markets. Interdependence has meant greater opportunities for states, but it has also meant greater restraints. It has effectively blurred the distinction between domestic and foreign affairs. The motto of the increasingly interdependent world in which we live may well be, as Stanley Hoffmann has written, "You can hurt me, and I you. But neither one of us can retaliate fully without harming himself."[10]

Developing countries and countries that until recently had communist-style economies understand that their economic well-being depends on their participation in this interdependent global economy, which in turn means playing the game according to Western rules. Most have accepted the view that greater prosperity and development depend on economic liberalization, and many are trying to open up their political systems as well. However economic relations among the industrial (and postindustrial) powers of the West play out—whether they take the form of economic warfare or only the relatively benign and mutually beneficial competitiveness of a liberal order—developing countries would appear to face much more difficult problems.

Although these problems have received somewhat more attention in films than economic relations among the developed market economy states have, in the real world they have received less. At least during the Cold War both East and West courted the countries of the Third World, providing many of them with various forms of aid in order to secure their support in the great ideological struggle. Those years of competitive courtship are recalled in a cynical statement by an African diplomat, speaking during a conference on poverty in David Hare's play, *A Map of the World*.

> We take aid from the West because we are poor, and in everything we are made to feel our inferiority. The price you ask us to pay is not money but misrepresentation. . . . the yellow press does not speak of Africa except

to report how a nun has been raped, or there has been a tribal massacre, or how we are slaughtering the elephants—the elephants who are so much more suitable for television programmes than the Africans—or how corrupt and incompetent such-and-such a government is. If the crop succeeds, it is not news. If we build a dam, it is called boring. . . . Boring. The white man's word for everything to which he does not wish to come to terms. Yes, he will give us money, but the price we will pay is that he will not seek to understand our point of view. Pro-Moscow, pro-Washington, that is the only way you see the world. All your terms are political, and your politics is the crude fight between your two great blocs.[11]

But even aid on these terms has largely come to an end. As the Soviet Union and later Russia lost both the capacity and the will to support Third World governments, the United States and to a lesser degree its European allies also lost their interest in doing so.

This transitional world—this world of complex interdependence—has made its way to the screen in a variety of films, although, as noted in the introduction, international economic relations have been less well and less frequently treated by filmmakers than many other aspects of international relations. Most of the films cited in this chapter are concerned with various aspects of the development issue, and particularly with those states and peoples that are most vulnerable in a world of complex interdependence. Among the themes that have attracted filmmakers, or that can be located as secondary elements of film plots, are responsibility for the plight of poor countries, draconian and ideologically driven measures for generating development, environmental and cultural tradeoffs of particular development policies, population flows resulting from the burden of economic hardship, and, of course, the human dimension of poverty.

Multinational Companies and the Global Marketplace

Before turning to these and related themes, another aspect of interdependence requires comment, both because it is intrinsically important and because it has surfaced in at least a few films: the revolution in technology and the fact that "the main creators and controllers of technology have increasingly become large, multinational corporations with more global reach than global responsibility."[12] The revolution in technology that bears such a large responsibility for the integration of the global marketplace has, of course, fascinated the film industry, which both makes use of it in the production and marketing of films and depicts its wonders in many of those films. (Some would argue that Hollywood is increasingly relying on technological wizardry rather than strong plot and good acting to turn a profit.) But the impact of this revolution in technology on trade and finance has largely been ignored by the industry. Today flows of paper have been replaced by electronic transactions that take place around the clock, picked up in one capital market when another shuts down for the night. . . . trading in yen futures or in General Motors stock goes on twenty-four hours a day and creates a single market. Daily foreign exchange flows amount to around *one trillion* dollars, and far outweigh the sums employed for the international purchase of goods and services or investments in overseas plants.[13]

Yet this truly dramatic aspect of the technological revolution and its impact on the way the world does business shows up on film only rarely and then obliquely. After all, drug dealers are among the few who still make large financial transactions the old-fashioned way, with paper currency; and drug dealers remain more interesting to the film industry than speculators on the exchanges in New York and Tokyo and Zurich.

But multinational corporations (MNCs)—companies based in one state while maintaining subsidiaries in other states—do occasionally make an appearance in films. MNCs are today both numerous (there are more than 10,000) and powerful (many have annual sales figures greater than the GNP of the majority of nation-states).[14] These corporations typically operate in several countries, own capital in several countries, control global trade, almost always place profits above loyalty to their home country, and must be acknowledged as among the most influential actors in contemporary international relations. Although they, too, have received relatively little attention from filmmakers, and for much the same reason that international finance has been ignored by the industry—a presumption of limited box office appeal—there have been a few film excursions into the world of MNCs and especially into the matter of foreign direct investment.

One such film is *Rising Sun,* Philip Kaufman's adaptation of Michael Crichton's best-selling novel. The book has been described as the author's "wake-up call to America,"[15] a xenophobic argument that Japanese economic practices pose a serious threat to the economic security of the United States. The word isn't used, but the charge, nonetheless, is "mercantilism," and in a particularly virulent form. The movie, which has "toned down the book's relentless insistence that the Japanese are intent on swallowing America whole,"[16] has two interrelated stories, one personal and the other political or corporate. The personal story, which need not detain us here, concerns the murder of a beautiful American call girl in the boardroom of the Nakamoto Corporation in Los Angeles and the efforts of two police detectives to solve the crime. Sean Connery plays the senior of the two detectives, John Connor, an old Japan hand who guides his young colleague, played by Wesley Snipes, through the intricacies of negotiating across the barriers of culture. The corporate story has greater relevance for the theme of economic interdependence. Nakamoto is an aggressive and highly successful Japanese conglomerate, which is engaged in controversial negotiations to acquire MicroCon, an American computer software company. The acquisition is highly controversial, both because it has national security implications that have stirred congressional interest and because it would enable Nakamoto to compete more successfully (and the inference is unfairly) with the U.S. computer industry. It is clear that Crichton and Kaufman are tapping into the anxiety with which many Americans have greeted Japan's foreign direct investment in the United States, especially in such high-profile cases as the sale to Japanese interests of Columbia Pictures (and Rockefeller Center, which the Japanese subsequently resold). That anxiety is given voice in the film by the police officer initially in charge of the investigation (Harvey Keitel). A reflexive Japan-basher, he is bitterly critical not only of Japanese culture and business practices but of what he perceives as U.S. willingness to roll over for a people he clearly regards as the enemy. When a Japanese guard in the Nakamoto building tries to impede the investigation, Keitel tells him that "we're still the fucking police in our own country," but shortly thereafter he laments to Connery that "we're giving the country away."

It can be argued that *Rising Sun* is ultimately more or less even-handed in its handling of the U.S.-Japanese relationship. Connery and Snipes may be sympathetic, but most of the Americans are either unscrupulous or incompetent or both. The Japanese may keep a bevy of attractive American women for their pleasure and associate with yakuza (gangsters), but they are portrayed as smart and successful businessmen. They gain their advantage through technology, as they have done in real life in fields such as robotics.[17] In the film, the Nakamoto building is a state-of-the-art facility in which hidden cameras and recording devices monitor everything, including the private conversations of Nakamoto's American counterparts during negotiations for acquisition of MicroCon. The solution to the murder of the call girl, which occured on the same boardroom table where the MicroCon negotiations took place earlier in the day, depends on the fact that the cameras were running during the crime (and that the video disk was subsequently and cleverly altered). The thesis of the film would not seem to be that the Japanese are the bad guys of international economic competition, but that, to quote Connery's "wise" assessment of the situation, "Business is war" and "We're in a war zone." This is obviously one perspective on the matter, but, as noted earlier, it is not an uncommon one.

The film raises another issue of importance in international economic relations, that of the ethics of accepting gifts—or bribes—in order to secure contracts.[18] In this case no contract is at stake, but the point is essentially the same. John Connor, who is investigating the crime, plays golf with the chairman of Nakamoto and then accepts from him the gift of membership in an exclusive and expensive country club. His colleague finds such behavior offensive in view of the fact that Nakamoto's officials are under suspicion, and he is not fully persuaded by Connor's explanation that golf is the way the Japanese do business and that, by implication, to refuse the gift would be rude.

Rising Sun is ultimately more of a mystery thriller than a film of ideas, but it does invite interesting debates about two matters: economic competitiveness and cross-cultural communication. The film's contribution to the latter issue will be revisited in Chapter 10.

Gung Ho is a very different kind of a movie, lacking the angry edge of *Rising Sun*. But it is related to *Rising Sun* in that its plot also turns on a case of foreign direct investment in the United States by a Japanese corporation and resulting tensions between the Japanese and the Americans. *Gung Ho,* directed by Ron Howard and starring Michael Keaton, is a comedy in which a Japanese company (Assan in the film, but the viewer can imagine Toyota or Honda or Nissan) takes over a failed automobile plant in Hadleyville, Pennsylvania, and thereby saves that American town from economic ruin. Along the way to the happy ending we are witness to the many difficulties American labor and Japanese management experience in working together.

Unlike *Rising Sun,* which tells us that the Japanese advantage lies in technology and business chicanery, *Gung Ho* attributes the success of America's economic challenger to superior work habits. The dialogue makes sure that the American audience will not miss the point. In one scene, the frustrated young Japanese executive (Gedde Watanabe) tells his plant foreman (Keaton), "I do not understand American workers. They come five minutes late, they leave two minutes early. They stay home when they are sick. They put themselves above company." By comparison, he tells Keaton (and us), "Japanese workers very loyal to company, ashamed when it does poorly." The Japanese tolerate no defects in the cars that roll off the assembly line; the Americans, by comparison, are quite willing to settle for the occasional lemon. In one exchange, an American worker insists that defects are something for the dealer to worry about, because every car can't be perfect. Keaton urges Watanabe to lighten up, to forget the zero defect policy; after all, he says, "It's just cars, not brain surgery."

Although *Gung Ho* is a comedy, and not a very subtle one at that, its central plot device—the decision of a Japanese company to build cars in the United States—reminds us of important facts about international economic relations. Japanese cars *have* made enormous inroads on the American automobile market, driving U.S. automakers to seek government relief in the form of import quotas and other restrictions on the importation of popular Japanese vehicles. One reason for the success of Japanese cars has been that on the whole they have had a better service record than American cars—they have had fewer defects. And many Japanese cars *are* built in the United States. A major reason for this development has been the desire of Japanese MNCs to avoid import restrictions.[19] Moreover, no matter where cars or other products are assembled, their parts were often manufactured in several countries. Domestic content rules have become important elements in negotiations between multinational corporations and host governments in an age when it is increasingly difficult to identify a car or other product as Japanese or German or American.

A multinational corporation also plays an important role in yet another recent film, *Disclosure*. Like *Rising Sun, Disclosure* is based on a novel by Michael Crichton and also reflects the author's interest in and knowledge of advanced computer-age technology. In this case, however, the MNC that occupies such an important place in the story line is American, not Japanese, and the foreign subsidiary is located in a Third World country, Malaysia. The setting for most of the action is a high-tech Seattle firm, DigiCom, where Meredith Johnson (Demi Moore) has just been appointed to a vice-presidency for which her former lover, Tom Sanders (Michael Douglas), thought he was in line. The principal element of the plot is Johnson's attempted seduction of Sanders and the resulting charges of sexual harassment, hers against him and his against her. What matters for international relations is that DigiCom is involved in negotiations for a merger with another firm, and the outcome of those negotiations hinges on its ability to demonstrate that a new CD-ROM drive it is developing will perform as promised. Presumably there would be no problem if the new product were being assembled in the United States; but DigiCom, like many an MNC, has farmed the task out to a subsidiary in Malaysia, where labor is cheaper.

It appears that DigiCom is experiencing fabrication problems with the production line in Malaysia, and the reason—according to a plot device that enables Sanders to triumph over the villainous Johnson in the film's denouement—is that the Malaysian workers have been installing chips by hand in a plant where the air quality is dirty, whereas automatic installers should have been used. The decision to use manual labor on the production line was taken in order to make the Malaysian government happy. MNCs have been much criticized for their negative impact on Third World economies, but the fictional DigiCom's experience in Malaysia suggests that countries that are host to MNC subsidiaries do possess some leverage. *Disclosure* is more interested in sexual harassment in the workplace and computer-generated special effects than it is in multinational corporations; it does, however, invite a discussion of the ways in which MNCs operate when they set up shop in developing countries.

Colonialism, Dependency, and Development

Malaysia is but one of many states generally described as "developing." The real Malaysia has fared far better than most of the states in that category, with classifiers of such things usually placing it just a step behind Asia's economically successful "Four Tigers" (South Korea, Taiwan, Singapore, and Hong Kong) and among the emerging newly industrializing countries, or NICs. The overwhelming majority of the world's states are developing countries; at the United Nations and its affiliated agencies they long ago banded together to form the Group of 77, a pressure group and voting bloc that today numbers close to twice the seventy-seven members present at its creation in 1964. They range from the oil-rich states of the Gulf to the desparately poor states of the African Sahel to more complex cases such as India and Mexico. These many and quite diverse states are often referred to collectively as the South, a label that not only makes an obvious reference to geography but also invites comparison with (and criticism of) the North.

The notion that the North is developed and the South developing is rooted in a conventional concept of development—"dynamic economic performance, modern institutions, the availability of abundant goods and services."[20] Development, in other words, is about economics. Most statesmen in the South, as well as those in the North, have subscribed to some variation of this conception. But as Denis Goulet has reminded us so eloquently, there are other ways of viewing development. He argues that "development is above all a question of values,"[21] but that all too often it is promoted and practiced in ways that are not respectful of the values of traditional societies.

> Traditional societies receive stimuli to change which clearly challenge their prevailing normative values. These stimuli present different ways of doing things: planting crops, educating children, or practicing hygiene. More fundamentally they introduce new objectives to human effort: to improve one's level of living, to obtain a "better" house or more food, to gain greater mobility so as to work and travel elsewhere. . . . All efforts to introduce modernity, efficiency, and technological rationality risk being destructive if change agents uncritically assume these qualities to be superior to those they supplant.[22]

The traditional approach to development has tended to be top-down, with the experts in the "development industry" (the International Monetary Fund, the World Bank, the U.S. Agency for International Development and its counterparts in other developed countries, as well as many universities and think tanks) prescribing and implementing programs and projects in and for developing countries. Some of these programs and projects would qualify as successes by almost any yardstick of measurement while others have been failures, not only on their own terms but because they have exacted a high cost in value destruction. In either case, this approach to the problem tends to view development as a product rather than as a process. Development theorists today generally prefer to emphasize people-centered development and to disparage the big industrial and infrastructure projects that were once the hallmark of development strategy.[23]

At the end of World War II, when the United Nations system came into being, the terms "developing" and its predecessor, "underdeveloped," had not yet become part of the vocabulary of international relations. Most of the countries that would later be called "developing" were still colonies without a separate international standing. The first priority of indigenous leaders was not development but self-determination. In important respects, the campaign for decolonization and political independence was related to Goulet's concept of development, inasmuch as it was based on the rejection of alien rule and hence the imposition of alien values. Political independence did not produce economic independence, however; the many countries that had finally broken free of the European metropoles found that they were still living with the legacies of colonialism. Scholars and statesmen began to talk of neocolonialism and of *dependencia*. Dependency theorists asserted that

> the under- or perverted development of the Third World and the development of the industrialized nations are intimately related. The poverty of the one is a consequence of the wealth of the other. . . . It is not the absence of education, infrastructure, capital, or foreign exchange per se that account for poverty; rather, these lacunae are a manifestation of a pernicious set of transnational interactions. The international order corrupts the economic, political, and cultural development of dependent areas.[24]

This view of the international economic order led to a concerted effort by the developing countries to create a New International Economic Order (NIEO). Although the NIEO agenda consisted of proposals to strengthen the economies of Third World states, it was also and more importantly, as Stephen Krasner has argued, a set of meta-power political demands.[25] The developing countries sought to make the international economic environment more predictable and more favorable to their interests by changing the "rules" by which international economic relations are conducted, substituting authoritative allocation of resources for market allocation. Thus, although they sought greater wealth, they also sought greater control over the processes whereby wealth is created and distributed.

It is important to note that the Third World wanted a more equitable distribution of power and wealth among *states*. The governments of these states stoutly resisted all efforts by the developed country governments to focus on *individuals*—that is, to make aid conditional upon "performance criteria to be met by recipient countries, if those performance criteria should concern the treatment of individuals."[26] Adamantly protective of their sovereignty, so recently won in many cases, the developing countries were not prepared to let the economically powerful states define for them what constitutes internal distributive justice. Thus the NIEO, that major effort to move development to the top of the agenda of the international community, was in the final analysis a basically conservative program, affirming "the view that in international affairs states, not persons, are the subject of moral and legal rights and duties."[27]

The Third World's efforts to modify the liberal economic order also clearly reflected a traditional, economically oriented conception of development. But running through the NIEO agenda—and through the contemporaneous Charter of Economic Rights and Duties of States and UNESCO's New World Information and Communication Order—was also a persistent thread of concern for the protection of the societal values of developing countries from the corrosive effects of Western influence. Colonialism had not been forgotten. Indeed, the Charter of Economic Rights and Duties of States proclaimed the duty of the West to make amends for its past exploitation of the South, and the NIEO spelled out just how that was to be accomplished. It is not a great exaggeration to say that in some ways the NIEO was an economic affirmative action program to compensate developing countries for the wrongs of the colonial era.

The New International Economic Order never came into being despite a decade of off-again, on-again negotiations; the South simply did not have the leverage to compel the North to make significant concessions. As we have seen, the liberal order the developing countries had wished to overhaul is now more firmly entrenched than ever. However, the legacy of colonialism, with its distortions of Third World economies and denial of opportunities for balanced growth, is still frequently cited as a major reason for the failure—or retardation—of the development process. Films have picked up and amplified this message, both in their recreation of historical events and in fictional accounts of European exploitation of the non-Western world. Three such films merit mention here.

One of these is *Gandhi,* discussed in greater detail in Chapter 3. The British government adopted policies toward "the jewel in the crown" that were intended to advance British economic interests and that had a stultifying effect on the development of India's own economy. This mattered not to London, which viewed India as an appendage of the mother country, not as a separate entity with its own economic future. The denial to India of an opportunity to become more economically self-sufficient is illustrated in the film first in the case of cloth and then in the case of salt. Cotton was grown in India, but clothing was made from that cotton in the great mill towns of the English midlands; Indians were expected to clothe themselves with English-made apparel, a policy Gandhi challenged by encouraging Indians to burn clothes made in England and make use of homespun. Indeed, Gandhi has often been depicted sitting at a spinning wheel, turning Indian cotton into homemade cloth for homemade clothing; what may appear to be a picture of quiet domesticity is in reality a picture of economic and political rebellion. The case of salt receives even more attention in the film. Britain forbade the Indians to make their own salt, requiring them instead to purchase it from government shops. Once again a policy crafted with home country economic interests in mind had the effect of making the colony an economic dependency. The Gandhi-led salt march was one of the more famous and effective challenges to crown policy, and this assertion of economic independence—with Indians soon busily making salt all over the country (and risking jail by doing so)—is well documented in the film.

Colonial officials frequently converted their colonies into plantations for the production of crops for European consumption. The English liked their coffee, tea, and chocolate, for example, so they turned Kenya into a coffee- and tea-producing colony and the Gold Coast (called Ghana at independence) into a cocoa-producing colony. This development of cash-crop production had two benefits for Europeans: it generated revenue for colonial administrations and met the home country's need for cheap sources of raw materials. The consequences for the colonies, later as independent sovereign states, were far from benign. These cash crops produce foreign exchange, of course, but prices are far from stable, terms of trade are frequently adverse,[28] and, what is often worse, the diversion of acreage from subsistence farming to cash crops makes it necessary for countries that might otherwise be reasonably self-sufficient in food production to rely on imports to feed their people.

Another cash crop, sugar, plays a critical role in the plot of *Burn*, another film that deals with the economics of colonialism. No other movie demonstrates so effectively the economic considerations that motivated the colonial powers, and it is doubtful if any other presents a more powerful indictment of colonialism. *Burn* takes place in the early part of the nineteenth century on a fictional Caribbean island known as Queimada. When the film begins, Queimada is a Portuguese colony with a slave economy and sugar as its most important product. The British send William Walker (Marlon Brando in one of his most interesting if least heralded roles) to Queimada, where, in order to capture the sugar trade for England, he foments a rebellion against the Portuguese. The leader of the rebellion, Jose Dolores (the nonprofessional Evaristo Marquez), is handpicked for that role by Walker because he clearly has the courage to stand up to the white man. But once the rebellion has succeeded and the Portuguese ousted, the principled but naive and uneducated Dolores has served his purpose; there will be no place for him in the new government. In a scene that captures succinctly an all-too-familiar attitude of the Europeans toward their colonial subjects, Walker confronts Dolores after negotiations over a new constitution have broken down. "Who'll govern your island?" he asks. "Who'll run your industries? Who'll handle your commerce?" He points to several of Dolores's men nearby, the implication clear that these tasks are way beyond them. "Civilization is no simple matter," Walker announces. "You can't learn its secrets over night. Today civilization belongs to the white man."

When Walker returns to Queimada ten years later, it is as an agent of the Antilles Royal Sugar Company, which in practice now controls the entire economy of the island country. But Jose Dolores has revived the revolution, and Walker's task this time is not to encourage rebellion but to suppress it. There is no longer any question of who is in control; Walker and the British sugar interests arrest and execute the president, invite the British to send an army, and use that army of redcoats to burn the cane fields, forcing the rebels into the open where they are mercilessly cut down. Dolores is captured and hanged after he chooses martyrdom over Walker's offer of exile. By having Walker stabbed to death on the dock at the film's conclusion, the director, Gillo Pontecorvo, lets us know that the revolution is not dead and that colonial exploitation is doomed.

The screenplay of *Burn* has much to say about the economics of colonialism. Early in the film, when Walker is trying to persuade Queimada's business leaders to support the rebellion against the Portugese, he poses the question of which is more economically efficient, domination by a colonial power, with its laws, taxes and commercial monopolies, or independence, with the freedom to trade with anyone you like and on terms dictated only by the prices on the international market. It is a reasonable question, and the response he wants, of course, is independence; but the result will once again be foreign domination, this time by British sugar interests. Later, just prior to Walker's second visit to Queimada, a voice-over tells us that, because no one wants to drink tea without sugar, the value of shares in sugar companies is continuing to rise and the increasingly powerful sugar companies are now able to assume responsibility for law and order in the colonies (very much as the British East India Company did for decades in India). The Antilles Royal Sugar Company proceeds to do just that in the second half of *Burn*. When Walker's strategy of burning the cane fields to flush out Dolores is questioned, he responds that fire cannot cross the sea, whereas ideas can. The plantations will come back and again be profitable, but if left unchallenged, Jose Dolores's message will spread with terrible consequences for the economic interests of the company.

The indictment of colonialism (and imperialism) in *Burn* gains some of its sharp edge from the simple integrity of Jose Dolores and the savagery of the tactics used to defeat the rebels. A much gentler depiction of the exploitation of cane cutters on the sugar plantations is to be found in Euzhan Palcy's impressive first film, *Sugar Cane Alley*. The setting is Martinique, and because that Caribbean island is a department of metropolitan France, *Sugar Cane Alley* is not technically a film about colonialism. But the distinction is not important for our purposes. Palcy is primarily concerned with telling the story of a young boy, very poor and very bright, who, with the help of a proud and doting grandmother, acquires the education that will enable him to escape the brutally hard life of the cane cutters. It is a charming story, well told, and one can enjoy the movie without giving a thought to its relevance for an understanding of the economics of development.

But *Sugar Cane Alley* has something important to say about development and, albeit indirectly, about neocolonialism. The laborers in the cane fields were originally slaves imported from Africa; by the 1930s, when the story takes place, slavery has long since been abolished but the descendants of those slaves, still toiling long hours for little pay, are little better off than their ancestors. One reviewer has succinctly summarized the situation: "Free of any obligation to care for their employees, the French neocolonialists who owned the fields could maintain their own standard of living by letting the global depression trickle down on their impoverished field hands."[29] We are witness to the callousness of overseers as they abitrarily dock the cutters' miserably low pay for the most trivial of reasons. One of the young boy's teachers is an old man who is something of an oral historian; it is he who makes it clear that the end of slavery only meant a change of masters, not true freedom.

Few films say so much about neocolonialism, or say it with such an economy of words and, ironically, with so little rancor. *Sugar Cane Alley* could easily have been a bleak and angry film. Instead, it is uplifting; "there's the humiliation of life under the overseer's whip, but there's also the discovery of surprising joys by resilient people."[30] Ultimately, this is a film that resonates with Goulet's conception of development, authentic only when it "aims at the full realization of human capabilities."[31]

Development by Decree

Once peoples living under colonial rule acquired political independence, they faced the question of how to go about the task of development. Most have found that this is a difficult question, far more difficult for many than the ending of colonial rule. Different countries adopted different development strategies. Some remained closely tied to the former metropole, their economies intertwined with those of the Europeans, many of whom remained behind in important commercial and administrative capacities. Others sought to distance themselves from the Western model of development, deliberately choosing approaches that seemed more in keeping with local culture (a representative example would be Tanzania's experiment with African socialism, called *ujamaa* in Swahili).[32] Some states became veritable kleptocracies, their rulers much more concerned with their personal lifestyles and Swiss bank accounts than with their countries' development. In some places, the perceived lack of legitimacy of colonial rule had led to a widespread conviction that it was acceptable, even honorable, to steal from the state; that attitude, unfortunately, sometimes carried over to the postcolonial era.[33] Almost all developing countries have at one time or another experienced the problem of importing technology that has proven inappropriate in the local context, and many have found themselves saddled with dual economies, in which enclaves of modernity, relative affluence, and cosmopolitan tastes exist alongside deep and abiding poverty. Almost all of these problems can be seen on the screen, although rarely as the focus of a film. Instead they are part of the background against which the filmmakers develop other themes that concern them. More interesting are those films in which governments adopt draconian development strategies, in which they seek forcibly to channel their country's development into some ideologically acceptable path and tolerate no dissent.

The countries in which this occurs need not be newly emancipated from colonial rule. In fact, the most familiar cases in recent years of what might be called enforced development have occurred in communist societies, and several of these have been captured on film. Stalin, Mao, and other communist dictators have pursued the development of their countries according to plans that brooked no compromise and left millions of their countrymen and women dead. There may have been worse examples of this approach to development than the one followed by the Khmer Rouge in Cambodia, but that case has been given the most penetrating coverage in a feature film. *The Killing Fields* was discussed at some length in Chapter 4, in terms of whether the international community should have intervened to put a stop to the slaughter.

Yet the Khmer Rouge was not simply or mindlessly killing people. That government had a plan—a development strategy—that called for nothing less than the eradication of all Western and even traditional Buddhist influences, the elimination of all loyalties other than loyalty to the ideals of the revolution, the emptying-out of the cities, and the creation of a simple, regimented agrarian society—in short, nothing less than the creation of new Cambodian men and women. The process whereby the Khmer Rouge sought to produce this result is depicted in horrifying detail in *The Killing Fields*. In perhaps the film's most powerful and unforgettable segment, Dith Pran, the unfortunate interpreter and assistant to an American war correspondent, struggles to survive in a brutal re-education camp and eventually escapes through a swamp literally filled with the bodies of thousands of his countrymen who have been killed because they have not met the standards of this new society. To watch the black-clad custodians of this hell on earth eye their prisoners for the slightest hint of deviation and then summarily haul them out of line and kill them is to understand that development, which we normally think of as a positive thing, can be terribly malevolent in the hands of fanatics.

As noted earlier, development strategy may be geared to the preservation of societal values or, in its preoccupation with modernization, be indifferent to them even if it does not consciously seek to destroy them. But the development strategy of the Khmer Rouge was something else altogether;

it sought the total extirpation of those values. We see something very similar in two other films dealing with the phenomenon of enforced development, *To Live* and *Larks on a String*. The former, by the Chinese director Zhang Yimou, is essentially the story of one Chinese family struggling to survive almost continuous political and social upheaval, from the civil war that brought the communists to power to the horrors of the Cultural Revolution. The focus of the film is on the trials and tribulations of a young couple, Fugui (Ge You) and Jiazhen (Gong Li), yet the difficult situations in which they find themselves as they age are often the consequence of the efforts of the Communist Party to channel Chinese development in a particular ideological direction. Their son is killed in an accident, but his presence at the accident site is due to pressure on even the children to help with smelting in order to reach a production quota in steel so that "in fifteen years we'll catch up with England and surpass America." Their daughter dies following childbirth because the Cultural Revolution is at its height and only untrained students and Red Guards are on duty at the hospital; all of the doctors have been branded as reactionaries and taken away to be re-educated (and ridiculed as they are paraded through the streets). Fugui himself is a lucky survivor. At the beginning of the film he impoverishes his family by gambling away their elegant home, but after the communist victory in the civil war, the man who won it from him is arrested and shot as a counterrevolutionary. Other friends and acquaintances are denounced as "capitalist roaders," and to avoid suspicion that he is a reactionary, Fugui must burn his treasured puppets.

Zhang Yimou is telling us that the human spirit can survive even such dreadful travesties of development as Maoism. Along the way, we are witness to the irony of a wedding between two hopeful young people, each clutching a copy of Mao's little red book, while a band plays and the crowd sings

> Nothing compares to the party's benevolence.
> Chairman Mao is dearer than Father and Mother.
> There's nothing as good as socialism;
> No ocean is deep as class feeling.
> Mao's thought is revolution's treasure;
> Whover opposes it we take as our enemy.

This is truly a sobering movie.

Larks on a String also deals with the efforts of a communist dictatorship to mold a new society. The film, by Czech director Jiri Menzel, was begun during the Prague Spring of 1968 when Alexander Dubcek and his colleagues were seeking to reform the repressive Communist Party regime in Czechoslovakia. When the Soviet Union intervened, the reform movement collapsed and the hard-line government was restored. Menzel's film was banned and was not seen by the public until 1989 when the Czechs rid themselves of communist rule. *Larks on a String* is very different in tone from *To Live*. Menzel lightheartedly mocks the communist authorities and satirizes their efforts to turn a group of bourgeois dissidents into good, class-conscious followers of the party line. The film is set in a junkyard, where some of these dissidents, including a professor (who refused to shred forbidden books), a public prosecutor (who believes in defendants' rights), and a Seventh-Day Adventist (who will not work on Saturdays), are forced to do manual labor. The Communist Party official who oversees the laborers explains that the scrap in the junkyard will be smelted down to make tractors, and then, referring to his "volunteer workers" of bourgeois origin, "we'll also smelt them down."

The junkyard clearly symbolizes communism. It is obvious that these dissidents, who would rather quote Kant than Marx and who are bemused by the phoniness of the system, will not become good communists. They are more interested in the women in an adjacent prison, and some of the movie's charm comes from the efforts of the men and the women to fraternize (the Adventist eventually gets to wed one of the women, and they are reunited at the film's end as co-workers in a coal mine—still prisoners, but still free in spirit). The official prescription for development is subtly satirized throughout the film. A prominently displayed slogan at the junkyard, "Work Is a Matter of Honor," seems just as false as the one at Burpleson Air Force Base in *Dr. Strangelove* announcing that "Peace Is Our Profession." As James Reid Paris has said of Menzel, "he makes us snicker at the inversions of a 'worker's paradise' in which laborers have no say, no personal freedom, and any 'impertinence' results in incarceration."[34]

Poverty and Migration

When most people think about development in the context of international relations, they probably have in mind efforts to overcome the abject poverty that characterizes the lives of perhaps as many as a billion people in what used to be called the Third World. The profile of poverty varies from place to place, but a great many of these people are malnourished, live in wretched housing with minimal sanitation and unsafe drinking water, are illiterate, and have limited life expectancies due to disease and starvation.[35] All countries have known poverty, and some affluent nations still have substantial pockets of poverty. Today, as in times past, peoples living in these conditions may live and die largely unnoticed by the world beyond their village or favela or ghetto. But some will seek to escape those conditions by migrating: sometimes only from farm and village to the city, but also from poor countries to other nations that are believed to hold the promise of a better life.

In John Ford's treatment of John Steinbeck's novel *The Grapes of Wrath,* nature and the Great Depression conspire against the Joad family, who flee the Dust Bowl and try to make a new beginning in California. Although this American classic is ultimately about social justice (and obviously not about international relations), we know that the Dust Bowl was more than a cruel trick of nature—that it was caused by human abuse of the land, just as much as the desertification of the African Sahel can be attributed to misuse by its human inhabitants. The film's treatment of the misery of the Depression reminds us that the great industrial powers have also known terrible poverty; it also makes a strong statement that such poverty need not be man's fate. Another Hollywood film of the same period, the screen adaptation of Pearl Buck's *The Good Earth,* has a very different setting (prerevolutionary China), but its central characters are also farmers whose life becomes a nightmare when a plague of locusts and a severe drought bring famine to the once-bountiful earth. In this case, the story line implies that these disasters are retribution for the wrongful actions of the peasant farmer who is the central figure in the plot; in real life, natural disasters, whatever their cause, can lead to terrible poverty and famine—and to population migration. One of the most famous cases of such migration occurred in the nineteenth century following the potato famine in Ireland, but the twentieth century has seen vastly larger numbers of people on the move for similar reasons, most of them coming from the countries of the Third World and going to neighboring countries in those same regions or to the economically more affluent North.

One of the best films about migration to escape poverty is *The Emigrants,* Jan Troell's epic about a Swedish couple who pull up roots and journey to the United States in the mid-nineteenth century. Karl Oskar and his wife (Max von Sydow and Liv Ullmann) face a never-ending struggle to make a rocky soil and a miserable climate productive, a struggle that keeps the couple always on the edge of despair. After a tragedy in which one of their young children dies, they make the momentous decision to leave the only home they have known and cross the ocean to a land they have only read about. This saga is a poignant reminder not only of how desperate the circumstances are that produce decisions to emigrate, but how hazardous the act of emigrating can be and how much that act, multiplied many times over, changes the face of the countries to which the emigrants move. Today, of course, many of those who leave their homes for economic reasons are transients, seeking jobs that will enable them better to support their families back home. Some are illegal immigrants and thus frequently the source of controversy and sometimes ugly politics in the countries to which they come.

These several patterns of migration and their consequences continue to attract moviemakers. Franco Brusati's *Bread and Chocolate* is a humorous examination of the guest worker phenomenon, as well as a satirical look at class prejudice and the problems of cultural misunderstanding. Stephen Frears's *My Beautiful Laundrette* reminds us that immigrants can be victims of racial prejudice and even violence, while at the same time demonstrating impressive adaptive skills. The latter film will be discussed in Chapter 10, when we turn to the subject of cross-cultural communication. Two films that deal with the subject of poverty-driven illegal immigration into the United States merit attention here, Gregory Nava's *El Norte* and Tony Richardson's *The Border*.

Both of these films highlight efforts of the United States to keep illegal immigrants out of the country. Indeed, the work of the border patrol and the ethics of the border guards, rather than the circumstances that induce the "illegals" to seek entry into the United States, are the focus of *The Border*. Nonetheless, both films have something important to say about development and the push-pull factors that encourage people to seek a better life in another country.

Although the residents of a Guatemalan Indian village in which the action of *El Norte* begins are not living in extreme poverty—the village is actually almost picturesque—they are oppressed by tyrannical landlords much like those in *Sugar Cane Alley*. One of them, who will be killed when the government cracks down on their protest, observes that "for the rich, the peasants are just a pair of arms." In any event, poverty is relative; the members of the family we get to know as the story unfolds have been looking at pictures of America's wonders in old copies of *Good Housekeeping* magazine and marvelling at life in a place where even the poorest people have flush toilets. When their father is killed, a young brother and sister, Enrique and Rosa, decide to go to "the North." The rest of the film is about their journey to California and their subsequent experiences as illegal immigrants, variously joyful, harrowing, and sad.

The segment of *El Norte* that will remain longest in the viewer's mind is the one in which Enrique and Rosa make their illegal crossing of the border through a long, rat-infested sewage tunnel. That, plus the air of danger that pervades Tijuana, where they and many other prospective immigrants seek "coyotes" to help guide them across the border, serves to remind us of the desperation with which so many decide to migrate. The film tells us nothing of the U.S. government's support for the unsavory regime in Guatemala, which fostered the conditions that led to the flight to "the North";[36] nor does it attempt to explore the volatile political issue of how to deal with the problem of illegal immigrants. It does, however, provide arresting snapshots of this particular aspect of the larger develoment problem, giving it an appealing human face.

The Border is also concerned with illegal immigration into the United States from Mexico and Central America, and the would-be immigrants on whom we focus are again a young brother and sister, the latter (played by Elpidia Carrillo) something of a madonna with child. The film has two

main and interrelated themes: the corruption of some of the U.S. border
patrol agents, who conspire with unscrupulous American businessmen in a
veritable slave trade in "wetbacks," and the efforts of one border patrol-
man, disgusted by the sordid business, to do something decent. This man,
Charlie (Jack Nicholson), is determined to reunite Carrillo with her baby,
who has been stolen by slavers intent on selling infants to childless couples. It is a grim and disturbing film, not only because it suggests that government officials may sometimes be corrupt. The young woman and her
baby attract our sympathy, but they only personalize a much larger problem that promises to become more acute, the problem of mass movements
of peoples from the Third World, where populations are exploding, to the
West. As Kishore Mahbubani has written,

> In the year 2000, out of a projected global population of 6.25 billion, 5
> billion will live in the Third World. . . . this population imbalance, ag-
> gravated by the enormous disparity in living standards, will be the fun-
> damental underlying cause of the new sorts of threats facing the Western
> world, ranging from migrations of the poor and disposessed to environ-
> mental damage, drugs, disease, and terrorism.[37]

These impoverished masses, growing at alarming rates and crowding up
against porous Western borders, are an inescapable reminder of interdependence. They also suggest that economic development in the Third
World is a necessary antidote for massive migrations from poor to affluent societies, and hence that the post–Cold War indifference in the West
to the problems of developing countries may be extremely short-sighted.

The Environment and Sustainable Development

The threat of environmental damage cited by Mahbubani is of concern not
only to the Western world. The industrial revolution gave rise to a world
view that Dennis Pirages calls "exclusionist." This world view

> is manifest in the beliefs that human beings exist apart from nature and
> that they are destined to dominate it, that the last four hundred years of
> growth and progress will be followed by another stretch of good fortune,
> and that there are few limits to resource-intensive industrial growth. This
> position, in a sense, exempts human beings from the laws of nature.[38]

This perspective, shaped by a seemingly endless series of scientific and
technological breakthroughs, tended for a long time to make human beings
oblivious to the reality of ecological limits. The environment was mal-
leable and could always be made to serve human needs, or so it seemed.
Although there remains a good deal of uncertainty about the urgency of

some threats to the environment, there is now overwhelming evidence that attention does need to be paid to environmental security. The industrialized countries of the North were slow in coming to this realization, and environmentally destructive development has left a terrible legacy in several places, nowhere more so than in Russia, Ukraine, and other parts of the former Soviet Union. There is a danger that this pattern may be repeated in the South as developing countries industrialize. Moreover, it now appears certain that population growth in the Third World will generate tremendous pressures on available water supplies, crop land, and energy resources. With one-third to nearly one-half the rapidly growing population of many developing countries under the age of fifteen,[39] it is all too easy to imagine governments trying to meet the needs of their people by adopting policies destructive of a fragile and resource-scarce environment. The consequences of such policies are unlikely to be confined to the Third World; the global commons is also at risk in our interdependent world. One commentator illustrates the complexity of the problem this way: "Bangladesh, worried about providing adequate sewerage for 115 million people, is unlikely to care much about global warming; Malawi, with one of the highest birthrates in Africa, is unlikely to accept that the elephant has a greater right to grazing land than its own hungry farmers."[40]

In 1992, the United Nations Conference on the Environment and Development (UNCED) was held in Rio de Janeiro; as the name suggests, it sought to link preservation of the environment with development of Third World countries. The term commonly used for the wedding of these two issues is "sustainable development."[41] If fully realized, sustainable development would presumably relieve countries like Bangladesh and Malawi of the kinds of dilemmas mentioned in the quotation above. UNCED produced a number of prospectively important agreements, although, as with the results of most such global conferences, the agreements are not self-enforcing and no international body has the authority to make states do what they are not prepared to do. Nonetheless, the Rio Summit demonstrated that all countries have a stake in preventing environmental degradation, even as it revealed considerable differences of opinion as to what should be done and when and by whom to make sustainable development possible.

The issue of sustainable development has been explored in a semibiographical film, *The Burning Season,* which makes an unusually strong statement on the subject. This John Frankenheimer film tells the story of Chico Mendes, the famous Brazilian union leader and environmental activist who led the fight for the preservation of the Amazon rain forest and was ultimately assassinated by his enemies. There is probably no environmental issue that has so captured the imagination of the public at large as the destruction of rain forests. It is a prime suspect in global warming, and it bears much of the responsibility for species extinction and the loss of opportunities for scientific research into the medicinal properties of the rich variety of plant life found there. *The Burning Season* hints at these issues, but it is primarily about conflicting development strategies.

Mendes, played in the film by Raul Julia, wants to preserve the rain forest for the rubber tappers. His opponents are developers who want to cut down and burn off the forest to make way for large cattle ranches. The developers, supported by the government, look forward to large earnings from the export of beef and are unconcerned with the displacement of the rubber tappers or with the long-term environmental consequences of their slash-and-burn policies. The debate in the film has been going on, with local variations, in developing countries from Brazil to Indonesia and from Costa Rica to Thailand. It is a debate about how to develop—about how best to earn hard currency to service debts, about where to settle rapidly growing populations and to cultivate the land for food to feed them. Although Frankenheimer quite understandably sides with Mendes, he tends to stack the deck by making all of his adversaries into unscrupulous, violent, and transparently evil men. But Mendes has it right when he tells the cutters with their chain saws that once the land is stripped of trees, the fragile soil—so dependent on the existing natural balance—will soon be useless. He is right again when he reminds the developers—and us—that ultimately development is about people, and that the victims of the government-sponsored switch from forest to pasture, from rubber to beef, will be the people of the Amazon basin.

The Chico Mendes story, as told in this film, reinforces an important point about sustainable development: that it is simply wrong to claim, as so many have, that poor people in developing countries are so preoccupied with their need to develop that they are more than willing to deplete natural resources. This view suggests that poverty itself is inevitably the cause of environmental problems. But, as two social scientists have argued, poverty is very often not the culprit.

> A small number of families in Brazil, Honduras, Zaire, Indonesia, and many other countries control economic and political power and use governmental power for private enrichment. . . . In these countries, the overlapping interests and identities of politicians and business people—commercial logging companies owned by congressional representatives, presidential relatives, and retired military officers—make for powerful lobbies in favor of continued exploitation.[42]

The Burning Season tells essentially the same story. Mendes and his fellow union workers may be poor and they are surely in favor of development, but they are the true environmentalists.

Robert Redford's *The Milagro Beanfield War* hardly qualifies as a major film about development. It is too whimsical (the star, according to several distinguished reviewers, is a large pink pig), and it makes no pretense of making a statement of universal applicability. Although not concerned with environmental issues and otherwise very different in both tone and purpose from *The Burning Season,* it presents interesting parallels with that film that deserve mention. In the first place, it too, shows a conflict between common, mostly poor people on the one hand and big developers with government support on the other. The developers of *Milagro* are building a giant recreation complex in the American southwest, complete with golf course and tennis courts; one of the "little" people, in an act of defiance, diverts water (a scarce commodity in that area, as in many developing countries) from the development project to irrigate his bean field. Now, as in *The Burning Season,* we have a volatile confrontation between the rich who seek profits in modernization and the poor who wish to preserve a more traditional way of life and relationship with the land. We know that if the developers win, property prices and taxes will rise dramatically and the residents of Milagro will have to leave. Here, as in the Frankenheimer film, one of the costs of development may be the dispossession of those most in need of it. *The Milagro Beanfield War* may be a comedy/fantasy, but beneath its light, almost gossamer surface lies a thoughtful message about the complexities of the development process.

Many of the films cited in this chapter have a subtext of cultural or ethnic tensions, suggesting that conflict over development strategy may divide people along cultural, ethnic, or racial lines. It is certainly one of the elements of *The Milagro Beanfield War,* in which the establishment is Anglo and the people of Milagro Hispanic. Perhaps the extreme example of development as a culturally divisive phenomenon is *Where the Green Ants Dream,* a product of the imagination of one of the industry's most idiosyncratic filmmakers, Werner Herzog. In this case, the conflict is between a mining company, which wants to conduct a series of test blasts for uranium in the Australian desert, and a group of Aborigines, who regard the land as sacred and block the tests because disturbing the ants may cause the end of the universe. As one reviewer describes the film, it is "a classic confrontation between ancient myth and modern technology, the spiritual and material, oppressor and oppressed, and finally between those who would preserve life and those who endanger it."[43] There is no question of Herzog's intent. The mining company represents Western economic imperialism, for whom develement means modernization and profits, even at the expense of the traditional values of indigenous peoples, whom the company does not understand and to whom it is indifferent. The Aborigines are, for Herzog, a more purely spiritual people whose function in the film is to prevent the spread of false progress. As with many of the films discussed in this book, what we witness on the screen is not intended to be a balanced debate, but rather the perspective of the screenwriter and the director (Herzog was both in this case). The result, of course, is a simplification of complex issues. But inasmuch as development can pose critical challenges to both nature and culture that are often slighted in film, *Where the Green Ants Dream,* for all of its heavy-handed symbolism, is a welcome stimulus to discussion of this important aspect of interdependence.

Development is ultimately about values as well as economics, and interdependence about cooperative international relations as well as competition for a larger piece of the global pie. Although these issues remain largely on the periphery of the industry's vision, there are a number of films that touch on them and offer insights into their complexity and increasing importance for a small planet.

Notes

1. Kennedy, *Preparing for the Twenty-First Century*, p. 127.
2. Maull, "Germany and Japan," p. 98.
3. Ikenberry, "The Myth of Post–Cold War Chaos," p. 81.
4. See Mearsheimer, "Why We Shall Soon Miss the Cold War."
5. Ikenberry, "The Myth of Post–Cold War Chaos," pp. 79–80.
6. Fukuyama, "The End of History?" p. 4. Fukuyama has developed the thesis of this article into a book, *The End of History and the Last Man.*
7. Fukuyama, *"The End of History?"* p. 16.
8. *Ibid.,* p. 18.
9. Hirsh and Henry, "The Unraveling of Japan Inc.," p. 12.
10. Hoffmann, *Primacy or World Order*, pp. 123–24.
11. Hare, *A Map of the World*, p. 40. Reprinted by permission of Faber and Faber, Ltd.
12. Kennedy, *Preparing for the Twenty-First Century*, p. 47.
13. *Ibid.,* p. 51.
14. Of the 100 largest economic units in the world as of the early 1990s, nearly half were MNCs. General Motors ranked twenty-fourth, ahead of Indonesia, Turkey, Argentina, South Africa, and Poland, among many other states. Among the other major MNCs in terms of annual sales were Royal Dutch Shell, Exxon, Ford, Toyota, IBM, General Electric, British Petroleum, Mobil, Hitachi, and Philip Morris. See Hughes, *Continuity and Change in World Politics*, p. 360 (data assembled from *Fortune,* the World Bank, and the U.S. Central Intelligence Agency).
15. See review by Canby, "Rising Sun," C1:4.
16. See review by Turan, "Plot Twists Cast Shadows," F1:2.
17. See Kennedy, *Preparing for the Twenty-First Century*, Ch. 5.
18. For a discussion of the problem of transnational bribery, see Leiken, "Controlling the Global Corruption Epidemic."
19. Ironically, Japanese incursion into the U.S. automobile market has contributed both to an increase in the number of Americans working in the auto industry and to the improvement in the quality of Detroit's cars; these trends help to explain why Japan-bashing is considerably more muted in the United States than it was only a few years ago. See Hirsh and Henry, "The Unraveling of Japan, Inc.," p. 16.
20. Goulet, "An Ethical Model for the Study of Values," p. 206.
21. *Ibid.,* p. 205.
22. *Ibid.,* p. 210, 215.
23. See Korten, *Getting to the 21st Century.* Korten defines development as "a process by which the members of a society increase their personal and institutional

capacities to mobilize and manage resources to produce sustainable and justly distributed improvements in their quality of life consistent with their own aspirations" (p. 67).

24. Krasner, *Structural Conflict*, pp. 82–83.

25. Krasner distinguishes between relational power and meta-power behavior in his *Structural Conflict*, p. 14. "Relational power behavior refers to efforts to maximize values within a given set of institutional structures; meta-power behavior refers to efforts to change the institutions themselves," i.e., to change the rules of the game.

26. Hoffmann, *Duties Beyond Borders*, p. 146.

27. *Ibid.*, p. 147.

28. "Terms of trade" refers to the ratio of the prices of goods a country sells to the prices of goods it buys. Raul Prebisch, the distinguished Argentine economist, advanced the argument, widely accepted among critics of the liberal economic order, that developing countries faced long-term deterioration of terms of trade as prices of their primary exports declined relative to prices of manufactured goods they imported.

29. Sheehan, "Sugar Cane Alley," p. 511. Joseph Zobel's novel (on which the film was based) is available in English as *Black Shack Alley* from Lynne Rienner Publishers.

30. *Ibid.*

31. Goulet, "An Ethical Model for the Study of Values," p. 206.

32. *Ujamaa* was primarily the vision of Tanzania's former president Julius Nyerere. In the countryside, peasants were forced to resettle in "Ujamaa villages," where they would live and farm together for the collective good and which would give them greater access to government services—schools, clinics, clean water, etc.

33. This is a point Ali Mazrui makes in "A Garden of Eden in Decay," one of the episodes in his provocative series for television, *The Africans.*

34. Paris, *Classic Foreign Films,* p. 245.

35. To put such poverty in perspective, it is useful to contrast the conditions in developing countries with those in developed countries. John Rourke contrasts the relative deprivation of Nigerians with Japanese. His data show not only that per capita GDP is $280 in Nigeria as opposed to $34,600 in Japan, but that infant mortality is twenty times higher in Nigeria, and only 40 percent of Nigerians enjoy safe drinking water (versus 99 percent in Japan). Rourke, *International Politics,* pp. 424–25.

36. For a critique of the U.S. role in Guatemala, see Jonas, "Dangerous Liaisons," pp. 144–60.

37. Mahbubani, "The West and the Rest," p. 6.

38. Pirages, *Global Technopolitics*, p. 8.

39. It has been estimated that roughly 45 percent of the total population of Africa is under the age of fifteen, while the percentage in Asia and Latin America is greater than 30 percent in both cases. See Cairncross, "Environmental Pragmatism," p. 38.

40. *Ibid.*, p. 46.

41. Sustainable development has been defined as an approach to economic growth that endeavors "to ensure that development meets the needs of the present without compromising the abilities of future generations to meet their own needs." See World Commission on Environment and Development, *Our Common Future,* p. 8.

42. Broad and Cavanagh, "Beyond the Myths of Rio," p. 66.

43. Review by K. Thomas, "Myth vs. Technology Down Under," Part 6, 7:1.

9

Ethics and International Law

The picture of international relations that emerges on most of the pages of this book is one of ubiquitous confict, much of it violent. This is not surprising in view of two salient facts. The first is that it takes place in an international system that knows no authority higher than that of the state and hence can be described as anarchical. The second is that films about international relations usually deal with conflict situations. The world is clearly not a Hobbesian world of the war of all against all, but it certainly seems to be characterized by Machiavellian statecraft. In other words, statesmen must do whatever they believe is necessary for the security and well-being of their own country, not that of an imagined international community. As Stanley Hoffmann has argued, "Raison d'etat is not an abdication of morality, but the proper morality of statecraft."[1] Is there room in such a world for ethical international politics? For international law? The answer is a qualified "Yes," and the attention given to these questions in films, often obliquely, argues for the inclusion in this book of a chapter on law and morality in international relations.

We often hear the states of the world described collectively as an international community, but the phrase is misleading. "A community of vocabulary is not the same thing as a community of values."[2] However, the absence of a true international community does not mean that states have no common interests or that ethical international relations are impossible. As noted in Chapter 1, the international system is also an international society. To quote again Hedley Bull's definition, an international society "exists when a group of states, conscious of certain common interests and common values, form a society in the sense that they conceive of themselves as bound by a common set of rules in their relations with one another, and share in the working of common institutions."[3] These rules create obligations to respect each other's sovereignty, to honor agreements, and to observe limits on the use of force against each other; states jointly participate in the various institutions necessary (if far from sufficient) for the effective functioning of these rules.

In effect, so this argument goes, there is some order in international relations, however imperfect and fragile, and that order exists because states *do* have some common interests and have developed rules and institutions to serve those interests. These shared interests may reflect common values, although there is abundant evidence that we are far from what might be called a common moral culture in international relations. Common interests also exist because all states, at least some of the time, are concerned about the consequences "of unrestricted violence, of the instability of agreements or of the insecurity of their independence or sovereignty."[4] A version of the golden rule would appear to operate in the relations of states—states have a common interest in behaving with restraint and observing basic rules of coexistence because they want other states to do so as well.

These common interests that make it possible to speak of an international society do not, of course, prevent war, ensure that treaties will be honored, or otherwise deter states from behaving in self-interested ways that are harmful to other states. Common interests do, nonetheless, exist and they have led to the formulation of rules ranging from informal "rules of the game," such as no first use of nuclear weapons, to formal multilateral treaties, such as those proscribing genocide and governing the right of innocent passage through maritime straits. Moreover, states have developed institutions to make the rules of international society more effective—institutions that run the gamut from informal arrangements such as the balance of power to formal organizations such as the United Nations and the World Trade Organization. Bull refers to these institutions as both expressions of states' willingness to collaborate and a means of sustaining that collaboration.[5]

Within the sovereign state, the preeminent institution for making and enforcing rules is the government. In international society there is no government. This absence of government leaves the member states as the principal institutions of international society; they have the primary responsibility for making such rules as there are, for enforcing them if they can, and for giving them whatever legitimacy they enjoy—that is, for seeing that the rules are not simply platitudes but reasonably effective guides to state behavior.

This absence of a central government leads some students of international relations to deny the existence of an international society. For them, it is a delusion to speak of rules and law when discussing international relations or the making of foreign policy. Power is unrestrained in the absence of a world-wide authority; although prudent statesmanship may achieve a certain global stability, wars will inevitably be fought "because wars are the way in which a world of multiple sovereignties transacts its basic business."[6]

This debate between those who subscribe to the concept of an international society and those who do not frequently takes the form of a debate about the existence, or at least the efficacy, of international law. Perhaps inevitably, this debate often turns on the issue of enforcement. Within states, the government enforces the law. It can do so because it possesses an overwhelming preponderance of force, and because it also enjoys a monopoly on the legitimate use of force. Internationally, there is no such government, much less one possessing a preponderance of force and enjoying a monopoly of the legitimate use of force. This inescapable fact confronts us with "the classic paradox of international law: with no serious police, and courts that depend on voluntary compliance, international law is as powerful as any national legal system with no police or courts would be."[7]

This deficiency of international law is, for many students of the subject, far from fatal. They would remind us that within states laws are obeyed less because individuals fear the police and the criminal justice system than because it is in their interest to do so—compliance is the norm, and the use of force by the police relatively rare. Similarly, states generally comply with international law; when they do not, they frequently deny that they have violated it or cite special circumstances that justify their actions (the tribute, some might say, that vice pays to virtue). As Bull argues so cogently, "The importance of international law does not rest on the willingness of states to abide by its principles to the detriment of their interests, but in the fact that they so often judge it in their interests to conform to it."[8] From this perspective, the absence of centralized enforcement capability does not make international law ineffectual, much less disprove its existence. The answer to the question, "Who is to enforce international law," is that the member states of international society themselves enforce it.

International society is still very limited, however, not so much in scope as in depth. It remains shallow; as Hoffmann argues, "the drama of international politics is that there is, as of now, no generally accepted alternative to Machiavellian statecraft."[9] According to those of an extreme realist persuasion, what ultimately matters in international relations is not that there is sometimes a mutuality of interests among states (arising out of concerns for reciprocity, complementarity, and predictability in their relations), but "that in the absence of self-restraint, power, in international affairs, is limited only by countervailing power."[10]

If realists are inclined to treat international law as merely epiphenomenal, they are even more dismissive of international morality, arguing that ethical foreign policy is impossible; if a state should try to conduct its relations with other states according to moral principles, the result would be an invitation to national disaster. Hans Morgenthau, the quintessential post–World War II realist, argued that

> the claim to universality which inspires the moral code of one particular group is incompatible with the identical claim of another group. . . . Thus, carrying their idols before them, the nationalistic masses of our time meet in the international arena, each group convinced that it executes

the mandate of history, that it does for humanity what it seems to do for itself, and that it fulfills a sacred mission ordained by providence, however defined. Little do they know that they meet under an empty sky from which the gods have departed.[11]

Law and morality are, of course, quite different. There is, for example, a well-established obligation in international law to respect the diplomatic immunity of properly accredited representatives from one state to another. Even if those representatives commit egregious offenses against the laws of the host state, they are not incarcerated, although their government may be asked to recall them. Everyone is familiar with stories of diplomats who take advantage of their immunity and regularly break local traffic and parking laws, while local officials gnash their teeth in frustration. Problems such as these are the price governments are prepared to pay in the interest of stability and reciprocity in the day-to-day conduct of interstate relations. When diplomatic immunity is violated, as it was so conspicuously in 1979 when the government of Iran conspired in the seizure of the American embassy and diplomatic staff in Teheran, the international community is quick to invoke international law against the offending state. In the Iranian hostage case, the International Court of Justice spoke out unequivocally (and unanimously), condemning this violation of one of the most basic elements of the law of nations.[12] A case can be made that observance of diplomatic immunity is also the moral or ethical thing to do, but that is really beside the point.

Duties Beyond Borders

For purposes of comparison, take the case of extreme poverty, in which thousands are dying every day from starvation and the diseases that afflict the severely malnourished. This is the kind of situation in which Western newspaper editorials and op ed pieces frequently seek to convince their governments that they have an obligation to step in and provide the assistance that will stop the dying. Those governments, wrestling with competing claims on their budgets, agonize over their obligation to help. But that obligation, if one exists, is moral and not legal. There are very few who would argue that international law requires the more affluent states to provide assistance to those states trying to cope with these human tragedies.

Or perhaps civil order breaks down; in the resulting chaos, various ethnic groups or tribes or clans slaughter each other in appalling numbers. In such situations innocent civilians are usually among the principal victims, their plight exacerbated as the combatants callously deprive them of food and medicine. The United Nations Security Council debates what to do, as do individual states with the resources to cope with the interrelated crises of violence and famine. Yet international law does not require that the international community respond, although it may provide legal justification for intervention should the will exist to take some sort of action. Whether there is a moral obligation to intervene is, once again, another story.

Some have argued that Western countries have a moral obligation to provide substantially more assistance to developing countries than they have done in the past (the duties enumerated in the Charter of Economic Rights and Duties of States are largely the duties of the North), asserting that that obligation has acquired legal as well as moral standing.[13] The rationale for this position is that resolutions of the UN General Assembly proclaiming these obligations, when adopted by overwhelming majorities and reiterated year after year, eventually achieve the status of law. Positivists would argue instead that international law is determined by state behavior—what states do, not what they say they should do. Western countries have not only fallen far short of meeting the targets set for them in these resolutions, but have frequently made it clear that they are in no way bound to meet those targets (or, in some cases, even to accept the principles upon which they are based).[14] International law is real enough, of course; it is simply limited in its scope and reach. The body of such law is slowly growing, via the negotiation and ratification of treaties and conventions, the customary practices of states, and the decisions of international and even national tribunals. It is possible at any given time to produce an inventory of international law—that is, to list the legal obligations of states in their dealings with each other.

But to do the same for international ethics would be impossible. Law presumably is not situational. If it exists, states are obligated to comply; if some of them do not, that fact does not negate the existence of law, it only demonstrates that enforcement mechanisms are lacking and that states can violate the law and escape punishment. Ethics *are* in fact situational, however, whether we like it or not. One state may feel a moral obligation to dispatch aid to a drought-stricken Ethiopia or a civil war–ravaged Rwanda, while another may not. Or the former may feel a moral obligation to provide aid to Ethiopia but not to Chad, or to Rwanda but not to Sudan, even if the situation in Chad and Sudan is objectively very similar to that in Ethiopia and Rwanda. Moreover, there is very likely to be disagreement over the existence of a moral obligation to extend aid. That debate will usually turn on the question of whether it is in the country's interest to provide aid, not whether there is a moral obligation to do so. Inasmuch as humanitarian intervention is almost certain to be costly, some people will oppose it—not just because it is not in the national interest, but because, in their view, it is immoral to send money overseas when there are people at home whose needs are also great. (Relative need is hard to assess, and in any event the statesman's highest duty is presumably to his own state and its people.)

Almost everyone would acknowledge that no matter how worthy the goal, a policy cannot be characterized as moral if the means used to achieve it are evil. The problem is that reasonable people can and do disagree as to what constitutes immoral means. There is still a great debate as to whether the means used to end the war in the Pacific in 1945—the atomic bombing of Hiroshima and Nagasaki—were moral or not. Difficult as it may be in specific situations to determine whether ends and means are moral, there may be an even more difficult moral issue. What if intervention to help the people of another country turns out to cost the lives of some of those providing the assistance? What if aid only serves to strengthen the grip of a despotic regime on its people? Are those policies still moral? We are now in the realm of what Stanley Hoffmann has called the ethics of consequences, to which we have already referred in Chapter 4. Much of the discussion of international morality focuses on the ethics of intentions, on whether the end sought is moral; helping desperate people to escape from terrible poverty or the horrors of civil strife are quite obviously moral ends. But there is always the danger that foreign policy based on an ethics of intentions will become in practice a tyranny of benevolence. Even if it does not, good intentions may still have immoral results for those one is seeking to help, for one's own state and its interests, for the larger international community. The bad consequences of good intentions may be foreseeable but ignored by those who make policy because their vision is limited by their worldview or by their preoccupation with domestic considerations. Or they may be unforeseeable simply "because of the huge political handicap of uncertainty."[15]

Given the nature of the international system, states typically have only limited moral choice in the conduct of their foreign policies. Stanley Hoffmann summarizes the problem this way:

> The closer the international system is to a jungle, the closer we are to the floor of survival, the less opportunity for choice we have, the more values we have to sacrifice, the more plausible the statesman's claim of necessity becomes, the more we will be tempted to accept "the morality of struggle"—and either resign ourselves to endless competition, or put a moral dressing on it, in either case restricting our duties to our own community and, at most, to its supporters or clients. On the contrary, the more moderate the system is, the greater the range of moral choice for all of us, the greater the possibility for the statesman to look at the world in terms other than us vs. them.[16]

The film industry has produced many films that raise questions about the ethical content of particular policies. Some do so quite deliberately; they are produced and directed by people who have a strong point of view and who make it quite clear that policies depicted on the screen are right or wrong. Other films are more or less neutral. Indeed, the makers of a film may not even have given much thought to the question of whether actions taken (or not taken) are moral. We are invited to lose ourselves in the action, or in the contest of wills, or in the fate of individuals, but not to wrestle with the question of whether the behavior of a government or its agents is ethical. Whether the film is ultimately judgmental or not, the viewer is entitled to ask hard questions: Is the decision to intervene on behalf of a particular government or an insurgency morally justifiable? Is the way a war is being waged moral? Is a policy supporting development at the expense of the environment or of important cultural values ethical? Although in some films the director has sought to answer such questions, we need not accept his or her position, but rather treat it as a challenge to debate. And in other films that do not concern themselves directly with the ethical dimensions of international relations, that challenge is still present, if less obviously so.

If the viewer is to consider questions such as those posed above about the place of ethics in international relations, it is useful to develop some criteria to raise the debate above the level of personal prejudice. Among those whose thoughts on these matters might be consulted are figures as diverse as Machiavelli and Kant; Stanley Hoffmann, who has already been cited several times, has provided a literate and balanced discussion of the issue, and one might also usefully peruse the annual volume of a thoughtful journal devoted exclusively to this subject, *Ethics and International Affairs*. It is almost certain, however, that not everyone will agree on whether the actions taken (or not taken) in any film about international relations are moral. Such is the hard and seemingly durable reality of conflicting moral values in a world often referred to as an international community but which still falls short of actually being one.

Hiroshima and the Atomic Bomb

A dramatic example is the atomic bombing of Hiroshima and Nagasaki at the end of World War II. After years of terrible warfare, the world was indeed close to Hoffmann's jungle, where opportunity for choice was presumably minimal, the statesman's claim of necessity most plausible. Yet few choices have occasioned so much anguished—and often angry—debate as Truman's decision to use the A-bomb; more than fifty years after the event, scholars, statesmen, and students of international relations are still arguing about it. Although the debate typically turns on the question of whether the use of the bomb was necessary to bring the war in the Pacific to an end without the loss of unacceptably large numbers of American lives, sooner or later we find ourselves in a debate over the morality of the bombing. Two films relevant to this subject are *Fat Man and Little Boy* and *Black Rain*. The former, discussed briefly in Chapter 6 on decisionmaking, is an American film, directed by Roland Joffe, which concerns the Manhattan Project that produced the atomic bomb. *Black Rain,* by the Japanese director Shohei Imamura, is set in that country in the years following the bombing and shows ordinary people trying to cope with the effects of radiation sickness.

In neither of these films is the primary purpose to brand the U.S. decision to use the bomb as immoral. Neither film is overtly judgmental. In fact, neither film is about either the decision to drop the bombs on Hiroshima and Nagasaki or the actual bombing (although *Black Rain* does devote a few minutes to the attack, that footage is more in the nature of background for the story that follows). In *Fat Man and Little Boy,* the war is still raging and it has already become, for all practical purposes, total war; the concept of noncombatant immunity had become, even before Hiroshima, a casualty of the massive air attacks in both European and Pacific theaters that had (quite intentionally) killed huge numbers of civilians. In the film the atomic bomb is still under development, its lethality has never been tested, and it has not yet acquired the terrible stigma it carries today. In *Black Rain,* the war is over; the bomb has achieved its purpose—the surrender of Japan—and the citizens of that country are trying to resume a normal life in the wake of war's destruction. Among the legacies of the war is radiation sickness, as people who were in or near the target cities give names and faces to the abstract calculations of the scientists at Los Alamos. In effect, these two films frame the momentous decision to launch the nuclear age at Hiroshima.

With the possible exception of Japan's military leaders in 1945, few would argue that the U.S. objective—to shorten the war and save lives—was immoral. President Truman and those of his advisers who counseled use of the bomb were, of course, thinking in terms of *American* lives. Although there was some postwar talk to the effect that the decision was taken to save the lives of as many as half a million Americans, military leaders in the United States never believed that the cost of an invasion would exceed 25,000 to 46,000 lives.[17] Nonetheless, those are substantial numbers, and Truman and his advisers

> did not have to be reminded of the danger of a political backlash in America if they did not use the bomb and the invasions became necessary. Even if they had wished to avoid its use—and they did not—the fear of later public outrage spurred by the weeping parents and loved ones of dead American boys might well have forced American leaders to drop the A-bomb on Japan.[18]

The question that still generates heated debate, however, is whether the means employed to achieve that end were immoral. Many believe they were, and not only in Japan. It has been argued that other means, presumably less immoral, were available but not pursued, including dropping the demand for unconditional surrender, continuing heavy conventional bombing, and waiting for the Soviet Union to enter the war. It has also been argued that the bomb should have first been dropped in a demonstration with Japanese observers present, or that the Japanese should have been forewarned so that civilians could be evacuated. Even many of those who believe that the attack on Hiroshima was necessary are less sure about the morality of the second bomb on Nagasaki. At a minimum, those who have challenged the morality of using the A-bomb view the means as disproportionate to the ends sought.

Physicists involved in the Manhattan Project whose opinions on the use of the bomb were sought did ultimately raise moral questions; this is a point made clear in *Fat Man and Little Boy,* although not explored in any depth (if it had been, the film's implicit critique of the bombings would have been much stronger). One of these physicists, Arthur Compton, observed that "It introduces the question of mass slaughter, really for the first time in history. It carries with it the question of possible radioactive poison over the area bombed. Essentially, the question of the use . . . of the new weapon carries much more serious implications than the introduction of poison gas."[19]

The comparison with poison gas reminds us that as science and technology make possible ever more terrible means of killing, so do they generate pressures to outlaw particular forms of warfare. Unfortunately, once the genie is out of the bottle, it is very difficult to put it back. In June 1945, the scientists who had questioned the use of the A-bomb quickly swallowed their misgivings. A special advisory panel including Compton and J. Robert Oppenheimer, director of the Los Alamos laboratory, announced that "We see no acceptable alternative to direct military use."[20] As noted above, in any assessment of the morality of a particular policy, the ethics of consequences must be considered. Inasmuch as no nuclear weapon had been used before, its full destructive consequences were necessarily matters of scientific conjecture. But Oppenheimer and his colleagues were well aware that both blast and radiation damage would be dramatic. *Fat Man and Little Boy* leaves the viewer with no doubt on this score, particularly with respect to the effects of nuclear radiation. In one of the film's dramatic "highlights," one of the scientists at Los Alamos dies a horrible death from the effects of a lab accident with radioactive material. Such a tragedy did in fact occur, although the film takes liberties with its timing in order to make it a catalyst for second thoughts among some of the scientists. So the immediate consequences were, at least in general terms, foreseeable. Indeed, they were the reason the bomb was developed and used.

We see these consequences in *Black Rain.* The viewer is asked to follow the lives of several people who survived the blast of the atomic bomb dropped on Hiroshima only to develop radiation sickness later. Some of these people inevitably die, and part of the tragedy is that the families who are the focus of the story must live their lives with terrible uncertainty about their own futures. Life, in effect, is a kind of living death, posing the question whether those who survived the bomb were in fact more fortunate than those who did not. This is a quiet film, and not an obviously angry one, but it does help to pose the question of whether the use of the A-bomb was moral. It may be argued, of course, that dying later from the effects of radiation is no worse than dying instantly from incineration, or that the atomic bombing of Hiroshima was no worse than the firebombing of Tokyo. From this perspective, what is immoral is, if not war itself, at least the use of weapons intended to kill noncombatants or which will almost certainly have the killing of noncombatants as a major side effect.

Other consequences were less foreseeable. The Truman administration had hoped that the attack would intimidate the Soviet Union, making it more cooperative in the postwar era. The result was, of course, exactly the opposite. The use of the bomb raised the curtain on the nuclear age, stimulating a frightening arms race with potentially deadly consequences not only for armies in the field but for humankind generally—an arms race that has been the focus of many movies, a fair number of which speculate on the nature of life on earth after a nuclear war. Following the saturation bombing campaigns, the Holocaust, and other wartime atrocities, Hiroshima and Nagasaki marked the end of any pretense that the old morality that sought to spare the lives of noncombatants had survived World War II. On the other hand, it could be argued that one of the consequences of the bombing has been an inoculation, born of the terrible lesson of August 1945, against the further use of nuclear weapons in combat.

Law and Morality in War and Deterrence

Discussion of the use of the atomic bomb against Japan—dramatic evidence of the abandonment of the principle of noncombatant immunity—inevitably calls to mind the "just war" doctrine, which, while acknowledging that war could not be prohibited, sought to impose restraints on both the ends and means of war.[21] According to this doctrine, first developed by St. Augustine and medieval scholastics, war was to be fought only for just causes (*jus ad bellum*). Thus wars were just when fought in self-defense or to punish wrongdoers (presumably in accordance with God's will). In the conduct of a just war, the means employed were to be proportional to the war's objectives and noncombatants were to enjoy immunity (*jus in bello*). It was understood that noncombatants might be killed, but their deaths were to be unintended. As Stanley Hoffmann demonstrates so persuasively in his analysis of the role of ethics in the use of force,[22] the just war doctrine is difficult to apply in the modern era, when ideology has raised the stakes in so many conflicts and technology has produced such destructive weapons.

Who is to say when the cause of war is just? The claim of self-defense is commonly invoked, the UN Charter's Article 51 providing justification for the claim. But it is a claim frequently abused by states that are not actually resisting an armed attack or pre-empting what is believed to be an imminent attack by a powerful adversary (for example, Israel's act of anticipatory self-defense in 1967). Thus the Soviet Union's invasions of Hungary and Czechoslovakia in 1956 and 1968 and the American invasions of Grenada and Panama in 1983 and 1989 were not moral simply because of an assertion of a right of self-defense.[23] These cases and others demonstrate the problems inherent in the application of the concept of *jus ad bellum*.

Similarly, if one accepts the view that the spread of international communism was an evil threatening not only the United States but the greater international social order—as the U.S. government did when it intervened in Vietnam and as General Ripper did when he launched the attack on the Soviet Union in *Dr. Strangelove*—would such a view make those wars just? Quite a few of the filmmakers who brought the Vietnam War to the screen, as well as Stanley Kubrick in the case of *Dr. Strangelove*, certainly did not think so. World War II is a different case; the war against Hitler's Third Reich and the Japanese militarists is very widely regarded as just, whereas the Vietnam War and many others since 1945, including the Soviet Union's aggression in Afghanistan, are far more controversial. But what does the view that the war against German and Japanese aggression in the 1940s was just say about the conduct of that war, about *jus in bello?*

> When people throw millions of men into the battlefield, and suffer enormous losses, and have to give themselves reasons for the horror, the stakes escalate; if you apply the principle that means are just as long as they are proportional to the stakes, once the stakes become defined as nothing less than the survival of mankind, or the victory of a sacred cause, the proportionality of means becomes a rather sinister joke. The best example is the dropping of the atomic bomb on Japan.[24]

No definitive answer to the question of whether the atomic bombing of Hiroshima and Nagasaki was morally justifiable is likely for precisely the reason alluded to in this quotation. The same is true of conventional bombing of the kind employed by Germany, Britain, and the United States in World War II; the overwhelming majority of the victims might have been noncombatants, but it can be argued that their deaths were largely unintended. (If they were intended, most of those killed were factory workers engaged in producing the sinews of war and hence were not really noncombatants.) The killing of large numbers of noncombatants by such raids might have brought the war to a quicker end, saving even more lives and qualifying as the lesser evil.

However one judges the morality of these aerial attacks, nuclear or conventional, the conduct of war has certain moral restraints. Indeed, some of these elements of *jus in bello* would appear to have acquired the status of international law, even if enforcement is at best uneven. It *is* unethical—and even unlawful—for soldiers on the ground to kill even one noncombatant whom they encounter while on patrol. Perpetrators of such battlefield crimes are clearly violating the laws of war, as Colonel Calley did at My Lai in the infamous Vietnam case. It has been argued that in modern wars it is virtually impossible to distinguish between combatants and noncombatants, and that the soldier who is overly meticulous about the distinction stands a good chance of being killed by a seemingly innocent child of ten or twelve. But the moral and legal position is clear enough, and is perhaps best illustrated in Brian DePalma's *Casualties of War.* Following a harrowing firefight, an American patrol led by Sergeant Meserve (Sean Penn) abducts a young Vietnamese girl from her village; the soldiers take turns raping her and eventually kill her. Whether the viewer is familiar with the laws of war or not, it is obvious that the behavior of Meserve and his colleagues is highly immoral. It also happens to be illegal, as the soliders discover when they are reported by a member of the platoon, Private Ericksson (Michael J. Fox), who did not participate in the rape but who has a troubled conscience because he did not intervene in a timely way to save the girl. Ericksson represents the effort to preserve some semblance of morality, even in the midst of a dehumanizing war, and he discovers that it is a difficult, even dangerous, mission. Meserve and the others are eventually tried and convicted by a U.S. military tribunal, reminding us that maintaining some standards of international morality and enforcing international law in a decentralized system depend primarily on the will of the member states themselves.

Other elements of *jus in bello* have been treated in films. One is the requirement that prisoners not be killed. The greatest blot upon Henry V's remarkable victory over the French at Agincourt was his order that French prisoners be killed. This order was given, historians tell us, because he was mistakenly under the impression that the prisoners were about to attack the English baggage train. Whether his action was justified or not, it is glossed over in the films based on Shakespeare's play, as it is in the play itself (Shakespeare wanted to lionize Henry, not depict him as a war criminal). The killing of prisoners activates the plot in Bruce Beresford's *Breaker Morant.* This film is set during the Boer War and focuses on the trial and execution of Australian soldiers who are responsible for killing prisoners. Beresford takes pains to demonstrate the anguished mental state of the Aussies (Edward Woodward and Bryan Brown), who are understandably outraged at the deaths of some of their own colleagues. He also invites sympathy for the men on trial by having them defended by a sincere but woefully inexperienced attorney. *Breaker Morant* belongs to that group of films like *Gallipoli* and *Paths of Glory* intended to condemn a system in which men in the ranks are made scapegoats by morally deficient superior officers. But like *Casualties of War,* it asks us to reflect on the paradox of trying to maintain ethical standards in the context of dehumanizing warfare.

So does *Lawrence of Arabia* in a gut-wrenching scene in the latter part of the film. Lawrence's Arab forces are on their way to Damascus when they encounter a Turkish column that has just slaughtered the inhabitants of a small desert village. Deeply shaken by the sight of the carnage at the village well, Lawrence yields to the entreaties of some of his men and, crying "Take no prisoners," leads them in a mercilessly savage attack on the column that ends only when all the Turks have been killed. In context, this act clearly violates *jus in bello*. The Turks, who pose no threat to Lawrence's troops, could easily have been taken prisoner or simply bypassed for the more important prize, Damascus. If what we witness on screen is not enough to impress the immorality of Lawrence's behavior upon us, the director has an American journalist who has been covering the war and reporting Lawrence's exploits come upon him, elbow-deep in blood in the aftermath of the massacre, and say in disgust "Oh, you rotten man. Let me take your rotten bloody picture for the rotten bloody newspapers."

Scenes that raise the issue of unethical conduct in the course of combat are common to a great many films, including *Apocalypse Now* and *Battle of Algiers*. In the former, the relevant scene is also one of the film's most famous, in which Colonel Kilgore (Robert Duvall) leads his squadron of helicopter gunships in a napalm attack on a Vietnamese village. This is not just one more instance of the deliberate killing of noncombatants. Kilgore, who launches his attack to the amplified strains of Wagner's "Ride of the Valkyries," derives obvious pleasure from the destruction of the village by fire ("I love the smell of napalm in the morning"). This is an unambiguously immoral moment in an ambiguously immoral war. In *Battle of Algiers,* we witness two bombings, one by the French and one by the Algerians, that kill many innocent people, including women and children (see Chapter 3 for a more detailed commentary). In both cases the explosives are carefully planted in places where they are sure to kill noncombatants as they go about their daily lives. The film makes no judgment about the means employed by the two sides in this war for independence, but the viewer is left with yet one more piece of visual evidence that when the stakes are high—as they were for both sides in this conflict—it is very difficult to maintain restraint on means.

A more complex debate surrounds the morality of nuclear deterrence. Since August 1945, nuclear weapons have been "used" primarily for purposes of deterrence (prestige or status is also a rationale for their possession); the fact that there has been no nuclear war or even a conventional war between states possessing nuclear weapons (other than by proxy) suggests that nuclear deterrence has worked and must therefore be regarded as moral both as to intent and consequences. It cannot be proved, of course, that the absence of war between the United States and the Soviet Union was due to the mutually perceived threat of nuclear annihilation.[25] In any event, critics of nuclear deterrence are less concerned with the nuclear wars that have not occurred than they are with the terrible consequences of such wars if deterrence should fail. In this view, nuclear war is so inherently immoral that, given the uncertainties of command, control, and decisionmaking under the stress of crisis—not to mention the possibilities of accident or unauthorized acts of terrorism—nuclear deterrence must be regarded as immoral. This is a conclusion with which many viewers of *Dr. Strangelove* or its more sober twin *Fail Safe* might well agree. In both films, nuclear weapons exist for purposes of deterrence, but in both cases deterrence fails. The reasons are different, but the results are more or less the same.

Carol Cohn has presented an interesting and troubling perspective on this issue.[26] She deconstructs the lexicon of the nuclear strategists and finds that they have developed a sanitized vocabulary of euphemisms that mask the horrors of nuclear war and protect those who are trained to deter (*and* fight) it from the necessity of living with the awful knowledge of those horrors. Thus, "countervalue" attacks are those aimed at cities and that will kill hundreds of thousands of civilians, "collateral damage" refers to civilian casualties caused by attacks on military targets, and "clean bombs" are those nuclear weapons that kill by blast rather than by radiation. The point, of course, is that if nuclear war begins to look so unexceptional, it will be that much easier to take the steps that will lead to such a war. The point is illustrated by General Turgidson in Kubrick's *Dr. Strangelove*. Turgidson (George C. Scott) is explaining to the American president what the country's options are after a psychotic general has launched an unauthorized attack on the Soviet Union. He urges the president to take advantage of the crisis to "hit the Russians with every thing we've got," claiming that the United States would survive the resulting war "with only modest and acceptable civilian casualties." When the president demurs, the general elaborates: "I don't say we wouldn't get our hair mussed. But I do say no more than ten to twenty million killed, tops, depending on the breaks." Thus is nuclear war reduced to the level of just another war, its unique horrors made commonplace. Cohn and Kubrick would no doubt insist that nuclear deterrence is immoral.

Another issue that raises a question about the place of morality in international relations is one of domestic politics (and hence of domestic morality), but it has arisen in the context of war and merits a few words in this book. In 1942, following the Japanese attack on Pearl Harbor and the beginning of the long and bitter Pacific war between the United States and Japan, the U.S. government interned large numbers of Nisei, or American citizens of Japanese descent, moving them from their homes in the

Pacific states to relocation camps. The reason for this controversial decision was, of course, a fear that these citizens would give their loyalty to the enemy rather than to their adopted country, that they might resort to acts of sabotage or otherwise disrupt the American war effort. In time, the United States came to regret this ill-considered action and sought to make amends, but it remains a blot on the country's conscience and a good example of a morally defective policy.

This policy, and the racial prejudice it revealed, has been powerfully evoked in a recent prize-winning novel, David Guterson's *Snow Falling on Cedars*.[27] The prejudice against Japanese Americans in the context of World War II came to the screen as early as John Sturges's *Bad Day at Black Rock* in 1954. But the nearest thing to a definitive film on the relocation of Japanese Americans during the war is Alan Parker's *Come See the Paradise*. This is a film about many things: a mixed marriage between an Irish American, Jack McGurn (Dennis Quaid), and a Japanese American, Lily Kawamura (Tamlyn Tomita); cultural differences and misunderstandings; and troubled and ocasionally violent labor relations in the United States during the Depression years. But it is also and most importantly about what happened to Japanese Americans during World War II, when they were summarily removed from their homes and sent to sterile camps in the desert where, surrounded by fences and closely monitored by soldiers, they tried to carry on normal lives. The film's principals react to the injustice of the relocation in various ways, but *Come See the Paradise* is ultimately a sober indictment of America's treatment of some of its own people and of the prejudices that made that mistreatment possible (as characters in both Guterson's novel and the film observe, German Americans were not sent to relocation camps during the war).

Human Rights on the International Agenda

In 1942, when the U.S. government interned Japanese-Americans, human rights had not yet become a prominent issue on the international agenda. Since World War II, that issue has acquired far greater salience, with the adoption of the Universal Declaration of Human Rights, the Covenants on Civil and Political Rights and on Economic, Social and Cultural Rights, and numerous conventions, such as those outlawing genocide and torture. State practice in respecting the rights of individuals lags well behind the obligations enunciated in these treaties and conventions, but only the most cynical would deny that there has been moral progress in what is one of the most difficult areas for the development of ethical international relations. After all, it is states and their governments that stand accused of depriving individuals of their civil and political rights and of failing to provide them with economic and social rights, and states and their governments typically do not welcome the interference of outsiders in what they regard as matters that fall within their sovereign prerogatives. Thus the international regime for human rights is essentially a declaratory regime, stipulating the rights of individuals and the obligations of states, and only rarely and to a very limited degree an implementation or enforcement regime.[28]

Economic and social rights have been promoted most vigorously by Third World states, which have tended to argue that they are more basic than civil and political rights and should receive priority attention. Because most Third World states do not have the capacity to fulfill these economic and social rights, they have sought without much success to shift the burden of responsibility for satisfying these rights to the Western (and former colonial) powers. This issue is discussed in Chapter 8. It is civil and political rights that command the attention of the international civil rights machinery, from the UN Human Rights Commission and the Committee on Human Rights[29] to regional commissions such as those in Western Europe and Latin America and to such nongovernmental organizations as Amnesty International. These bodies are the scene of an ongoing struggle to expose and condemn the abuses by governments of individual rights ranging from arbitrary arrest and imprisonment to denial of freedom of speech and assembly. One of the principal foci of international efforts on behalf of human rights has been the practice of torture, the subject of a 1984 United Nations convention.

Although the film does not itself depict either torture or the efforts of the international community to intervene on behalf of victims of a cruel regime, *The Official Story* is one of the most provocative treatments of the human rights issue. It concerns the torture and disappearance of thousands of Argentine citizens at the hands of the military junta in the so-called "dirty war" against alleged subversives during the 1970s and 1980s; these practices were clearly immoral and in violation of basic principles of international human rights law. This troubling film by Luis Puenza focuses on the terrible awakening of an Argentine school teacher, Alicia (Norma Aleandro), to the realization that her adopted daughter was very probably born in prison to one of the *desaparecidos* (those who simply disappeared, never to be heard from again, during the dirty war). Moreover, in the course of her efforts to discover the truth about the child, she comes to realize that her husband has been involved in the evil work of the junta. To compound the tragedy further, she also meets a woman who is probably the child's grandmother during a demonstration by the "Grandmothers of the Plaza de Mayo," a group organized to protest the traffic in children of the *desaparecidos*. As one reviewer commented, it is the purpose of the film "to frame a parable about the individual's relationship to totalitarianism," and it does this by telling the story of a woman who "descends from serenity . . . to a final, harrowing acknowledgement that her privileged life was based on willed blindness."[30] *The Official Story* is not overtly a film about international relations, but it makes a powerful statement to the effect that some forms of state behavior are so intrinsically offensive that they must necessarily become the concern of the larger international community.

The widespread violations of the most basic human rights that provide the context for *The Official Story* are also central to the plot of John Boorman's *Beyond Rangoon*. This film is set in Burma (Myanmar), a reclusive Asian nation that achieved international notoriety when the military dictatorship refused to accept the electoral victory of Aung San Suu Kyi's National League for Democracy, placing the brave woman under house arrest for six years and cracking down hard on those seeking greater political freedom for their country. Aung San Suu Kyi subsequently received the Nobel Peace Prize in 1991 for her efforts on behalf of democratic rule in Burma. In an early scene in the film, she is shown challenging the military in a peaceful demonstration, an act of conspicuous courage that makes a strong impression on an American doctor, Laura Bowman (Patricia Arquette). Bowman has come to Burma in an effort to overcome her grief following the tragic death of her husband and son, and *Beyond Rangoon* is basically the story of her gradual recovery of a sense of purpose in her life as she confronts the brutality of the military regime. The young doctor is witness to the sickening slaughter of people whose only crime is that they speak out on behalf of democracy; soon she too finds herself on the run from the soldiers of the rogue regime. At the film's conclusion, Bowman and an older Burmese professor and dissident who has befriended her, and whose life she has saved, cross over into Thailand and safety, barely surviving a murderous artillery barrage at the border.

Like *The Official Story, Beyond Rangoon* has little to say about the international response to the violations of human rights by the government. But the international community has in fact acted to condemn and isolate Burma, and the film effectively captures the brutal suppression of dissent that led to that response. It took some time before revulsion over events in Rangoon led to action, but by early 1997 the United Nations Human Rights Commission had unanimously condemned the military government, the European Union had suspended favorable trading benefits, companies such as Apple and PepsiCo had pulled out of Burma, and the United States had imposed sanctions, prohibiting other U.S. companies from investing in that country. Inevitably, questions have been raised as to why Burma has been treated as a pariah while "business as usual" has characterized relations with China, which also has brutally suppressed political dissidents. The answer, of course, lies in the fact that China, unlike Burma, is a rapidly growing power in world affairs and an important trading partner of the United States and other Western countries. Deflecting criticism of the double standard, U.S. Secretary of State Madeleine Albright contended that the United States has "consistent principles and flexible tactics."

Human rights issues play a pivotal role in several other movies, including films as different as *The Killing Fields* and *Judgment at Nuremberg*. In both of these cases, violations of rights reached genocidal proportions, which clearly transformed the issue from a domestic one to a concern of the larger international community. However, the genocide practiced by the Khmer Rouge and depicted so graphically in *The Killing Fields* met with no effective international response; nor have more recent instances of genocide in places such as Rwanda and Burundi stirred the international community to effective action, in spite of the fact that the United Nations Convention on Genocide was adopted as long ago as 1948 at the height of international revulsion over the Holocaust.[31] Several films have dealt with the Holocaust, the one case of genocide that did produce a strong if belated international response in the form of trials and punishment for some of those responsible for planning and implementing Hitler's "final solution." *The Wannsee Conference* depicts the chillingly casual planning by the Nazis to exterminate the Jews, and *Schindler's List* is the most memorable of the films showing the implementation of that plan (although its focus is on a man whose intervention saved many Jews). However, the film that deals most directly with the efforts of the international community to hold the perpetrators of the Holocaust responsible for that monstrous violation of international morality and international law is Stanley Kramer's *Judgment at Nuremberg*.

Kramer's film is about the trials held at Nuremberg after World War II, in which the leaders of the Third Reich were charged with war crimes, conspiracy to commit aggressive war, crimes against peace, and crimes against humanity. The film does not deal with the major trials of such prominent Nazis as Hermann Goering, Joachim von Ribbentrop, Julius Streicher, Ernst Kaltenbrunner, and Albert Speer. Instead, Kramer creates a fictional trial of four German judges who had systematically violated the most basic canons of justice while implementing the policies of an inhumane regime. The Nuremberg trials were inevitably controversial. For some, they were merely victors' justice. After all, most of the charges against the defendants, and especially that of crimes against humanity— the crime with which the four judges were charged, were of dubious legal status. At the time the Nazis were systematically engaged in what would become known as the Holocaust, there was no international law that forbade Germans from killing German Jews. Despite the absence of codified international law, the prosecution argued that there existed a moral consensus against genocide. The American prosecutor, Robert Jackson, contended that although there was no judicial precedent for the charges, "the real complaining party at your bar is Civilization."[32]

Judgment at Nuremberg has been faulted, along with many of Kramer's films, for being a message film, and a heavy-handed one at that. And it is long and largely confined to the courtroom. But much of the dialogue in that courtroom, as the prosecution and defense make their cases, has something important to say about both law and morality. The defense attorney, Hans Rolfe (Maximillian Schell in an Academy Award–winning performance), insists that the judges were only doing their duty under the law of the state, and that if they were to be found guilty, so must much of the international community, including British and American statesmen. The prosecuting attorney, Colonel Lawson (Richard Widmark), is unsparing in his attempts to portray the judges as monsters, even showing the court film footage of the horrors of the concentration camps to which many of the judges' victims were sent to perish. The most prominent of the German judges, Ernst Janning (Burt Lancaster), refuses to enter a plea because he will not recognize the authority of the court; but in the end he rises, "in an outburst of soul-searching, to pinpoint the real guilt of all who rationalized or ignored the inhumanity of Nazism," himself included.[33] Two of the film's most powerful scenes involve the testimony of two people victimized by the system; Montgomery Clift and Judy Garland turn their moments on the witness stand into powerful if sad indictments of the inhumanity of Nazism.

In the end it is the senior judge, Spencer Tracy's Dan Heywood, who sums up Kramer's message as well as the need for *some* ethical standards in our anarchic world: "This, then, is what we stand for—truth, justice, and the value of a single human being." Yet the film also reminds us of the limits on moral choice in the conduct of foreign policy. Near the end of the film, we are told that the Soviets are creating trouble over Berlin; with the Cold War heating up, one of the characters suggests to the judges that the United States will need the support of the German people and so should not antagonize them by being too harsh in their verdict. Tracy rejects this advice, and all four judges are sentenced to life imprisonment. In real life, whatever the merits of the argument that the law applied at Nuremberg was ex post facto, the trials succeeded in creating international law. The principles that emerged from the Nuremberg trials were thus even more important than the convictions of Nazi leaders.

Unfortunately, the Nuremberg trials (and their counterparts in the Far East) have not prevented further war crimes. The legal and moral standards established at that time did not lead to the establishment of another war crimes tribunal until the UN Security Council, in Resolution 808, decided to create one to deal with gross violations of international humanitarian law in the former Yugoslavia in the early 1990s.[34] This means that international law has been violated with impunity in a great many cases over a great many years. Moreover, even where a tribunal has been established, it faces a huge problem that did not confront the allied powers at Nuremberg: most of the alleged war criminals (and all of the major ones) in Bosnia, Croatia, and Serbia are not in custody; given the political situation, so unlike that after World War II, it is highly unlikely that many of them will ever appear in the dock.[35]

The Issue of Distributive Justice

Distributive justice also raises important ethical questions but has almost never been the explicit focus of feature films. Viewers must decide whether in a particular situation depicted on screen there are what amount to duties beyond borders. For example, a film that confronts the viewer with scenes of deep and persistent poverty in a developing country may raise the question of what, if anything (and by whom), should be done about that poverty. Luis Bunuel's *Los Olvidados,* Hector Babenco's *Pixote,* and Mira Nair's *Salaam Bombay* all tell us about children living in conditions of extreme poverty and turning to street crime in Mexico, Brazil, and India, respectively. The three films are very different from one another, but all can leave the viewer with the feeling that one of the tragedies of developing countries is that so many of their children—who make up such a large percentage of their large populations—are doomed to live lives of poverty, scavenging, vagrancy, and even violent crime. These films have nothing to say about whether those governments should do more about the situation, or about whether the more affluent countries or international financial institutions have an obligation to provide more economic assistance. But they are a reminder both of the reality of grinding poverty and the survival skills of those living with it, and they may well invite discussion of the causes and consequences of poverty, as well as of responsibility for eradicating it. An altogether different film, as well as a more conventional one, is Peter Weir's *The Year of Living Dangerously.* It too provides a picture of Third World poverty, this time in Indonesia. But unlike the others, this film assigns blame. Billy Kwan (Linda Hunt in an Oscar-winning role) is the conscience of the film, a photographer who is deeply disturbed when an Australian reporter whom he has befriended betrays a trust; even more importantly, Billy is angry that the Sukarno government has betrayed the trust of the Indonesian people. In one of the dramatic highlights of the film, Billy, who has seen too much malnutrition and misery up close, unfurls a large banner that reads "Sukarno, feed your people," only to be killed by the police for this challenge to the president.

The Year of Living Dangerously, while fictional, actually does cover the final years of the Sukarno regime. The Indonesian president had once been a leader of the Third World movement, but he came to grief in part due to a failure to deal with his country's postindependence problems. The issue of poverty and responsibility for alleviation of its worst aspects is also on display in Roland Joffe's *City of Joy.* In this case, the director of *The Killing Fields* turns his attention to India, where a corrupt system also helps to perpetuate the misery of millions of decent people. But in *City of Joy* there is a change agent at work, a disillusioned American doctor, Max Lowe (Patrick Swayze), who becomes involved in running a free clinic in a Calcutta ghetto. Dr. Lowe does not, of course, wipe out the poverty in

India's largest city, but he does inspire the Indians to challenge a local "mafia" that has been preying on them, so that by movie's end the clinic is back in operation and there is hope once more in the "city of joy." Viewers may come away from this film with two quite contradictory reactions. Some will find the film inspirational; others will be irritated that, once again, as Shohat and Stam have argued in *Unthinking Eurocentrism,* it is a white Western hero who has saved the peoples of a benighted Third World country from themselves, thus demonstrating the superiority of Western culture and fortitude. However one responds to the story, *City of Joy,* like *Pixote, The Year of Living Dangerously,* and other films set in so-called developing countries, raises important questions about distributive justice.

Whether rich countries have a moral obligation to provide for a more equitable distribution of the world's economic resources or not—whether aid in one form or another should be a matter of duty or only of charity— is a matter about which there is much disagreement. Some find the capitalist system itself to be immoral while others, standing that argument on its head, locate injustice in government efforts to "throttle the signals which the market gives."[36] One has only to raise the subject of conditionality by the International Monetary Fund[37] to generate an argument between those who defend it as an essential if temporarily painful way to ensure economic stability and those who see it as cruel in its consequences for the people affected and hence immoral. Those in the latter group can be said to favor a "do no harm" view of the responsibility of rich countries and international financial institutions. This position comes through in *The Burning Season,* the film about Brazilian activist Chico Mendes. Having become an international celebrity, albeit an uncomfortable one, Mendes goes to the United States to attend a meeting of the Inter-American Development Bank, hoping it can help him stop the construction of a highway through the rain forest. What he discovers is not only that the international bankers spend lavishly while his rubber tappers live in poverty, but that the bankers' conception of development is closer to that of the developers he has been fighting back home than it is to his own. Whether the bank's lending policies are immoral is left to the viewer to decide, but there has been no shortage of criticism of the international financial institutions for not factoring the environmental impact into decisions regarding loans. Instead, they constantly exhort developing countries to increase exports, and since "exports tend to be natural-resource intensive . . . the frenzy to ship more goods overseas accelerates environmental degradation."[38]

The question of whether moral behavior can exist in a world of sovereign states and, if so, under what conditions, has no easy answers, but films may help to focus the search for answers. Films have had less to say about the role of law in the relationships among those sovereign states, but occasionally a film does remind us that, whatever the difficulty of enforcement, "to deny that international law exists . . . as a system of binding legal rules flies in the face of all the evidence."[39] This assertion of the existence of international law comes not from an idealist, but from the "father" of post–World War II realism, Hans Morgenthau. The study of international relations may not begin with an inquiry into law and morality, but it would be woefully incomplete were they not included.

Notes

1. Hoffmann, *Duties Beyond Borders*, p. 23.
2. *Ibid.*, p. 20.
3. Bull, *The Anarchical Society*, p. 13.
4. *Ibid.*, p. 67.
5. *Ibid.*, p. 74.
6. Fromkin, *The Independence of Nations*, p. 145.
7. Rosenberg, "Tipping the Scales of Justice," p. 56.
8. Bull, *The Anarchical Society*, p. 140.
9. Hoffmann, *Duties Beyond Borders*, p. 24.
10. Fromkin, *The Independence of Nations*, p. 30.
11. Morgenthau, *Politics Among Nations*, p. 263.
12. United States Diplomatic and Consular Staff in Teheran (United States v. Iran), 1980, I.C.J. 3.
13. See, for example, Bedjaoui, *Towards a New International Economic Order*.
14. Following adoption of the Charter of Economic Rights and Duties of States by the UN General Assembly over strongly voiced U.S. opposition, U.S. spokespersons at subsequent UN meetings regularly made a point of disavowing the Charter every time some delegate invoked it in a speech.
15. Hoffmann, *Duties Beyond Borders*, p. 33.
16. *Ibid.*, pp. 35–36.
17. Bernstein, "The Atomic Bombings Reconsidered," p. 149.
18. *Ibid.*
19. Quoted in *ibid.*, p. 143.
20. *Ibid.*, p. 145.
21. For the most widely cited work on the just war doctrine, see Walzer, *Just and Unjust Wars*.
22. Hoffmann, *Duties Beyond Borders*, Ch. 2.
23. See, for example, Maechling, "Washington's Illegal Invasion."
24. Hoffmann, *Duties Beyond Borders*, pp. 50–51.
25. John Mueller argues in his book *Quiet Cataclysm* that the containment policy of the United States, with its massive military build-up, was not necessary to achieve the collapse of the Soviet Union and international communism.
26. Cohn, "Sex and Death," and "Slick 'Ems, Glick 'Ems."
27. Guterson, *Snow Falling on Cedars*.
28. See Donnelly, "International Human Rights." In another essay, Donnelly argues that "there is . . . no evidence of a growing willingness of states or intergovernmental organizations to act to impose international human rights norms on recalcitrant states." See "State Sovereignty and International Intervention," p. 145.
29. The Human Rights Commission, composed of elected representatives of UN member states, is the UN's principal organ with a responsibility for ascertaining

patterns of human rights violations and challenging states to explain their abusive policies toward their own citizens. The Committee on Human Rights is an ostensibly uninstructed expert committee created under the UN Covenant on Civil and Political Rights; it can hear petitions from persons whose states have accepted the Covenant's optional protocol allowing such challenges to their governments' policies.

30. Schickel, "The Official Story," p. 513.

31. Adoption of conventions such as this one does not automatically create international legal obligations; ratification by the number of states prescribed in the Convention is required. The Convention on Genocide entered into force on January 12, 1951, and now has more than 100 parties. The United States did not ratify the Convention until 1988.

32. Falk, Kolko, and Lifton, *Crimes of War*, p. 87.

33. Spoto, *Stanley Kramer, Film Maker*, p. 228.

34. See Meron, "The Case for War Crimes Trials in Yugoslavia," for a discussion of the legal case.

35. See Thornberry, "Saving the War Crimes Tribunal"; Meron, "Answering for War Crimes"; and Scheffer, "International Judicial Intervention," in which the author also discusses the case for an international criminal court.

36. Hoffmann, *Duties Beyond Borders*, p. 168.

37. Conditionality refers to the conditions to which governments must agree before the International Monetary Fund will lend them money to cope with their balance of payments problems. These conditions typically include controlling inflation, reducing government spending (often by eliminating subsidies), and eliminating budget deficits.

38. Broad and Cavanagh, "Don't Neglect the Impoverished South," p. 29.

39. Morgenthau, *Politics Among Nations*, p. 273.

10

The Clash of Cultures

In the summer of 1993, only shortly after the end of the Cold War, *Foreign Affairs* published an article by distinguished political scientist Samuel P. Huntington entitled "The Clash of Civilizations?"[1] This essay quickly turned into a lightning rod for the community of academics and practitioners in the field of international relations, many of whom rushed into print to demonstrate that Huntington had gotten it all wrong. It is doubtful if any recent essay about international relations, with the possible exception of Francis Fukuyama's announcing the end of history,[2] has generated so much heated discussion. What caused all the commotion was Huntington's thesis that in the coming years, the conflicts that dominate world affairs will no longer be ideological or economic in nature. Instead, "the great divisions among humankind and the dominating source of conflict will be cultural. Nation states will remain the most powerful actors in world affairs, but the principal conflicts of global politics will occur between nations and groups of different civilizations. . . . The fault lines between civilizations will be the battle lines of the future."[3] This sweeping prediction has served to give culture a prominence in debates about international relations it has not previously enjoyed. Yet culture has long been a critical secondary factor in shaping the way the international system works. We can see the clash of cultures as states and peoples define friend and foe, welcome or reject immigrants, succeed or fail at the negotiating table, and communicate or engage in a dialogue of the deaf in literally dozens of situations, ranging from the board room to the sidewalk cafe.

Huntington defines a civilization as

> the highest cultural grouping of people and the broadest level of cultural identity people have short of that which distinguishes humans from other species. It is defined both by common objective elements, such as language, history, religion, customs, institutions, and by the subjective self-identification of people. . . . The people of different civilizations have different views on the relations between God and man, the individual and

the group, the citizen and the state, parents and children, husband and wife, as well as differing views of the relative importance of rights and responsibilities, liberty and authority, equality and hierarchy. These differences are the product of centuries.[4]

We know that cultural differences have influenced the course of history by influencing the ways in which states and peoples have reacted to other states and peoples. Moreover, we also know that cultural differences manifest themselves in subtle but important ways, which can compound the difficulties of reconciling divergent interests between states as well as individuals. One does not have to accept Huntington's vision to appreciate the problems that may arise in intercultural relations when Americans insist on getting to the point while their Japanese interlocutors seem more indirect and evasive, or when those same Americans value punctuality while their Mexican counterparts seem less worried about adhering to a tight schedule.

It could be argued, however, that in a world made dramatically more compact by modern means of communication and transportation, cultural homogenization is a more plausible future than Huntington's clash of civilizations. Benjamin Barber uses the term "McWorld" to characterize this process of homogenization; what he has in mind is the fact that peoples everywhere are increasingly mesmerized by "fast music, fast computers, and fast food—with MTV, Macintosh, and McDonald's."[5] This phenomenon is sometimes called the "Coca-colaization" of the world, another way of saying that aspects of the world's unique cultures are being overwhelmed by Western consumer culture. In other words, the fact that we may still speak a multitude of languages may be less important than the fact that we all wear jeans and otherwise sport "all of the insignia of the global market."[6] Another social scientist has called attention to a different area in which a Western-influenced universal culture appears to have taken root. Diplomats, Raymond Cohen suggests,

> seem to belong to an exclusive fraternity. They dress in similar elegant suits, flash the same charming smiles at photo opportunity sessions, and often speak elegant Harvard- or Oxford-accented English. When they express themselves in those invariant and familiar phrases about "friendly and constructive talks," the inevitable conclusion presents itself: these people share a common (elitist) language, way of life, and outlook on the world; they are members of the diplomatic club.[7]

Both Barber and Cohen go on to make the point that, despite superficial similarities of dress, taste, and manner, there is no universal culture. Jihad, or religious and cultural war in the name of difference, is still a stronger force than McWorld, and intercultural dissonance all too frequently undermines the best efforts of diplomats. Culture may not be the most important factor dividing the states and peoples of the world, but cultural differences can and do reinforce and compound other factors that generate and prolong conflicts. They are likely to continue to do so, in spite of a shrinking world and superficial cosmopolitanism.

Encounters with Indigenous Peoples

Thanks to the relative ease of travel to the far corners of the world, a wealth of studies by cultural anthropologists, and the availability on public television and cable of beautifully produced documentaries, many people in many countries have at least some knowledge of cultures very different from their own—what people wear, what they eat, what they do from dawn until dusk and from birth until death. That knowledge is, of course, typically superficial and no guarantee of immunity from cultural misunderstanding. But we know more about other cultures than did participants in cross-cultural encounters in more primitive times. Some of these earlier encounters have been brought to the screen in memorable demonstrations of the clash of culture.

The films depicting Columbus's "discovery of America" necessarily include his initial encounter with the very different peoples of the New World. Shortly after coming ashore following two months at sea, Columbus and his men meet the inhabitants of the place he was to call San Salvador. Neither party has ever seen anything like the other—the sailors, with their white skins and bearded faces, their European clothes of the period and their muskets, facing the Indians, who are nearly naked, their bodies darker and painted, their weapons more primitive but still very deadly spears and arrows. We do not know how this encounter we see on the screen will end, and neither, presumably, did those who were present in 1492. The tension is finally broken by nervous laughter, brought on, one assumes, by the mutual realization that "the others" look slightly ridiculous. Thus do these dissimilar cultures break the ice. We are led to believe, in spite of the language barrier and the total ignorance of each other's beliefs and practices, that the culture gap—really a chasm—can be bridged. Although the films show us a generally peaceable relationship in the beginning, harsher reality follows: when he returns on his second voyage, Columbus finds that all thirty-nine of the men he had left behind on Hispaniola have been killed. This clash of cultures would be repeated again and again as the Europeans explored and probed the far corners of the earth in search of gold and converts to Christianity.

No film better captures the clash of cultures between Old and New Worlds than Bruce Beresford's *Black Robe*. In this case, the locus of contact is New France (now Quebec) and the events in the film take place in the 1630s. *Black Robe* is about the efforts of the Jesuits to convert the

Huron Indians to Catholicism, or "one religious culture's attempts to understand, compromise, and transform another."[8] The film follows a lone Jesuit priest, Father LaForgue (Lothaire Bluteau), accompanied by a young French adventurer and a group of loyal Algonquin Indians, on a fifteen-hundred-mile journey, much of it by canoe, to a remote Huron mission. The beautiful autumnal weather turns cold, the river freezes, most of the Algonquins desert, and Father LaForgue and the remnants of the party are captured and tortured terribly by an Iroquois war party. Rarely has missionary work seemed less rewarding. But the film's greatest value lies in what it has to say about cultures whose understanding of each other is superficial at best. One reviewer comments that "Best of all is the film's evenhanded depiction of the baffling otherness of both native and French cultures. Neither culture is morally privileged; each is presented to the viewer in its undiluted strangeness, as it was to the other in 1634."[9] We see the cultures of the several Indian tribes—Algonquin, Iroquois, Huron—through the eyes of the Jesuit priest, and French culture through the eyes of the Indians. We are not seduced into believing that the French are superior (although the savagery of the Iroquois torture may well test that judgment for some viewers); the Catholicism preached by the Black Robes (as the Jesuits were called because of their cassocks) was both utterly joyless and more intolerant than the native religion, and the diseases brought by the French were devastating to the Indians, who had not developed immunity to them. This last point is underscored near the film's end, when Father LaForgue finally reaches the Huron mission in the dead of winter and finds many of its inhabitants dying of smallpox. It is a depressing ending to a beautiful but disturbing film, one that has much to say about the clash of cultures, and especially about cultural imperialism as practiced by missionaries intent on converting the "heathen" to the one true faith, or, as one reviewer describes it, collecting souls the way trappers bag pelts.[10]

Missionaries have often been the focus of films about the clash of cultures. *The Mission,* discussed at some length in Chapter 2, is also concerned with the work of the Jesuits, this time in eighteenth-century South America. The Guarani Indians have become converts in this film and live in well-ordered missions that look superficially like transplanted European communities, but they have retained their traditional style of dress and many of their traditional practices, so that the process of acculturation is somewhat fragile. The film begins with one of its most powerful scenes, which tells the viewer that Jesuit efforts to convert the Indians in this faraway place will not be easy. A Jesuit priest has been crucified by the Indians, and this human cross is put into the river above the giant Iguazu Falls; he floats downstream with the current and then plunges over the edge and falls a seemingly interminable distance to his death in the roiling waters below. Quite obviously, these are cultures that will have trouble understanding each other.

The Jesuits, led by Jeremy Irons, do succeed in their efforts to convert the Guarani, however, but the representatives of the Spanish and Portugese governments are unwilling to believe that these Indians can transcend their primitive culture and become like the Europeans. At a hearing to decide the future of the Jesuit mission, a young Guarani boy, nearly naked and very obviously non-European, sings church music with a beautiful soprano voice. This attempt by the Jesuit order to demonstrate the success of the mission is curtly dismissed by the ranking Spanish official. When asked by the papal legate how he can refer to the child as an animal, he replies that a parrot can be taught to sing. "This is a child of the jungle," he insists, "an animal with a human voice. These creatures are lethal and lecherous. They will have to be subdued by the sword and brought to profitable labor by the whip." Rarely has one culture been so contemptuously dismissed by a representative of another in a feature film.

Black Robe and *The Mission* depict encounters between Europeans and more "primitive" cultures in what might be called early times. But such encounters still occur today, and these more contemporary instances of relations between different cultures have also found their way to the screen.[11] One example of such an encounter occurs in Hector Babenco's *At Play in the Fields of the Lord*. This film is also about missionaries, although in this case they are evangelical Protestants.

At Play contains two interrelated plots. Louis Moon (Tom Berenger), a Cheyenne Indian by birth and now a bush pilot for hire, comes to the Amazon on a government-supported assignment to bomb a Niaruna Indian village, driving its inhabitants away so that the land can be exploited by the white man. Moon somewhat improbably gets in touch with his Indian roots and, instead of bombing the Niaruna, parachutes into their village and goes native, even shedding his Western clothes in the process. (*At Play,* which for many minutes of its overlong running time resembles a live action version of a *National Geographic* article, probably contains more full-frontal nudity, both male and female, than any other feature film.) Moon adapts relatively well to the Niaruna culture; the Niaruna accept him rather than kill him because they regard him as a god, Kisu Mu, since he came to them from the sky. The second plot concerns the efforts of two missionary couples (John Lithgow and Daryl Hannah, Aidan Quinn and Kathy Bates) to make Christians of the Niaruna. Unlike Moon, these four are never at home in the Brazilian jungle, nor do they ever develop any understanding of the people they are trying to convert. The two couples quarrel endlessly among themselves, regard Catholics as the enemy, and at film's end conclude, in the words of perhaps the most thoughtful of the missionaries, Quinn, that "it would have been better for them [the Niaruna] never to have known us." This is a sentiment with which most members of the audience are likely to agree.

At Play in the Fields of the Lord is perhaps the ultimate example of the cultural hubris of missionaries and the complete failure of cross-cultural communication. The senior missionary, Lithgow, has no respect for the people he wants to convert to Christianity. He refers to one group of Indians who have already been converted as "a meek and stupid people," and later, expressing his frustration with the Niaruna, says angrily that "not one soul realizes that God loves them—they're as savage now as they ever were." The wife of the younger missionary, Bates, is out of control through much of the film, absurdly prudish, frequently hysterical, a cross her long-suffering husband must bear. The other wife, Hannah, turns out to be the cause of sickness and death among the Niaruna when, surprised by Moon while taking a nude swim, she kisses him, transmitting a flu germ he then passes on to the members of his adopted tribe. Like the Hurons in *Black Robe,* the Niaruna have not developed an immunity to the white man's diseases; that single kiss spells doom for the Indians. Relations between the Niaruna and the missionaries, always tense, deteriorate rapidly following the fatal kiss. Many of the Niaruna die, but their village is bombed after all, Quinn is killed, and Berenger is left to ponder the meaning of this madness in "the heart of darkness." It is clear that time is running out for the Niaruna, and by implication for all "primitive" indigenous peoples— peoples the dominant culture sees only as obstacles to progress.

Modern Western culture meets traditional indigenous culture in a number of other films, of which two merit mention here: Werner Herzog's *Where the Green Ants Dream* and Jamie Uys's *The Gods Must Be Crazy.* The first takes place in Australia and concerns the great culture gap between that country's white settler population and the Aborigines. The other, a slapstick film that is a throwback to the Keystone Kops era, focuses on the encounters of an African bushman with some of the absurdities of white civilization. Neither film is literally about international relations, but the gap between the cultures portrayed on the screen is so great that viewers can easily imagine that what they are watching is an aspect of international relations in microcosm. As in *At Play in the Fields of the Lord,* the Aborigines in *Where the Green Ants Dream* and the Bushmen in *The Gods Must Be Crazy* are so unlike the European settler communities that we know that cross-cultural communication will be extremely difficult. In Herzog's film, the white developers are very future-oriented. They want to blast in order to determine where it will be economical to mine for uranium, a mineral with twentieth- and twenty-first century uses. The Aborigines are preoccupied with "the ancient origins of life and the landscape, stretching back into the infinite past, the Dreaming."[12] Their belief system, with its respect for both ancestral spirits and the land itself, has sustained them in a harsh environment since a time long before the white man came to Australia. Blasting and mining are not only acts of desecration; they can destroy the Aboriginal cosmos. The culture of the Aborigines is so far removed from that of the miners as to be absolutely incomprehensible. Even surface differences between the cultures are dauntingly great. In spite of

Western clothes, the Aborigines are almost as unlike the whites in appearance as the Klingons and Ferengi are unlike the peoples of earth in the *Star Trek* series; their musical instrument, the didjeridu, produces a strange, droning sound totally alien to Western ears; and the Aboriginal practice of sitting silently for hours on end in the presence of the bulldozers is deeply disturbing to the miners. In *Where the Green Ants Dream,* there is clearly little possibility of communication across the barrier of cultural differences.

The Gods Must Be Crazy also introduces us to two cultures that appear light years apart in their development, but there is an important difference. In *Where the Green Ants Dream,* the director has given the central role to a decent geologist who tries to understand the Aborigines; consequently, the viewer is invited to look at the Aboriginal culture through the sympathetic but uncomprehending eyes of the dominant white culture. In *The Gods Must Be Crazy,* the viewer's perspective is that of a Bushman, Xi, and the dominant white culture is made to appear incomprehensible. Xi belongs to a simple hunter-gatherer culture living in harmony with nature in the bleak, unforgiving Kalahari desert of Botswana. His life is contrasted with that of the whites in the nearby urban metropolis of Johannesberg, where modern technology may have made life easier but also has made it more complex and subject to breakdown. The directors' sympathies in both of these films clearly lie with the more primitive of the two cultures, but whereas in *Green Ants* the dominant culture is thoughtless and threatening, in Uys's film the dominant culture is made to appear ridiculous. The two cultures do not conflict in the latter film in the way that they do in *Green Ants,* but communication between them is difficult nonetheless. Because *The Gods Must Be Crazy* is ultimately a benign comedy, neither the Bushman hero nor the bumbling white leading man is culturally insensitive, and they do manage to cooperate despite the cultural gulf that separates them.

The Bushman's contact with the white world is set in motion when the pilot of a small plane drops an empty Coke bottle into a Bushman village. Initially useful, the Coke bottle becomes a source of dissension in a heretofore happy community. We are being told that the intrusion of modern civilization into the lives of more primitive peoples will have negative effects. At film's end, after many adventures and misadventures, the Bushman hero throws the troublesome Coke bottle away over the rim of Victoria Falls, symbolically restoring tranquility and order to the simple (and obviously preferable) culture of the Bushmen.

Parenthetically, it should be noted that *The Gods Must Be Crazy* has been criticized for being racist. The basis for this charge is twofold. In the first place, a sub-plot in the film involves civil strife between a black African government and black African guerrillas, and it is clear that the director—a white South African—has no respect for either. Moreover, the critics say, the Bushmen are treated paternalistically; "all these people scurrying around the landscape of Southern Africa, colliding in pratfalls, constitute a distorted microcosm of the clash of peoples and ideologies that is in reality deeply tragic."[13] But when it comes to satire, Uys is clearly an equal opportunity critic. Indeed, it is the whites who behave most foolishly, and Xi is the most sensible person in the film. The main white characters, while inept bumblers, are his true friends and never treat Xi condescendingly.

Culture is also a factor in mainstream films about colonialism, such as *Gandhi* and *A Passage to India*. In these films, the subject peoples in the colonies understand the European colonizers much better than the Bushmen appear to understand the white men in *The Gods Must Be Crazy*. When Gandhi and Jinnah and Nehru argue with British officials in *Gandhi*, for example, they do so as well-educated professionals, as intellectual equals. The principal conflicts appear to be economic and political, but those conflicts are exacerbated by the inescapable reality of cultural differences and by the cultural arrogance of the Europeans. British colonial officials typically wish to preserve the cultural gap, refusing to mix socially with the native population and treating them with condescension when they interact. We are witness to this assertion of cultural superiority in virtually all of the films about the colonial era, several of which are discussed in Chapter 3, although filmmakers are no longer likely to accept it uncritically and typically take the side of those who challenge it. It should be noted that colonialism almost always involved the domination of whites over darker-skinned peoples, so that race became the most obvious, if not the only, manifestation of cultural difference and racism a major element in the clash of cultures. Film is a medium through which this point has been made most effectively.

Migration and Cross-Cultural Tensions

One does not need to turn to colonialism or to the work of missionaries or to encounters between modern and primitive cultures in the outback or desert to find misunderstanding and conflict between peoples of different cultures. The clash of cultures occurs today in the large cities and small towns of the Western world, as those countries become hosts to immigrants and refugees from other countries and other cultures. We know that guest workers from countries like Turkey have been harassed in Germany, that Algerians have encountered rude treatment in France, that immigrants from Mexico and Central America are increasingly the target of restrictive measures in the United States, that peoples from South Asia often find the welcome mat withdrawn in England. Migration has, of course, been going on since before the beginning of recorded history, and it has repeatedly brought different cultures into contact and conflict with each other. But the phenomenon of cultural mingling and resultant tensions due to population flows in our own time has recently captured the interest of a variety of filmmakers. Among the many films to address this issue, four merit special mention. They are *El Norte, Alamo Bay, My Beautiful Laundrette,* and *Romper Stomper.*

All of these films comment in thought-provoking ways about cultural assimilation, the first two set in the United States, the third in the United Kingdom, and the fourth in Australia. The United States and the United Kingdom have complex traditions regarding immigration, but they have been relatively receptive to newcomers, the United Kingdom because of its association with non-European members of the British Commonwealth and the United States because "Americans prided themselves on being the land of religious and political liberty, and, above all, because the growing economy needed the immigrants' labor."[14] Australia's experience with immigration from places other than "the mother country" has been more limited. Yet all three countries have recently been troubled by hostile reactions from the established citizenry to newcomers from Third World countries whose cultures are different from their own. There is no question but that these conflicts are in part the product of economic anxiety. The newcomers appear to be competitors for scarce jobs, especially at the lower end of the economic scale, and are resented, especially by those who are themselves economically marginal within the larger society.

The movement in the United States to curb benefits to immigrants, particularly those from Latin America, is certainly fed in considerable measure by economic considerations. But there are strong cultural overtones to the debate over immigration policy, and it is no accident that the people commonly identified by the media and politicians as the threat that must be contained are overwhelmingly Hispanic and culturally distinguishable. This is not the place to discuss cultural stereotypes, but there has been a fairly widespread tendency to resort to sterotyping in the debate about immigration policy. The film *El Norte,* discussed at some length in Chapter 8, does not concern itself with this debate, but in its final segment it does suggest the plight of illegal immigrants from Central America. A Guatemalan brother and sister, Enrique and Rosa, are trapped in menial jobs, badly handicapped by their ignorance of the English language, and confused by the behavior of the thoughtless *gringos,* who are only too happy to pay cheap wages to people they know are illegals but care nothing for them as individuals. *El Norte* does not stress the issue of culture, but it is a pervasive presence throughout the film and especially in the Los Angeles section, where there is a near-total failure of communication between the white Angelenos and Enrique and Rosa; the former simply take for granted the superiority of their own culture, making no effort to understand these newcomers to their city.

Louis Malle's *Alamo Bay* also concerns itself with the plight of immigrants to the United States, but in this case the newcomers are not viewed as a welcome source of cheap labor but as economic competitors, and they are greeted with violence. The immigrants in *Alamo Bay* are Vietnamese, not Hispanics, and they have settled on the Texas coast. The circumstances of their coming to the United States are very different from those which brought Enrique and Rosa from Guatemala. Following its withdrawal from the Vietnam War, the United States felt an obligation to provide a haven for those Vietnamese who had worked with U.S. forces and who were at risk after the communist takeover of their country. In the years following the end of the war, many Vietnamese found their way to the United States; although their numbers have never been more than a small fraction of those from Latin America, they too have encountered problems of acceptance and assimilation.

As with most of the films discussed in this book, *Alamo Bay* examines the larger conflict by focusing on the relationships among individuals, in this case three residents of a Texas fishing village: Shang Pierce (Ed Harris), a financially troubled shrimper; Glory (Amy Madigan), Shang's former high school sweetheart, whose father buys shrimp from the Vietnamese as well as the Anglos; and Dinh (nonprofessional actor Ho Nguyen), an enterprising Vietnamese shrimper whose success ultimately drives Shang to desperate measures. Malle presents the Vietnamese as honest, hard-working people; the whites, on the other hand, fall into two camps—those who are sympathetic to the Vietnamese and willing to help them get established, and those who are bent on driving "the gooks" out of town. The conflict between the cultural communities turns nasty when the Anglo fishermen boycott Glory's business and then, egged on by the local chapter of the Ku Klux Klan, resort to force against Dinh and his friends. The scene that best captures the unwillingness of members of the dominant culture to accept the Vietnamese takes place in a bar. Dinh enters the bar, where he hopes to buy a motor for a crab boat from one of the white fishermen. When he orders a beer, he is refused service. The bartender says, "Look, this is an American bar. We're plumb out of brew." As one critic has observed, that line "neatly highlighted the bartender's equating white racism with Americanism."[15] The owner of the motor regards it as an affront that a Vietnamese should try to buy it, and the fishermen beat Dinh up and throw him out of the bar. The scene will evoke memories of the problems confronting black Americans when segregation prevailed in the United States, and reminds us that racial and cultural prejudice are hard to exorcize. It is encouraging that Glory, a white Texas woman, emerges as the film's hero, but *Alamo Bay* remains a disturbing commentary on the clash of cultures.

Stephen Frears's *My Beautiful Laundrette* provides the viewer with a very different experience. It is totally unlike *Alamo Bay* in story line, character development, and tone; its setting, a working-class neighborhood in South London, is far removed from the Gulf coast of Texas. But it too is relevant to an understanding of intercultural relations and the problems facing immigrants as they seek to make a new life for themselves in the West. The immigrants in this case are Pakistanis. Unlike the Vietnamese in Malle's film, the principal representatives of the immigrant community in Frears's film have achieved considerable economic success, some of it by dubious means; good entrepreneurs that they are, they see London "as a city ripe for conquest."[16] Much of the film is taken up with family life and business dealings in the Pakistani community and with a homosexual affair between an ambitious young Pakistani, Omar (Gordon Warnecke), and a white friend trying to get away from his past as a street hooligan, Johnny (Daniel Day-Lewis). Omar and Johnny take over a rundown laundromat and turn it into a glitzy, neon-lighted place called "Powders," a name that suggests both the detergents used there and the drug sales which made the venture possible.

My Beautiful Laundrette also has its dark side, involving the conflict between the two cultures and the issue of cultural identity. Johnny's former pals are young, restless skinheads and punks who get their kicks by "Paki-bashing." Unhappy with their life in Thatcherite England and looking for scapegoats, they lash out at the Asians in their midst, smashing the laundrette's windows and beating up on Johnny because he has gone over to the enemy. It matters not that the Pakistanis are successful; in fact, that only raises the level of frustration among the punks. They seem to feel that it is important that there be someone they can look down upon, and the Pakistanis—outsiders of another culture—fill that role. However, Frears and his screenwriter, Hanif Kureishi, are not interested in indicting the British people as a whole for cultural insensitivity and Paki-bashing. Instead their film is a celebration of the immigrant community, reminding us that "the cultural history of the twentieth century is the story of outsiders—the exiled, the disenfranchised, the oppressed, the ignored,"[17] and insisting that the outsiders can achieve success and assimilation in spite of the obstacles placed in their path. *My Beautiful Laundrette* is ultimately one of the most optimistic of the films dealing with the clash of cultures.

There is no optimism in Geoffrey Wright's *Romper Stomper.* Set in Melbourne, this Australian-made film shares with *Alamo Bay* and *My Beautiful Laundrette* the issue of Asian immigrants trying to make it in a predominantly Caucasian society and the resistance of a white-supremacist sub-culture to their presence. *Romper Stomper* is extremely violent. Throughout the film, Wright's camera puts the audience right in the middle of nearly non-stop, no-holds-barred conflict between neo-Nazi skinheads and the "gooks" they are determined to drive out of the country. What we see is, quite literally, war. The skinheads sport Nazi-style tattoos and decorate their quarters with swastikas. Their leader, Hando (Russell Crowe), reads to his girlfriend from *Mein Kampf*, is obsessed with the danger of racial blood poisoning, and tells one of the immigrants that "This is not your country" before beating him to a pulp. In addition to its violence and its percussive musical score, the film is full of ironic touches: just prior to a scene in which his home is attacked by the skinheads, a wealthy Australian is listening to the sublime duet by two Asian (Ceylonese or Sri Lankan) pearl fishers in Bizet's opera *Les Pecheurs de Perles;* and in the climactic scene on a Melbourne beach, complete with a furiously burning car and the violent death of the skinheads' leader, Japanese tourists alight from their bus to take pictures of the carnage.

Intercultural conflict as an aspect of international relations is a common theme in a great many films in addition to those discussed above. Indians from East Africa, driven out of Uganda and resettling in the United States, conflict with black Americans in *Mississippi Masala;* white Americans conflict with Japanese Americans in *Come See the Paradise,* and do so even before the Japanese attack on Pearl Harbor. Although films about conflict between black and white Americans (e.g., Spike Lee's *Do the Right Thing*) or black and white South Africans (e.g., Euzhan Palcy's *A Dry White Season*) are rarely about international relations, they also serve as a reminder that, while race need not be a defining characteristic of a culture, peoples of different races frequently may be said to belong to different cultures as well.

Studies in Culture Shock

The problems of intercultural relations on display in most of the films previously discussed have occurred when peoples from so-called Third World countries interact with peoples of European descent. But it is also possible that cultural differences may present problems when the government and citizens of one country with a predominantly European population confront those of another. There is, for example, no shortage of both anecdotal evidence and serious scholarship to the effect that relations between the French and the Americans—or the French and the British, or the French and Germans—have occasionally been strained not only by conflicts of interest but by attitudes that can only be described as culturally based. This cultural dimension of relations between white peoples of a presumably shared European heritage is usually subordinate to other issues in films. But one relatively recent film, *Moscow on the Hudson,* made culture its central focus.

This Paul Mazursky film looks sympathetically at the travails of a Russian saxophonist who defects to the United States when the touring circus with which he performs visits New York. The Cold War is still very much alive, and the hero, Vlad Ivanoff (Robin Williams), must outwit the KGB agents who accompany the troupe precisely for the purpose of preventing defections. One is reminded of the measures the Soviet government took for so many years to make sure that its citizens would not defect to the West, including the practice of requiring the personnel in its UN mission and even Soviet members of the UN secretariat to live in a tightly controlled compound outside New York City. Vlad makes his escape in Bloomingdale's, and as Pauline Kael observed in her review of the film, Mazursky uses the department store "as a temple of the mouth-watering temptations of capitalist decadence."[18] Bloomingdale's is more than a metaphor for American consumerism in this case; it is there, during those frantic minutes when he is trying to make good his defection, that Vlad becomes involved with the people who will become his surrogate family. They are a mixed lot, a cross-section of the city's (and the country's) population: an Italian girl who is a salesperson in the store, a black security guard originally from Alabama, and a Cuban immigration lawyer. Indeed, it quickly becomes apparent that while New York may not be a melting pot, it certainly is a tossed salad. Vlad tells the girl, Lucia (Maria Conchita Alonso), that "Everybody I meet is from somewhere else." She replies, quite simply, "That's America."

The film has a bittersweet quality. Its point is not that life in the United States is wonderful, or that Vlad is lucky to have left the drab and regimented life of a communist society behind him. Instead, Vlad discovers that he has traded one kind of misery for another, that good jobs are hard to find, that people can be indifferent and even cruel, that life in the big city can be lonely. At one point he observes that in Russia he at least knew who the enemy was. Vlad's New York odyssey is not unlike the experience of many other people, including, of course, many long-time Americans who discover that they are less happy in new cities and new homes than they had expected to be. But Vlad is experiencing culture shock. It begins when he comes into New York with the circus troupe; as their bus drives through the city, Vlad and his fellow performers stare out the windows in amazement at the weird kaleidoscope of sights on New York's throbbing streets. He has left one culture behind and suddenly finds himself struggling to come to terms with a vastly different one, made all the more confusing by the fact that it is really a melange of many cultures and that he is but one of many strangers in a strange land.

Moscow on the Hudson is a more sober and truthful rendering of the East-West culture wars than Ernst Lubitsch's 1939 confection, *Ninotchka*. In that film, Greta Garbo and several of her compatriots come to Paris to negotiate the return to the Soviet Union of some valuable jewels, only to be mesmerized by the glamour of the City of Light (and, in Garbo's case, by an ever-so-smooth Melvyn Douglas). Moscow is a dreary place in both films, but Paris is too good to be true, and the only thing delaying Garbo's flight to the West is that she is a good communist. The Soviet Union is now defunct, of course, and Soviet-style communism is in disrepute, so it is unlikely that we shall soon be seeing more films like *Moscow on the Hudson,* much less like *Ninotchka.* Some Russians may, of course, still find the West more attractive than their homeland, but if they come, the KGB will presumably not be shadowing them all the way and most will probably have experiences more like Vlad's than Ninotchka's.

Of the many films that explore intercultural relations, it is doubtful if any make the gulf between cultures look more unbridgeable than Brian Gilbert's *Not Without My Daughter.* Set in Iran in the 1980s following the revolution that overthrew the Shah's regime and brought Islamic funda-mentalism to power, the film is based upon the true story of a marriage be-tween an American woman and her Iranian husband that goes terribly wrong when they visit his family in the Iran of the Ayatollah Khomeini. Like virtually all movies about the clash of cultures, this one focuses on interpersonal rather than intergovernmental relationships. But this time the interpersonal conflict mirrors all too accurately the conflict between the two countries, and in its relentlessly angry portrayal of postrevolutionary Iran, the film captures the American revulsion over the practices of a mil-itant Islamic society. Context is critically important in the case of *Not Without My Daughter.* In 1979, during the revolution, Iranian students seized the American embassy in Teheran and took embassy personnel hostage. The Iranian government, instead of acting to protect the Ameri-cans, took the side of the students and the result was the notorious hostage crisis, which dragged on for over a year. The American public, under-standably angry and frustrated with the situation, was subjected to a cram course on Iran and Islam, and in the circumstances it is not surprising that little attempt was made to provide a balanced perspective on either coun-try or religion.

Not Without My Daughter reflects this anti-Iranian and anti-Islamic bias, and will certainly be offensive to those who believe that Iran is a much more complex case and Islam one of the world's great faiths. Yet the film does fairly accurately convey the views of many Westerners regarding the culture of Islamic fundamentalism. Its strongly stated thesis that the two cultures are so antithetical as to preclude understanding and compro-mise has its real-life counterpart in the continuation of mutual antagonism between the U.S. and Iranian governments. This antagonism continues nearly two decades after the revolution, in spite of the fact that many ob-servers believe that the revolution has burned itself out and that Iran and the United States might well make common cause against Saddam Hus-sein's regime in Iraq. Samuel Huntington, in his much-discussed essay on the clash of civilizations, claims that one of the most important fault lines or flash points for crisis and bloodshed in the decades ahead is the one di-viding Western and Islamic civilizations.[19] A U.S. Iranian specialist, writ-ing in a recent issue of *Foreign Affairs,* argues that Islamic fundamental-ists cannot and should not be accommodated, that the United States should stop trying to "find and encourage fundamentalists who do not believe that God's word is law and that Washington is the cultural font of evil."[20] Such people simply do not exist, he contends, and goes on to ask how it is possible to compromise when Western human rights and Islamic *sharia,* both of which are inalienable, collide.[21]

This conflict between Western and Iranian cultures, their conceptions of human rights and responsibilities, and the place of God's will in the public life of the society is present in almost every scene of *Not Without My Daughter.* Betty Mahmoody (Sally Field) reluctantly accompanies her Iranian doctor-husband Moody (Alfred Molina) and their daughter Mahtob to Iran so that his family may meet her and see the little girl. The scene that greets them when they step off the plane in Teheran is a great shock to Betty and Mahtob, who only know the very different environment of Michigan. All of the women are dressed in the chador, a drab garment that covers the whole body and the hair; they present Betty with a chador, which she puts on in front of a huge poster of the Ayatollah Khomeini, who seems to be glaring down at her. In fact posters of the Ayatollah are everywhere, a constant reminder of the new Islamic order; the morals police assail Betty on the street for not having her hair properly covered, and the women in Moody's family regard her with stern disapproval throughout the film. Betty tells her husband that the culture seems primitive, and Moody reminds her that "all religious beliefs seem primitive when they're not your own."

These early scenes are but a prelude to the crisis that unfolds when Moody announces that he has decided that they will remain in Iran and that Mahtob will be raised as a Muslim; "Islam," he declares, "is the greatest gift I could give my child." Betty is horrified: "This is a backward, primitive country," she tells her husband, and sets about the nearly impossible task of smuggling Mahtob out of Iran and back to the States. She discovers that because she is married to an Iranian she is regarded as an Iranian citizen, and that all rights are those of the husband. Moody turns violent when Betty seeks help from the American interest section of the Swiss embassy; supported by his family, he locks Betty in her room and takes Mahtob away. In scenes that are painful to watch, Moody is portrayed as an exceedingly abusive spouse, but in this culture there would seem to be no place for Betty to turn for help. Eventually, she is put in touch with a sympathetic Iranian who facilitates a harrowing escape from this nightmare, an escape helped in no small measure by Betty's own dogged determination to save her daughter from that "primitive, backward country" and the fanatic family of the husband she never really knew.

Not Without My Daughter is an example of filmmaking with a pronounced point of view, and as such will produce different reactions in different people. The husband is given a few lines that argue for understanding of and respect for cultural differences, but the story line and the direction of the film as a whole clearly support the view that fundamentalist Islam has few if any redeeming features. The two cultures are on a collision course in this film, and it is the culture of Western civilization, with its emphasis upon individual freedom and the separation of church and state, that enlists the viewer's support. It should be noted, however, that in one area at least the film makes clear that Iran is *not* a primitive, backward country; the Muslim call to prayer has been recorded on a cassette and is played over a loudspeaker, a subtle reminder that Ayatollah Khomeini laid the groundwork for his revolution with the dissemination of taped messages throughout Iran.

Japan and the United States: Cultural Dissonance

There has been very little dialogue between the United States and Iran since the hostage crisis, but this is a special case. Representatives of different cultures are constantly engaged in efforts to communicate with each other at many different levels, including that of intergovernmental negotiations. It is does not follow, however, that successful communication has been achieved simply because two parties speak the same language and understand the literal meaning of the words that pass between them. As Raymond Cohen has argued, "for a message to be correctly understood there must be sufficient similarity, if not identity, between the intention of the sender and the meaning attributed by the receiver,"[22] something that is almost always more problematic when the communication takes place across the boundaries of culture. Cohen then elaborates: "Cultural strangers can rely on no shared experience of family, church, schooling, community, and country. Their national histories, traditions, and belief systems may or may not concur. When they communicate there can be no guarantee that the meanings encoded by one and decoded by the other are at all related."[23] Dissonance in communication between cultures is particularly likely, as we have observed, when the parties are Western and non-Western. In his discussion of negotiating across cultures, Cohen identifies three factors that contribute to a failure to communicate successfully. Although his focus is diplomatic negotiations, these factors also operate as impediments to successful communication in other areas, as illustrated especially in films about U.S.-Japanese relations.

   These three factors are well known to students of cross-cultural communication and have been observed firsthand, if not fully understood, by increasingly large numbers of ordinary people in their travels and encounters with "foreigners." Each may be expressed as a dichotomy between "our" approach to communication and "theirs": between a culture with an individualistic ethos and one with a collectivistic or interdependent ethos, between a low-context culture and a high-context culture, and between regimented and leisurely conceptions of the importance of time.[24]

Differences between a culture that gives priority to individual rights and one that stresses the primacy of obligations to the group or community are among the most important impeding intercultural communication. The former values individual self-expression and encourages the questioning of authority; it believes in equality and mobility, taking the view that status is acquired rather than inherited; it holds that obligations are defined by contract, not custom. The collectivistic culture makes very different assumptions, beginning with the basic notion that individual freedom is constrained by duties to the group and that the individual's relationship to that group is inherited rather than acquired. Such a culture emphasizes respect for tradition and authority, avoidance of confrontation, and the importance of preserving face, or the individual's standing in the eyes of the group. These differences cannot simply be set aside when persons from cultures with such deeply ingrained beliefs seek to communicate; the interlocutors bring these culturally dissonant beliefs to the dialogue as surely as they do the interests that dictate their formal agendas. The United States is the classic example of an individualistic culture, while Japan's culture is clearly collectivistic by comparison.

The concept of low-context and high-context cultures, developed in a famous work by Edward T. Hall,[25] introduces yet another important factor into the problem of intercultural communication. Once again, the United States and Japan provide excellent illustrations. Low-context communication—the American way—involves saying what one means, not "beating around the bush." Language is important for its factual content, not for the social function of cultivating personal relationships. What matters is what is said; there is little need to search for hidden meanings or watch for nonverbal signals. A high-context culture like that of the Japanese approaches verbal exchanges, whether in private conversation or public negotiation, rather differently. There is a strong aversion to the direct, blunt approach in communication, with the result that words are weighed very carefully and the speaker, anxious to avoid offense, often prefers evasion to precision. As the name implies, context is very important; more is going on than simply the sending of a message, including an effort to cultivate or preserve social harmony—hence the predilection for exaggerated expressions of courtesy and much small talk before getting down to business. When persons from low-context and high-context cultures meet and talk, they frequently misunderstand and sometimes even resent each other because they are insensitive to this important dimension of communication.

The third factor complicating intercultural communication is different perceptions of time. Some cultures—and once again the United States is the prime example—live by the clock, ever preoccupied with schedules and deadlines. Time is indeed money. "In an individualistic culture like the United States, grounded in personal fulfillment and the work ethic, 'getting things done' is the prevailing value, and life is a treadmill of achievement."[26] Moreover, Americans are an ahistorical, future-oriented people, generally viewing the past as largely irrelevant to the quest for solutions to today's problems. But time is viewed differently in some other cultures, where the rhythms of nature are more important than the ticking of the clock and where "past humiliations . . . are not consigned to the archives but continue to nourish present concerns."[27] For such cultures, the urgency with which Americans approach tasks is alien to them. In this case, Japan provides less of a contrast than it does in the other two dichotomies discussed above, although the Japanese do tend to be more conscious of history and its humiliations for their country than do Americans.

These cultural dichotomies may be observed in several of the films mentioned heretofore in this chapter. But two other films, both about U.S.-Japanese relations, make perhaps the most insightful contributions to an understanding of this aspect of international relations. These films are *Gung Ho* and *Rising Sun,* both of which were discussed in Chapter 8 because they deal with economic competitiveness between the United States and Japan. Both are concerned with the presence of Japanese corporations in the United States and with problems that representatives of the two cultures have in understanding each other and negotiating solutions to their differences. *Gung Ho* is a comedy and *Rising Sun* a high-tech mystery yarn, but each in its own way has something of interest to say about intercultural communication, and especially about the conflict between individualistic and collectivistic cultures and between low-context and high-context cultures.

In Ron Howard's *Gung Ho,* the clash of cultures takes place in an automobile plant in fictional Hadleyville, Pennsylvania. The plant has been closed down and the town is dying until a Japanese company decides to take over the plant, saving Hadleyville but creating a minor cultural war when the workers rebel at Japanese management practices and expectations. The conflict of cultures begins when Hunt Stevenson (Michael Keaton), a fast-talking foreman, arrives in Japan to persuade the board of Assan Motors to reopen the plant. In real life, of course, Stevenson would have been a poor choice as salesman for Hadleyville; the Japanese culture venerates age and wisdom, whereas Stevenson is young and lacks status. But he is also brash and anything but subtle in his sales pitch. While the older Japanese board members listen silently (and, by the looks on their faces, disapprovingly), he plunges straight into his pitch, lacing it with crude humor. At the end of his remarks he invites the members of the board to raise questions, and is clearly discomforted when they remain stonily silent. The Keaton character is the quintessential representative of the low-context American culture, with its emphasis on getting right to the point and its obliviousness to nonverbal cues. He has not done his homework on the high-context Japanese culture, and if this were not a comedy in which the screenplay necessarily dictates another outcome, Assan Motors would never choose to come to Hadleyville.

But come it does, and when the plant reopens we become witness to the conflict between the individualistic nature of American culture and the collectivistic nature of Japanese culture. The Japanese management wants to instill in the workers a sense that they are a part of a team and that they owe their first loyalty to the company. They rotate the workers around among the different jobs on the assembly line, organize group calisthenics at the start of the work day, and do not tolerate radios, cigars, or the reading of newspapers on the job. Accustomed to "doing their own thing," the American workers chafe under these rules. Stevenson tries to intercede on their behalf, at one point arguing that "Americans like to feel special." In its own heavy-handed way, *Gung Ho* gives us a short lesson on an important difference between American and Japanese cultures.

The director has loaded the film with brief scenes that caricature cultural differences. When Stevenson and his girlfriend (Mimi Rogers) are invited to dinner by his boss (Gedde Watanabe), all of the Japanese wives leave the room when it comes time to talk business; she does not get the cultural message and insists on staying for the discussion, which quickly turns into a disaster for Stevenson and his relationship with both her and the Japanese management team. The American workers find the Japanese practice of eating with chopsticks amusing, and the audience is reminded that most Americans do not share the Japanese taste for sushi and seaweed. Even the problem of understanding the vernacularisms in each other's language is lampooned. When Stevenson tries to see his boss, the Japanese secretary tells him that it is not a good day to do so; uncertain of how to say it, she consults her Japanese-English dictionary and then informs him that the boss is "between a rock and a hard on." The audience laughs, but the film has scored another point for the proposition that communication across the barrier of culture can be difficult.

Rising Sun, although a very different kind of film, also explores the problems of intercultural communication, particularly those that occur during negotiations between high-context and low-context cultures. As noted in the comment on this film in Chapter 8, a prostitute has been murdered in the boardroom of a Japanese corporation's Los Angeles headquarters during the course of a lavish reception attended by important American politicians. The company, anxious to avoid adverse publicity, insists that her death is simply the result of a drug overdose and wants the matter handled quietly; the Los Angeles Police Department, in the person of outspoken lieutenant Tom Graham (Harvey Keitel), who detests the Japanese, is equally determined that the police conduct the investigation in their own way. A young police liaison officer, Web Smith (Wesley Snipes), and a senior officer, John Connor (Sean Connery), who is an old Japan hand, arrive to take charge of what promises to be a delicate investigation.

En route to the crime scene, Connor tutors Smith on the subtleties of negotiating with the Japanese, describing their relationship as that of *sempai* and *kohai,* an older, superior man and his younger, subordinate colleague. Unlike Graham, whose belligerent and threatening style is a veritable caricature of a low-context culture's approach to communication, Connor is sensitive to the context in which the dialogue is taking place and seeks to develop a relationship of trust with the Japanese. Alert to the importance the Japanese attach to the preservation of social harmony and to the significance of body language, Connor has told Smith not to lose his temper and not to use big arm movements, both unacceptable practices in a high-context culture; however, when the Japanese spokesman for the company, Ishihara, is uncooperative, Connor violates his own advice and flies into a rage, coercing him into cooperation. When Smith comments on this, Connor explains that he purposely acted out-of-control in order to help Ishihara save face in front of his boss.

Later in the film, when it becomes apparent that Ishihara has disgraced the company by giving the investigators a doctored video disc of the murder, its senior officials quietly distance themselves from him in the climactic meeting in the boardroom. He is thus shamed and humiliated in front of everyone, and this loss of face is, in the eyes of a culture like Japan's, a fate almost literally worse than death. Thus the film ends as it began with a commentary on the importance of face in high-context, collectivistic cultures. *Rising Sun,* like *Gung Ho,* can hardly be said to offer a textbook analysis of cross-cultural communication, and both films have been criticized for their oversimplified portrayal of Japanese culture. However, if one makes due allowance for the filmmakers' license to present complex issues in a few broad brush strokes, these films make valuable comments about intercultural relations and they should invite a more thoughtful inquiry into an important aspect of international relations.

Huntington may well be wrong in his insistence that in the years ahead "the great divisions among humankind and the dominating source of conflict will be cultural."[28] But we can be sure that culture will continue to play an important role in relationships among states and peoples, and that other sources of tension will be exacerbated by culturally-based misunderstandings and failures of communication. Whether films take the clash of cultures as their principal theme or not, it will remain an important subtext in numerous films of interest to students of international relations.

Notes

1. Huntington, "The Clash of Civilizations?" pp. 22–49.
2. Fukuyama, "The End of History?"
3. Huntington, "The Clash of Civilizations?" p. 22.
4. *Ibid.,* pp. 24, 25.

5. Barber, "Jihad v. McWorld," pp. 53–55; the author has further developed this conflict in a subsequent book, *Jihad v. McWorld.*

6. Barber, "Global Multiculturalism and American Experiment," p. 51.

7. R. Cohen, *Negotiating Across Cultures*, p. 3.

8. Axtell, "Black Robe," p. 78.

9. *Ibid.*

10. Review by Rafferty, "True Believers: Black Robe," p. 122.

11. Perhaps the most extreme instance of the clash of cultures in our time occurs, not in a film, but in a wickedly satirical novel, Richard Dooling's *White Man's Grave.*

12. Isaacs, *Australia's Living Heritage*, p. 8.

13. Peter Davis, quoted in Peary, *Cult Movies 3*, p. 105.

14. Reimers, *Still the Golden Door,* p. 1.

15. Culhane, "Louis Malle," pp. 28–31.

16. Powers, "My Beautiful Laundrette," p. 295. In the film, Nasser, a kind of Pakistani godfather, teaches his nephew "how to squeeze the tits of the system."

17. *Ibid.*, p. 297.

18. Kael, "Circus," p. 138.

19. Huntington, "The Clash of Civilizations?"

20. Shirley, "Is Iran's Present Algeria's Future?" p. 33.

21. *Ibid.*

22. R. Cohen, *Negotiating Across Cultures*, p. 20.

23. *Ibid.*, p. 21.

24. In the discussion of these dichotomies, the author draws heavily upon Raymond Cohen's provocative study, *Negotiating Across Cultures.*

25. Hall, *Beyond Culture.*

26. R. Cohen, *Negotiating Across Cultures*, p. 28.

27. *Ibid.*, p. 29.

28. Huntington, *"The Clash of Civilizations?"* p. 22.

11

The Domestic Roots
of International Relations

The roots of the foreign policy of a state often lie deep within the social fabric of that country, nourished by geography and by history and reflecting both national traditions and mood swings among the population. Thus phenomena that may seem at first blush to be purely internal and unrelated to international relations can have an important influence on the course of world affairs. Societal attitudes with foreign policy implications are shaped over time by such factors as whether borders have provided protection or been a standing invitation to invasion; whether or not there is a history of remembered humiliations at the hands of other states and peoples; whether the population is largely homogeneous or riven by divisions of ethnicity, race, religion, or class; whether there is a tradition of governmental stability or one of chronic turmoil and upheaval; whether or not social institutions exist that enhance the quality of life and sustain a sense of community; even whether the citizenry is largely literate or illiterate. Societies differ from each other in many ways that can have a bearing on the foreign policies of states. A liberal civil society, for example, provides a different context for the development of a state's role in world affairs than a Marxist or Islamic society or a society characterized by authoritarian populism.[1]

A classic example of the thesis that foreign policies are rooted in societal factors is the influence of the U.S. frontier and the country's long period of westward expansion in the nineteenth century; it is possible to describe the role of the United States in world affairs without reference to this phenomenon, but it would be a mistake to underestimate its importance. Another very different example is provided in the case of France. That country's relations with trading partners and with fellow members of the European Union are affected by the fact that French farmers are able to demonstrate their great influence by effectively blocking highways with their tractors in protest of government farm policies. Russian society is caught today in a difficult period of transition between a regimented

228 International Relations on Film

communist past and a future whose outlines are still hard to discern. A truly democratic civil society may yet emerge, but until it does, mafia entrepreneurship[2] is likely to thrive in Russia with important implications for that country's external relations. Japanese pacifism and Swiss neutrality are not merely policy choices arrived at after debate and negotiation, but products of beliefs that are by now so deeply entrenched as to be core elements of the national ethos. Examples of societal forces such as these could be multiplied many times over.

Some of the societal factors shaping the way states view their role in the world are obviously more enduring than others. Geography, it has been argued, is destiny. Peoples living in countries far removed from the major centers of international contact and conflict are likely to view the world differently than peoples in countries closer to the epicenter. Peoples living in countries where nature is harsh or fickle tend to have different priorities than peoples in countries where the climate is benign and the land bountiful. The literature on international relations is replete with references to the fact that Russia lacks warm water ports and has hard-to-defend western borders, that Spain has long been isolated from the rest of Europe by the Pyrenees, that Japan has a severely limited supply of the natural resources necessary to sustain an industrial power, and that Saudi Arabia is blessed with vast pools of oil beneath desert sands. Many of these factors have become less salient over time, but they often continue to exercise significant influence over a country's world outlook.

No societal forces are immutable, although some are subject to change more easily or quickly than others. The volatility of social and political institutions in times of national stress—for example, the experience of Germany during the Weimar Republic and Hitler's rise to power, is so common as to need no documentation. When the resulting ideological friction is so great as to paralyze those institutions, civil war or dictatorship is a distinct possibility. In a recent essay, Charles S. Maier distinguishes that situation, which he calls a political crisis, from what he sees as a major change in the constellation of societal forces within Western democracies as we near the end of the twentieth century.[3] He refers to this latter change as a moral crisis. It is clear that the phenomenon Maier is talking about runs both widely and deeply through many democracies—that it is more than simply a matter of replacing liberals with conservatives or vice versa in the halls of government. He argues that what has been taking place is "a profound shift of public attitude along three dimensions: a sudden sense of historical dislocation, a disaffection with the political leadership of all parties and a recurring skepticism about doctrines of social progress."[4]

The end of the Cold War deprived governments and peoples of their sense of great purpose; the euphoria that accompanied the collapse of communism quickly turned to irresolution, as demonstrated by the feeble and uncertain responses to crises in Bosnia, Somalia, Rwanda, and elsewhere. Citizens seem to have lost confidence in government and in the political classes, and have been hacking away at the legitimacy of those in public office; with varying degrees of anger and enthusiasm, they have been embracing what Maier terms "territorial populism," with its frequently intolerant undercurrents.[5] Related to this dimension of moral crisis has been a decline in the belief that social problems can be solved and a mounting indifference, if not outright hostility, to the condition and claims of minorities, outsiders, and the less fortunate. In effect, so this argument goes, the societal values and habits that have given direction and purpose to the Western democracies at least since World War II are now in question. Insofar as this is true, we can expect to see a ripple effect in the relations among states.

Whether ferment within societies produces political or moral crises or not, the societal level of analysis is important to an understanding of international relations, especially so in the case of the larger powers and what Anthony Lake has termed "backlash" states, that is, "recalcitrant and outlaw states that not only choose to remain outside the family but also assault its basic values."[6] The societal forces at work in different countries have of course been the subject of countless films, and only some of those films can be considered relevant to international relations. But even when links exist between those societal forces and a country's foreign policy, the linkage is so rarely mentioned that the moviegoer will usually have to make a considerable effort to make the connection. Some films offer insights into national character and national values relevant for an understanding of the sources of foreign policy, even if foreign policy is not the subject of those films. Moreover, the kind of movies made in a country and the kind of movies its citizens turn into box office blockbusters can also tell us something about the way the country visualizes its interests and its role in world affairs. Is it irrelevant to an understanding of the U.S. view of the world in the 1990s that Americans have recently been shelling out enormous sums of money to see big budget action thrillers involving terrorists, drug dealers, soldiers of fortune, and ex–Cold Warriors, all armed with the most sophisticated and deadly high-tech weaponry imaginable?

This chapter will focus on only a few of the many films that might be cited under a broad definition of the "domestic roots of international relations." Many of the films discussed in earlier chapters—films that more obviously pertain to international relations—have something to say about societal factors as sources of foreign policy. For the most part, these films will not be revisited in the following pages. The emphasis will instead be on films that are not overtly about international relations, but which highlight conditions and factors within countries that have contributed to the way those countries perceive the world beyond their borders and are in turn perceived by others.

American Exceptionalism and the Frontier Legacy

From its infancy in the late eighteenth century, the United States has enjoyed a degree of geographic isolation from the rest of the world that has
been denied to all of the other great or near-great powers. Moreover, it had
in the first century of its existence an opportunity to expand westward almost unimpeded until it occupied a large part of a continent rich in fertile
soil, mineral resources, a beneficent climate, navigable rivers, natural harbors—indeed, nearly all the requisites of rapid growth and prosperity. Although the slavery issue and the Civil War obviously constitute a very important qualification, it is fair to say that the United States grew from a
cluster of loosely confederated colonies on the Atlantic littoral to a continental and then global power with relative ease. Little wonder that the
American people came to believe in "the myth of America's uniqueness as
a nation and a force in the world,"[7] in what Louis Hartz has called the doctrine of American exceptionalism.[8] Michael Hunt has argued that the
United States has a foreign policy ideology that took shape during the
country's formative years and which continues to dominate the thinking of
the foreign policy establishment.[9] Dissecting this ideology, he identifies
three core ideas: a view of the American mission that equates the cause of
liberty with the pursuit of national greatness, a view of other peoples informed by a belief in the hierarchy of races, and a view of political and social change that abhors revolution.[10] This thesis, which locates the roots of
modern-day American foreign policy in the country's history, makes a
provocative contribution to the proposition that the societal level of analysis offers a useful perspective on state behavior in world affairs.

It is doubtful if there is any one film that can be said to validate
Hunt's position or that of any of the other scholars who have inquired into
the domestic roots of American foreign policy. But a case can be made that
the search for such a film should begin with that quintessential American
contribution to the medium, the western. In 1989, when Tony Thomas published his study of the "wild west" on film,[11] he estimated that the number of westerns made since the coming of sound was close to 3,500, and
that figure excluded movies made for television. This astonishingly large
output, most of it set between the Civil War and the end of the nineteenth
century, led Thomas to claim that "More six-shooters have been fired,
more cattle rustled, more banks and stagecoaches held up, more cowboys
have brawled in saloons, more wagons have rumbled westward, more Indians have been shot from ponies and more cavalry have ridden to the rescue in the movies than the real West ever knew."[12] He goes on to assert
that "of all the depictions of American life put on film, the western is the
least accurate and the most romanticized."[13] Few would question that conclusion, and John Ford, usually regarded as the greatest director of westerns, would not be among them. Ford is responsible for the famous line in

The Man Who Shot Liberty Valance: "When the legend becomes fact, print the legend." What matters in westerns is not what happened as the Americans settled the vast expanses of land between the Mississippi River and the California coast, but the meaning of what happened.

And what is that meaning? One critic explains that

> Westerns appeal so much to us because they are explorations of who we are, dramas in which America's soul, the national identity, hangs in the balance. Epic in its scope, the Western is taken seriously because the fate of its protagonists becomes the fate of our nation. . . . The Westerner embodies the myth that we can perpetually start over in this new land to be shaped by our measurements.[14]

Most westerns unfold in a wide-open landscape, a frontier between the civilization men (and a few women) have left behind and the untamed country that lies ahead. This is the land of sagebrush, desert, mountains, and the "big sky" into which Americans pushed as they created their continental empire and developed the values and beliefs about themselves that helped to shape their country's conception of its role in world affairs.

Many westerns could be cited for their contribution to our image of this process. Only one will be mentioned here, and it is Ford's *The Searchers,* generally thought of as one of the finest examples of the genre. The film is set in Ford's beloved Monument Valley; although it was hardly on any of the major trails followed by settlers of the American west, its great empty spaces and imposing red rock formations help the viewer imagine the magnitude of the task of settling the west and the fortitude of those who undertook that task. This beautiful but austere country is very sparsely inhabited; there are only a few homesteaders and, of course, there are Indians. In fact, it is a Comanche raid on a family of homesteaders, in which three of the family are massacred and two young girls kidnapped, that leads to the five-year search (and gives the film its title). The searchers are Ethan Edwards (John Wayne) and Marty (Jeffrey Hunter), the former a loner and a racist, the latter the adopted son of the massacred family and part Cherokee. Marty insists on accompanying Ethan in his search for Debbie, the surviving daughter (her sister has been raped and killed by the Indians), because he knows that Ethan will kill her if he finds her because she has been defiled by having intercourse with the Comanche chief, Scar.

Ethan illustrates Hunt's thesis about the American belief in a hierarchy of race.

> Just as Southern whites spawned virulent strains of negrophobia, frontier whites were the source of the most intense and violent Indian hating. And though their resort to fraudulent or violent methods collided with humanitarian principles and legal agreements (including formal treaties),

the federal government and, it seems fair to say, most Americans endorsed
or acquiesced in the practice of Indian extermination and removal.[15]

But Ethan's search is not only for Debbie; it is also a search for self-
purification. Ethan catches up with Scar and kills him, but when he finds
Debbie he no longer feels the need to kill her too. Instead he carries her
back to the foster family that will take her in, and, still the outsider in a
frontier now becoming "civilized," he turns and walks away alone at film's
end. Thus Ethan represents not only a racist strain in American society, but
also America's struggle to rid itself of racism. That struggle is still in evidence as the United States debates immigration policy, and there are people in the Third World who would probably find evidence of it in U.S. foreign aid policy, in the American response to humanitarian crises in Africa,
and in U.S. support for the United Nations, with its overwhelming majority of states from the non-Western, non-Caucasian world.

Westerns like *The Searchers* remind us that Americans were long preoccupied with the task of westward expansion, not the problems of the rest
of the world. Although it has been argued that the United States became
isolationist during the first century of its existence, the truth is more complicated. Frances Fitzgerald has claimed that "isolationism was merely a
tropism to the south and west rather than to the east;"[16] national expansion
continued after the closing of the frontier. The sense of manifest destiny
that came to be associated with the settlement of the west acquired a missionary quality that became a major part of the rationale for the annexation
of the Philippines and hegemonic policies in the Caribbean and Central
America. "This evangelical mission was not just the substance of American policy," Fitzgerald writes. "For many it was the spirit of the nation itself."[17] Thus westerns such as *The Searchers* indirectly underscore Hunt's
thesis that in the nineteenth century the United States developed a foreign
policy ideology that pursued national greatness by "pitching the tents of
liberty farther westward and farther southward,"[18] remaking other peoples
in our image.

In the Shadow of the Cold War

Societal forces are also on display in other films made in and about the
United States that arguably reflect its approach to international relations.
The McCarthy era—that brief but deeply disturbing period from the late
1940s through the mid-1950s—was mentioned briefly in Chapter 5 on espionage and subversion, but merits further comment here. This was a period during which the country seemed to abandon its customary common
sense and civility; the communist scare and the frequently reckless charges
of those who would exploit it produced political and social turmoil in the

body politic that both reflected anxiety about the state of international relations and colored the way in which Americans saw the world. The wave of virulent anticommunism and heightened suspicion of those with leftist leanings produced a considerable number of films; in time those who were under attack fought back, producing films of their own. Most of the films in the first category, such as *My Son John* and *Big Jim McClain,* were so patently meretricious and polemical as not to justify further comment. Sam Fuller's *Pickup on South Street* is an altogether more interesting example of this type of filmmaking, and is discussed in Chapter 5.

The counterattack is best seen in Nicholas Ray's baroque western, *Johnny Guitar,* which on the surface is not at all about McCarthyism. But in its own clever and decidedly unusual way, it is, as Danny Peary argues, "a serious indictment of McCarthyite mob hysteria and bigotry, controversial because Ray and screenwriter Philip Yordan dared attack the reactionary political climate of 1954 by subverting what had always been a politically conservative genre."[19] Viewed on one level, this is simply an unusual western in which the two principal antagonists are women— Vienna (Joan Crawford), who runs a gambling establishment and awaits the arrival of the railroad that will make her rich, and Emma (Mercedes McCambridge), who represents the status quo, opposes the railroad, and hates Vienna both for her politics and for the men in her life. But the characters in the film are also meant to represent the various players in the drama of McCarthyism's witch hunt. Emma and the cattlemen and townspeople who side with her are the ones conducting the witch hunt; when Emma organizes a posse to capture Vienna, the posse becomes a surrogate for the House Un-American Activities Committee (HUAC). Vienna and her former (and future) lover, Johnny Guitar (Sterling Hayden), symbolize the progressive element, condemned as suspected communists or "fellow travelers" during the McCarthy era. Just as HUAC forced witnesses to testify against others and resorted to guilt by association, so do Emma and her posse bully people into squealing and even lying to save their own skins. Once a loose woman, Vienna has reformed, but "as it was with suspected communists who had long given up their left-wing affiliations, she finds it impossible to live down her past."[20]

Johnny Guitar may well be the best film commentary on the McCarthy phenomenon, capturing as it does the intense convictions and terrible excesses of those years. Like McCarthy, who was eventually undone by his own demagogic excesses and censured by the Senate, Emma is shot dead by Vienna at film's end after her fellow vigilantes lose their stomach for her fight. And it is an interesting sidelight that Sterling Hayden, the title character in the film and an actor who was later to portray the psychotic anticommunist general who launches a nuclear strike against the USSR in *Dr. Strangelove,* was himself once a communist who had to clear himself by confessing this past indiscretion to the FBI. Hayden survived the witch hunt; not all Hollywood personalities or other Americans were so fortunate.

One other film from those feverish days in the 1950s also merits mention. It is Don Siegel's *Invasion of the Body Snatchers*. (The picture was remade by Philip Kaufman just over twenty years later, after the red scare had largely dissipated, but the remake, although well done, is less relevant to the issue at hand than the original.) *Invasion of the Body Snatchers* is one of the best of the science fiction films that were so popular in the 1950s, and like others of that genre, it is about the dehumanization of ordinary people by alien forces. Large seed pods appear mysteriously in the small California town of Santa Mira, and while its residents are asleep the pods gradually turn into replicas of them. Soon virtually all of the people are zombie-like versions of their former selves, looking exactly as they did before but lacking all emotions. The film's hero, Dr. Miles Bennell (Kevin McCarthy), struggles desperately to stay awake so that he will not also become a pod person (his girlfriend succumbs near the end in one of the film's truly shocking moments). He also tries to warn the outside world about what is happening, no easy task considering that the whole community is singlemindedly bent on preventing him from doing so. Meanwhile, truckloads of the pods continue to arrive by night, suggesting that it is only a matter of time until not only Santa Mira but all of California and eventually the United States will be taken over.

Siegel always denied that the *Invasion of the Body Snatchers* was a film with a political message, but that did not prevent the critics from concluding that it was an allegory of the politics of the McCarthy era. Indeed, the film produced two diametrically opposed interpretations. For some it was an anticommunism film, warning America that the country was in danger of being taken over by cold, calculating, regimented, and emotionless communists who would deprive people of their freedom of thought and turn them into obedient servants of an authoritarian regime. Others were equally convinced that it was an anti-McCarthy film, in which the pod people were the anticommunist zealots of the day, demanding adherence to their conception of the truth and relentlessly destroying the careers (and lives) of those who did not conform.[21]

This is a lot of baggage for a modest, low-budget film to carry, but the very fact that so many were ready to read so much into it is a good indication of the extent to which the red scare had become a major societal issue, helping to shape national politics and complicating the task of conducting foreign policy in the turbulent early years of the Cold War. To cite but one example of this impact, the United States not only worried about communists in the agencies of its own government, but also insisted on the ideological purity of American citizens working for the United Nations secretariat, even if this meant violating the principles on which an international civil service is based. The films made during the McCarthy era and reflecting the anxieties then rampant provide an excellent illustration of what Richard Hofstadter has called the paranoid style in American politics.[22] They also tend to illustrate the thesis that while Americans may support reform, their own historical experience had produced an aversion to radical politics and to revolutionary change that has repeatedly found expression in both domestic and foreign policy.[23] Thus, ironically, the McCarthyites believed that they had to prevent a revolution from the left, while their opponents argued that the tactics of the McCarthyites were themselves nothing less than revolutionary and hence un-American.

Vietnam, Watergate, and Wall Street

The Vietnam War and the Watergate crisis created a turbulence within American society that lasted well beyond the conclusion of the war and the resignation of Richard Nixon. America's other twentieth-century wars also generated debates about U.S. involvement, produced casualties that left a legacy of grief, and spawned their share of postwar revisionist thinking about alternative scenarios. But no war opened such painful wounds within U.S. society as the one in Vietnam, and this was not only because the United States lost that war. In fact, the societal rift over the war came years before the last American soldier left Vietnam and the communist victory was secured. The Vietnam War is discussed in several earlier chapters, as is the film that more than any other recaptures the crisis over American involvement in that war, *Born on the Fourth of July.*

The Oliver Stone film is not about the war itself, but about the trauma that U.S. participation in the war visited upon American society. It uses one young American, Ron Kovic (Tom Cruise), to demonstrate the breakdown in the country's nearly reflexive support for military resistance to the spread of international communism. Initially a gung-ho volunteer for service in Vietnam, Kovic is seriously wounded in combat; parayzed from the waist down, he returns home to a country that is beginning to question its government's policy and becomes part of the antiwar movement. The rift in U.S. society over the military presence in Vietnam and its conduct of the war was deep and long lasting. It was not until the end of Operation Desert Storm in 1991 that an American president, George Bush, was able to say, "By God, we've kicked the Vietnam syndrome once and for all."[24] That societal rift is brought to us on screen in *Born on the Fourth of July,* where angry antiwar demonstrators challenge traditional notions of what constitutes patriotism. Of course the screen version of those demonstrations does not begin to capture either the scale or the depth of the tensions that rocked the country in the late 1960s. Nor does it bring us the debacle of the Democratic Party's national convention in Chicago in 1968 or tell us anything about the muddied referendum on the war that led to Richard

Nixon's narrow victory over Hubert Humphrey, tarnished by his linkage to the Johnson administration and its conduct of an increasingly unpopular war. Yet Stone's film, through Kovic's personal pilgrimage, does manage to convey something of the trauma that gripped the society in those years.

So does that director's more recent film, *Nixon*, which, like virtually all of his films, stirred instant controversy upon its release. Stone's biopic of the thirty-seventh president of the United States touches upon most of the highlights of Nixon's political life and invites the audience to accept as fact some speculative embellishments that reflect the director's fascination with conspiracy theories. There is more than a little foreign policy in this film, including Nixon's famous trip to China, which led to normalization of relations for the first time since the communist victory of 1949, and a fair amount of screen time for Nixon's formidable secretary of state, Henry Kissinger. But the film's contribution to understanding the role of societal forces in shaping foreign policy is largely the result of what it has to say about the conduct of the war in Vietnam and the Watergate scandal, which led to a presidential resignation for the first time in American history.

Here, as in *Born on the Fourth of July,* we are made aware of the anti-war movement and the fact that it has forced the administration to seek a way to extricate the United States from Vietnam without conceding defeat. In a key scene in the film, Nixon (Anthony Hopkins) finds himself confronted by a group of demonstrators at the Lincoln Memorial; never comfortable in such face-to-face meetings, he tries unsuccessfully to bridge what has become an unbridgeable gap between opponents of the war and his own Machiavellian strategy for ending it. Once again we are reminded that American society had been shaken to its roots by the controversy over the war.

The Watergate affair inevitably provides the climactic drama of the film. In spite of Nixon's now-infamous defense, "I am not a crook," Watergate not only destroyed his presidency but also sent shock waves through a country already reeling from the assassinations of President Kennedy, his brother Robert, and Martin Luther King, and from the domestic turmoil unleashed by racial conflict and the Vietnam war. Stone's film walks us step by step through the several phases of the coverup by Nixon and his top aides that turned a bungled burglary into a major constitutional crisis. It is not a flattering portrayal of government in action. Critics have differed in their assessment of the film's treatment of Nixon, but the very fact that it produced such a vigorous national debate, not only in the movie reviews but in the editorials and op ed pages of America's newspapers, confirms the view that the Watergate crisis and the president it brought down still occupy a prominent place in the country's memory and exercise a powerful hold on its imagination.

Another earlier film, *All the President's Men,* also offers insights into the Watergate affair and, more importantly, into the critical role of investigative journalism in exposing corruption in high places and thereby shaping public opinion. This 1976 film by Alan Pakula, in which Robert Redford and Dustin Hoffman play the *Washington Post* reporters, Bob Woodward and Carl Bernstein, who broke the story, focuses exclusively on their efforts to obtain the information their managing editor needs to authorize publication of the story. Needless to say, none of the people involved in the coverup wants to talk to Woodward and Bernstein; this is quite understandable, both because of the possibility, confirmed by subsequent events, that some of them may wind up in jail if the truth gets out, and because the reporters are so irritating in the way they badger people for information. Yet the success of Woodward and Bernstein has led to a dramatic increase in investigative reporting by the staffs of major newspapers and hence to much closer scrutiny of government officials, political parties, interest groups, corporate leaders, and influential public figures. The result has been a series of stories that have made the American people more skeptical and even more cynical about the nation's institutions, and has contributed to the decline in the perceived legitimacy of those institutions, a point made by Charles S. Maier in a work cited earlier in this chapter. *All the President's Men* does not carry the Watergate story through to the Congressional hearings, the revelation about Nixon's tapes, or the resignation to avoid impeachment, but it does suggest the ways a pluralistic society's views of its institutions are shaped by one of those institutions, the much-maligned media.

Nixon's preoccupation with Watergate and the survival of his presidency inevitably had an effect on the country's foreign policy. It was a huge distraction, making it difficult for the government to anticipate and react in a timely way to international developments of concern to the nation. It seems clear, for example, that the United States was caught off guard when the countries of the developing world mounted their campaign for a New International Economic Order in 1974. Fixated on Watergate, and with a secretary of state who was not much interested in development issues, the Nixon administration was ill-prepared to assume a leadership role in the North-South debate that ensued at the United Nations.[25]

Another film that explores some of the societal forces that define the United States is *Wall Street,* yet another of Oliver Stone's filmed commentaries on the nation's flaws. "Wall Street" has long been more than the name of the street on which the New York Stock Exchange happens to be located; it has come to stand for the influential financial interests of the U.S. economy—the heart of free market capitalism. The *Wall Street Journal* is one of the most widely read newspapers in the country, if not the world, and millions of investors follow the stock market quotations emanating from Wall Street as religiously as they do the fortunes of their alma mater on the football field or their child's soccer team on Saturday mornings. What Wall Street has to say about the nation's health is arguably as important as—if not more important than—what the government's leaders in Washington have to say. Yet Stone's film is bent on showing us the dark side of Wall Street and capitalism, and especially on exposing what Susan Strange has termed "casino capitalism."[26]

The film's antihero is highly successful Wall Street "legend in his own time" Gordon Gekko (Michael Douglas), who has made a fortune buying and selling companies and has become a hero and mentor to a cocky and ambitious young broker, Bud Fox (Charlie Sheen). But Gekko does not play by the rules; he is a man who not only has no scruples about how he makes his money but does not care how many people he destroys in the process. Gekko is clearly intended to be the fictional counterpart to such real-life white-collar criminals as Ivan Boesky and Michael Milken. His philosophy is summed up in a speech he gives during a shareholders meeting of the Teldar corporation. Announcing that he intends to take over the company, he spits out his creed in typically unsubtle Stone fashion: "Greed is good. Greed works." And then, to make sure no one misses the point, "Greed will not only save Teldar Paper but that other malfunctioning corporation called the U.S.A."

Fox eventually realizes that he has made a pact with the devil when, after helping Gekko acquire Blue Star Airline for which his father (Martin Sheen) works, he discovers that Gekko never intended to build the airline up as promised. "Why do you need to wreck this company?" he asks, and Gekko fires back, "Because it's wreckable." The film is full of one-liners that hammer home Stone's critique of capitalism run amok. Gekko tells his now-disillusioned disciple that it's a zero sum game they're playing, one in which somebody wins and somebody loses, and then sums up his disdain for those who are naive enough to follow the rules, saying "It's not a democracy, it's a free market."

Wall Street is, of course, an American morality play, and Fox, who at film's end is headed to jail himself, helps the government nail Gekko. Although the film is technically only about a fictional inside trader on Wall Street who finally gets his just desserts, it can also be read as an indictment of the Reagan revolution and its contribution to the culture of greed that swept the United States in the 1980s. As one critic who is not especially fond of Stone's work commented, "Like those turn-of-the-century muckraking novels illustrating such social ills as corruption in railroads (*The Octopus*) and meat-packing (*The Jungle*), Stone's work is searing in immediate impact, then of historical (rather than artistic) value once the particular problem has passed."[27] Whether that particular problem has passed or not is, of course, still debatable.

In an age of economic interdependence and the globalization of the market place, it is impossible to confine the consequences of such a mentality of greed to a single country. Its impact may be felt far and wide in such things as the price of goods and services, employment levels, environmental safety, and even the economic prosperity and growth of other countries. Moreover, it became conventional wisdom in many quarters that the United States was suffering in international economic competition because too much emphasis was placed on making money by buying and selling corporations rather than by producing better products. "I create nothing," Gordon Gekko says, "I own it." This is the important message of *Wall Street,* in which Oliver Stone uses Gordon Gekko to tell us what he thinks is wrong with American capitalism.

The Totalitarian State: Nazism and Fascism

The utility of societal analysis for understanding international relations is also on display in films set in other countries. Only a few of these films will be discussed here, but the windows they open onto conditions in Nazi Germany, Stalinist Russia, China during the Cultural Revolution, South Africa under apartheid, and Argentina under the military junta—all during the decades of turmoil in the twentieth century—should contribute to a fuller and clearer picture of the domestic roots of international relations.

One of the great tragedies and great puzzles of the twentieth century was the descent into Nazi barbarism of Germany, a country whose gifted people have contributed so much to what we think of Western civilization. Hitler's rise to power, which brought to the world history's most devastating war and the horrors of the Holocaust, has been blamed variously on the harsh terms of the Treaty of Versailles, the political chaos and economic distress of the post–World War years, the weakness of the Weimar Republic, Hitler's own personal magnetism, the naiveté of a reactionary and vacillating opposition, and a disillusioned public only too willing to embrace a man and a party outspokenly committed to "national renewal." Once Hitler had been named chancellor, he moved quickly to consolidate his power, suppressing parties of the left, using the excuse of the Reichstag fire to abolish fundamental rights and freedoms, and unleashing violence and terror against Jews, communists, and anyone who incurred the disfavor of an increasingly authoritarian regime. A lot of people who were not themselves Nazis contributed by their silence and acquiescence to Hitler's success, and this particular aspect of the German story in the 1920s and 1930s has been brought to the screen in Istvan Szabo's film, *Mephisto.*

Mephisto tells the story of a German actor whose career develops in parallel with Hitler's. In the film's early scenes, in pre-Hitler Germany, Hendrik (Klaus Maria Brandauer) works in a provincial theater, supports the communist party, and, through a combination of acting skill and driving ambition, attains a certain status in important social circles. Unfortunately, Hitler's star is also rising. When he comes to power, Hendrik's former associates lose favor and are driven underground or into exile.

Hendrik is revealed as an opportunist whose desire to reap glory as an actor and stage director leads him to shed his old beliefs and embrace the new regime. For his troubles, he is appointed director of the German state theater. Hendrik must know that the Nazis are evil in view of what they have done to his friends and the interpretive restraints they place upon his productions of such German classics as Goethe's *Faust*. But, in the words of one reviewer, he is "perhaps the screen's quintessential portrait of the artist as weak-willed, slimy opportunist, prostituting, corrupting, and destroying himself by inches as he toadies to a fascist regime."[28] Hendrik tries to ignore the awful things that are happening in Germany, but he comes to realize that, although he plays the role of Mephistopheles on stage, he is, in real life, cast in the role of Faust and has indeed sold his soul to the devil. The devil in the film is a sadistic minister in the Nazi regime whom we are clearly meant to identify with Herman Goering, and few characters mentioned in this book are as unequivocally evil as he (especially as played by Rolf Hoppe). It might not have been possible for most Germans to stand up to Hitler, and it certainly would not have been easy. But Hendrik in *Mephisto* reminds the viewer of such brilliant German artists as the world-famous orchestral conductor Herbert von Karajan, men (and women) who chose, whether out of conviction or overweening ambition and self-regard, to put their talent and reputations at the service of the Nazis and thereby helped give them a legitimacy they never deserved.

This legitimation of Hitler had very real consequences for Germany's neighbors and ultimately the rest of Europe. The German people might not initially have flocked to Hitler because of his vision of *lebensraum*, but the fact that men like Hendrik went along with him only served to legitimize his obsession with expansion to the east. After consolidating his hold on the country, Hitler turned his attention to preparation for the war that would not only provide that living space but give Germany dominance over the whole of Europe. The result was disaster on an unprecedented scale, not at all what the German people had in mind when they gave their support, enthusiastically or by default, to the author of *Mein Kampf*.

A variant of this moral blindness is on display in another film, set primarily in England during the 1930s. The film is the Merchant and Ivory version of Kazuro Ishiguro's prize-winning novel, *Remains of the Day*. Stevens (Anthony Hopkins) is a butler in the service of Lord Darlington, a member of that decaying social order known as the British aristocracy. Moreover, he wishes to be the perfect butler, and for Stevens that means suppressing his own opinions; he runs Darlington Hall with but one thought in mind, to make it run like clockwork for his employer. As it happens, Lord Darlington is a Nazi sympathizer, and Stevens dutifully serves the needs of his distinguished guests, most of them fellow advocates of appeasement, while they discuss the great issues of the day. Never does it occur to Stevens to listen to the conversations of these "important people," much less question the wisdom of Lord Darlington. At one point Lord Darlington, who is influenced by British fascist and anti-Semite Sir Oswald Mosley, tells Stevens to dismiss two young Jewish housemaids; the butler promptly does so. When the housekeeper, Miss Kenton (Emma Thompson), objects, Stevens tells her that Lord Darlington has studied the Jewish question, and that if he has concluded that Jews are bad people then it is necessary to trust him and dismiss them. It is not that Stevens is anti-Semitic, only that he will not permit himself to think or act except in the context of his conception of the butler's role. In a perceptive analysis of the film, Richard Grenier reaches the following conclusion: "The parallels between the total surrender of will by the perfect butler to his employer and the total surrender of will of the Nazis to their *Fuehrer* are left implicit, but I believe they are the intellectual substructure of *The Remains of the Day*."[29] This film makes an obvious companion to *Mephisto,* not only in its criticism of the failure to speak out against Nazism but in its commentary on a larger social pathology—the accommodation of evil by otherwise good people. This phenomenon has surely had a bearing on the course of relations among states as well as on the domestic politics of states.

   In *Mephisto,* Hendrik must abandon his communist sympathies in order to ingratiate himself with the Nazi regime. The conflict between these two ideologies is hinted at but never developed. That conflict is the very essence of Bernardo Bertolucci's epic film, *Novecento (1900).* Over five hours long when originally released, *Novecento* still runs to more than four hours in the most widely available print, and easily qualifies as the longest film to be discussed in these pages. Bertolucci is a Marxist, and this is very much a film about class struggle. The director fills his large, colorful canvas with the political and social turmoil of his native Italy between 1900 and the end of World War II. The film is all about conflict—between rich and poor, between landowners and peasants, and especially between socialists and communists on the one hand and fascists on the other. *Novecento* has a huge international cast, but at the heart of its conflicts are two men born on the same day (January 1, 1900) in the North Italian province of Emilia-Romagna—Alfredo (played as an adult by Robert DeNiro) and Olmo (played as an adult by Gerard Depardieu). Emilia-Romagna was at the beginning of the century a traditionally socialist and communist region, where farmers organized and forced concessions from landlords, but it was also the region in which Benito Mussolini, originally a socialist but later the founder of the fascist movement, was born.[30] Olmo is born into a family of peasants who are avowed socialists; he becomes an activist on behalf of the peasants and, together with his earthy socialist girlfriend Anita (Stefania Sandrelli), leads the struggle against the landowners and later the fascists. Alfredo, the son of a wealthy landowner, is far more passive politically than Olmo, but his passivity is tantamount to an implicit backing of the increasingly powerful fascists. This passivity costs him the love of his wife Ada (Dominique Sanda) and leads at film's end to his trial at the hands of Olmo and the peasants.

As one interpreter of Bertolucci's films observes, the clash "between the different classes and personalities is indicative of a wider national discord. From this potentially explosive social tension, fascism will rise, promising law and order."[31] Fascism is personified in *Novecento* by Attila (Donald Sutherland), the foreman on Alfredo's land. There is nothing subtle about the way Attila's part is written, directed, or played. He is a monster. As Bertolucci himself has said, Attila represents "not only Italian fascism but universal fascism."[32] In the framing passages of the film, both taking place following the liberation of Northern Italy in 1945, Attila is first captured by the peasants and then killed by them in strangely surrealistic scenes. Thus do Marxism and the masses triumph over fascism and the cruelly repressive landowners in Bertolucci's version of the great social struggle of the twentieth century.

The Totalitarian State: Stalinism and Maoism

Novecento is one of those big sprawling works like *Gone with the Wind* and *Doctor Zhivago* that purport to lay bare the vicissitudes of a society by following the lives of several individuals. In the end, none of those individuals matters as much as the film's real "hero," peasant communism. Communism as portrayed here is a very different matter from the communism practiced in the Soviet Union, first under Lenin and then under Stalin, and as depicted in a film such as Ivan Passer's *Stalin*. Of course the communists were never in power in the Italy of *Novecento*, although Bertolucci wants us to know that they would have ruled humanely if they had been. The situation was very different in Russia; once he had won the fight for power following Lenin's death, Stalin clamped upon that country a totalitarian dictatorship so comprehensive and severe that, in the words of biographer Robert Conquest, "When he died in 1953 he left a monster whose own death throes are not yet over, more than a generation later."[33]

The film *Stalin* begins in the heady days of the Bolshevik revolution and ends with the dictator's death; in the course of its nearly three hours of running time, the camera rarely strays far from Stalin (played by Robert Duvall) as he maneuvers to gain power and then exercises it ruthlessly to destroy almost everyone around him. Passer and others associated with the making of the film have made a major effort to achieve verisimilitude. Not only are many of the settings authentic; most of the actors were obviously chosen for their physical resemblance to the historical figures they are playing; documented events from Stalin's family life, even some that are quite minor, are carefully recreated. Most importantly, we are treated to a reasonably accurate, if necessarily simplified, picture of Stalin's paranoia and its consequences. He manages over the course of the film, as he did in real life, to kill off almost all of the inner circle of communist leaders who jockeyed for position after Lenin's death—Trotsky, Kirov, Kamenev, Zinoviev, Bukharin, and, for good measure, the heads of the secret police who do Stalin's bidding to eliminate the others. Some of these men were Stalin's rivals at one time or another, with different conceptions of how to proceed with the creation of the communist state; but even when there was no evidence, Stalin saw conspiracies against him on every hand. Arrested on trumped-up charges, most were the victims of show trials in which they were coerced into confessing imaginary crimes and then shot. Nor was it only the party leaders who were destroyed by the terror of the 1930s. Stalin personally masterminded the liquidation of millions of "enemies of the people," almost invariably on false charges.

Although *Stalin* is a biographical film, and hence more about the dictator and his troubled relationships with family and important comrades than about Russian society (we see very little of the average factory worker or collective farmer), the impact of Stalinist policies was so great that the film qualifies as a useful commentary on the social forces that defined the Soviet Union for decades. The terror affected not only its victims, but the population as a whole: "Millions lived year after year in an insane world of denunciation and hysteria. . . . The massive system of threats and rewards—at least the reward of survival—conditioned the minds of millions into an almost Pavlovian submission to the state's insistences, and not seldom an acceptance, with relief, of the state's false enthusiasms."[34] Although the film deals only briefly with the brutal policy of collectivization, enough is said to remind the viewer that the country was thrown into economic and social turmoil when Stalin decided to secure his own power and at the same time build socialism by waging civil war against the peasants. His fight against the peasants included policies consciously designed to create a famine; that famine claimed millions of lives and also produced "the greatest and most massive of the falsifications of Stalinism"[35]—his denial that any famine existed, with severe penalties, including death, for anyone who mentioned the word. In the film, the principal voice we hear defending the peasants is Stalin's wife, Nadezhda (Julia Ormond). For her temerity, Nadezhda, who had been increasingly disillusioned by her husband's cruelty, is treated rudely and humiliated by her husband in front of many guests; she shoots herself that night. Stalin, who is shown to be as abusive to his wife and son as he is to political rivals, will henceforward insist that she betrayed him.

Stalin's abandonment of the relatively pragmatic and gradualist policies of Lenin and his ruthless extermination of real and imagined adversaries contributed in the long term to the collapse of both the state and the party. His purge of the Red Army left the country woefully unprepared for

Hitler's attack in 1941; when the magnitude of German military successes became apparent, Stalin retreated into his dacha and into denial, a point dramatized in the film. Eventually Soviet forces prevailed and Stalin does deserve some credit for the victory in the Great Patriotic War. When he died in 1953, the people of the Soviet Union, conditioned by years of lies and struggle, mourned his passing and the crowds attending his funeral were so large that many were crushed to death. This strange and misguided adulation is hinted at in *Stalin*. It is more dramatically presented in another film about the Stalinist era, *The Inner Circle.*

Passer's film makes it clear in several scenes that Stalin enjoyed watching films. Andrei Konchalovsky's *The Inner Circle* turns that interest into a plot device. Ivan Sanshin (Tom Hulce) is a young man who becomes Stalin's film projectionist, a post that enables him to observe some of the dictator's machinations at first hand. Ivan idolizes Stalin, and for much of the film refuses to accept the mounting evidence that he is in fact a cruel despot.[36] When his wife asks him whom he loves more, her or Stalin, Ivan replies, without hesitation, "Stalin." This film confirms the sad truth that otherwise decent people can be mesmerized by tyrannical leaders like Stalin. After all, Winston Churchill and Franklin D. Roosevelt good-naturedly called him "Uncle Joe."

Stalin and *The Inner Circle* are really Western films about the Soviet Union, although the latter was shot with the cooperation of Russian authorities, much as Bernardo Bertolucci's *The Last Emperor* was filmed with the cooperation of the communist government in Beijing. One of the more interesting films about Stalinism to be made in Russia by Russians is Vitaly Kanevski's *Freeze–Die–Come to Life,* produced at the very end of the communist era. Its critique is more oblique than that of the other two films; even so the film encountered some resistance from the authorities and had to be made on a low budget with out-of-date film stock. Stalin never makes an appearance, yet it is doubtful if the dismal world he created in the Soviet Union has ever been more effectively shown on screen. *Freeze–Die–Come to Life* takes place near the end of World War II in a remote Russian coal-mining town that is "rubble-strewn, mud-covered, poverty-stricken, and Communist-oppressed."[37] It is not clear who is worse off, the workers, the "enemies of the state" incarcerated in a nearby labor camp, or prisoners of war in another camp. The principals in the film are a young boy and a young girl not yet in their teens; the harrowing life they lead, "with everyone on guard against theft, assault, starvation, and freezing to death,"[38] is a chilling reminder of the terrible misrule of the Stalinist era.

Stalin's impact reached for beyond his own people. Although *Stalin, The Inner Circle,* and *Freeze–Die–Come to Life* are primarily concerned with events within the Soviet Union, Stalin, like Lenin before him, was committed to the export of revolution, even if it was necessary first to contend with the situation at home. Stalin gained control of the Comintern by the early 1930s and with it "a powerful instrument for political and propagandist intervention in the West and in the world as a whole."[39] The Soviet experiment had from its very beginning attracted the interest and often the fervent support of many in the West, especially intellectuals disillusioned with what they regarded as flawed economic and social arrangements in their own countries. These people, whom Paul Hollander has called "political pilgrims,"[40] allowed their conviction that the cause was right to blind them to the magnitude of the atrocities being perpetrated in the name of communization in the Soviet Union. They in turn became the targets of anticommunist movements and policies, so that one of the important international consequences of the establishment of a communist regime in Russia was the sharpening of social and political divisions in other countries.

The relationship between the Soviet Union and the West during and after World War II would have been difficult even without Stalin, but his own paranoia and deviousness certainly exacerbated that relationship. The countries in Eastern Europe that fell under Soviet domination after the war were given no choice but to reproduce the Stalinist model. In short, the Soviet Union created by Lenin and Stalin had a great impact upon the rest of the world, inspiring some with the illusion of swift progress under tight centralized control while frightening others with policies nurtured by national paranoia and millennarian theory. The relevance of the societal level of analysis for an understanding of international relations has perhaps no more compelling illustration than this one.

China provides us with the twentieth century's other great experiment with communism. Although *The Last Emperor* allows us to follow a somewhat specialized course in Chinese history, tracing as it does the life of the last Manchu emperor to occupy the Dragon Throne in Peking's (now Beijing's) Forbidden City, it is less relevant for understanding China's role in world affairs than other, more recent films made in China by Chinese directors. Bertolucci's epic shows us how the boy emperor Pu Yi, after losing his throne, was later used by the Japanese as puppet-emperor in Manchuoko (Manchuria), was incarcerated as a war criminal, and was finally "reeducated" by Mao's communist government. Bertolucci would apparently have us believe that at the end, as Pu Yi lives out his days as a simple gardener, "his repentance was genuine, and that what some might disparage as Communist brainwashing actually cleaned away his decadence and healed him."[41] That impression may reflect Bertolucci's political views or his need to accommodate the Chinese government, which was in effect serving as official host during the filming. In any event, *The Last Emperor,* while a treat for the eye, tells us less about China than *Farewell, My Concubine,* which is also a film of epic proportions.

The latter film, directed by Chen Kaige, likewise unfolds over roughly half a century, including the coming to power of the communist regime. It takes the viewer through the great upheaval known as the Cultural Revolution from 1966 through 1976, and it is this part of the film—as well as the efforts of the Communist Party to censor it—that make *Farewell, My Concubine* especially important as a window onto international relations. The film's plot concerns the lives of two male members of the Beijing Opera, who from the very beginning of their training have been locked into specific roles, the one that of kingly heroes, the other that of delicate women, including the concubine of the film's title. The one who plays the concubine, Cheng Dieyi (Leslie Cheung), believes that the offstage relationship of the two actors should mirror that of king and concubine on-stage, and he is fiercely jealous when his partner, Duan Xiaolou (Zhang Fengyi), takes a wife. The vicissitudes of this triangular relationship become the heart of the film, but that relationship is played out on a political landscape that culminates in the Cultural Revolution. As one reviewer writes,

> In the fifty-odd years spanned by the film, the nature of everyday life changes so frequently, and so radically, that the characters remain perpetually off balance, unsure of how to react. At every stage of their history, Cheng and Duan are subject to some kind of tyranny: first, the feudalistic authority of the warlord era, represented by their despotic teacher; later, the occupying army of imperialist Japan; and, finally, the enforced comformity of Mao's Communist regime.[42]

The Cultural Revolution had a powerful impact on China and upon directors like Chen Kaige. Chen wanted to evoke that turbulent period in his work and he does so, including one scene in which "the Red Guards successfully reduce their initially decent victims to desperate, panicked wrecks, each furiously denouncing old friends and lovers as counter-revolutionaries."[43] A film such as *Farewell, My Concubine* "that holds up a mirror to the Cultural Revolution, no matter how objectively, reminds a battered Chinese population that devastating political movements have become a way of life under Communism, and there is still no system of laws, no guarantee of basic democratic or human rights, to prevent these destructive forces from being loosed again."[44]

The treatment of this subject in film has been deeply troubling to the Chinese government. Although Chen's film shared the top prize at the 1993 Cannes Film Festival, it was promptly banned in China and then subsequently unbanned, although in a slightly censored form. Had it not been for the fact that banning the film was hurting China's image just when it was conducting a vigorous campaign to bring the Olympics to Beijing in 2000, it is quite possible that the Chinese public would still not be allowed to view it. Indeed, when the government censorship authorities rescinded their ban, they also issued a warning that any film portraying the communist system in a bad light would not be approved for public viewing. With

the Soviet Union dead and Stalin largely discredited by his own succes-
sors, it may now be possible for the excesses of the communist regime in
Russia to be presented on screen by Russian filmmakers without fear of
censorship or reprisal. China shows no signs of being ready to follow suit.
Presumably we shall have to wait quite a bit longer before we see a Chi-
nese-made film dealing even obliquely with Tiananmen Square or the subsequent government crackdown on dissidents in that country.

At the end of the twentieth century, China has adopted a more open
economic system, but politically it remains repressive, adamant in its denial of individual freedoms. The result is that China poses a dilemma for
other countries, which must decide whether trade or a concern for human
rights is the highest foreign policy priority in dealing with that country.
Whatever the outcome of this debate in particular countries (trade is usually the winner), Sinologists are engaged in another debate with implications for international relations in the early twenty-first century and beyond. It concerns whether the world's most populous country can make the
economic and political transition to modernity without collapsing and
breaking up, as the Soviet Union did.[45] Either way, Chinese turbulence, so
vividly portrayed on film, seems certain to continue to have repercussions
well beyond China.

Apartheid, Militarism, and the Authoritarian Regime

Few films are as instructive about the utility of the societal level of analysis for an understanding of international relations as those that depict life
under authoritarian rule. In addition to those dealing with life under
despotic governments in twentieth-century Germany, Russia, and China,
two other cases deserve special attention. The one concerns South Africa
under the apartheid regime, and the other Argentina under the junta in the
1970s and 1980s. The former story has perhaps been given its most interesting film treatment in *A Dry White Season*. The latter has been brought
to the screen most compellingly in *The Official Story,* a film discussed
briefly in Chapter 9 when the subject was ethics and international law.

There have been numerous other films about apartheid in South
Africa, including *Sarafina, The Power of One, Cry Freedom,* and *A World
Apart*. It is a subject that inevitably found its way to the screen, both because this indisputably evil system stirred the conscience of filmmakers
and because it spawned violent conflicts and personal dramas of the kind
the film industry is drawn to. Apartheid came to prominence as a perennial
issue on the agenda of the United Nations and other international organizations in the 1960s, after the Sharpeville Massacre drew international attention to South African racism and decolonization brought independence
to several dozen African countries. These states immediately made the end

of apartheid a primary goal of their diplomacy, and a global network of human rights organizations helped to focus attention on the plight of black South Africans. The government in Pretoria argued that its racial policies were strictly an internal matter in which the international community had no right to interfere. That argument was overwhelmingly rejected in a multitude of resolutions by the General Assembly and other bodies, as well as through the adoption of economic sanctions by governments and policies of disinvestment by major corporations. South Africa achieved the dubious distinction of becoming the world's number one pariah state. It was not until 1994 that the policy of systematic and comprehensive discrimination against non-whites came to an end and Nelson Mandela became the country's first black president. But during the long decades when apartheid was the law of the land, the white supremacy regime brutally suppressed any political activity by members of the black majority while much of the white citizenry lived and worked in relative comfort, well insulated from the realities of life (and death) in the black townships outside the country's major cities, where black urban residents were forcibly relocated.

All of this is on display in *A Dry White Season,* director Euzhan Palcy's second feature film (her first, *Sugar Cane Alley,* is discussed in Chapter 8). The film begins with a recreation of the famous 1976 uprising in Soweto. We are witness to the decision of a young black student to join a demonstration against second-rate education for blacks, a demonstration that escalates into a tragedy with worldwide repercussions when the police slaughter the demonstrators. Among those killed is the young student, and when his father, Gordon (Winston Ntshona), persists in seeking the truth about his son, he, too, becomes a victim of police brutality. It is at this point that Ben du Toit (Donald Sutherland), a white schoolteacher who lives in a pleasant suburb and is blissfully unaware of the way blacks are routinely treated, decides to investigate the death of Gordon, who had been his gardener. His inquiries are brushed aside by the authorities, but he persists; with the help of a wise black taxi driver (Zakes Mokae), who sneaks him into Soweto, he discovers that Gordon was tortured to death by the sadistic police. Finally aware of the horrors of the system, Ben seeks justice. Needless to say, he doesn't get it, despite the efforts of an anti-apartheid barrister, Ian McKenzie (Marlon Brando); the inquest is a travesty of justice, demonstrating the extent to which the government is prepared to go to preserve white supremacy.

Ben's search for truth and justice costs him his wife, who supports the status quo, his job at the school, and ultimately his life. His only triumph is that he is able to get the story of Gordon's murder out of the country and into the hands of a sympathetic journalist; to accomplish even this, he has to outwit his own daughter, who loves her father but betrays him because she "just wants everything back to normal." *A Dry White Season* is the story of a country in the grip of a great social malady, and a reminder that commitment to change means "risking being subject to all the dangers, injustice and suffering of those who have been so systematically victimized."[46] The miracle is that the Afrikaners and Mandela's African National Congress were finally able to overcome such an unpromising history and effect a transfer of power to the country's black majority. Not only did this bring an end to a terrible injustice; it also lanced a boil that had long infected world politics.

Argentina is another country whose political and social turmoil have attracted filmmakers. After many years, the popular musical *Evita* finally came to the screen in late 1996, bringing with it Andrew Lloyd Weber's version of the complex relationship between the Argentine people and the Perons. A much more interesting film for our purposes is *The Official Story*, which, like many of the films cited in this chapter is not really about international relations at all. Luis Puenzo has given us a powerful film about the reign of Argentina's military junta and its campaign against alleged subversives, over 9,000 of whom became *desaparecidos,* people who disappeared, never to be seen again. The film actually takes place after the collapse of the dictatorship, brought on by the disaster of its ill-fated attempt to capture the Falklands (Malvinas) Islands in 1982. But the roots of the plot lie in the fact that many of the children of parents who were among the *desaparecidos* were put up for adoption, and that the adopted daughter of the film's central character, Alicia (Norma Aleandro), is, unknown to her, very probably one of them. Puenzo does not try to resolve the personal dilemma that becomes the focus of the plot, but instead wants to encourage the viewer to reflect upon the relationship between the individual and an evil regime. Thus Alicia is in important respects like Ben du Toit in *A Dry White Season.* Both have been living comfortable lives, unconcerned with the terrible things their government has done to other people; both are schoolteachers who have uncritically shared conventional wisdom with their students instead of raising hard questions. Both of these basically decent but naive people finally have their consciousness raised, but their awareness comes late and the cost is almost unbearably high.

For many years the military dictatorship in Argentina survived because there were many people like Alicia who were by and large indifferent to its behavior as long as they were not themselves affected. The junta's dirty war that produced the *desaparecidos* ultimately did help to weaken its legitimacy at home and brought it into disrepute internationally.[47] The disaster in the Falklands hastened the end of the dictatorship and the reestablishment of democratic institutions. The departure of generals does not always mean the arrival of real democracy, however. Tina Rosenberg, writing more generally about the replacement of military dictatorships by elected civilian governments, has argued that elections do not necessarily mean democratization.[48] Contrasting what she calls countries of inhabitants and countries of citizens, she finds that in all too many countries, elections are not accompanied by the development of civic institutions the people can use to solve their problems. The result is a kind of sham democracy in which true citizenship cannot flourish. This phenomenon influences international relations in many ways.

Most films reflect the political and social climate of the countries and the time period in which they were made. *The Official Story* is clearly a post-junta film, just as *Freeze–Die–Come to Life* is obviously a product of the post-Stalinist era. In democratic societies, films can be made which are critical of prevailing political and social attitudes, as several of the U.S.-made films cited in this chapter demonstrate. But it is hardly surprising that even in democratic societies films will tend to mirror the mood swings of the country. The rebellion against "the system" in the United States as opposition to the war in Vietnam mounted was celebrated in films that made heroes of outlaws and nonconformists. The popularity of *Bonnie and Clyde, Easy Rider,* and *Butch Cassidy and the Sundance Kid,* all made in the late 1960s, speaks volumes about the national mood of that time. Similarly, with Ronald Reagan in the White House and proclaiming that "It's morning in America," Hollywood embraced the new conservatism with films such as *Top Gun* and *Rambo: First Blood Part II.* John Belton provides us with a succinct capsule commentary on the significance of the latter film:

> If America lost the Vietnam war back in 1975 on both the military and political fronts, Rambo won it for us in the mid-1980s, single-handedly killing hundreds of the enemy and rescuing a chopperful of American MIAs. President Reagan led the cheering for the film. After Lebanese terrorists released 39 American hostages, Reagan declared, "I saw *Rambo* last night. I know what to do the next time this happens."[49]

The films cited in this chapter are only the tip of a very large iceberg of films that comment indirectly on international relations and do so by highlighting conditions within states which help to define those states as actors in world affairs. It may be objected that virtually all of the films cited in this chapter are about man's inhumanity to man, about despotisms or dysfunctional states and societies. The plea is "Guilty as charged." There are, of course, films that present positive, upbeat pictures of particular societies and it is possible that the characteristics portrayed are a contributing factor in the benign role those states play or are alleged to play in world affairs. But the connection is usually harder to make, and in any event this commentary on the domestic roots of international relations is only intended to stimulate further debate on the subject—one that seems certain to lead to the discovery of yet other relevant films.

Notes

1. For a discussion of this thesis, see Gellner, *Conditions of Liberty*. Although there is no single definition of civil society, it may be simply defined as "that arena of social engagement which exists above the individual yet below the state." See Wapner, "Politics Beyond the State," pp. 312–13.

2. The phrase is that of Michael Ignatieff. See Ignatieff, "On Civil Society," p. 136, for his review of Gellner.

3. Maier, "Democracy and Its Discontents," pp. 48–64.

4. *Ibid.*, p. 54.

5. Maier defines territorial populists as those who "rally supporters in reaction to the fragmentation of social cohesion. . . . They contest the perceived diffusion of decision-making to supranational authorities or offshore enterprises. They promise to restore a sense of identity and to repatriate decisions to a cohesive community on a familiar home territory." *Ibid.*, p. 61.

6. Lake, "Confronting Backlash States," p. 45. Lake was President Clinton's assistant for National Security Affairs when he wrote this essay.

7. Ravenal, *Never Again*.

8. Hartz, *The Liberal Tradition in America*.

9. Hunt, *Ideology and U.S. Foreign Policy*.

10. *Ibid.* Hunt organizes a major portion of his book around these themes: Chapter 2 is entitled "Visions of National Greatness"; Chapter 3, "The Hierarchy of Race"; and Chapter 4, "The Perils of Revolution."

11. T. Thomas, *The West that Never Was*.

12. *Ibid.*, p. 9.

13. *Ibid.*

14. Mellen, "The Western," p. 471.

15. Hunt, *Ideology and U.S. Foreign Policy*, p. 53.

16. Fitzgerald, "The American Millennium," p. 261.

17. *Ibid.*, pp. 274–75.

18. Hunt, *Ideology and U.S. Foreign Policy*, p. 40. Hunt is quoting Senator Albert Beveridge.

19. Peary, *Cult Movies 3*, p. 171.

20. *Ibid.*, p. 172.

21. This conflict of interpretations of the film is discussed in *Ibid.*, pp. 157–58.

22. Hofstadter, *The Paranoid Style in American Politics*.

23. For a discussion of the American view of the perils of revolution, see Hunt, *Ideology and U.S. Foreign Policy*, Ch. 4.

24. Quoted in Boo, "Wham, Bam, Thanks Saddam," p. 19.

25. For a discussion of the North-South debate and the Third World's quest for a New International Economic Order, see Chapter 8 and such other sources as Krasner, *Structural Conflict;* Rothstein, *Global Bargaining;* and Gregg, "The Politics of International Economic Cooperation and Development."

26. Strange, *Casino Capitalism*. Her description of this phenomenon begins on page 1: "The Western financial system is rapidly coming to resemble nothing so much as a vast casino. Every day games are played in this casino that involve sums of money so large that they cannot be imagined. . . . In the towering office blocks that dominate all the great cities of the world, rooms are full of chain-smoking young men all playing these games. Their eyes are fixed on computer screens flickering with changing prices. They play by intercontinental telephone or by tapping electronic machines. . . . The financial casino has everyone playing the game of Snakes and Ladders."

27. Brode, *The Films of the Eighties*, p. 205.

28. Wilmington, "Mephisto," p. 477.

29. Grenier, "Servants, Masters, and the Art of Bantering," p. 66.

30. See Tonetti, *Bernardo Bertolucci*, pp. 142–68, for an interesting commentary on the historical context as well as quotes from Bertolucci about the film.

31. *Ibid.*, p. 156.

32. *Ibid.*, p. 159.

33. Conquest, *Stalin*, p. 325.

34. *Ibid.*, p. 206.

35. *Ibid.*, p. 164. Conquest quotes the Russian publication *Novy Mir*, 9, 1989.

36. If there is anyone who comes across as an even more horrible specimen of humanity than Stalin in *Stalin* and *The Inner Circle*, it is Lavrenti Beria, onetime head of the NKVD, who personally and with obvious pleasure executes Stalin's victims with a pistol at close range in the former film and seduces and beds Ivan's wife in the latter. The viewer is left to decide whether Roshan Seth or Bob Hoskins is more effectively cast in the role of this utterly repulsive man. Beria was executed shortly after Stalin's death, much as he had executed countless others.

37. Cardullo, "Life and Nothing But," p. 482.

38. *Ibid.*

39. Conquest, *Stalin*, p. 172.

40. Hollander, *Political Pilgrims*.

41. Kael, "The Manchurian Conformist," p. 99.

42. Rafferty, "Blind Faith," p. 121.

43. Canby, "Action, History, Politics," C22.

44. Tyler, "Who Makes the Rules in Chinese Movies?" Section 2, p. 19.

45. See, for example, Goldstone, "The Coming Chinese Collapse," and Huang, "Why China Will Not Collapse," pp. 35–52 and 54–68, respectively; Segal, "China's Changing Shape," pp. 43–58.

46. K. T. Thomas, "Dry Season," Part 6, p. 1(5).

47. Maechling, "The Argentine Pariah," pp. 69–83.

48. Rosenberg, "Beyond Elections," pp. 72–91.

49. Belton, *American Cinema/American Culture*, p. 316. This book as a whole is valuable for its extended discussion of the way films reflect changing societal values in the United States.

12

Epilogue

International relations is about many things, but it is also about continuity and change. Each of the themes addressed in the preceding chapters has been a staple of international relations *and* of scholarly discourse about international relations for a considerable period of time. Wars are still fought, states still assert their sovereign prerogatives, spies still seek to ferret out other countries' secrets, cultural differences still complicate international negotiations, and so on. And all of these themes continue to generate articles and monographs and even the occasional magnum opus by scholars, not to mention the memoirs of practitioners as they retire from government service and succumb to the urge to "set the record straight" or burnish their own reputations. As we contemplate the world around us, there are times when it is tempting to say that the more things change, the more they are the same.

Yet all these aspects of international relations are also characterized by change. The principal players, both globally and regionally, change over time. New nongovernmental and transnational actors arrive upon the scene. The ongoing revolutions in science and technology create new opportunities as well as new problems. Perhaps most important, the function of the state itself changes; economic strategy is becoming more important than military strategy, the acquisition of markets more important than the acquisition of territory. These changes are leading, according to one distinguished political scientist, to the rise of the "virtual state,"[1] a state that "depends as much or more on economic access abroad as it does on economic control at home,"[2] a state that increasingly "specializes in modern technical and research services and derives its income not just from high-value manufacturing, but from product design, marketing, and financing."[3] This is a different world than the one that arose from the ashes of World War II, not to mention the world of Wilson or Bismarck or Metternich.

Films reflect both continuity and change in international relations. They remind us that issues on the global agenda today were also present in times past, troubling earlier generations of citizens and policymakers as well as they do our own. But they also demonstrate that the ways in which those issues are perceived and addressed vary over time as the players become more numerous, distances shrink, knowledge expands, the tools of statecraft become more sophisticated, and the "rules" of international behavior undergo stress in the crucible of conflict. It is worth noting that the twentieth century has been both a century of unsurpassed international turbulence *and* the century in which moving pictures were invented and came of age. The growth of the film industry, and the emergence of the movies as a powerfully influential element of popular culture, has paralleled the unfolding drama on the world's stage—a drama that has brought us two world wars of almost unimaginable destruction, the long clash of irreconcilable ideologies that followed the Russian Revolution, the terrible tyrannies of Hitler and Stalin, the economic and social devastation of the Great Depression, the ominous arrival of the atomic age, the end of colonialism and the postcolonial crisis of development and governance, and the revolution in communication that has transformed the world of commerce and weakened the sovereign state. Filmmakers have tracked these events, providing the public with vivid and often controversial accounts of this troubled century, becoming in effect one of the major sources of information about the world we live in and the forces that have shaped our lives.

Historical License and Eurocentrism Revisited

In the first chapter of this book, a cautionary note was raised with respect to the liberties filmmakers take with history. Not only do they have to crowd events that may have taken place over days or even years into the space of two or three hours, but they must necessarily be selective in doing so. Those who shape history for the screen may also be inventive, speculating on what might have happened when the evidence is inconclusive or on motivation when historical figures are long dead, left no record, or sought to put themselves in a favorable light. There is no reason why films employing such inventiveness cannot be useful for the student of international relations. As one critic has observed, "The Hollywood historical film will always include images that are at once invented and yet may still be considered true; true in that they symbolize, condense, or summarize larger amounts of data; true in that they carry out the overall meaning of the past that can be verified, documented, or reasonably argued."[4] Although there are clearly limits to the exercise of artistic license (even if it is not always clear where those limits lie), a case can be made that filmmakers who exercise their imagination when reconstructing the past may make a more useful contribution to public discourse about the past than those who seek refuge in arid objectivity.[5]

No attempt has been made in these pages to question the historical accuracy of all of the films under discussion. To have done so would have led to a very different kind of a book, not to mention one of much greater length. But the issue is sufficiently important to justify a few words by way of example about a film that illustrates the dilemma facing the filmgoer. That film is Costa-Gavras's *Missing,* which was discussed at some length in Chapter 4 on civil strife and intervention. This is a film, it will be recalled, that tells the story of an American businessman's search for his missing son in Chile during the right-wing military coup that overthrew the elected socialist government of Salvador Allende in 1973. It turns out that the son has been executed, presumably by the Chilean military. *Missing* is based on the real-life experience of Ed Horman, whose frustrating search for his son, Charles, led him to believe that the U.S. government had been involved in the coup, that U.S. officials knew what had happened to Charles but withheld information from him, and even that those officials may have had something to do with the young man's death. Horman sued several U.S. officials, but, unable to obtain CIA documents that might have helped the prosecution, he ultimately dropped his suit. The film, in effect, became his vindication.

Costa-Gavras accepted Ed Horman's version of events and insisted that "The story is true and is based upon true facts."[6] Yet the director could not know that everything presented or strongly suggested in the film was true. Horman himself, while convinced of his claims, was never able to prove them. That the Nixon administration was hostile to Allende and pursued policies designed to undermine his regime is well documented, especially in the report of a Senate select committee issued in 1975. But whether the U.S. government participated directly in the coup, much less in Charles Horman's death and an effort to cover it up, remains an intriguing but unproven theory. And many film critics, not to mention foreign policy analysts and government officials, took Costa-Gavras to task for his one-sided interpretation of the case. It seems clear enough that the director wanted to "alert audiences to the broader problem of U.S. covert operations around the world and the tragic consequences they sometimes created,"[7] and that he found in the Horman case a useful vehicle for doing so. *Missing* is ultimately a troubling film, not only because of its indictment of U.S. interventions in support of military dictatorships, but because of the director's claim that artistic license entitled him to present conjecture as truth.

Films like *Missing* have the virtue of provoking discussion and stimulating further inquiry. Films depicting important figures and events in history can also serve another purpose, illustrated by another film that received attention earlier in this book. *Patton,* which is discussed in Chapter 7 on war, began life on Hollywood's drawing board as a tribute to a military hero. But the film was a long time in the making; before it reached the movie houses in 1970, the American public had become disillusioned with the war in Vietnam, and a film glorifying the military no longer seemed like such a good idea. The result was a shift in the film's treatment of Patton; where once it was to have celebrated his virtues, now it would be a more complex examination of his faults as well. Robert Brent Toplin, in his study of Hollywood's use and abuse of American history, argues that *Patton* became something of a Rorschach test, "allowing people with diverse points of view to read their own messages into the multidimensional story about a complex figure from history."[8] Whether films are made with such deliberately ambivalent messages in mind, they may serve this purpose, stimulating debate that can help create a better understanding of the complexities of international relations.

Patton may have given the public a picture of a complicated figure, but one viewer who saw only the courageous war hero was Richard Nixon. Other national leaders have been fascinated with films, including Joseph Stalin, of whom a biographer observes, "Films played an important role in his daily life, in some ways more important than reality."[9] But it is doubtful if any national leader became as obsessed with any one film as Nixon did with *Patton*. It was released during a time when the president was wrestling with the intractable problem of Vietnam, and more particularly with the question of whether to expand the war into Cambodia. Nixon made his decision to go into Cambodia only days after seeing *Patton* for the second time; although Schaffner's film cannot be blamed for that momentous decision, which led to massive student demonstrations and the tragedy at Kent State University, Nixon himself frequently invoked Patton as a model of courage, unafraid to make difficult decisions and pursue them singlemindedly in spite of criticism. Indeed, Nixon not only saw the film many times, he repeatedly urged his staff and others to see it; his secretary of state, William Rogers, observed "that the president was a walking ad for the movie."[10] It is not unreasonable to assume that Nixon cast himself as a latter-day Patton and wanted others to see him that way, too. *Patton* is thus among that small handful of films that merit attention because they not only mirror international relations but in modest ways might have had some influence on those relations.

It was also suggested in this book's opening chapter that any effort to use films in order to gain a better understanding of international relations must take into account the possibility of a Eurocentric bias, especially when those films portray events in the developing world. Here, as with the caveat about historic license, no effort has been made to remind the reader of that bias in the discussion of each film to which it might apply. But it is important that the possibility of such bias be kept in mind. While Eurocentric filmmaking is usually criticized for its negative portrayal of Third World peoples and practices (and for its depiction of Westerners as heroes and agents of change in the Third World), the indictment may need to be broadened in view of a recent trend. That trend is illustrated by Hector Babenco's *At Play in the Fields of the Lord,* discussed in Chapter 10. In this film, there is a role reversal. The indigenous Indians of the rainforest are no longer the weak or bad or foolish people who inhabit so many of the films that critics of Eurocentrism object to. Nor are the white missionaries the wise and good men and women who will bring civilization to these benighted people. Instead, the Indians have been romanticized, their way of life idealized, while the Westerners have been cast in the role of *mauvais sauvages.* Thus does *At Play* become an exercise in political correctness. It does not seem to matter that the notions of the good savage and the bad savage are Western in origin, and that the film overcompensates in an understandable effort to get away from old and discredited stereotypes. There is an element of condescension in this approach, just as there is in more conventional Eurocentric films. We see it at work in a variety of film genres, including revisionist Westerns such as *Dances with Wolves,* but however refreshing such films may be, we need to remember that the effort to be politically correct does not guarantee the absence of bias.

Films Omitted, Films Yet to Come

Inevitably, there are films that have been overlooked in the preceding chapters, films that could have been included in the discussion of international relations on film. Although more than one hundred films have been cited, many others that have something of interest to say about our subject are regrettably absent from the discussion. One thinks, for example, of David Lean's *Doctor Zhivago* and Warren Beatty's *Reds,* both of which look at the lives of individuals caught up in that great social and political cataclysm known as the Russian Revolution, certainly one of the major events of the twentieth century. Many would argue that war has been more than adequately treated by the many films already mentioned in the book, but others may miss such memorable films as Lean's *Bridge on the River Kwai* and Robert Altman's *M.A.S.H.,* each of which in its very different way makes the point that war is a form of insanity. Space might also have been found for John Frankenheimer's *The Manchurian Candidate,* which, in addition to its contribution to the American debate about political conspiracies, also looks at the phenomenon of brainwashing that became part of the national vocabulary after the Korean War.

Three other films otherwise overlooked in the preceding chapters also deserve mention for their commentary on important transitions: Andrzej Wajda's *Ashes and Diamonds* (Poland, having just emerged from the horrors of World War II, is about to enter the long, dark era of communist rule and subservience to the Soviet Union); Rainer Werner Fassbinder's *The Marriage of Maria Braun* (the title character becomes a metaphor for

Germany's recovery from the war and the "economic miracle" that made it rich and restored it to the status of a world power); and Norman Jewison's *The Russians Are Coming The Russians Are Coming* (the belligerent patriotism of the early Cold War gives way to the cautious cooperation of detente). A case might also be made for mention of the depiction of life under Nazi military occupation in two very different films, Louis Malle's tragic (and semi-autobiographical) *Au Revoir les Enfants* and Jiri Menzel's sensitive blend of comedy and tragedy, *Closely Watched Trains*.

And then there are Peter Weir's *Green Card* and Ang Lee's *The Wedding Banquet*, each of which examines in a lighthearted way the extent to which some people may go to obtain a green card in order to live and work in the United States. Also among the missing in this book are such interesting and variously important films as Michael Curtiz's *Charge of the Light Brigade*, which makes no claim to historical truth but can be read as an argument against appeasement and concessions to terrorists, and Satyajit Ray's *Distant Thunder*, which explores the effects of a terrible war-induced famine on an Indian village and that country's caste system. In a longer and more comprehensive book, there would surely have to be room as well for Costa-Gavras's *Z*, Alain Resnais's *La Guerre Est Finie*, Agnieszka Holland's *Europa, Europa*, Margarethe von Trotta's *Rosa Luxemburg*, Nikita Mikhalkov's *Burnt by the Sun*, Tomas Gutierrez Alea and Juan Carlos Tabio's *Strawberry and Chocolate*, and even Ernst Lubitsch's *To Be or Not to Be*.

The list of films that have been "neglected" could go on for many pages. The number of films relevant for an understanding of international relations will continue to grow as filmmakers mine old familiar topics and explore newly emergent issues. Terrorism, for example, is likely to remain on the agendas of governments and on the minds of individual citizens as long as terrorists ply their frightening and indiscriminate trade; inasmuch as there is no evidence that terrorism is on the wane, we may expect to continue to see it on our movie screens. Exhibit number one is Stuart Baird's *Executive Decision*, in which Islamic terrorists are foiled at the last minute in their attempt to lay waste America's east coast megalopolis with a nerve toxin. The manner in which they are foiled is unbelievable, but the film does manage to convey a message that terrorists now have at their disposal weapons of mass destruction that are hard to defend against[11] (as well as the less original message that, at least in Hollywood, Arabs remain the usual suspects).

War, like terrorism, will continue to attract the attention of filmmakers. Old wars that have already been the subject of numerous films will be revisited, and more recent wars will begin to make their appearance on screen. A case in point is the Gulf War of 1991 between Iraq and the UN-endorsed, U.S.-led coalition. Operation Desert Storm has already produced a much-discussed film, Edward Zwick's *Courage Under Fire*. This film, with its focus on the question of whether a female officer (played by Meg

Ryan) deserves a posthumous medal for bravery in combat, does not address any of the larger issues of international politics raised by the war in the Gulf, but it is likely to be only the opening salvo in film treatment of that conflict.

Another emergent issue that is a natural candidate for the movies is the spread of infectious diseases. The success of the World Health Organization in eradicating diseases like smallpox and a widespread belief that other diseases like cholera could be geographically sequestered led in time to an overconfidence on the public health front that has been shattered first by AIDS and then by Ebola.[12] With so many people on the move worldwide, and with "unwanted microbial hitchhikers" tagging along,[13] silent killers are not only once more among us but they are getting a lot of media attention. Wolfgang Petersen's *Outbreak,* starring Dustin Hoffman, demonstrates that films about these silent killers, especially when they entail a breathless race against the clock, are prospectively good box office. They may also, if incidentally, make a modest contribution to a better understanding of the complexities of contemporary international relations.

There are other themes or issues that, regrettably, seem somewhat less likely to find their way to the screen, at least not in a substantial number of films. One is the subject of women in positions of responsibility for major decisions about war and peace and high finance. Liberal feminists have objected to the relative paucity of women in positions of power, and films about international relations have mirrored reality, rarely depicting women as prominent decisionmakers. Inasmuch as a few women have in fact risen to important posts, including that of prime minister,[14] it is not inconceivable that we shall begin to see films that reflect that fact. *Courage Under Fire,* in which the heroine is a female pilot in the U.S. Air Force, and the *Star Trek: Voyager* series, in which the commander of the Federation's starship is a woman, may be small straws in the wind. Essentialist feminists may have to wait longer for films to present their perspective. They argue that women, because of their biological essence, bring a different perspective to decisionmaking, one informed by their experience with nurturing and characterized by their preference for cooperation over conflict. Thus far, however, most of the better-known women who have made it to the top and who may be models for the next generation of filmmakers have been largely indistinguishable from their male counterparts in the way they have run the ship of state.

We have also had very few films that adopt the postmodernist position, which would argue that multiple realities exist in the case of any phenomenon in international relations. This perspective would welcome a *Rashomon*-like approach to filming international relations, telling the audience about issues and events from various points of view and leaving it to the viewer to decide where the truth lies. Such an approach is not unknown in films, but it is not easy to bring it off successfully, and sometimes filmmakers who think they have done so have in fact done no such thing. Oliver Stone, for example, insisted that he had employed the *Rashomon* technique in *JFK*. But he made no attempt to present different theories about Kennedy's assassination; had he done so, those theories would almost certainly have been mutually contradictory *a la Rashomon*.[15] In the absence of feminist and postmodernist films, the realist school will continue to be the one best served by the medium when the film industry turns its attention to international relations.

Whatever the future brings in the way of new films, there are already so many films available with international relations themes or sub-themes that there is little danger that anyone will run out of opportunities to learn more about international relations by going to the movies or curling up on the couch in front of the VCR. In some instances the film's relevance for an understanding of international relations may be impossible to miss; in other cases it may be tucked away in a clever bit of dialogue or in a secondary plot, and may therefore require that the viewer pay closer attention. Some of the lessons may be slanted, requiring a suspension of judgment and further inquiry into the situation unfolding on the screen. Other lessons will be presented in metaphorical fashion, necessitating translation into the vocabulary of the international relations field. But if approached with an open mind, a healthy skepticism, and a certain affection for the movies, knowledge even of a subject as large and complex as international relations can be enhanced by films. And the process of acquiring that knowledge can be fun.

Notes

1. Rosecrance, "The Virtual State," pp. 45–61.
2. *Ibid.*, p. 52.
3. *Ibid.*, p. 47.
4. Rosenstone, "JFK: Historical Fact/Historical Fiction," p. 509.
5. See Toplin, *History by Hollywood,* pp. 1–22, for a discussion of the two sides of this argument.
6. *Ibid.*, p. 111.
7. *Ibid.*, p. 105.
8. *Ibid.*, p. 175.
9. Conquest, *Stalin,* p. 295.
10. Toplin, *History by Hollywood*, pp. 172–75.
11. Laqueur, "Postmodern Terrorism," pp. 24–36.
12. Garrett, "The Return of Infectious Disease," pp. 66–79.
13. *Ibid.*, p. 69.
14. Among the women who have achieved political prominence in recent years are Great Britain's Margaret Thatcher, Israel's Golda Meier, India's Indira Gandhi, Norway's Gro Brundtland, Pakistan's Benazir Bhutto, Turkey's Tansu Ciller, and Japan's Sadako Ogata (the latter with the United Nations).
15. For a discussion of Stone's contention regarding *Rashomon* and *JFK*, see Toplin, *History by Hollywood*, pp. 45–78.

Appendix: The Films

Across the Pacific. 1942. Dir. John Huston. With Humphrey Bogart, Sydney Greenstreet, Mary Astor. English. B & W. 98 min. A fictional Japanese plan to attack the Panama Canal along with Pearl Harbor on December 7, 1941, is foiled by Bogart, a counterspy who must conceal his true mission in order to outwit the film's villain, a Japanophile who is covertly serving as a spy for the enemy.

Alamo Bay. 1985. Dir. Louis Malle. With Ed Harris, Ho Nguyen, Amy Madigan, Donald Moffatt. English. Color. 99 min. Vietnamese shrimpers on the Texas coast face discrimination from white fishermen who resent their presence and ultimately resort to violence to drive them out of town. Film provides a disturbing commentary on the clash of cultures and racial prejudice in what used to be called America's melting pot.

Alexander Nevsky. 1938. Dir. Sergei Eisenstein. With Nikolai Cherkasov, Nikolai Okhlopkov, Alexander Abrikossov. Russian with English subtitles. B & W. 108 min. Propaganda film about invasion by Teutonic knights in the thirteenth century was designed to mobilize Russian nationalism in the period immediately prior to World War II. Nevsky appeals to the people to rise up against the foe, not just as defenders of their villages but as Russians.

All Quiet on the Western Front. 1930. Dir. Lewis Milestone. With Lew Ayres, Louis Wolheim. English. B & W. 132 min. Still impressive adaptation of Remarque's antiwar novel takes place during World War I and follows a group of German recruits through their passage from idealism and enthusiasm for war to disillusionment and, for many, death in the trenches and cratered battlefields of the Western Front.

All the President's Men. 1976. Dir. Alan Pakula. With Robert Redford, Dustin Hoffman, Jason Robards, Hal Holbrook. English. Color. 139 min.

This story of the exposure of the Watergate break-in and subsequent coverup by two *Washington Post* reporters focuses attention on the investigative journalism that has done so much to make Americans skeptical and even cynical about their nation's institutions.

Apocalypse Now. 1979. Dir. Francis Ford Coppola. With Martin Sheen, Marlon Brando, Robert Duvall, Sam Bottoms. English. Color. 153 min. Coppola presents the Vietnam War as a surreal and often terrifying trip into Conrad's *Heart of Darkness.* The film both captures the "myriad horrors of the unexpected" in modern warfare and makes this particular war seem utterly futile and a terrible waste.

Ashes and Diamonds. 1958. Dir. Andrzej Wajda. With Zbigniew Cybulski, Eva Kryzerska, Adam Pawilkowski. Polish with English subtitles. B & W. 105 min. Film takes place just as World War II is ending and Poland is about to exchange German domination for that of a Soviet-supported communist regime. The "hero" represents the disillusionment of a generation raised on war.

At Play in the Field of the Lord. 1991. Dir. Hector Babenco. With Tom Berenger, John Lithgow, Aidan Quinn, Daryl Hannah, Kathy Bates. English. Color. 186 min. The plight of indigenous Indians in the Brazilian rain forest is the film's focus; developers want their land, Christian missionaries want their souls, and the white man's diseases, for which they have no immunity, decimate the tribe.

Au Revoir les Enfants. 1987. Dir. Louis Malle. With Gaspard Manesse, Raphael Fejto, Philippe Morier-Genoud. French with English subtitles. Color. 82 min. Malle's autobiographical film is set in a Catholic boarding school in France during German occupation. A new pupil is Jewish, a fact that gradually becomes known to his young friend and to German soldiers, leading to a tragic denouement.

Battle of Algiers. 1966. Dir. Gillo Pontecorvo. With Yacef Saadi, Jean Martin, Brahim Haggiag. French and Arabic with English subtitles. B & W. 125 min. Powerful treatment of the Algerian fight for independence from France is noteworthy for its realistic, nearly documentary look. Rarely has violence in the name of nationalism (and by those defending the status quo) been so strikingly and memorably captured on film.

Battle of Britain. 1969. Dir. Guy Hamilton. With Michael Caine, Trevor Howard, Christopher Plummer, Laurence Olivier, Ralph Richardson, Robert Shaw. English. Color. 133 min. A recreation of the air battle in which the RAF repelled the Luftwaffe and saved England from invasion, the film is among those demonstrating the fact that by 1940 the world had entered the age of total war.

Before the Rain. 1994. Dir. Milcho Manchevski. With Rade Serbedzija, Katrin Cartlidge, Gregoire Colin. Macedonian, Albanian, and English with English subtitles. Color. 112 min. Set in the former Yugoslav republic of Macedonia, the film's three interlocking stories mirror the ethnic and religious hatreds that have ravaged Bosnia and Croatia and threaten to spread to other parts of the Balkan tinderbox.

Beyond Rangoon. 1995. Dir. John Boorman. With Patricia Arquette, U Aung Ko, Frances McDormand. English. Color. 100 min. The well-documented violation of human rights by Burma's brutal military regime is the focus of this film, in which a young American doctor, despondent in the wake of a personal tragedy, recovers a sense of purpose in her life by helping a Burmese dissident escape.

Bird of Paradise. 1932. Dir. King Vidor. With Joel McRae, Delores Del Rio, John Halliday, Richard Gallagher. English. B & W. 80 min. A classic example of Eurocentric filmmaking that is embarrassing by today's standards, Vidor's early talkie about a romance between a white sailor and a South Seas woman takes for granted the right of the civilized Western world to dominate exotic and primitive peoples.

Black Rain. 1989. Dir. Shohei Imamura. With Yoshiko Tanaka, Kazuo Kitamuro, Etsuko Ishihara. Japanese with English subtitles. B & W. 123 min. Sober account of the aftermath of the atomic bombing of Hiroshima concentrates on the shattered lives of a few of the survivors, most of whom suffer from radiation sickness and many of whom eventually die. The film does not preach, but it does invite reflection on the morality of the decision to use the bomb.

Black Robe. 1991. Dir. Bruce Beresford. With Lothaire Bluteau, Aden Young, Sandrine Holt, Tantoo Cardinal. English. Color. 101 min. The film concerns a Jesuit priest's epic seventeenth-century journey through the Canadian wilderness to convert the Huron Indians to Christianity. It makes a vivid statement about the clash of cultures during the time when European beliefs and values were being transported to other parts of the world.

Black Sunday. 1977. Dir. John Frankenheimer. With Robert Shaw, Bruce Dern, Marthe Keller. English. Color. 143 min. Terrorism has provided the plot line for numerous films, among them this story of a fictional attempt by terrorists to wreak havoc at the Super Bowl. As with many such films, the conflict between Arabs and Israelis and their supporters is the catalyst for what we see on screen.

Das Boot. 1981. Dir. Wolfgang Petersen. With Jurgen Prochnow, Herbert Gronemeyer, Klaus Wennemann. English (dubbed). Color. 150 min. The claustrophobic and often desperate nature of submarine warfare in World War II is effectively captured in this German film, which reminds us of the ongoing revolution in technology and its consequences for the conduct of war.

The Border. 1981. Dir. Tony Richardson. With Jack Nicholson, Harvey Keitel, Elpidia Carrillo. English. Color. 107 min. The border of the title is that of the Rio Grande river, the scene of a never-ending flood of humanity seeking to cross over into the United States from Mexico. The conflict between cynicism and corruption and compassion for human suffering is at the heart of this film about the dilemma of illegal immigration.

Born on the Fourth of July. 1989. Dir. Oliver Stone. With Tom Cruise, Willem Dafoe, Kyra Sedgwick. English. Color. 145 min. A young, gung-ho patriot's attitudes toward his country's involvement in Vietnam undergo a dramatic transformation when he returns home from the war a paraplegic. The film's value lies in its teatment of the growing antiwar sentiment in the United States, a phenomenon which shaped the outcome of that war and U.S. foreign policy post–Vietnam.

Bread and Chocolate. 1974. Dir. Franco Brusati. With Nino Manfredi, Anna Karina. Italian with English subtitles. Color. 112 min. Bittersweet comedy in which an Italian worker obtains jobs in Switzerland in order to support his family back home. Like many guest workers in Europe in recent decades, he finds himself caught up in conflicts of class and culture in this poignant look at a very real contemporary issue.

Breaker Morant. 1979. Dir. Bruce Beresford. With Edward Woodward, Bryan Brown, Jack Thompson. English. Color. 107 min. A controversial court-martial is the centerpiece of this film, set at the end of the Boer War. Three Australian soldiers are on trial for killing a Boer prisoner, and we are asked to reflect on whether it is possible to maintain some semblance of law and morality even in the context of dehumanizing warfare.

The Bridge on the River Kwai. 1957. Dir. David Lean. With Alec Guiness, William Holden, Sessue Hayakawa. English. Color. 162 min. British prisoners of war, under their proud colonel's misguided leadership, build a railway bridge for their Japanese captors in Burma during World War II. The relationship between the colonel and the Japanese camp commander is the most intriguing part of this film about the madness of war.

The Burmese Harp. 1956. Dir. Kon Ichikawa. With Shoji Yasui. Japanese with English subtitles. B & W. 116 min. Antiwar film focuses on a patrol of Japanese soldiers in Burma at the close of World War II. In a tribute to human dignity amidst the unspeakable horrors of war, one of the soldiers undergoes a spiritual conversion and undertakes the insurmountable task of burying his country's war dead.

Burn. 1969. Dir. Gillo Pontecorvo. With Marlon Brando, Evaristo Marquez, Renato Salvatori. English. Color. 113 min. Film explores the economic motivations of the colonial powers, in this case England, which foments a revolution on a Caribbean island to facilitate capture of the sugar trade and later represses that revolution when it gets out of hand. Those who see the roots of the failure of development in colonialism will find this film especially compelling.

The Burning Season. 1994. Dir. John Frankenheimer. With Raul Julia, Sonia Braga, James Edward Olmos. English. Color. 123 min. The story of Brazilian labor leader Chico Mendes and his fight to preserve the Amazon rain forest and the jobs and way of life of the rubber tappers offers the viewer a debate between alternative development strategies. Frankenheimer sides with the environmentalists.

Cal. 1984. Dir. Pat O'Connor. With Helen Mirren, John Lynch, Donal McCann. English. Color. 102 min. Film humanizes the long-running conflict between Catholics and Protestants in Northern Island, focusing on a love affair between a lonely Catholic boy and the widow of a man killed by the IRA. Its depiction of civil strife in a place that has known little peace for many years is a disturbing contribution to film literature on nationalism and its complexities.

Casablanca. 1942. Dir. Michael Curtiz. With Humphrey Bogart, Ingrid Bergman, Claude Rains, Paul Henreid. English. B & W. 103 min. Film classic is much more than the story of a romantic triangle set in the backwaters of World War II. The singing of the "Marseillaise" is a powerful evocation of nationalist sentiment, and the intrigue that takes place at Rick's cafe is a reminder of the conflicts that occupy the gray area between peace and war.

Casualties of War. 1989. Dir. Brian DePalma. With Sean Penn, Michael J. Fox. English. Color. 120 min. The rape and murder of an innocent girl by an American patrol in Vietnam ultimately results in courts-martial of the soldiers. En route to that denouement we are made aware of how fine the line is between man and savage in the moral quagmire of modern warfare.

The Charge of the Light Brigade. 1936. Dir. Michael Curtiz. With Errol Flynn, Olivia DeHaviland. English. B & W. 117 min. One must look elsewhere for an historically accurate discussion of the suicidal charge by British caval-rymen at Balaclava during the Crimean War; Curtiz's fictional explanation has its roots in a massacre on the far-off Indian frontier that must be avenged. Some view the film as a message that appeasement does not pay.

City of Joy. 1992. Dir. Roland Joffe. With Patrick Swayze, Pauline Collins, Om Puri. English. Color. 134 min. Poverty and its causes and cures are the focus of this film set in Calcutta's ghetto. On one side is a corrupt system that perpetuates the misery of the people; on the other is an American doctor who runs a free clinic and tries to inspire the Indians to take back their city.

Clear and Present Danger. 1994. Dir. Phillip Noyce. With Harrison Ford, James Earl Jones, Willem Dafoe. English. Color. 141 min. A CIA-backed paramilitary force launches an attack on the Colombian drug cartels, and Ford ultimately lays responsibility for authorizing the attack on the president himself. Film's importance lies in its commentary on the threat posed to state sovereignty by international drug trafficking and on the issue of deniability in decisionmaking.

Closely Watched Trains. 1966. Dir. Jiri Menzel. With Vaclav Neckar, Josef Somr, Jitka Bendova. Czech with English subtitles. B & W. 92 min. Men-zel's film, set in German-occupied Czechoslovakia during World War II, is both comedy and tragedy. Its appeal lies in its demonstration that life goes on and people grapple with age-old problems even under the shadow of war's tensions.

Come See the Paradise. 1990. Dir. Alan Parker. With Dennis Quaid, Tam-lyn Tomita. English. Color. 135 min. A romance between an American man and a Japanese-American woman is dramatically interrupted by the intern-ment of Japanese Americans after Pearl Harbor. The film takes an un-equivocal stand against the internment, forcing us to take a hard look at this black mark in U.S. history. It also sheds light on the clash of cultures.

Confessions of a Nazi Spy. 1939. Dir. Anatole Litvak. With Edward G. Robinson, George Sanders, Paul Lukas, Francis Lederer. English. B & W. 110 min. One of the first American films to attack the Nazis, *Confessions* focuses on the German-American Bund and its role in spying for Germany in the 1930s; loosely based on real-life FBI investigations and trials of Nazi sympathizers.

The Counterfeit Traitor. 1961. Dir. George Seaton. With William Holden, Lilli Palmer, Hugh Griffith. English. Color. 140 min. During World War II a Swedish businessman is pressed into undercover work in Germany for the British; he survives his assignment but at great personal cost. Rarely has the game of international relations looked less moral than in this nerve-racking adventure.

Courage Under Fire. 1996. Dir. Edward Zwick. With Denzel Washington, Meg Ryan. English. Color. 120 min. An early entry on a list of what will presumably be a number of films about Operation Desert Storm. Plot concerns whether a female officer deserves a posthumous medal for bravery in combat, and could signal an increase in attention to women as key players in international relations.

The Day that Shook the World. 1977. Dir. Veljko Bulajic. With Christopher Plummer, Maximilian Schell, Florinda Bolkan. English. Color. 111 min. Film follows the lives of Serbian student revolutionaries as they plan the assassination of the heir to the Austrian throne, which set in motion events leading to World War I. It captures some of the combustible nationalism that has kept the Balkans in flame.

The Desert Fox. 1951. Dir. Henry Hathaway. With James Mason, Cedric Hardwicke, Luther Adler. English. B & W. 87 min. Story of the much-honored German field marshal, Erwin Rommell, presents him as a highly respected commander who comes to believe that Hitler's orders are madness and pays with his life for his principled disloyalty.

Disclosure. 1994. Dir. Barry Levinson. With Michael Douglas, Demi Moore, Donald Sutherland. English. Color. 129 min. Film about sexual harassment in the computer industry also has something important to say about multinational corporations. The U.S. company in question uses a subsidiary in Malaysia for production purposes, a fact that figures prominently in the resolution of the film's central conflict.

Distant Thunder. 1973. Dir. Satyajit Ray. With Soumitra Chatterji, Babita, Sandya Roy. Bengali with English subtitles. Color. 100 min. A story of how famine, caused by a war we never see, affects an Indian village and particularly a Brahmin doctor and his family. Desperate with hunger, the villagers beg, steal, and prostitute themselves, and the doctor is humbled when he realizes that his caste is irrelevant.

Don Carlo. 1983 production. Conductor James Levine. With Placido Domingo, Nicolai Ghiaurov, Mirella Freni, Ferruccio Furlanetto. Italian with English subtitles. Color. 214 min. In Verdi's grand opera with an explicitly political theme, the confrontation scene between King Philip of Spain and the Grand Inquisitor captures superbly the presumably hierarchical international system prior to the Peace of Westphalia.

Dr. Strangelove. 1963. Dir. Stanley Kubrick. With Peter Sellers, George C. Scott, Sterling Hayden, Slim Pickens. English. B & W. 93 min. Kubrick's black comedy, in which a psychotic American general launches an unauthorized nuclear attack on the USSR, provides a veritable clinic on deterrence theory, the problems of command and control, and that high-wire act known as crisis decisionmaking. In this film, Murphy's Law is much in evidence.

Doctor Zhivago. 1965. Dir. David Lean. With Omar Sharif, Julie Christie, Geraldine Chaplin, Rod Steiger, Tom Courtenay. English. Color. 197 min. Epic story unfolds against the background of the Russian Revolution. Those events transform the lives of all the film's principals—as well as those of the Russian people—as they struggle to survive in the face of the forces convulsing their country.

The Dogs of War. 1981. Dir. John Irvin. With Christopher Walken, Tom Berenger. English. Color. 104 min. Film has something to say about the brutal dictatorships that all too often followed the retreat of colonial empires; but it also shows, with perhaps too much approbation, the role mercenaries in the pay of Western interests have played in the affairs of such states.

A Dry White Season. 1989. Dir. Euzhan Palcy. With Donald Sutherland, Janet Suzman, Marlon Brando, Zakes Mokae. English. Color. 107 min. Palcy's film documents the evil of apartheid and the gradual awakening of the conscience of white South Africans that contributed to the De Klerk-Mandela settlement. It reminds us that domestic issues resonate internationally—in this case shaping global views of human rights.

Duck Soup. 1933. Dir. Leo McCarey. With the Marx Brothers, Margaret Dumont, Louis Calhern. English. B & W. 70 min. The Marx Brothers are at their zaniest in a film that is, of course, not to be taken seriously. But it also is about the insanity of war, the occasionally irrational pretexts for war, and, perhaps most importantly (if most absurdly), the consequences of entrusting the affairs of state to irresponsible leaders.

El Norte. 1983. Dir. Gregory Nava. With Dana Villapando, Zaide Silvia Gutierrez, Ernesto Cruz, Eracia Zepada. Spanish with English subtitles. Color. 139 min. A Guatemalan brother and sister become illegal immigrants in the United States, fleeing tyrannical landlords and a repressive government at home and drawn by the promise of "the wonders" of the country to the north. Film is one of several that focus on migration as escape from the problems of developing countries.

The Emigrants. 1971. Dir. Jan Troell. With Max von Sydow, Liv Ullmann. English (dubbed). Color. 151. This epic of Swedish emigration to the United States in the mid-nineteenth century addresses an aspect of international relations that continues to shape the contemporary international system. An interesting companion to more recent films showing the United States as mecca for migrants from very different countries and regions.

Executive Decision. 1996. Dir. Stuart Baird. With Kurt Russell, Halle Berry, Steven Segal, David Suchet. English. Color. 132 min. Terrorism does not seem to be on the wane, either in the real world or on the screen. In this recent entry, Islamic terrorists attempt to devastate the east coast of the United States with a nerve toxin, only to be foiled by a bit of improbable mid-air heroics.

Farewell, My Concubine. 1993. Dir. Chen Kaige. With Leslie Cheung, Zhang Fengyi, Gong Li. Chinese with English subtitles. Color. 157 min. The story of the lives of two male members of the Beijing Opera covers half a century, during which they are caught up in and influenced by their country's turbulent history. Most interesting is the film's presentation of the impact of China's Cultural Revolution.

Fat Man and Little Boy. 1989. Dir. Roland Joffe. With Paul Newman, Dwight Schultz, John Cusack. English. Color. 127 min. This is the story of the Manhattan Project, which ushered in the atomic age and the ever-present threat of nuclear annihilation. Few scientific breakthroughs have so transformed world politics or made us so aware of the inexorable "progress" of science and technology and their impact on the world we live in.

The Final Cut. 1995. Dir. Mike Vardy. With Ian Richardson, Diane Fletcher, Nick Bramble. English. Color. 200 min. In this insightful look at foreign policy decisionmaking, a fictional British prime minister seeks to gain his place in history by masterminding a settlement of the very real Cyprus crisis. Unfortunately, he is also totally unscrupulous; when his self-serving plan for the island country backfires, he resorts to a military intervention that turns into a disaster.

Fires on the Plain. 1959. Dir. Kon Ichikawa. With Eiji Funakoshi, Osamu Takizawa. Japanese with English subtitles. B & W. 105 min. Like the director's *The Burmese Harp,* this disturbing antiwar film also focuses on the plight of Japanese soldiers in the final days of World War II. While most are reduced by hunger to animal-like savagery, the film's hero faces inevitable death with dignity.

Forbidden Games. 1952. Dir. René Clement. With Brigitte Fossey, Georges Poujouly. French with English subtitles. B & W. 87 min. While there is very little war footage, this remains one of the most powerful antiwar films ever made. It is the story of a small girl, orphaned when her parents are killed in a harrowing opening scene, who is taken in by a French farm family. The girl deals with her grief and confusion by creating a pet cemetery.

Foreign Correspondent. 1940. Dir. Alfred Hitchcock. With Joel McRae, Laraine Day, Herbert Marshall, Herbert Basserman. English. B &W. 120 min. Film was released early in World War II when Great Britain had its back against the wall and the United States was still neutral. Hitchcock's eve-of-war story was both a spy thriller and an appeal to the Americans to get involved before the lights went out all over the world.

1492: Conquest of Paradise. 1992. Dir. Ridley Scott. With Gérard Depardieu, Armand Assante, Sigourney Weaver. English. Color. 150 min. A big, sprawling epic, *1492* covers Columbus's three voyages to the new world and provides a glimpse of Spanish mercantilism. Its primary value lies in the debate it invites about Eurocentrism in the film industry's treatment of encounters between Europeans and other peoples in the age of exploration (and later colonization).

The Fourth Protocol. 1987. Dir. John Mackenzie. With Michael Caine, Pierce Brosnan, Joanna Cassidy. English. Color. 100 min. This is a "what-if" film that assumes the availability of small, portable atomic bombs and has a KGB agent plan the detonation of one in England. The plan is ultimately foiled, but it serves as a warning that nuclear terrorism is a very real possibility.

Freeze–Die–Come to Life. 1989. Dir. Vitaly Kanevski. With Pavel Nazarov, Dinara Drukarova, Yelena Popova. Russian with English subtitles. B & W. 105 min. The terrible conditions in Russia under Stalin are chronicled in this story of the lives of two children in a remote coal-mining town during World War II. Film is one of the most telling of Russian-made critiques of Stalinism.

Gallipoli. 1981. Dir. Peter Weir. With Mel Gibson, Mark Lee. English. Color. 111 min. Australian film criticizes the British command for the disaster that befell Aussie troops during the Allies' ill-fated effort to gain control of the Dardanelles in World War I. But the film also celebrates the valor of the men killed at Gallipoli and decries the terrible waste of these young lives.

Gandhi. 1982. Dir. Richard Attenborough. With Ben Kingsley, Trevor Howard, John Mills, John Gielgud, Roshan Seth. English. Color. 187 min. Epic biography of one of the major figures of the twentieth century contains memorable scenes of the challenge of nationalism to the stubborn colonial mentality. But it is also a painful reminder of the sharp and enduring divisions that often underlie the nationalist impulse.

The Gods Must Be Crazy. 1984. Dir. Jamie Uys. With Marius Weyers, Sandra Prinsloo, Xao. English. Color. 109 min. Film follows the peregrinations of a Kalahari Bushman as he tries to get rid of a troublesome artifact of civilization—a Coke bottle—and encounters the many absurdities of that civilization in the process. The value of this unique film lies in its running commentary on the contrast of cultures.

The Good Earth. 1937. Dir. Sidney Franklin. With Paul Muni, Louise Rainer. English. B & W. 138 min. Film adaptation of the Pearl Buck novel is set in prerevolutionary China, where the principal characters lose their crops to drought and a plague of locusts. In the film as in the real world, natural disasters bring famine and poverty in their wake.

Grand Illusion. 1938. Dir. Jean Renoir. With Jean Gabin, Pierre Fresnay, Erich von Stroheim, Marcel Dalio. French with English subtitles. B & W. 111 min. Film is among the great antiwar classics, although more concerned with the collapse of social and political values than it is with traditional war themes. The conflict between the European class system and patriotism is at the heart of this denunciation of war.

The Grapes of Wrath. 1940. Dir. John Ford. With Henry Fonda, Jane Darwell, John Carradine. English. B & W. 128 min. The Joad family flees the Dust Bowl during the Great Depression in film version of Steinbeck's commentary on social justice in America. Film reminds us that the land is a fragile resource, subject to misuse by its human inhabitants, often with tragic consequences.

Green Card. 1990. Dir. Peter Weir. With Gérard Depardieu, Andie McDowell. English. Color. 108 min. Foreign nationals desiring to stay and work in the United States must obtain a "green card"; needless to say, the demand is great. In this comedy, a Frenchman enters into a marriage of convenience with a New Yorker in order to get his card, and the relationship inevitably ripens over the course of the film.

Gung Ho. 1986. Dir. Ron Howard. With Michael Keaton, George Wendt, Gedde Watanabe. English. Color. 111 min. A Japanese company takes over an American automobile plant and a clash of cultures ensues when the new management expects the assembly line workers to adapt to Japanese policies. Workers rebel against efforts to put loyalty to company above the assertive individualism characteristic of American culture. This is a comedy with a serious subtext.

Gunga Din. 1939. Dir. George Stevens. With Cary Grant, Douglas Fairbanks, Jr., Victor McLaglen. English. B & W. 117 min. Action-adventure epic is a classic example of now politically incorrect celebration of empire and the capacity of Western (in this case British) heroes to outthink and outfight hordes of malevolent Third World types. Rarely has Eurocentrism in a film been clearer, although everyone has his tongue firmly planted in cheek.

Heartbreak Ridge. 1986. Dir. Clint Eastwood. With Clint Eastwood, Marsha Mason. English. Color. 130 min. American invasion of the small island country of Grenada in 1982 provides the climax of this entry in the list of films dealing with U.S. interventions in Central America and the Caribbean. However, film is more about the Eastwood character's checkered military career than it is about U.S. foreign policy.

Henry V. 1989. Dir. Kenneth Branagh. With Kenneth Branagh, Emma Thompson, Paul Scofield, Ian Holm, Derek Jacobi. English. Color. 138 min. Highlight of this interpretation of one of Shakespeare's better historical plays is the Battle of Agincourt, which demonstrates most effectively that war has always been hell. The film also reminds us that the reasons for which wars have been fought and the ways in which they have been fought have changed dramatically.

Henry V. 1944. Dir. Laurence Olivier and Reginald Beck. With Laurence Olivier, Renee Asheson, Leslie Banks, Leo Genn, Robert Newton. English. Color. 134 min. This version of the Shakespeare play, made during World War II, remains the favorite of many because of Olivier's stirring performance and the imaginative framing device in which the play begins and ends on the stage of London's Globe Theatre.

The House on 92nd Street. 1945. Dir. Henry Hathaway. With William Eythe, Lloyd Nolan, Signe Hasso. English. B & W. 89 min. A documentary-style treatment of tenacious and ultimately successful FBI efforts to thwart a Nazi spy ring in the United States during the early years of World War II. Propaganda-like celebration of the FBI also introduced audiences to the techniques employed by the agency and was the first film to deal with espionage aimed at acquiring atomic secrets.

Invasion of the Body Snatchers. 1956. Dir. Donald Siegel. With Kevin McCarthy, Dana Wynter. English. B & W. 80 min. Made during the era of

Cold War paranoia, this low-budget science fiction movie about an invasion of seed pods that take over the minds and bodies of Americans has been interpreted as both anticommunist and anti-McCarthy.

Indochine. 1992. Dir. Regis Wargnier. With Catherine Deneuve, Linh Dan Pham, Jean Yanne, Vincent Perez. French with English subtitles. Color. 156 min. This is a film about a lovers' triangle in colonial Vietnam that threatens to destroy all the parties. But its value for international relations lies in its story of the communist uprising against the French colonial overlords, which would culminate in the long war for liberation against first France and then the United States.

The Inner Circle. 1992. Dir. Andrei Konchalovsky. With Tom Hulce, Lola Davidovich, Bob Hoskins. English. Color. 139 min. Stalin's film projectionist idolizes the Soviet leader and for much of the film refuses to believe the evidence that he is a cruel despot. This film makes the point that otherwise decent people can be mesmerized by tyrants.

The Ipcress File. 1965. Dir. Sidney Furie. With Michael Caine, Nigel Greene, Guy Doleman. English. Color. 107 min. Spy film is more realistic than its contemporaries featuring James Bond. A product of the Cold War years, it deals with the issue of kidnapping and brainwashing of prominent scientists and suggests that even spies working for allies could be adversaries.

Johnny Guitar. 1954. Dir. Nicholas Ray. With Joan Crawford, Sterling Hayden, Mercedes McCambridge. English. Color. 116 min. Baroque Western features the traditional rivalry between railroad interests and cattlemen, with two women as principal protagonists. Film's importance lies in its allegorical treatment of the anticommunist witch hunt in the United States; in this case the film sides with the opponents of McCarthyism.

Judgment at Nuremberg. 1961. Dir. Stanley Kramer. With Spencer Tracy, Maximilian Schell, Burt Lancaster, Richard Widmark, Judy Garland, Montgomery Clift. English. B & W. 187 min. Film depicting the trial of Nazi judges accused of war crimes following World War II raises important issues regarding the creation and application of international law, as well as more fundamental questions of individual responsibility in the face of orders from a cruel and inhumane regime.

Khartoum. 1966. Dir. Basil Dearden. With Charlton Heston, Laurence Olivier. English. Color. 136 min. An Islamic zealot conducts a jihad against the forces of empire in this colorful rendering of a disaster for British colonialism in the Sudan in the late nineteenth century. A good example of Eurocentrism in filmmaking, as well as a cautionary tale about the perils of imperialism.

The Killing Fields. 1984. Dir. Roland Joffe. With Sam Waterston, Haing Ngor, John Malkovich. English. Color. 142 min. Film about the relationship between a U.S. journalist and his Cambodian interpreter is most notable for its harrowing account of the genocide perpetrated by the Khmer Rouge. It raises important questions about the morality of both intervention and nonintervention in that tragic country.

Larks on a String. 1990. Dir. Jiri Menzel. With Vaclav Neckar, Jityka Zelenohorska. Czech with English subtitles. Color. 96 min. Film mocks communist rule and mounts a satirical attack on efforts to re-educate rebellious bourgeois dissidents in Eastern Europe. Set in an industrial junkyard where the dissidents are forced to do manual labor, this allegory of the failure of communism celebrates love while deriding the workers' paradise.

The Last Emperor. 1987. Dir. Bernardo Bertolucci. With John Lone, Joan Chen, Peter O'Toole. English. Color. 164 min. The film version of the strange life of China's last emperor encompasses the Chinese civil war, the emperor's brief access to "power" as puppet ruler of Manchuria under Japanese occupation, and ultimately his role as a mere gardener in Beijing in the communist era.

Lawrence of Arabia. 1962. Dir. David Lean. With Peter O'Toole, Omar Sharif, Alec Guinness. English. Color. 225 min. Set in World War I in the Middle East, this epic transcends the story of one charismatic figure to shed light on the clash of cultures, diplomatic treachery, and the nature of war. Although these issues tend to be dwarfed by the spectacle, they are what make the film important for an understanding of international relations.

Lord of the Flies. 1963. Dir. Peter Brook. With Roger Allen, Tom Chapin, Roger Elwin. English. B & W. 90 min. Adaptation of the Golding novel is a frightening statement about politics under conditions of anarchy, and can be viewed as a metaphor for a society without legitimate authority or for the international system in which Hobbes's war of all against all prevails.

A Man for All Seasons. 1966. Dir. Fred Zinnemann. With Paul Scofield, Leo McKern, Robert Shaw, Orson Welles. English. Color. 120 min. Henry VIII's chancellor, Sir Thomas More, refuses to take an oath supporting the Act of Succession and is executed as a consequence. Film invites discussion about issues of both internal and external sovereignty in the period before Westphalia.

The Manchurian Candidate. 1962. Dir. John Frankenheimer. With Frank Sinatra, Lawrence Harvey, Angela Lansbury. English. B & W. 127 min. Film takes a hard, cynical look at U.S. politics during the Cold War. It begins with brainwashing of captured U.S. soldiers during the Korean War and culminates in an attempted assassination of a presidential candidate by one of them.

The Marriage of Maria Braun. 1978. Dir. Rainer Werner Fassbinder. With Hanna Schygulla, Klaus Lowitsch, Ivan Desny. German with English subtitles. Color. 120 min. Fassbinder intended his film to be a metaphor for Germany in the years after World War II. The woman of the title, hardened by life's vicissitudes, becomes prosperous, mirroring her country's "economic miracle." Germany, the film argues, has survived and recovered from the catastrophe of the war, but only at great cost.

M.A.S.H. 1970. Dir. Robert Altman. With Donald Sutherland, Elliott Gould, Sally Kellerman, Robert Duvall. English. Color. 116 min. Irreverent comedy takes place at a mobile field hospital during the Korean War; a frenetic antiwar, antiestablishment film confronts the viewer with badly wounded soldiers and zany surgeons trying to preserve their sanity in the midst of carnage.

Mephisto. 1981. Dir. Istvan Szabo. With Klaus Maria Brandauer, Rolf Hoppe, Karin Boyd. English (dubbed). Color. 134 min. Set in Germany as Hitler comes to power in the 1930s, Szabo's film uses a single figure—a self-centered actor—to demonstrate that a failure to oppose evil will have terrible consequences for those who choose to "go along" and, by extension, for the country and the world. One of the best films to expose the seeds of disaster in the small, selfish acts of ordinary people.

Midnight Express. 1978. Dir. Alan Parker. With Brad Davis, John Hurt, Randy Quaid. English. Color. 120 min. A young American is jailed in Turkey for smuggling hashish, and the film is an account of his incarceration and ultimate escape from a wretched prison. This cautionary tale of the perils of the drug business is likely to be best remembered as an attack on the abuse of U.S. citizens in foreign countries.

The Milagro Beanfield War. 1988. Dir. Robert Redford. With Ruben Blades, Sonia Braga, John Heard, Christopher Walken. English. Color. 118 min. Fanciful comedy about a confrontation between developers and the little people struggling to make a living on their land in the American southwest reflects a larger, universal problem. The film's value also lies in its humorous depiction of cultures in conflict.

Missing. 1982. Dir. Costa-Gavras. With Jack Lemmon, Sissy Spacek. English. Color. 122 min. When an American businessman investigates the disappearance of his son in Chile during a military coup, it gradually becomes apparent that the U.S. government may have been implicated in the young man's death. Film raises important questions regarding clandestine intervention in the affairs of another state and a government's responsibility to its own citizens.

The Mission. 1986. Dir. Roland Joffe. With Robert DeNiro, Jeremy Irons. English. Color. 125 min. Film set in South America in the eighteenth century works on several levels, including that of conflict between faith and greed; value for international relations lies in its demonstration of the fact that Westphalian norms were for a long time different for Europeans than they were for peoples of other countries and cultures.

Mississippi Masala. 1991. Dir. Mira Nair. With Denzel Washington, Sarita Choudhury, Roshan Seth. English. Color. 117 min. Although primarily about the prejudices that threaten the love affair between an African American man and an immigrant Indian woman in the U.S. south, film begins with a memorable recreation of the expulsion of Asians from Uganda after independence that offers insights into the darker side of nationalism.

Moscow on the Hudson. 1984. Dir. Paul Mazursky. With Robin Williams, Alejandro Rey, Maria Conchita Alonso, Clevant Derricks. English. Color. 107 min. Bittersweet comedy focuses on the trials and tribulations of a Russian defector to America. It is an effective dissection of the plight of immigrants in the land of opportunity and an interesting commentary on the cultural stew that is the United States.

My Beautiful Laundrette. 1985. Dir. Stephen Frears. With Daniel Day Lewis, Gordon Warnecke, Safred Jaffrey, Roshan Seth. English. Color. 94 min. Film about the Pakistani community in London is a comedy with a raw edge; Pakistanis are shown dealing with white punk Paki-bashers, making money off the Anglos, and otherwise demonstrating that society's outsiders can make it even if they never become part of the dominant culture.

Night of the Shooting Stars. 1982. Dir. Paolo and Vittorio Taviani. With Omero Antonutti, Margarita Lozano. Italian with English subtitles. Color. 107 min. During the last days of the Italian campaign in World War II, the citizens of a small village flee from their Nazi occupiers. A battle in a wheatfield between fascists and resistance fighters makes a memorable statement about war—that it often pits families and neighbors against each other and is thus doubly tragic.

1900. 1977. Dir. Bernardo Bertolucci. With Robert DeNiro, Gerard Depardieu, Dominique Sanda, Donald Sutherland. English. Color. 255 min. Two Italian boys, born on the same day at the turn of the century, become engaged in a class struggle as adults that is an allegory of the turmoil that has wracked Italy during the twentieth century. Fascists are pitted against socialists and communists in this huge, sprawling saga of life, love, and politics in the Mussolini era.

Ninotchka. 1939. Dir. Ernst Lubitsch. With Greta Garbo, Melvyn Douglas, Ina Claire. English. B & W. 108 min. In this lighthearted meeting of East and West, the lure of Paris and romance eventually overcomes Garbo's commitment to communist ideology. Lubitsch obviously had fun satirizing the rigid, drab, and humorless Soviet regime in this prewar film.

Nixon. 1995. Dir. Oliver Stone. With Anthony Hopkins, Joan Allen, Powers Booth, Paul Sorvino, James Woods, Ed Harris. English. Color. 191 min. Controversial film treatment of one of the most controversial U.S. presidents is most important for its perspective on Watergate, which forced Nixon's resignation and helped shape the country's cynicism about its government. Nixon also goes to China and expands the war in Vietnam in the course of this lengthy film.

Not Without My Daughter. 1990. Dir. Brian Gilbert. With Sally Field, Alfred Molina, Sheila Rosenthal. English. Color. 107 min. An American woman visits postrevolutionary Iran with her Iranian husband and young daughter, only to find that the husband intends to remain there and keep the daughter with him. In this highly controversial film, the gulf between Iran's fundamentalist Islamic culture and that of the secular United States is so great as to seem unbridgeable.

The Official Story. 1985. Dir. Luis Puenzo. With Norma Aleandro, Hector Alterio, Analia Castro, Chunchuna Villafane. Spanish with English subtitles. Color. 110 min. After the Argentina junta's "dirty war" in which thousands of alleged subversives simply disappeared, a woman comes to suspect that her adopted daughter may be the child of one of the *desaparecidos* and that her husband had been involved with the evil regime. Film opens a window on this infamous human rights issue.

Outbreak. 1994. Dir. Wolfgang Petersen. With Dustin Hoffman, Rene Russo, Morgan Freeman. English. Color. 128 min. Based on widely circulated accounts of the frightening Ebola virus. Although the virus appears to have originated in Africa, the film implies that we are all potentially at risk as people move about in our increasingly interdependent world.

Passport to Pimlico. 1948. Dir. Henry Cornelius. With Stanley Holloway, Margaret Rutherford, Hermione Baddeley. English. B & W. 84 min. Post–World War II British comedy takes place in a London neighborhood that discovers—as a result of an ancient treaty—it is really an independent country. Locals opt for independence from the crown to escape rationing, but customs officials move in and crises follow. A spoof of sovereignty run amok.

Paths of Glory. 1957. Dir. Stanley Kubrick. With Kirk Douglas, Adolph Menjou, George Macready, Ralph Meeker. English. B & W. 89 min. Powerful antiwar film and blistering indictment of military politics contains one of the most effective presentations of trench warfare and its futility. Heart of the film is the trial and execution of three hapless soldiers chosen at random for failure of French troops to persevere in a doomed assault on an impregnable German position.

Patton. 1970. Dir. Franklin Schaffner. With George C. Scott, Karl Malden. English. Color. 171 min. U.S. General George Patton was a flamboyant figure who knew how to win battles, but he was also a tyrannical egotist who inspired anger as well as awe. Film presents both qualities, and also contains a series of battle sequences that help to provide a picture of what World War II was like in the European and African theaters.

Pickup on South Street. 1953. Dir. Sam Fuller. With Richard Widmark, Jean Peters, Thelma Ritter. English. B & W. 81 min. Classic B movie from the McCarthy era suggests that the enemy is in our midst and that even thieves and other losers will behave as patriots when they realize the stakes. Film reflects Hollywood's involvement in the frenzy over communist subversion.

Pixote. 1981. Dir. Hector Babenco. With Fernando Ramos da Silva, Jorge Juliao, Gilberto Moura. Portuguese. Color. 127 min. Grim tale of poverty and social dysfunction, set in the streets of São Paulo, Brazil. A group of homeless young boys, including the ten-year-old of the title, survive by theft, drug dealing, pimping, and even murder. A devastating look at the grimmer aspects of life in the great cities of the developing world.

Platoon. 1986. Dir. Oliver Stone. With Charlie Sheen, Tom Berenger, Willem Dafoe. English. Color. 120 min. This Vietnam War film brings the horrors of war home to viewers as few other films do. The conflict is not only with the enemy, but between two sergeants, very different men who compete for the allegiance of the platoon and demonstrate the devastating impact of war upon the men who fight it.

Pork Chop Hill. 1959. Dir. Lewis Milestone. With Gregory Peck, Harry Guardino, Rip Torn, George Peppard. English. B & W. 98 min. The story of a bloody offensive to capture and hold a Korean hill, which had little military value, but "had" to be taken for its psychological impact on the peace negotiations taking place in nearby Panmunjon.

Raiders of the Lost Ark. 1981. Dir. Steven Spielberg. With Harrison Ford, Karen Allen, Denholm Elliott, John Rhys-Davies. English. Color. 115 min. This is a prime example of a film that critics of Eurocentrism complain about. They argue that Indiana Jones is nothing but an archetypal Western adventurer who boldly intervenes in a benighted Third World country (Egypt), saving a priceless artifact for the benefit of Western civilization.

Rambo: First Blood, Part II. 1985. Dir. George Cosmatos. With Sylvester Stallone, Richard Crenna. English. Color. 93 min. Ex–Green Beret Stallone rescues American POWs from the Vietnamese (and the Russians) in this revisionist film for those in the United States who believe that the war in Vietnam could and should have been won. The violence is nonstop, the body count staggering.

Reds. 1981. Dir. Warren Beatty. With Warren Beatty, Diane Keaton, Jack Nicholson. English. Color. 195 min. A love affair between radical American journalists is played out against the backdrop of the Russian Revolution. Film has much to say about the appeal of communism to many Americans who saw in it a dawning of a more socially and economically humane era.

Reilly: The Ace of Spies ("Prelude to War"). 1983. Dir. Martin Campbell. With Sam Neill, David Suchet, Jeananne Crowley. English. Color. 51 min. This episode from the television series depicts the coming of war between Japan and Russia in 1904, and offers a stunning illustration of the failure of deterrence and a classic demonstration of the proposition that officials who see only what they expect to see in the behavior of an adversary are often destined for unpleasant surprises.

Remains of the Day. 1994. Dir. James Ivory. With Anthony Hopkins, Emma Thompson, James Fox, Christopher Reeve. English. Color. 134 min. Merchant-Ivory film provides a commentary on moral blindness during the ominous rise of Nazism. The accommodation of evil by otherwise good people is illustrated by the perfect British butler, committed to the service of his Nazi-sympathizing master.

Rising Sun. 1993. Dir. Philip Kaufman. With Sean Connery, Wesley Snipes, Harvey Keitel, Cary-Hiroyuki Tagawa. English. Color. 129 min. This film illustrates U.S. paranoia over Japanese economic influence but deals most significantly with differences between U.S. and Japanese business practices and problems of communicating across the cultural divide.

Romper Stomper. 1992. Dir. Geoffrey Wright. With Russell Crowe, Daniel Pollock, Jacqueline McKenzie. English. Color. 88 min. White supremacist Australian skinheads quite literally make war on Asian immigrants in this frenetic, violent commentary on the conflict of cultures in Western countries facing a tide of migration from the Third World.

The Russia House. 1990. Dir. Fred Schepisi. With Sean Connery, Michelle Pfeiffer, Roy Scheider, Klaus Maria Brandauer. English. Color. 126 min. Film version of a John LeCarré novel of espionage was produced just as the Cold War was ending, and argues that personal relationships can breach the barriers of ideological conflict. Inevitably, the principals, who are not spies, are soon caught up in a dangerous game much bigger than they are.

The Russians Are Coming, the Russians Are Coming. 1965. Dir. Norman Jewison. With Carl Reiner, Alan Arkin, Eva Marie Saint, Theodore Bikel. English. Color. 127 min. A Soviet submarine runs aground on a New England island, setting off panic and manic patriotism among the locals. Film comedy finds grounds for optimism in the common humanity of the two Cold War rivals.

Saigon: Year of the Cat. 1983. Dir. Stephen Frears. With Frederic Forrest, Judi Dench, E. G. Marshall. English. Color. 106 min. The war in Vietnam is winding down, and the Viet Cong is poised to capture Saigon. In this adaptation of the David Hare play, U.S. officials wait too long to evacuate the embassy, with the result that many Vietnamese loyal to the United States are left behind to an uncertain fate.

Salvador. 1985. Dir. Oliver Stone. With James Woods, James Belushi, Elpedia Carrillo, Michael Murphy. English. Color. 122 min. This is a searing indictment of El Salvador's death squads and official U.S. support of the Salvadoran government during that country's civil war. Film includes fictionalized accounts of such real life events as the murder of Archbishop Romero and the rape-killing of American nuns.

Scorpio. 1972. Dir. Michael Winner. With Burt Lancaster, Alain Delon, Paul Scofield. English. Color. 114 min. In this espionage thriller, a CIA operative is allegedly a double agent working for the Soviets. Film's sympathy lies with the double agent rather than the CIA, and both the double agent and his KGB counterpart are contemptuous of their governments' policies and methods.

The Sea Hawk. 1940. Dir. Michael Curtiz. With Errol Flynn, Brenda Marshall, Claude Rains, Flora Robson. English. B & W. 144 min. Adventure yarn tells a fictionalized story of English efforts to keep Spanish ambitions at bay in the sixteenth century, culminating in the defeat of the Armada. Film was an early World War II propaganda piece designed to bolster British morale in a dark hour.

The Searchers. 1956. Dir. John Ford. With John Wayne, Jeffrey Hunter, Vera Miles, Ward Bond. English. Color. 144 min. Ford classic merits inclusion in this volume because it reflects factors that have shaped America's self-image and perception of world. Here we have manifest destiny, a vast and open frontier, rugged individualism, simmering racial tensions, and, of course, a culture of guns.

Senso. 1954. Dir. Luchino Visconti. With Alida Valli, Farley Granger, Massimo Girotti, Heinz Moog. Italian with English subtitles. Color. 115 min. Set during the Italian Risorgimento, lush and operatic Visconti film is primarily about an ill-starred romance between a Venetian woman and an Austrian officer. The treatment of Italian nationalism, then in full cry, makes the film relevant here.

Seven Days in May. 1963. Dir. John Frankenheimer. With Burt Lancaster, Frederic March, Kirk Douglas. English. B & W. 117 min. Film with a Cold War theme suggests that the United States was vulnerable to an attempted coup by a military faction that would not tolerate any hint of weakness (e.g., a disarmament treaty) where the Soviet adversary was concerned. Democratic values prevail, but it is a close call.

Spies. 1928. Dir. Fritz Lang. With Rudolf Klein-Rogge, Willy Fritsch, Gerda Maurus, Lupu-Pick. Silent with English titles. B & W. 88 min. Silent film is really the first major attempt by the industry to portray the world of spies. Lang demonstrates many of the tricks of the spy's trade, although the motives of the master spy are never clear and the country for which he works is never revealed.

The Spy Who Came in from the Cold. 1965. Dir. Martin Ritt. With Richard Burton, Oskar Werner, Claire Bloom, Peter Van Eyck. English. B & W. 110 min. Film treatment of the LeCarré novel is unrelievedly serious and grim, and makes the point that spying is a morally ambiguous enterprise in which it is hard to tell who are the good guys and who are the bad guys.

The Spy in Black. 1939. Dir. Michael Powell. With Conrad Veidt, Valerie Hobson, Sebastian Shaw. English. B & W. 82 min. Spy drama was released shortly before World War II, but takes place during World War I as the Germans seek information in Scotland about the movements of the British fleet. One of the few films of the genre in which the spies have real personalities and show mutual respect.

Stalin. 1992. Dir. Ivan Passer. With Robert Duvall, Maximilian Schell, Julia Ormond, Jeroen Krabbe. English. Color. 174 min. Much of the film focuses on Stalin's family relationships, but it also exposes his paranoia and ruthlessness, which led to the elimination of his colleagues in the Soviet hierarchy in the 1930s. Value of film lies in its examination of a tyrannical personality who shaped world politics in the twentieth century.

Star Trek ("Balance of Terror"). 1966. Dir. Vincent McEveety. With William Shatner, Leonard Nimoy, DeForest Kelley, Mark Lenard. English. Color. 51 min. This episode of the original *Star Trek* series deals with a war between the Romulans, who make war because it is in their nature, and the crew of the *Enterprise,* which accepts the argument that "it is better to attack now than defend later."

Star Trek: The Next Generation ("The Klingon Trilogy"). 1990, 1991. Several directors. With Patrick Stewart, Michael Dorn, Robert O'Reilly. English. Color. 51 min. each episode. Problems of third-party mediation are on display in this series, in which Picard must decide a dispute between two Klingon factions. He manages to alienate both sides and must in the end even abandon the Federation's neutrality, which—like that of the UN in Bosnia—ultimately proves impossible.

Star Trek VI: The Undiscovered Country. 1991. Dir. Nicholas Meyer. With William Shatner, Leonard Nimoy, Christopher Plummer, Kim Cattrall. English. Color. 113 min. This entry in the series of *Star Trek* films provides the viewer with many unmistakable references to interstate relations on earth in the twentieth century. The plot revolves around peace negotiations between the Federation and the Klingons and efforts by some on both sides to sabotage them.

State of Siege. 1973. Dir. Costa-Gavras. With Yves Montand, Renato Salvatori, O. E. Hasse, Jacques Webber. French with English subtitles. Color. 120 min. One of a number of films about covert U.S. intervention in Latin America; based on the kidnapping and execution of an American adviser in Uruguay by leftist rebels. The adviser turns out to be an unsavory character, and the director's sympathies lie with the rebels.

Sugar Cane Alley. 1983. Dir. Euzhan Palcy. With Gary Cadenet, Darling Legitimus, Douta Seck. French with English subtitles. Color. 103 min. A charming story of a self-sacrificing woman who is determined that her grandson shall escape the canefields of Martinique through education; this film also has a message about colonialism and development, showing that the end of slavery has not meant the end of bondage for black cane cutters.

The Tall Blond Man with One Black Shoe. 1972. Dir. Yves Robert. With Pierre Richard, Jean Rochefort, Mireille Darc. French with English subtitles. Color. 90 min. This film about spies focuses on bungling in high places and invites us to find humor in the ineptitude of those who would manage a country's foreign policy. The Aldrich Ames case suggests that the French farce may not be all that far off the mark.

Three Days of the Condor. 1975. Dir. Sydney Pollack. With Robert Redford, Faye Dunaway, Cliff Robertson, Max von Sydow. English. Color. 118 min. A product of the Watergate era in American politics, when the CIA and FBI were under fire for abuse of power, this film is highly critical of "The Agency," which has spawned a rogue plot within its ranks and is prepared to stoop to murder to cover up that plot.

To Live. 1995. Dir. Zhang Yimou. With Ge You, Gong Li. Chinese with English subtitles. Color. 132 min. In this film by China's best-known director, a young couple struggles to survive almost continuous political and social upheaval. Mao's determination to channel China's development in ideologically correct directions has tragic results for this couple and, by implication, millions of others.

Tora! Tora! Tora! 1970. Dir. Richard Fleischer, Toshoa Masuda, Kinji Fukasaku. With Martin Balsam, Soh Yamamura, Joseph Cotton, Tatsuya Mihashi. English and Japanese with English subtitles. Color. 144 min. A joint U.S.-Japanese re-creation of the attack on Pearl Harbor, the film also presents events leading up to the attack. Not an in-depth analysis of the causes of the war, film nevertheless demonstrates the importance of perceptions and communication.

Triumph of the Will. 1935. Dir. Leni Riefenstahl. German with English subtitles. B & W. 122 min. Documentary of Nazi Party rallies in Nuremberg in 1934 transforms reality into "repellent Wagnerian legend." Perhaps the most famous propaganda film ever made, it is a commentary on nationalist fervor and a demonstration of the capacity of cinema to contribute to that fervor.

Twelve O'Clock High. 1949. Dir. Henry King. With Gregory Peck, Hugh Marlowe, Gary Merrill. English. B & W. 132 min. Primarily about the strain of command, this film of the air war over Germany in the 1940s reminds us that the ongoing revolution in warfare produces ever more powerful means of destruction, some of which have ended any pretense that noncombatants can be spared.

Twilight's Last Gleaming. 1977. Dir. Robert Aldrich. With Burt Lancaster, Richard Widmark, Charles Durning, Paul Winfield. English. Color. 146

min. Premise of this film is that during the Vietnam War the U.S. government secretly endorsed a strategy of limited warfare around the world in order to deter the Soviet Union. An air force general threatens nuclear war unless this plan is made public. Film underscores the problem of making nuclear deterrence credible.

Under Fire. 1983. Dir. Roger Spottiswoode. With Nick Nolte, Gene Hackman, Joanna Cassidy. English. Color. 127 min. The Sandinista rebellion against the Somoza regime in Nicaragua provides the context for two interventions, one by the U.S. government in support of the regime and the other by American journalists who abandon their objectivity to help the rebels. Film makes a case for revolution by depicting government forces as brutal and the life of the people as wretched.

Vukovar. 1994. Dir. Boro Draskovic. With Mirjana Jokovic, Boris Isakovic. Serbian and Croatian with English subtitles. Color. 94 min. The Serbs and Croatians are modern-day Capulets and Montagues in this Balkan "Romeo and Juliet." The war in what used to be Yugoslavia destroys the Croatian town of Vukovar as it did in real life, with terrible consequences for the lives of a young couple of mixed backgrounds.

Wall Street. 1987. Dir. Oliver Stone. With Michael Douglas, Charlie Sheen, Martin Sheen. English. Color. 126 min. Stone takes a critical look at casino capitalism as practiced in America and the culture of greed in the Reagan era. An unscrupulous Wall Street broker breaks all the rules on his way to fame and fortune until a disillusioned protégé finally blows the whistle.

The Wannsee Conference. 1987. Dir. Heinz Schirk. With Robert Artzhorn, Friedrich Backhaus, Gerd Bockmann. German with English subtitles. Color. 85 min. A chilling re-creation of the 1942 meeting at which members of the Nazi Party, the SS, and the German bureaucracy planned the systematic extermination of 11 million Jews. Most disturbing is the totally matter-of-fact manner in which the Holocaust is discussed and planned.

Watch on the Rhine. 1943. Dir. Herman Shumlin. With Paul Lukas, Bette Davis, George Coulouris. English. B & W. 79 min. Film version of the Lillian Hellman play focuses on the prewar efforts of a member of the anti-Nazi German underground to raise money in the United States to help his colleagues in Germany. The message: it isn't sufficient to be antifascist; people must be willing to do something about it.

Waterloo. 1971. Dir. Sergei Bondarchuk. With Rod Steiger, Christopher Plummer, Jack Hawkins. English. Color. 122 min. A compelling look at warfare in the early years of the nineteenth century, following the mobilization of mass armies. It begins with Napoleon's return from exile on Elba to lead the old guard in one last campaign, and concludes with the spectacle of one of history's more famous battles.

The Wedding Banquet. 1993. Dir. Ang Lee. With Winston Chao, Michael Lichtenstein, May Chin. Chinese and English with English subtitles. Color. 108 min. A young woman enters into a marriage of convenience so that she can obtain the green card that will allow her to work in the United States. The problem is that her "husband" already has a gay lover, and the deception quickly spirals out of control.

Wedding in Galilee. 1987. Dir. Michel Khleifi. With Ali Mohammed El Akili. Hebrew and Arabic with English subtitles. Color. 113 min. Palestinians living under Israeli rule strike a deal that allows an extension of curfew so that a marriage may be celebrated. In spite of tensions between the two communities, the film demonstrates the common humanity of Jews and Arabs and is ultimately hopeful.

Where the Green Ants Dream. 1985. Dir. Werner Herzog. With Bruce Spence, Wandjuk Marika, Roy Marika. English. Color. 99 min. Efforts of white developers to mine for uranium in Australia's outback encounter resistance from Aborigines who regard the land as sacred ground. Herzog's sympathies clearly lie with the Aborigines in this film about conflicting cultural values and the meaning of development.

The Wild Geese. 1978. Dir. Andrew McLaglen. With Richard Burton, Roger Moore, Richard Harris, Hardy Kruger. English. Color. 132 min. Mercenaries in the employ of Western businessmen intervene in force in a fictional African country to unseat a brutal and corrupt regime. Although the businessmen prove to be duplicitous and the mission turns into a disaster, the film romanticizes the soldier of fortune.

Wilson. 1944. Dir. Henry King. With Alexander Knox, Charles Coburn, Geraldine Fitzgerald, Cedric Hardwicke. English. Color. 154 min. Biopic about the U.S. president who came to grief over ratification of the League of Nations Covenant is interesting for its scenes of Wilson trying to bring the Allies and the U.S. Senate around to his view of the proper postwar world order.

The Year of Living Dangerously. 1983. Dir. Peter Weir. With Mel Gibson, Sigourney Weaver, Linda Hunt. English. Color. 115 min. Set in Indonesia on the eve of the revolution against Sukarno's government, this is another in a series of films about poverty and turmoil in Third World countries in which journalists play critical roles as observers (and sometimes as participants).

Yes, Prime Minister ("A Diplomatic Incident"). 1987. Dir. Sydney Lotterby. With Paul Eddington, Nigel Hawthorne, Derek Fowldes. English. Color. 30 min. Episodes in this BBC comedy series all focus on the contest of wills between a well-meaning but none-too-bright British prime minister and his devious cabinet secretary. In this one, the British and French have a dispute over sovereignty in the Channel tunnel and the French try to circumvent both British law and international law.

Yes, Prime Minister ("The Grand Design"). 1986. Dir. Sydney Lotterby. With Paul Eddington, Nigel Hawthorne, Derek Fowldes. English. Color. 30 min. The British prime minister, uncomfortable with his authority to make nuclear war by merely pressing a button, decides he prefers to build up Britain's conventional forces rather than modernize its nuclear arsenal. A clever dialogue about the problem of making nuclear deterrence credible.

Yes, Prime Minister ("One of Us"). 1986/1987. Dir. Sydney Lotterby. With Paul Eddington, Nigel Hawthorne, Derek Fowldes. English. Color. 30 min. In this episode, the prime minister learns that the late head of British intelligence was passing secrets to Moscow. It turns out that the cabinet secretary had earlier conducted an investigation that exonerated the man now revealed as a traitor; the title of the episode explains why that investigation was so perfunctory.

Yes, Prime Minister ("A Victory for Democracy"). 1987. Dir. Sydney Lotterby. With Paul Eddington, Nigel Hawthorne, Derek Fowldes. English. Color. 30 min. This episode contains one of the best short lessons on the dynamics of foreign policy decisionmaking. The careerists in the British Foreign Office do their best to keep the prime minister and the foreign secretary in the dark as they deal with a crisis in a fictional Commonwealth country and a vote at the United Nations.

Zulu. 1964. Dir. Cy Endfield. With Stanley Baker, Michael Caine, Jack Hawkins. English. Color. 138 min. Reenactment of the 1879 battle of Rorke's Drift, when barely one hundred British soldiers held off attacks by four thousand Zulu warriors at this African outpost of empire. Endfield salutes the heroism of both the British and the Zulus in this evocation of a dramatic chapter from the saga of imperialism.

Bibliography

Allison, Graham T. *Essence of Decision: Explaining the Cuban Missile Crisis.* Boston: Little, Brown, 1971.

Arnson, Cynthia J. *Cross-Roads: Congress, the Reagan Administration, and Central America.* New York: Pantheon Books, 1989.

Axtell, James. "Black Robe." In Mark C. Carnes, ed., *Past Imperfect: History According to the Movies.* New York: Henry Holt, 1995.

Barber, Benjamin. "Global Multiculturalism and the American Experiment." *World Policy Journal* 10:1 (Spring 1993): 47–55.

———. "Jihad v. McWorld." *The Atlantic* 269 (March 1992): 53–63.

———. *Jihad v. McWorld: How the Planet Is Falling Apart and Coming Together and What This Means for Democracy.* New York: Times Books, 1995.

Bedjaoui, Mohammed. *Towards a New International Economic Order.* New York: Holmes & Meier, 1979.

Belton, John. *American Cinema/American Culture.* New York: McGraw-Hill, 1994.

Benson, Sheila. "Making of the Atomic Age." *Los Angeles Times* (October 20, 1989).

Berkowitz, Bruce D., and Jeffrey T. Richelson. "The CIA Vindicated: The Soviet Collapse Was Predicted." *The National Interest* 38 (Winter 1994/95): 36–47.

Bernstein, Barton. "The Atomic Bombings Reconsidered." *Foreign Affairs* 74:1 (January/February 1995): 135–52.

Betts, Richard K. "The Delusion of Impartial Intervention." *Foreign Affairs* 73:6 (November/December 1994): 20–33.

Blainey, Geoffrey. *The Causes of War,* 3rd ed. New York: Free Press, 1988.

Blight, James G., David A. Welch, and Bruce J. Allyn, eds. *Castro, the Missile Crisis and the Soviet Collapse.* New York: Pantheon Books, 1993.

Boo, Katherine. "Wham, Bam, Thanks Saddam." *Washington Quarterly* (April 1991): 14–19.

Brecher, Michael, and Jonathan Wilkenfeld. "Crisis in World Politics." *World Politics* 34 (April 1982): 380–417.

Broad, Robin, and John Cavanagh. "Beyond the Myths of Rio." *World Policy Journal* 10:1 (Spring 1993): 65–72.

———. "Don't Neglect the Impoverished South." *Foreign Policy* 101 (Winter 1995/96): 18–35.

Brode, Douglas. *The Films of the Eighties.* Secaucus, N.J.: Citadel Press, 1990.

Bull, Hedley. *The Anarchical Society.* New York: Columbia University Press, 1977.

287

Cairncross, Frances. "Environmental Pragmatism." *Foreign Policy* 95 (Summer 1994): 35–52.

Canby, Vincent. "Action, History, Politics and Love Above All." *New York Times* (October 8, 1993).

————. "Deneuve as a Symbol of Colonial Epoch." *New York Times* (December 24, 1992).

————. "Rising Sun: A Tale of Zen and Xenophobia in Los Angeles." *New York Times* (July 20, 1993).

Cardullo, Bert. "Life and Nothing But," "Black Rain," "Freeze–Die–Come to Life." *Hudson Review* 44 (Autumn 1991): 475–84.

Carnes, Mark C. "Hollywood History." *American Heritage* 46:5 (September 1995): 74–84.

————, ed. *Past Imperfect: History According to the Movies*. New York: Henry Holt, 1995.

Chopra, Jarat, and Thomas G. Weiss. "Sovereignty Is No Longer Sacrosanct." *Ethics and International Affairs* 6 (1992): 95–117.

Cohen, Eliot A. "The Mystique of U.S. Air Power." *Foreign Affairs* 73:1 (January/February 1994): 109–24.

Cohen, Raymond. *Negotiating Across Cultures: Communication Obstacles in International Diplomacy*. Washington: United States Institute of Peace, 1991.

Cohn, Carol. "Sex and Death in the Rational World of Defense Intellectuals." *Signs* 12 (1987): 687–718.

————. "Slick 'Ems, Glick 'Ems, Christmas Trees, and Cookie Cutters: Nuclear Language and How We Learned to Pat the Bomb." *Bulletin of the Atomic Scientists* 43:5 (June 1987): 17–24.

Conquest, Robert. *Stalin: Breaker of Nations*. New York: Penguin Books, 1992.

Craig, Gordon A., and Alexander L. George. *Force and Statecraft*, 3rd ed. New York: Oxford University Press, 1995.

Craik, T. W., ed. *King Henry V.* London: Routledge, 1995.

Crowdus, Gary, ed. *The Political Companion to American Film*. Chicago: Lakeview Press, 1994.

Culhane, John. "Louis Malle: An Outsider's Odyssey." *New York Times Magazine* (April 7, 1985): 28–31, 68.

Curtis, Bruce. "The Wimp Factor." *American Heritage* (November 1989): 40–50.

Damrosch, Lori Fisler, ed. *Enforcing Restraint: Collective Intervention in Internal Conflicts*. New York: Council on Foreign Relations Press, 1993.

Darnton, Robert. "Danton." In Mark C. Carnes, ed., *Past Imperfect: History According to the Movies*. New York: Henry Holt, 1995.

De Weerd, Harvey. "Strategic Surprise and the Korean War." *Orbis* 6 (Fall 1962): 435–52.

Donnelly, Jack. "International Human Rights: A Regime Analysis." *International Organization* 40:3 (Summer 1986): 599–642.

————. "State Sovereignty and International Intervention: The Case of Human Rights." In Gene M. Lyons and Michael Mastanduno, eds., *Beyond Westphalia? State Sovereignty and International Intervention*. Baltimore: The Johns Hopkins University Press, 1995.

Dooling, Richard. *White Man's Grave*. New York: Farrar, Straus and Giroux, 1994.

Dornbusch, Rudi. "Euro Fantasies." *Foreign Affairs* 75:5 (September/October 1996): 110–24.

Dreyfuss, Robert. "The CIA Crosses Over." *Mother Jones* 20:1 (January 1995): 38–41, 71.

Durch, William J., ed. *The Evolution of U.N. Peacekeeping: Case Studies and Comparative Analysis*. New York: St. Martin's Press, 1993.

————. *U.N. Peacekeeping, American Policy, and the Uncivil Wars of the 1990s.* New York: St. Martin's Press, 1997.

Dyson, Freeman. *Weapons and Hope.* New York: Harper and Row, 1984.

Falk, Richard. "Toward Obsolescence: Sovereignty in the Era of Globalization." *Harvard International Review* 17:3 (Summer 1995): 34–35, 75.

Falk, Richard, Gabriel Kolko, and Robert Jay Lifton, eds. *Crimes of War: A Legal, Political Documentary, and Psychological Inquiry into the Responsibility of Leaders, Citizens, and Soldiers for Criminal Acts in Wars.* New York: Random House, 1971.

Farnsworth, Elizabeth. "Chile: What Was the U.S. Role? More than Admitted." *Foreign Policy* 2 (Spring 1974): 127–41.

Feldstein, Martin. "Why Maastricht Will Fail." *The National Interest* 32 (Summer 1993): 12–19.

Fitzgerald, Frances. "The American Millennium." In Sanford J. Ungar, ed., *Estrangement: America and the World.* New York: Oxford University Press, 1985.

————. "Apocalypse Now." In Mark C. Carnes, ed., *Past Imperfect: History According to the Movies.* New York: Henry Holt, 1995.

Fromkin, David. *The Independence of Nations.* New York: Praeger, 1981.

Fukuyama, Francis. "The End of History?" *The National Interest* 16 (Summer 1989): 1–18.

————. *The End of History and the Last Man.* New York: Free Press, 1992.

Fussell, Paul. "Patton." In Mark C. Carnes, ed., *Past Imperfect: History According to the Movies.* New York: Henry Holt, 1995.

Garrett, Laurie. "The Return of Infectious Disease." *Foreign Affairs* 75:1 (January/February 1996): 66–79.

Garthoff, Raymond L. *Reflections on the Cuban Missile Crisis*, rev. ed. Washington: Brookings Institution, 1989.

Gelb, Leslie H., and Morton H. Halperin. "The Ten Commandments of the Foreign Policy Bureaucracy." In Steven L. Spiegel, ed., *At Issue: Politics in the World Arena.* New York: St. Martin's Press, 1984.

Gellner, Ernest. *Conditions of Liberty: Civil Society and Its Rivals.* London: Penguin, 1994.

Glenny, Misha. "Heading Off War in the Southern Balkans." *Foreign Affairs* 74:3 (May/June 1995): 98–108.

Goldstein, Joshua S. *International Relations*, 2nd ed. New York: HarperCollins, 1996.

Goldstone, Jack A. "The Coming Chinese Collapse." *Foreign Policy* 99 (Summer 1995): 35–52.

Gottlieb, Gidon. *Nation Against State: A New Approach to Ethnic Conflict and the Decline of Sovereignty.* New York: Council on Foreign Relations, 1993.

————. "Nations Without States." *Foreign Affairs* 73:3 (May/June 1994): 100–112.

Goulet, Denis. "An Ethical Model for the Study of Values." *Harvard Educational Review* 41:2 (May 1971): 205–27.

Gregg, Robert W. "The Politics of International Economic Cooperation and Development." In Lawrence S. Finkelstein, ed., *Politics in the United Nations System.* Durham, N.C.: Duke University Press, 1988.

Grenier, Richard. "Servants, Masters, and the Art of Bantering." *The National Review* 35 (Spring 1994): 65–72.

Gurr, Ted Robert. *Minorities at Risk: A Global View of Ethnopolitical Conflicts.* Washington: United States Institute of Peace, 1993.

Guterson, David. *Snow Falling on Cedars.* San Diego: Harcourt Brace, 1994.

Hall, Edward T. *Beyond Culture*. Garden City, N.Y.: Anchor Press, 1976.

Hamilton, John Maxwell. *Main Street America and the Third World*. Cabin John, Md.: Seven Locks Press, 1986.

Harbottle, Thomas. *Dictionary of Battles*. New York: Stein and Day, 1971.

Hare, David. *A Map of the World*. London: Faber & Faber, 1982.

Harff, Barbara. "Minorities, Rebellion, and Repression in North Africa and the Middle East." In Ted Robert Gurr, ed., *Minorities at Risk: A Global View of Ethnopolitical Conflicts*. Washington: United States Institute of Peace, 1993.

Hartz, Louis. *The Liberal Tradition in America*. New York: Harcourt, Brace and World, 1955.

Hermann, Charles. *International Crises: Insights from Behavioral Research*. New York: Free Press, 1972.

Hilsman, Roger. "Does the CIA Still Have a Role?" *Foreign Affairs* 74:5 (September/October 1995): 104–16.

Hirsch, Foster. "Fuller, Sam." In Gary Crowdus, ed., *The Political Companion to American Film*. Chicago: Lakeview Press, 1994.

Hirschman, Albert O. *Exit, Voice and Loyalty: Responses to Decline in Firms, Organizations, and States*. Cambridge, Mass.: Harvard University Press, 1970.

Hirsh, Michael, and E. Keith Henry. "The Unraveling of Japan, Inc." *Foreign Affairs* 76:2 (March/April 1997): 11–16.

Hoffmann, Stanley. *Duties Beyond Borders: On the Limits and Possibilities of Ethical International Politics*. Syracuse: Syracuse University Press, 1981.

———. *Primacy or World Order: American Foreign Policy Since the Cold War*. New York: McGraw-Hill, 1978.

Hofstadter, Richard. *The Paranoid Style in American Politics*. Chicago: University of Chicago Press, 1979.

Hollander, Paul. *Political Pilgrims: Travels of Western Intellectuals to the Soviet Union, China, and Cuba 1928–1978*. New York: Oxford University Press, 1981.

Holsti, K. J. *International Politics: A Framework for Analysis*, 7th ed. Englewood Cliffs, N.J.: Prentice Hall, 1995.

Huang, Yasjeng. "Why China Will Not Collapse." *Foreign Policy* 99 (Summer 1995): 54–68.

Huffhines, Kathy Schulz, ed. *Foreign Affairs: The National Society of Film Critics' Video Guide to Foreign Films*. San Francisco: Mercury House, 1991.

Hughes, Barry B. *Continuity and Change in World Politics*, 2nd ed. Englewood Cliffs, N.J.: Prentice Hall, 1994.

Hunt, Michael H. *Ideology and U.S. Foreign Policy*. New Haven: Yale University Press, 1987.

Hunter, Allan, ed. *Movie Classics: From Silent Screen to Today's Screen Hits*. Edinburgh: W & R Chambers, 1992.

Huntington, Samuel P. *The Clash of Civilizations*. New York: Simon and Schuster, 1996.

———. "The Clash of Civilizations." *Foreign Affairs* 72:3 (Summer 1993): 22–49.

Ignatieff, Michael. "On Civil Society: Why Eastern Europe's Revolutions Could Succeed." *Foreign Affairs* 74:2 (March/April 1995): 128–36.

Ikenberry, G. John. "The Myth of Post–Cold War Chaos." *Foreign Affairs* 75:3 (May/June 1996): 79–91.

Iriye, Akira. "Tora! Tora! Tora!" In Mark C. Carnes, ed., *Past Imperfect: History According to the Movies*. New York: Henry Holt, 1995.

Isaacs, Jennifer. *Australia's Living Heritage*. Sydney: Ure Smith Press, 1984.

James, Alan. *Sovereign Statehood*. London: Allen & Unwin, 1966.

Janis, Irving L. *Victims of Groupthink: A Psychological Study of Foreign Policy Decisions and Fiascos.* Boston: Houghton Mifflin, 1972.

Janis, Irving L., and Leon Mann. *Decision-Making: A Psychological Analysis of Conflict, Choice, and Commitment.* New York: Free Press, 1977.

Jervis, Robert. *Perception and Misperception in International Politics.* Princeton: Princeton University Press, 1976.

Jervis, Robert, Richard Ned Lebow, and Janice Gross Stein, eds. *Psychology and Deterrence.* Baltimore: The Johns Hopkins University Press, 1985.

Jonas, Susanne. "Dangerous Liaisons: The U.S. in Guatemala." *Foreign Policy* 103 (Summer 1996): 144–60.

Kael, Pauline. "The Border." *New Yorker* (February 1, 1982).

———. "Circus." *New Yorker* (April 16, 1984).

———. "The Manchurian Conformist." *New Yorker* (November 30, 1987).

———. "Pig Heaven." *New Yorker* (July 28, 1986).

———. "Potency." *New Yorker* (January 22, 1990).

Keegan, John. *The Face of Battle.* New York: Penguin Books, 1976.

Kennedy, Paul. *Preparing for the Twenty-First Century.* New York: Vintage Books, 1994.

Kincade, William H. "On the Brink in the Gulf: Part 1, Onset of the 'Classic' 1990 Crisis." *Security Studies* 2:2 (Winter 1992): 163–200.

Korten, David. *Getting to the 21st Century: Voluntary Action and the Global Agenda.* West Hartford, Conn.: Kumarian Press, 1990.

Krasner, Stephen D. *Structural Conflict: The Third World Against Global Liberalism.* Berkeley: University of California Press, 1985.

Krepinevich, Andrew. "Cavalry to Computer." *The National Interest* 37 (Fall 1994): 30–42.

Lake, Anthony. "Confronting Backlash States." *Foreign Affairs* 73:2 (March/April 1994): 45–55.

Lapidoth, Ruth. "Redefining Authority: The Past, Present, and Future of Sovereignty." *Harvard International Review* 17:3 (Summer 1995): 8–11, 70–71.

Laqueur, Walter. "Postmodern Terrorism." *Foreign Affairs* 75:5 (September/October 1996): 24–36.

Lebow, Richard Ned. *Between Peace and War: The Nature of International Crises.* Baltimore: The Johns Hopkins University Press, 1981.

———. "Miscalculation in the South Atlantic: The Origins of the Falklands War." In Robert Jervis, Richard Ned Lebow, and Janice Gross Stein, eds., *Psychology and Deterrence.* Baltimore: The Johns Hopkins University Press, 1985.

Leiken, Robert S. "Controlling the Global Corruption Epidemic." *Foreign Policy* 105 (Winter 1996–1997): 55–76.

Lewis, David Levering. "Khartoum." In Mark C. Carnes, ed., *Past Imperfect: History According to the Movies.* New York: Henry Holt, 1995.

Lind, Michael. "In Defense of Liberal Nationalism." *Foreign Affairs* 73:3 (May/June 1994): 87–99.

Lloyd, Ann, ed. *Seventy Years at the Movies.* New York: Crescent Books, 1988.

Lorenz, Konrad. *On Aggression.* New York: Bantam Books, 1966.

Lyons, Gene M., and Michael Mastanduno, eds. *Beyond Westphalia? State Sovereignty and International Intervention.* Baltimore: The Johns Hopkins University Press, 1995.

McCarty, John. *Thrillers: Seven Decades of Classic Film Suspense.* Secaucus, N.J.: Citadel Press, 1992.

Maechling, Charles, Jr. "The Argentine Pariah." *Foreign Policy* 45 (Winter 1981/82): 69–83.

————. "Washington's Illegal Invasion." *Foreign Policy* 79 (Summer 1990): 113–31.

Mahbubani, Kishore. "The West and the Rest." *The National Interest* 28 (Summer 1992): 3–12.

Maier, Charles S. "Democracy and Its Discontents." *Foreign Affairs* 73:4 (July/August 1994): 48–64.

Malcolm, Noel. "The Case Against 'Europe'." *Foreign Affairs* 74:2 (March/April 1995): 52–68.

Mandelbaum, Michael. "The Reluctance to Intervene." *Foreign Policy* 95 (Summer 1994): 3–18.

Marius, Richard. "A Man for All Seasons." In Mark C. Carnes, ed., *Past Imperfect: History According to the Movies*. New York: Henry Holt, 1995.

Marshall, Monty G. "States at Risk: Ethnopolitics in the Multinational States of Eastern Europe." In Ted Robert Gurr, ed., *Minorities at Risk: A Global View of Ethnopolitical Conflicts*. Washington: United States Institute of Peace, 1993.

Maull, Hanns W. "Germany and Japan: The New Civilian Powers." *Foreign Affairs* 69:5 (Winter 1990/1991): 91–106.

Mearsheimer, John. "Why We Shall Soon Miss the Cold War." *The Atlantic Monthly* 266:2 (August 1990): 35–50.

Mellen, Joan. "The Western." In Gary Crowdus, ed., *A Political Companion to American Film*. Chicago: Lakeview Press, 1994.

Meron, Theodore. "Answering for War Crimes." *Foreign Affairs* 76:1 (January/February 1997): 2–8.

————. "The Case for War Crimes Trials in Yugoslavia." *Foreign Affairs* 72:3 (Summer 1993): 122–35.

Miller, Lynn H. *Global Order: Values and Power in International Politics*, 3rd ed. Boulder: Westview Press, 1994.

Morgan, Patrick M. "Saving Face for the Sake of Deterrence." In Robert Jervis, Richard Ned Lebow and Janice Gross Stein, eds., *Psychology and Deterrence*. Baltimore: The Johns Hopkins University Press, 1985.

Morgenthau, Hans J. *Politics Among Nations*, 5th ed. New York: Alfred A. Knopf, 1973.

Mueller, John. *Quiet Cataclysm*. New York: HarperCollins, 1995.

Mullerson, Rein. "Self Defense in the Contemporary World." In Lori Fisler Damrosch and David J. Scheffer, eds., *Law and Force in the New International Order*. Boulder: Westview Press, 1991.

Naipul, V. S. *A Bend in the River*. New York: Alfred A. Knopf, 1979.

Nathan, James A., ed. *The Cuban Missile Crisis Reconsidered*. New York: St. Martin's Press, 1992.

Nicolson, Harold. *The Congress of Vienna: A Study in Allied Unity 1812–1822*. New York: The Viking Press, 1946.

Nye, Joseph S., Jr. *Understanding International Conflicts: An Introduction to Theory and History*. New York: HarperCollins, 1993.

O'Brien, Conor Cruise. "The Wrath of Ages: Nationalism's Primordial Roots." *Foreign Affairs* 72:5 (November/December 1993): 142–49.

Ohmae, Kenichi. "The Rise of the Region State." *Foreign Affairs* 72:2 (Spring 1993): 78–87.

Osborne, Charles. *The Complete Operas of Verdi*. New York: Alfred A. Knopf, 1970.

Paris, James Reid. *Classic Foreign Films: From 1960 to Today*. Secaucus, N.J.: Citadel Press, 1993.

———. *The Great French Films*. Secaucus, N.J.: Citadel Press, 1983.

Peary, Danny. *Alternate Oscars*. New York: Delta, 1993.

———. *Cult Movies 3: Fifty More of the Classics, the Sleepers, the Weird and the Wonderful*. New York: Simon and Schuster, 1988.

———. *Guide for the Film Fanatic*. New York: Simon and Schuster, 1986.

Pirages, Dennis. *Global Technopolitics: The International Politics of Technology and Resources*. Pacific Grove, Calif.: Brooks/Cole Publishing Co., 1989.

Powers, John. "My Beautiful Laundrette." In Kathy Schulz Huffhines, ed., *Foreign Affairs: The National Society of Film Critics' Video Guide to Foreign Films*. San Francisco: Mercury House, 1991.

Putnam, Robert D. "Diplomacy and Domestic Politics: The Logic of Two-Level Games." *International Organization* 42:3 (Summer 1988): 427–60.

Quirk, Lawrence J. *The Great War Films*. Secaucus, N.J.: Citadel Press, 1994.

Rafferty, Terrence. "Blind Faith." *New Yorker* (October 11, 1993).

———. "The Spy Game." *New Yorker* (December 31, 1990).

———. "True Believers: Black Robe." *New Yorker* (November 18, 1991).

Ravenal, Earl. *Never Again: Learning from America's Foreign Policy Failures*. Philadelphia: Temple University Press, 1978.

Reimers, David. *Still the Golden Door: The Third World Comes to America*. New York: Columbia University Press, 1985.

Rosecrance, Richard. "The Virtual State." *Foreign Affairs* 75:4 (July/August 1996): 45–61.

Rosenau, James. "Sovereignty in a Turbulent World." In Gene M. Lyons and Michael Mastanduno, eds., *Beyond Westphalia? State Sovereignty and International Intervention*. Baltimore: The Johns Hopkins University Press, 1995.

Rosenberg, Tina. "Beyond Elections." *Foreign Policy* 84 (Fall 1991): 72–91.

———. "Tipping the Scales of Justice." *World Policy Journal* 12:3 (Fall 1995): 55–64.

Rosenstone, Robert A. "JFK: Historical Fact/Historical Fiction." *American Historical Review* 97:2 (April 1992): 506–11.

Rossiter, Clinton. *The American Presidency*. New York: Harcourt Brace, 1956.

Rothstein, Robert L. *Global Bargaining: UNCTAD and the Quest for a New International Economic Order*. Princeton: Princeton University Press, 1979.

Rourke, John. *International Politics on the World Stage*, 6th ed. Guilford, Conn.: Dushkin, McGraw Hill, 1977.

Rovere, Richard. *Senator Joe McCarthy*. New York: Meridian Books, 1960.

Rubenstein, Leonard. *The Great Spy Films*. Secaucus, N.J.: Citadel Press, 1979.

Rubin, Barry. *Modern Dictators*. New York: McGraw-Hill, 1987.

Russett, Bruce, and Harvey Starr. *World Politics: The Menu for Choice*, 5th ed. New York: W. H. Freeman, 1995.

Saccio, Peter. *Shakespeare's English Kings*. New York: Oxford University Press, 1977.

Said, Edward W. *Covering Islam: How the Media and the Experts Determine How We See the Rest of the World*. New York: Pantheon Books, 1981.

Scheffer, David J. "International Judicial Intervention." *Foreign Policy* 102 (Spring 1996): 34–51.

Schickel, Richard. "The Official Story." In Kathy Schulz Huffhines, ed., *Foreign Affairs: The National Society of Film Critics' Video Guide to Foreign Films*. San Francisco: Mercury House, 1991.

Schraeder, Peter J., ed. *Intervention in the 1980s: U.S. Foreign Policy in the Third World*. Boulder: Lynne Rienner Publishers, 1989.

Segal, Gerald. "China's Changing Shape." *Foreign Affairs* 73:3 (May/June 1994): 43–58.

Seth, Ronald. *The Anatomy of Spying.* New York: E. P. Dutton, 1963.

Sheehan, Henry. "Sugar Cane Alley." In Kathy Schulz Huffhines, ed., *Foreign Affairs: The National Society of Film Critics' Video Guide to Foreign Films.* San Francisco: Mercury House, 1991.

Sherr, James. "Cultures of Spying." *The National Interest* 38 (Winter 1994/95): 56–62.

Shirley, Edward. "Is Iran's Present Algeria's Future?" *Foreign Affairs* 74:3 (May/June 1995): 28–44.

Shohat, Ella, and Robert Stam. *Unthinking Eurocentrism: Multiculturalism and the Media.* New York: Routledge, 1994.

Shulsky, Abram, and Gary J. Schmitt. "The Future of Intelligence." *The National Interest* 38 (Winter 1994/95): 63–73.

Sigmund, Paul E. "Chile: What Was the U.S. Role? Less Than Charged." *Foreign Policy* 2 (Spring 1974): 142–56.

Silberman, Robert. "Stone, Oliver." In Gary Crowdus, ed., *The Political Companion to American Film.* Chicago: Lakeview Press, 1994.

Small, Melvin, and J. David Singer. *International War: An Anthology,* 2nd ed. Chicago: Dorsey Press, 1989.

———. *Resort to Arms: International and Civil Wars, 1916–1980.* Beverly Hills: Sage, 1982.

Smith, Eivind. "A Higher Power: Supranationality in the European Union." *Harvard International Review* 17:3 (Summer 1995): 12–14, 71–72.

Smith, Tony. *The Pattern of Imperialism: The United States, Great Britain and the Late Industrializing World Since 1815.* New York: Cambridge University Press, 1981.

Snyder, Jack L. "Perceptions of the Security Dilemma in 1914." In Robert Jervis, Richard Ned Lebow, and Janice Gross Stein, eds., *Psychology and Deterrence.* Baltimore: The Johns Hopkins University Press, 1985.

Spoto, Donald. *Stanley Kramer, Film Maker.* New York: G. P. Putnam's Sons, 1978.

Spruyt, Hendrik. "Decline Reconsidered: The Complex Nature of Modern Sovereignty." *Harvard International Review* 17:3 (Summer 1995): 36–39.

Strange, Susan. *Casino Capitalism.* New York: Basil Blackwood, 1986.

Thomas, Kevin. "'Dry Season' a Potent Look at South Africa." *Los Angeles Times* (September 22, 1989).

———. "Indochine: An Intimate Spectacle." *Los Angeles Times* (December 25, 1992).

———. "Myth v. Technology Down Under." *Los Angeles Times* (April 5, 1985).

Thomas, Tony. *The Great Adventure Films.* Secaucus, N.J.: Citadel Press, 1976.

———. *The West That Never Was.* Secaucus, N.J.: Citadel Press, 1989.

Thornberry, Cedric. "Saving the War Crimes Tribunal." *Foreign Policy* 104 (Fall 1996): 72–86.

Thucydides. *History of the Peleponnesian War,* trans. R. Warner. New York: Penguin Books, 1977.

Tonetti, Claretta Micheletti. *Bernardo Bertolucci.* New York: Twayne Publishers, 1995.

Toplin, Robert Brent. *History by Hollywood.* Urbana: University of Illinois Press, 1996.

Tucker, Robert W. *The Inequality of Nations.* New York: Basic Books, 1977.

Turan, Kenneth. "Das Boot." In Kathy Schulz Huffhines, ed., *Foreign Affairs: The National Society of Film Critics' Video Guide to Foreign Films.* San Francisco: Mercury House, 1991.

———. "Plot Twists Cast Shadows Over 'Rising Sun'." *Los Angeles Times* (July 30, 1993).

Tyler, Patrick E. "Who Makes the Rules in Chinese Movies?" *New York Times* (October 17, 1993).

Vermilye, Jerry, ed. *500 Best British and Foreign Films*. New York: William Morrow, 1988.

———. *The Great Italian Films*. Secaucus, N.J.: Citadel Press, 1994.

Walzer, Michael. *Just and Unjust Wars: A Moral Argument with Historical Illustrations*. New York: Basic Books, 1977.

Wapner, Paul. "Politics Beyond the State: Environmental Activism and World Civic Politics." *World Politics* 47:3 (April 1995): 311–40.

Ward, Geoffrey C. "Gandhi." In Mark C. Carnes, ed., *Past Imperfect: History According to the Movies*. New York: Henry Holt, 1995.

Warren, Spencer. "Your 100 Best Conservative Movies." *The National Review* (March 11, 1996): 55–61.

Weiss, Thomas G., and Jarat Chopra. "Sovereignty Under Seige: From Intervention to Humanitarian Space." In Gene M. Lyons and Michael Mastanduno, eds., *Beyond Westphalia? State Sovereignty and International Intervention*. Baltimore: The Johns Hopkins University Press, 1995.

Weiner, Tim. "Smart Weapons Overrated, Study Concludes." *New York Times* (July 9, 1996).

Wilmington, Michael. "Mephisto." In Kathy Schulz Huffhines, ed., *Foreign Affairs: The National Society of Film Critics' Video Guide to Foreign Films*. San Francisco: Mercury House, 1991.

———. "Salvador Has Action as Loud as Its Words." *Los Angeles Times* (April 10, 1986).

Wilson, Edward O. *Sociobiology: The New Synthesis*. Cambridge, Mass.: Harvard University Press, 1975.

Wilson, Jeremy. *Lawrence of Arabia: The Authorized Autobiography of T. E. Lawrence*. London: Minerva, 1989.

World Commission on Environment and Development. *Our Common Future*. New York: Oxford University Press, 1987.

Wriston, Walter. "Technology and Sovereignty." *Foreign Affairs* 67:2 (Winter 1988/89): 63–75.

Zimmerman, Warren. "The Last Ambassador." *Foreign Affairs* 74:2 (March/April 1995): 2–21.

Index

297

About the Book

This welcome exploration of the ways in which feature films depict the various aspects of international relations considers the utility of the feature film as a vehicle to dramatize issues and events, challenge conventional wisdom, rouse an audience to anger, and even revise history.

Gregg makes a strong case for the value of films as a window on the real world of international relations. Focusing on ten issues—each the subject of a chapter—he provides an overview of each, discusses the major concepts that have been employed by scholars to understand and explain it, and points to the trends that have characterized the evolution of international relations in the area. In each case, he cites feature films and then uses them to illustrate the ways in which popular culture has illuminated those concepts and trends.

An appendix of the approximately 150 films discussed in the text provides a brief summary of contents and relevance, as well as information about directors, casts, and dates of release.

The book is intended for use in international relations courses, as well as a souce of ideas for teachers seeking new ways to enliven course materials. It should also be of interest to anyone concerned with the ways in which popular culture depicts the world we live in.

Robert W. Gregg is professor in the School of International Service, American University. His numerous publications include *About Face? The United States and the United Nations.*